Tin-Pots and Pirate Ships

TIN-POTS AND PIRATE SHIPS:
Canadian Naval Forces and German Sea Raiders 1880–1918

Michael L. Hadley and Roger Sarty

McGill-Queen's University Press
Montreal & Kingston • London • Buffalo

© McGill-Queen's University Press 1991
ISBN 0-7735-0778-7

Legal deposit first quarter 1991
Bibliothèque nationale du Québec

Printed in Canada on acid-free paper

This book has been published with
the help of a grant from the
Social Science Federation of Canada,
using funds provided by the
Social Sciences and Humanities
Research Council of Canada.
Publication has also been assisted
by the Canada Council under its
block grant program.

Canadian Cataloguing in Publication Data

Hadley, Michael L. 1936–
Tin-pots and pirate ships

Includes bibliographical references.
ISBN 0-7735-0778-7

1. Canada. Royal Canadian Navy – History.
2. Canada – History, Naval.
3. World War, 1914–1918 – Naval operations, Canadian.
4. World War, 1914–1918 – Naval operations, German.
I. Sarty, Roger Flynn, 1952–   .   II. Title.

FC231.H33 1990   359'.00971   C90-090220-5
F1028.5.H33 1991

This book was typeset in 10/12 Baskerville with
Caslon Open-Face display by Q Composition.

Contents

Preface

"Tin-Pots" and "Pirate Ships" recall a once-pervasive Canadian attitude toward two navies that confronted each other in the First World War: the Canadian and the German. Canadians regarded their own naval forces as woefully inadequate and the opponent as a powerful band of marauding outlaws that defied international law and convention. Such catch-phrases served their purpose as an expression of public sentiment, but they did little to clarify the real issues at stake. The journalistic epithets reveal much, however, about the passions and fears surrounding public debate in those days and hint at the fascinating and complex determinants of Canada's naval policy and practice. Examined in the context of Germany's naval plans and operations against North America, Canada's early naval forces gain a distinctive profile.

The military history of Canada's unmilitary people records the emergence of two Canadian navies in two world wars.[1] In each case, international events compelled an unprepared nation to build a fleet. Much has been written about the second navy, which grew a hundred-fold from six fighting ships in 1939 to one of the largest Allied fleets in the years 1943–5. Yet the achievements and shortcomings of this better-known "Corvette Navy" and its post-1945 successors cannot be understood without knowledge of the much earlier struggles to develop a policy, a fleet, and a tactic. This is especially true of the crucial years 1914–18, when Canada's first wartime navy was built. But little has been written about the important beginnings of Canadian naval experience. Examination of these roots reveals patterns and events that prefigure in often surprising detail the naval experience of later years; it lends some credence to the popular wisdom that history repeats itself.

In the Canadian context at least, one comes upon chronic prob-

lems. One finds recurrent situations in which the government and
its navy tried to determine their own sovereign policy, only to be
thwarted by external forces beyond their control. In attempting to
pursue a self-determined maritime defence policy, Canada had to
grapple with the obvious factors of geography, internal political rival-
ries, and social and economic circumstances – and face the hard fact
that whatever its success in these areas, its senior alliance partners
ultimately dictated the terms. So it was in both world wars. Indeed,
much that historians have identified as shaping the Canadian navy's
development and operations in 1939–45 had already determined the
character of the effort in 1914–18.

Central to both events was Canada's complete unpreparedness for
war. This was particularly so on the eve of the First World War.
Neither of the two ageing cruisers that constituted the entire Canadian fleet in 1914 – the 3,400-ton *Rainbow* on the west coast and the
11,000-ton *Niobe* on the east – was anything like ready for operations
when war broke out. Quite apart from the poor condition of these
ships, the 350 officers and seamen of the regular force amounted to
but one-half of the war complement of the larger vessel alone. Even
if the two ships had been completely efficient, they were utterly
inadequate for the protection of the longest national coastline in the
world, not to mention the voluminous and valuable trade that plied
Canada's shores and adjacent waters. And why should they have
been? The British fleet had always been the ultimate guarantee of
Canadian security; and from the beginning of British rule over the
northern part of North America in the eighteenth century Canadians
had regarded the sea as the avenue by which the Royal Navy would
come to the rescue in times of need.

Situated at the North Atlantic centre of British seapower, Canada
felt itself more secure against seaborne attack than any other part
of the empire. Britain had the most powerful navy in the world
and a global network of operating bases on which the sun never
set. Then, too, Canada took comfort in its great distance from any
possible European conflict. The port of Halifax, one of the finest
natural harbours in the world, and easier of access than any other
large harbour on the Atlantic coast, lay a long way from Europe,
across a forbidding ocean: some 2,400 miles of open water separated
the port on a great circle route from Belfast and Liverpool; coastal
routes ran inland into the vast Gulf of St Lawrence and up the
huge river to Montreal, almost a thousand miles distant – some two
hundred miles further than the run from Halifax to Bermuda. From
a Canadian perspective, these extensive maritime routes were entirely safe.

The origins of Canadian naval organization therefore lay not so much in the fear of war as in peacetime imperatives arising from significant differences in British and Canadian maritime interests.[2] Most Canadians at first saw no need for a maritime force more formidable, or more costly, than the government's exceedingly modest and unprofessional civilian marine service which tended lighthouses and supervised the fisheries. During the Anglo-American war scare of 1861, Britain had expanded its North America and West Indies Squadron to forty vessels, including eight battleships; it had massively reconstructed the fortifications that defended the squadron's bases at Halifax and Bermuda and had strengthened the army garrisons to 2,000 men each.[3] These steps were designed to defeat the strongest fleet and landing force the Americans could have sent to seize the bases and thereby isolate Canada from the British support without which it could not survive.

Defence of the vast maritime communications of the empire would soon stretch the Royal Navy to the limit as other imperial powers – Germany, Russia, the United States, and France – competed for colonial wealth and built new ocean-going navies. The revolution in warship design during the 1850s–1880s – from wood to iron and steel construction, from sail to steam propulsion, from solid-shot, muzzle-loading cannon to explosive projectiles and rifled breech-loading guns – allowed competing powers to narrow the margin of British maritime supremacy. This threw the Royal Navy's strategy and tactics into disarray.[4] The vulnerability of the global web of trade and coaling stations to the new types of enemy warships brought British authorities to address the defence of empire systematically and as an integrated whole. On one issue the British government was decided from the outset: the self-governing colonies would simply have to help carry the increased burden of naval defence. The transformation thus thrust on Canada was in no sense an orderly process but a groping amid uncertainties and constantly shifting circumstances.

The great whirlwinds of debate about naval defence in Canada during the last years before the First World War produced but a penny-whistle navy. No longer fearing the territorial ambitions of the once-threatening United States, Canada was reassured by a new phase of friendship. No other immediate threats remained; more than ever, the naval defence question became one of assistance to Britain in meeting remote dangers, particularly those from Germany. The possibility of such far-reaching commitments fired emotions in Canada about a number of crucial issues: about Canada's place in the world, the kind of country it should be, and about its relationship to the Mother Country.

Several varieties of Canadian nationalism emerged; attitudes toward military relations with Britain cut to the heart of the differences among them. The inability of Canada's political leaders to resolve these conflicts explains the sorry state of the Royal Canadian Navy in 1914. In the parry and thrust of debate and controversy, both in the House of Commons and in the public arena, Canada's naval service was frequently pilloried. For some, the "Tin-Pot Navy" of 1910 had by 1918 become little more than a "Bum Boat Fleet."

Yet within four years of the outbreak of hostilities the naval service had in fact not only gone a long way toward fulfilling national objectives; it had contributed significantly to alliance warfare. Ultimately, however, it was no match for the submarine: a lethal new maritime weapon that had brought the Great Power navies to the brink of defeat. This new engine of war marked the last in a series of shifts in the geostrategic picture. By the late nineteenth century the advent of steam navigation had paradoxically limited the range of traditional surface warships by making the new vessels dependent on coaling stations and the quality of coal they provided. Industrialization and the naval arms race then focused the Royal Navy's attention on home waters around Great Britain and made long-range, large-scale operations virtually unnecessary; Britain's navy now operated as a blocking force that provided even greater security for Canada. The new weapon, the diesel submarine, then undercut the blockade and extended the range – and now made it possible for "cruisers" to operate freely once again.

The German undersea cruiser – at first a mythical danger, then a genuine threat, and finally an actual presence on the Atlantic coast – compelled Canada to act. But Canadian options were defined in both peace and war by the assistance that Britain was willing or able to provide. As it turned out, the Canadian government could procure only small vessels by 1918. This was not the fleet that the government or the navy had wanted; nor was it adequate by any objective measure. Still, the depredations of the "Kaiser's Pirates," as Allied newspapers and propagandists labelled the submarine raiders, demonstrated that Canada did indeed need a navy; they even helped to define what kind of navy it should be.

This book is about the impact of the German threat, both imagined and real, on Canadian naval development. It is about the influence of Britain and the United States on the capabilities and operations of a young Canadian navy. We have a good deal to say about how the German navy responded to the challenge of far-distant operations and about its actual operations in Canadian and American waters. In doing so, we provide a full account of the journeys of the commercial submarine *U-Deutschland* and the combat U-boat U-53 into American waters and their impact on Canadian policy.[5]

A logical starting point for the Canadian story – one indeed suggested by the existing literature – might have been the Anglo-German
naval crisis of 1909. After all, it was this event that triggered the
founding of the Canadian navy in the following year. But our research
revealed that the threat of overseas raiders played a much larger role
than hitherto appreciated in the naval question in Canada prior to
1909. It further emerged that these earlier discussions had influenced
the debates of 1909–13 in ways not previously understood. Indeed,
it became clear that Germany's plans as early as 1889 for war against
the United States included increasingly detailed provisions for action
against Canada.

Historians have virtually ignored Canada's anti-submarine warfare
during the First World War, even though it constituted the country's
principal naval commitment of those years.[6] Gilbert Tucker's official
history of the Canadian naval service has remained the major work
of Canadian historiography for nearly forty years.[7] This fine book
still commands authority on many subjects but concentrates unduly
on the operations of Canada's two cruisers early in the war as they
strove to assist the Royal Navy in suppressing German surface raiders.
While recognizing that the unshakable dominance of Britain's surface fleet had triggered Germany's u-boat offensive, Tucker offers
only cursory treatment of the Canadian navy's subsequent efforts
to develop an anti-submarine fleet to meet the German threat. He
nowhere examines unpublished German sources, and he does not
mention the fact that u-boats operated in Canadian waters – and sank
ships within a few miles of major east coast ports. Nor does he provide
any sense of the scope of the Canadian navy's role in organizing and
defending the merchant ship convoys that ultimately defeated the u-
boats. Over 1,900 ships sailed in convoy from Halifax, Sydney, and
Quebec in 1917–18; they carried over 11.5 million tons of vital cargo
to Britain and nearly half a million troops.[8] Published records omit
or only touch on much more: the profound public and official alarm
at the possibility of submarine attacks in the years 1915–17; the bitter
recriminations by the Canadian government at Britain's failure to
provide more adequate assistance in organizing anti-submarine
defences; and the emergence of strong nationalism in the Canadian
navy in response to ill-informed or heavy-handed actions by the
British Admiralty.

Nor have historians of other nations done little more than glance
at u-boat operations in North American waters. Admittedly, the large
literature on the us response to u-boat warfare has grown increasingly rich during the last three decades, with the opening of archives
and the application of new analytical methods. But their focus

remains on diplomacy and politics – how the u-boat offensive precipitated American entry into the war – rather than on naval operations.[9] Thus the best published sources on u-boat activities in North American waters remain the unanalytical and incomplete account produced by the us Navy in 1920 and the documents published by a congressional committee that same year.[10] As might be expected, the theme has inspired pot-boilers about "German Subs in Yankee Waters" that add nothing to the historical record.[11] The British and German official naval histories of the First World War are of high quality and place long-range u-boat operations in context. But they mention the North American theatre only briefly, and Canada scarcely at all.[12]

Still there is no doubt that Germany's naval leaders – Admiral Tirpitz, Admiral Henning von Holtzendorff, and Kaiser Wilhelm ii himself – were as deeply interested in wartime operations against North America as they had been in the grand pre-war plans. The dominance of the British surface fleet soon demonstrated to the Germans just how unrealistic their earlier plans had been. Yet even then, their ambitions for transatlantic u-boat operations were far from modest. They hoped to sever the flow of vital war supplies and troops from North America to the Allied armies in Europe, to isolate North America by cutting transatlantic transmission cables, to tap North American resources for the central powers, and to sow such panic among the populations of the United States and Canada that they would force their governments to urge Allied councils to sue for peace.

We first became interested in the subject of our book while studying the operations of German u-boats in Canadian waters during the Second World War. In treating the large and complex submarine war of 1939–45 we faced the greatest difficulty when integrating and interpreting the vast and rich documentation available from both sides of the conflict. How much easier, we thought, to master the small-scale events of 1914–18 and their prelude in the closing decades of the nineteenth century. We anticipated a simple task – and we were wrong.

To be sure, the documentation ultimately proved rich and rewarding, but it was random and scattered. For example, the kind of detailed periodic reports from Canadian ships and establishments that had formed the backbone of documentation for the Second World War proved no longer extant for the First World War. All that survives from the once-extensive files of reports amounts to a few dozen pages of copies, and several sheafs of brief notes, made by the naval historical section of National Defence Headquarters during the 1950s and early 1960s. Thus began the complicated and laborious task of piecing these fragments together with scraps of operational material that happened to have survived elsewhere – in policy files, personal papers, and army records and in British and American archives.

So too in German sources – found from Freiburg to Sylt and Berlin. While the original files often proved more substantive than their Allied counterparts, their use also demanded a good deal of sleuthing; this led to as many dead ends as rich rewards. U-boat log-books and war diaries are a case in point: uneven and idiosyncratic compared to similar records of 1939–45, they begged as many questions as they answered. Details in the hastily scribbled and virtually illegible log of the submarine cruiser U-155 (ex-*U-Deutschland*), for example, could be reconstructed only through a long process of linguistic analysis and word association; U-156 was sunk and took its logs to the bottom of the ocean, thus casting us back on circumstantial evidence in official reports, newspapers, and post-war briefs.

Some readers might argue that we offer here not one book on the rise of Canadian naval forces against the German threat, but two or even three: the early development of the Canadian navy and its role in the Great War; German raids off the coasts of Canada and the eastern United States; the US navy's reaction to these raids. Certainly, we deal with a number of complex themes: the navies of both Canada and Germany – the "Tin-Pots" and "Pirate Ships" of our title – as well as the influence of Britain and the United States on Canada's maritime defence policies and practice. Perhaps only one of the "books" presented here provides the kind of gun-smoke and derring-do some readers expect from naval histories and memoirs.

But in the naval affairs of Canada at least, the sailor is neither fast off the mark nor quick on the draw. The first shot in anger – often with whatever ships and weapons happen to be available from some previous war – follows an often tortuous political and bureaucratic process from concept to deed. Ultimately, the muzzle-flash derives its meaning from the events, personalities, and issues that trigger the belated war-like act. In our approach, Canadian naval operations begin in the politics of isolation. Having chosen to recount in a single work the full narrative from 1880 to 1918, we have divided

it into the "books" that might have been. The reader may either start
with the preconditions of combat or more readily turn to where
operations begin.

While shedding additional light on the attitude of German leaders
toward Canada and the United States, we have above all endeavoured
to illuminate not only the efforts of Canadian naval leaders but also
the constraints within which they worked. Four key Canadian figures
proved particularly important: G.J. Desbarats, deputy minister of the
naval service; Admiral C.E. Kingsmill, director of the naval service;
Captain Walter Hose, who commanded the anti-submarine flotilla in
1917–18; and Commander R.M. Stephens, a senior staff officer at
naval headquarters in Ottawa with responsibility for a variety of tasks,
including mobilization and intelligence.

   Ultimately, however, the burden of naval operations fell most heavily on the shoulders of the ships' crews – not only of the u-boats and
the Canadian patrol craft but also of the fishing craft and merchant
ships that the Germans destroyed. At this level, the gaps in the evidence are large and often unbridgeable. Yet we have never forgotten
that in the final analysis this is a sailors' story.

Michael L. Hadley
Roger Sarty

Acknowledgments

We wish to thank the following people whose assistance and encouragement have helped make this book possible. Dr W.A.B. Douglas, director, Directorate of History, National Defence Headquarters, Ottawa; the staff of the National Archives of Canada, in particular, Ms Barbara Wilson and Mr Glenn Wright; Mr Richard von Doenhoff and Mr Allan Rilley, US National Archives; Dr Dean Allard, former director, US Navy Operational Archives, together with staff members Messrs Cal Cavalcanti and Mike Walker; Dr Phillis Blakeley, Public Archives of Nova Scotia; Mr Bruce Ellis, curator, The Army Museum, Halifax; Ms Marilyn Gurney Smith, curator, Maritime Command Museum, Halifax; Dr Ron MacDonald, archivist, Halifax Defence Complex, Parks Canada, together with former member Mr Joe Greenough; the Public Archives of British Columbia, especially Dr Patrick Dunae; Commander Arthur Pomeroy, RNVR (Ret'd); staff of the history department, Metropolitan Toronto Central Reference Library; Mr David Brown, British Ministry of Defence; the staff of the Bundes- und Militärarchiv, Freiburg, Germany; and Dr Günther Reibhorn, Salzburg, Austria.

We are especially indebted to those pioneering members of the Naval Historical Section, which combined with the Army and Air Force historical sections in 1966 to form the Directorate of History at National Defence Headquarters in Ottawa. Their collections, compilations, and written narratives have made Canadian naval history possible. We acknowledge the late Mr E.C. Russell and the members of his founding staff: the late Mr Thor Thorgrimsson and Messrs Hartley Brown, Philip Chaplin, and J.D.F. Kealy. We are equally indebted to the pioneering work of Mr Horst Bredow, founder and executive director of the Federal Republic of Germany's U-Boot-Archiv, Stiftung Traditionsarchiv Unterseeboote, Cuxhaven.

For critical reading of the original manuscript we thank Dr Norman Hillmer, senior historian and acting director, Directorate of History, National Defence Headquarters, Ottawa; Dr Marc Milner, Department of History, University of New Brunswick; and Dr Barry Hunt, Department of History, Royal Military College of Canada, Kingston, Ontario. For helpful, imaginative suggestions we acknowledge our copy-editor, Mr John Parry.

Research was supported by grants from the Social Sciences and Humanities Research Council of Canada and from the University of Victoria, Victoria, British Columbia.

Vice-Admiral Henning Von Holtzendorff, chief, Admiralty Staff, 1915–18 (Horst Bredow, U-Boot-Archiv, Cuxhaven, Federal Republic of Germany)

Rear-Admiral (later Vice-Admiral) Sir Charles E. Kingsmill, director 1910–21 of the Naval Service of Canada. (Directorate of History [DHIST], Department of National Defence [DND], negative 0-776-2)

Control room of U-155 (ex-*Deutschland*) (Horst Bredow, U-Boot-Archiv)

HMCS *Grilse*. This converted fast yacht, purchased surreptitiously in New York by the Montreal millionaire and RNCVR officer J.K.L. Ross, served continuously in the Atlantic patrols from the summer of 1915 until war's end. She carried two twelve-pounder quick-firing guns, a fourteen-inch torpedo tube just forward of the aft gun, and, on the stern, depth charges. (National Archives of Canada, negative PA 133293)

Commander Walter Hose as commanding officer of cruiser HMCS *Rainbow*. Promoted captain, he commanded the Atlantic coast patrols in 1917–18. (DHIST, DND, negative E-36927

U-53 at anchor in Newport, Rhode Island, 7 October 1916. Note USS *Birmingham* in the background. (United States National Archives, 19-N-13-5-43)

U-156 with 5.9-inch (15-cm) guns fore and aft (Horst Bredow, U-Boot-Archiv)

German dreadnought division in line-ahead, with torpedo-boat destroyers sweeping through the column (Horst Bredow, U-Boot-Archiv)

German submarine freighter *U-Deutschland* (Horst Bredow, U-Boot-Archiv)

German cruiser SMS *Bremen* transiting the Kaiser-Wilhelm-Kanal (now Nord-Ostsee-Kanal, or Kiel Canal) (Horst Bredow, U-Boot-Archiv)

German reprint of "American cartoon on [*U-Deutschland's*] successful breach of the British block-ade" of the US coast

as vordere 15-Zentimeter-Geschütz von U 117. Auf dem hintere
ntennenmast sieht man den Ausguckposten im Beobachtungskorb sitze

U-17. View of forward 5.9-inch (15-cm) gun. Note lookout in the crow's-nest atop
the antenna mast. (Horst Bredow, U-Boot Archiv)

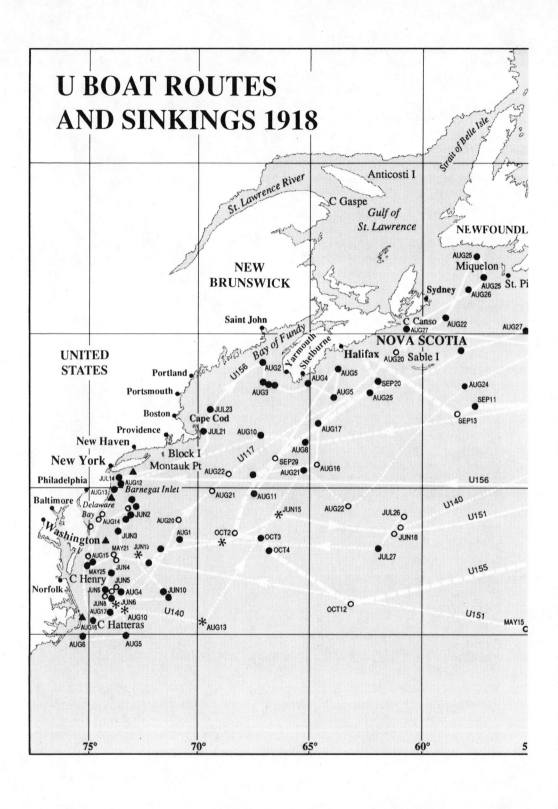

U BOAT ROUTES
AND SINKINGS 1918

Strait of Belle Isle

Anticosti I

St. Lawrence River

C Gaspe

Gulf of
St. Lawrence

NEWFOUNDL

AUG25 ●

Miquelon

NEW
BRUNSWICK

Sydney

AUG25
AUG26

St. Pi

Saint John

C Canso
AUG27

AUG22

AUG27

UNITED
STATES

Bay of Fundy

Yarmouth
Shelburne

Halifax

NOVA SCOTIA

AUG20 ○

Sable I

●

Portland

U156

AUG2 ●
●

AUG4

AUG5

SEP20

AUG24

Portsmouth

AUG3

AUG5
AUG25

SEP11

Boston ●

JUL23 ●

SEP13 ○

Cape Cod

JUL21 ○

AUG10 ●

AUG17 ●

Providence ●

New Haven

Block I

AUG8 ●

New York

Montauk Pt

U117

SEP29 ○

AUG16 ○

U156

Philadelphia

JUL14 ○

AUG22 ○

AUG21 ●

Baltimore

AUG12 ▲

Barnegat Inlet

AUG13 ○

AUG21 ○

AUG11 ●

JUN2 ○

AUG20 ○

JUN15 ✳

AUG22 ○

JUL26 ○

U140

Delaware
Bay

AUG14 ○

Washington ▲

JUN3

AUG1

OCT2 ○

OCT3 ●

JUN18 ○

U151

MAY21

JUN13

✳

OCT4 ●

AUG15 ○

JUN4

JUL27 ●

U155

MAY25 ○

JUN5

C Henry

JUN5 ●

AUG4 ○

JUN10 ●

Norfolk ●

AUG17 ○

JUN6 ✳

OCT12 ○

U151

JUN8 ●

AUG10

U140

MAY15

AUG16 ▲

C Hatteras

AUG13 ✳

AUG6 ●

AUG5

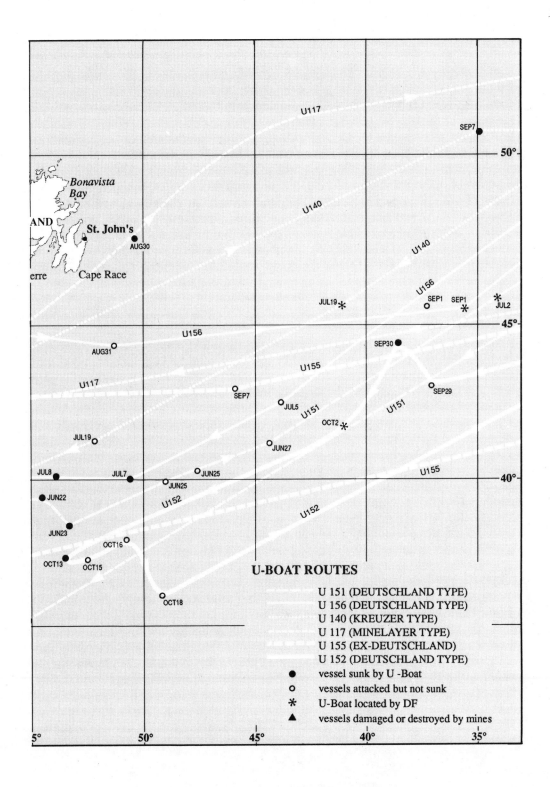

U117

SEP7 ●

50°

*Bonavista
Bay*

Bonavista
Bay

AND

St. John's

erre   Cape Race

AUG30 ●

U140

U140

U156

JUL19 ✳   SEP1 ○   SEP1 ✳   ✳ JUL2

45°

U156

AUG31 ○

SEP30 ●

U155

U117

SEP7 ○   JUL5 ○ U151   SEP29 ○

U151

OCT2 ✳

JUL19 ○   JUN27 ○

U155

JUL8 ●   JUL7 ●   JUN25 ○

40°

JUN25 ○

U152

JUN22 ●

U152

JUN23 ●

OCT16 ○

OCT13 ●   OCT15 ○

U-BOAT ROUTES

OCT18 ○

	U 151 (DEUTSCHLAND TYPE)
	U 156 (DEUTSCHLAND TYPE)
	U 140 (KREUZER TYPE)
	U 117 (MINELAYER TYPE)
	U 155 (EX-DEUTSCHLAND)
	U 152 (DEUTSCHLAND TYPE)
●	vessel sunk by U -Boat
○	vessels attacked but not sunk
✳	U-Boat located by DF
▲	vessels damaged or destroyed by mines

5°   50°   45°   40°   35°

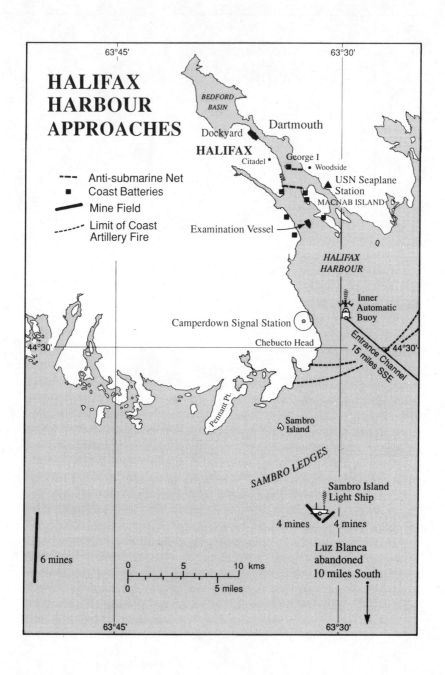

HALIFAX
HARBOUR
APPROACHES

63°45'

63°30'

BEDFORD
BASIN

Dockyard   Dartmouth

HALIFAX

Citadel •   George I

• Woodside

USN Seaplane
Station

MACNAB ISLAND

--- Anti-submarine Net
■ Coast Batteries
— Mine Field
---- Limit of Coast
     Artillery Fire

Examination Vessel

HALIFAX
HARBOUR

Inner
Automatic
Buoy

Camperdown Signal Station

Entrance Channel
15 miles SSE

44°30'   44°30'

Chebucto Head

Pennant Pt.

Sambro
Island

SAMBRO LEDGES

Sambro Island
Light Ship

4 mines   4 mines

6 mines

0   5   10 kms

0   5 miles

Luz Blanca
abandoned
10 miles South

63°45'   63°30'

PART ONE
Imperial Rivalries
1880-1914

– 1 –
Canada's Splendid Isolation

"The Latest Improvements in Scientific Warfare" reached Halifax on 6 July 1881 in what the Halifax *Morning Chronicle* called a "Grand Torpedo Attack."[1] The headlines announced a major test of a new weapon in the fortress town's defences. Military authorities had timed this thrilling event to climax the governor-general's visit to the imperial town. Thousands of people thronged the shoreline, from Freshwater to Point Pleasant Park, and the slope up to the summit of the Citadel, with its commanding view of the harbour. Others watched the war game from boats, steamers, and tugs, while some four hundred more held tickets for the governor-general's vantage-point on George's Island. How well could Halifax defend itself against assault forces from the sea? The military hoped to provide an answer with a realistic scenario.

The idea of the mock attack was simple. According to the well-briefed press report, "an enemy's squadron, taking advantage of a thick fog, had passed the entrance to the harbor unperceived, and intended to take possession of the Dockyard and the magazines." The defenders had meanwhile seeded the approaches with "torpedoes," or what we now call mines. The lone corvette HMS *Tenedos*, a converted wooden steam sloop with two seven-inch rifled muzzle-loader guns, represented an enemy squadron. On this occasion she enjoyed the brilliant sunshine of a glorious July morning instead of the fog for which the war-game scenario called. The audience watched as *Tenedos* anchored off the first "torpedo" and sent a boat's crew to reconnoitre the dangerous waters. Armed with grappling hooks for tearing the electric cables connecting the mines from their control station on shore, the men probed the channel. This was precisely the method that a secret German memorandum had recommended His German Majesty's Ship (SMS) *Elisabeth* use to combat moored mines in Panama in 1878: either a steam pinnace with trawls or two rowboats moving abreast, with a weighted line suspended between them.[2] But in the British exercise at Halifax the enemy "accidentally" exploded a mine, thereby awakening the garrison to its imminent danger and triggering a withering mock battle between the attacking "squadron" and the artillery ashore.

By all accounts the experiment was a great success. In the *Chronicle*'s words: "The roar of the heavy guns to the immediate spectators was perfectly deafening. The simultaneous explosion of ... mines was a grand sight, producing novel sensations to those unaccustomed to torpedo displays. The sudden upheaval of large masses of water ... carrying with it all kinds of debris, mud and fish ... accompanied by the angry rumbling roar of the explosion gave the spectators a faint idea of the grandeur ... and horrors of modern warfare." But the tumult had destroyed all the mines. The make-believe enemy slipped through the cleared passage and reached its ultimate target. Halifax faced defeat. But for the moment that did not really seem to matter: the governor-general had been "highly delighted and edified" by the operation.

The British garrison at Halifax lay nearly a thousand miles from Ottawa. In the consciousness of Canadian leaders it was even more remote than that. However glad they might be of the free security afforded by the fortress and by the Royal Navy squadrons on the western Atlantic and eastern Pacific, they had no desire whatever to help pay the expensive costs. Nor did they see any mitigating reasons for substantial defence spending. Prime Minister Sir John A. Macdonald had explained the position in 1880 to Britain's Royal Commission on the Defence of British Possessions and Commerce Abroad. He pointed out that the United States was the only nation that could conceivably threaten the Dominion's survival and that Canada was undefendable against an American invasion. But he regarded war with the United States as "virtually an impossibility" because of "a gradual improvement in the feeling" between the two North American neighbours.[3]

In any event, Macdonald added, the Canadian government was already fulfilling its responsibilities by maintaining a strengthened land militia, as arranged with Britain in 1865. As the prime minister reminded the commissioners, the imperial government had "pledged itself [in 1865] to exercise, in case of war, the whole military and naval force of the Empire in the protection of Canada."[4] For this reason he did not fear even cruiser raids by countries involved in any foreseeable European war. He quickly dismissed the commissioners' suggestion that Canada might none the less help with the increasing burden of imperial defence. To his mind, any permanent commitment of that kind would only arouse isolationist sentiments among his electorate. Much better, he advised, to await the spontaneous outpouring of loyalty that would come with an actual military crisis.

The commission had tried to explain that technology had changed the old strategic principles: in an era of telegraphic communications, of steam warships and rail transport, war could break out suddenly and develop quickly. Prudent defence therefore required that full preparations be completed in peacetime. Macdonald remained unconvinced. He would not even commit Canadian land units to reinforce British garrisons: neither at Halifax nor at the smaller British naval base at Esquimalt on the west coast of British Columbia. As he rather narrowly insisted, Britain maintained these stations and its squadrons to serve its own needs, not those of Canada.

But, as Macdonald well knew, that was beside the point. The royal commission had after all been established to address doubts raised by the Anglo-Russian confrontation of 1877–8. Russia had been preparing to arm fast steamers for raids on the virtually unprotected global web of seaborne trade and colonial coaling ports which Britain's economy, and indeed her very survival, depended.[5] The crisis had raised the spectre of the Royal Navy's inability to safeguard British overseas interests and to protect the colonies in a modern war.

Reports of Russian plans to operate in Canadian waters in 1878 had sharpened Ottawa's sense of menace.[6] Canada's appeal for Royal Navy cruisers to defend the Gulf of St Lawrence elicited a disturbing response: none would be available if war broke out. Indeed the Admiralty warned of the possibility of "much mischief being done ... by a single [enemy] cruiser notwithstanding great efforts to capture her."[7] Admiralty therefore enjoined Canada to arm the fast steamers of its own merchant marine for coastal and trade defence. This was the one concession that Macdonald had made to the British royal commission in 1880: if provoked, Canada would of course arm fast steamers for local security.[8] It had also been clear from his other remarks at the time that two fundamentals governed any Canadian defence initiative: it should arouse no political controversy and should cost very little.

Behind the scenes, however, the governor-general, the Marquis of Lorne, was urging a scheme that would cause his ministers difficulties on both counts. His duplicitous reports had led Admiralty to believe that Canada was actually more positively disposed than Macdonald had led it to believe. According to the viceroy's version, Canadians might recruit seamen for service aboard British ships and even begin their training in Canada.[9] For reasons that are still obscure, Macdonald accepted from the Admiralty in 1881 the twenty-year-old seventeen-gun screw corvette HMS *Charybdis*. Driven by sail and an auxiliary steam-engine, with deck guns mounted for broadside firing, she marked a fascinating transition in nineteenth-century ship construction. She was the first purpose-built warship ever owned by the Dominion of Canada.[10] Unwilling to appear ungrateful to the British, Canadians did not bother to examine the vessel until after her official acceptance on 2 December 1880. With her boilers burned out after seven-and-a-half years on the China Station, she was a dubious gift.

After an extensive but by no means complete refit to prepare her for what turned out to be a very rough Atlantic crossing, she reached her new home port of Saint John, New Brunswick, on 26 July 1881. The local press greeted her without enthusiasm.[11] Here the defect-ridden hulk lay unused. It was thus she gained her notoriety, at one point breaking loose in a storm and creating havoc in the harbour. The local press decried "Canada's White Elephant" and denounced the squandering of public money "to bring this rotten tub across the ocean, without ... any idea of what is to be done with her."[12] The unwarranted expense provoked the wrath of the Liberal opposition against Macdonald's supposed ambitions for a "war fleet." Taking great delight in facing a House that offered no opposition to his motion to send her back to Britain, the Hon. Malcolm Cameron lampooned the whole decision-making process that had led to the delivery of "this terrible monster."[13] "I am not quite sure ... where the flash of genius originated that suggested the propriety of the acquisition of this valuable piece of property," he facetiously mused in the Commons on 27 February 1882. *Charybdis*, a hulk that Cameron had pilloried as "utterly unfit for any service," was quietly returned to the Royal Navy a few months later.

It was no grand scheme of imperial co-operation that ultimately gave rise to an enduring Canadian maritime force, but rather the mundane question of fish. The Dominion government had commissioned and armed six schooners under the Department of Marine and Fisheries in 1870 in order to prevent US vessels from fishing the rich inshore areas of the Maritimes and the Gulf of St Lawrence. The Americans had excluded themselves from the zone in 1866 by revoking the 1854 treaty for reciprocal trade with the British colonies; but the Royal Navy had been reluctant to apprehend poachers for fear of provoking American enmity. The arrest of twelve American vessels by Canadian government schooners in 1870 did much to persuade the United States to settle the fisheries dispute in the Anglo-

American Treaty of Washington of 1871. Once the US Senate had ratified the treaty two years later, Canada promptly disbanded the so-called Marine Police. This temporary, makeshift response, evoked only when the need for action had become inescapable, typified the Canadian reaction to international crises.[14]

A fresh dispute arose when the United States renounced the fisheries articles of the treaty in 1885. Faced again with British reluctance to antagonize the Americans, Canada raised a new Fisheries Protection Service during the 1886 and 1887 seasons. Patrols by eight to ten schooners and small steamers helped induce the United States to conclude yet another fisheries treaty in 1888; but obstreperous US senators refused to ratify the document, compelling Canada to maintain the patrols for a further twenty years.[15]

Thus through pressure of circumstances, and not by design, the Fisheries Protection Service became a permanent institution. It proved useful not only in controlling American access to Canadian waters but in the general management and regulation of the fisheries as well. Although manned by merchant seamen, the fisheries "cruisers" were actually performing a function normally carried out by her majesty's warships.

It seemed but a short and logical step to convert the flotilla into a naval service. This idea was promoted by a retired Royal Navy officer who had commanded one of the steamers in the fisheries patrol and who had taken charge of the whole force in 1888. He conceived a practical scheme for procuring small torpedo gunboats that could serve as naval training ships and patrol the fishing banks in peacetime; they would carry armament heavy enough to provide useful defence in war. Macdonald and his minister of marine and fisheries encouraged the idea, but the British Admiralty did not.[16]

Admiralty's reasons were not as fickle as they appear. British policy was changing, and the concept of colonial navies for local coast and harbour defence now seemed faulty. The revolution in naval architecture and weaponry had stabilized itself by the late 1880s: a few distinct classes of warship had emerged from the experimental designs of the previous two decades. Unlike earlier types, the new warships had uniformly good seakeeping qualities and could manoeuvre together in powerful squadrons on the high seas. Supported by modern communications, Admiralty could now exercise centralized control. It could concentrate the squadrons against enemy fleets or raiders even before they had reached imperial territory or inflicted critical losses on seaborne trade. Faced with increasing competition from both Russia and France, Britain had to insist on large-scale and continuous expansion of the Royal Navy. Britain's Naval Defence Act of 1889

constituted a watershed in providing for construction of eight battleships and forty-two cruisers in fulfilment of a new "two-power standard": the British fleet should be at least equal in numbers of major
warships to the combined strength of the next two largest navies.[17]

The costs of such competition exceeded the capacities of the self-
governing colonies. It would have helped little even if they had been
able to finance and operate the latest types of warship, for the very
existence of flotillas under the control of colonial governments flew
in the face of the new naval doctrine. Tethering warships to the
protection of particular localities created two grave disadvantages:
the enemy could either evade them completely or defeat them in
detail.

As the Admiralty suggested at the Colonial Conference of 1887,
imperial resources could be most effectively and economically mar-
shalled against the growing menace of foreign fleets by other means:
the colonies need only pay annual subsidies in order to finance expansion of the Royal Navy. This scheme was energetically promoted by
members of the imperial union movement, which had emerged during the 1880s in response to alarm at Britain's declining military
strength. Armed strength was becoming the definitive measure of a
nation's moral and material fibre. In this heady environment, the
notion of the youthful, vital colonies voluntarily joining hands with
the beleaguered Mother Country found tremendous emotional
appeal in some circles. The cause gained a powerful voice in the
British government in 1895 when Joseph Chamberlain took up the
colonial portfolio. He was determined to achieve closer imperial military union.[18]

Canada had long since become the focus of opposition to such subsidies to imperial defence. Indeed, several prominent Canadian imperialists were among the concept's most trenchant critics. Significantly,
they found no conflict in principle between Canadian nationalism
and loyalty to the empire. Thus the only conceivable model for closer
union lay in a partnership between equals – not colonial subservience
to British interests and needs. Their views were in fact not far
removed from those that Macdonald had presented to the defence
royal commission in 1880 and that most Canadian prime ministers
would echo until the 1940s.

Imperialists in Canada were irritated by British suggestions that
Canada was a defence liability and therefore owed cash payments in
compensation. The contrary seemed the case. The dominion's
friendly relations with the United States had made it an anchor of
security; they allowed the pursuit of economic development that

strengthened the empire far more than the marginally increased naval forces that subsidies might finance. Yet the imperialists in Canada still regarded military relations with Britain in romantic, spiritual terms; the essence of this emotional attachment was faith in the willingness of Canadians to fight for the Queen at the moment of crisis. For this reason they argued that emphasis on a cash nexus could only erode loyal sentiments; after all, taxation without representation had caused the thirteen colonies to rebel.[19]

The most searching Canadian analysis of the big-ship blue-water strategy came from a prominent imperial unionist and onetime officer in the Royal Navy, H.J. Wickham of Toronto. In a speech before the Canadian Military Institute in 1894 he argued that in the event of war the Royal Navy would necessarily place a low priority on Canada's needs:

Come what may, the British navy must be kept up to a strength to cope with any two of the Navies of Europe, and that quite irrespective of the size and importance of colonial trade. If the naval scares which have taken place in England recently mean anything, they mean that the English people are apprehensive that their navy is not being kept up to the standard which will ensure the safety of the British Isles ... So far as one can judge, if it comes to a war with a first-rate power, every ship not required to actively engage the enemy or watch his ports will be required, not to protect colonial trade in the distant parts of the world, but to ensure a supply of food and raw materials for the inhabitants of the British Isles, and that being the case it is only reasonable, if the colonies are to be called upon to contribute to the expense of the British Navy, that a plan shall be worked out that will ensure their interests being properly safeguarded.[20]

What Wickham proposed went some distance toward creation of colonial navies. The overseas and British governments, he suggested, should jointly subsidize fast merchant steamers. These vessels would strengthen imperial economic ties by providing a high-class commercial service; on the outbreak of war they could quickly mount armament and defend distant colonial waters while the main British fleet was elsewhere engaged. The crews of the steamers would be recruited from the colony they served and enlisted in the Royal Naval Reserve for training.[21] Canadian imperialists had consistently argued that in any imperial federation, trade must figure at least as prominently as defence, for the greatest threat to Canada lay not in military attack but in economic absorption by the United States. Wickham played a leading role in organizing the Toronto branch of the Navy League at the end of 1895, shortly after the parent body was founded in

Britain. As we will see, the German Navy League provided the inspiration.

Wickham's armed–merchant cruiser scheme, which the Toronto branch adopted, received sympathetic airing through the British league. One leading member, the prominent naval reformer Lord Brassey, had shown profound understanding of Canada's antipathy toward imperial defence subsidies as early as 1892. He and other British reformers now began to promote a scheme not far removed from Wickham's. Concerned about the shortage of reservists available to complete the manning of the Royal Navy in wartime, they urged that Royal Naval Reserve divisions be organized among the seafaring populations of the colonies. At the outbreak of war, these crews could then mobilize ships of the British reserve fleet, which British foresight would have stationed at overseas ports to train the divisions. The scheme was promoted by the British Empire League, an organization of moderate unionists opposed to defence subsidies; it had a substantial Canadian membership.[22]

The Toronto branch of the Navy League at once claimed a share in the authorship of the scheme but dissociated itself in one important particular: it wanted a distinct Canadian force. For some time the Torontonians had been insisting that the colonial organizations come under undivided colonial control in peacetime. Adherence to the Royal Navy's regulations and standards, they argued, was tantamount to assuring integration into British command in war.[23] The Toronto branch now wanted a distinct Canadian Naval Militia rather than recruitment of Canadians into the Royal Naval Reserve.

This change reflected developments that had originated with the British army. After the brief Anglo-American war scare of December 1895–January 1896, the army had endeavoured to reform the moribund Canadian land militia and to revive interest within the British government in defending Canada against the United States. In doing so, the soldiers were attempting to counteract the increasingly predominant naval view of imperial defence. The army held that the vast international border in North America – the empire's longest continental frontier – was one potential theatre of war where ocean fleets could not directly intervene. In such a large-scale land conflict, colonial troops would be an invaluable reinforcement. Even raw troops could be trained more quickly than a useless colonial navy could be built. For this reason, the army had consistently encouraged development of colonial forces. Moreover, it exerted an important influence by lending qualified officers to colonial militias for key positions and for command.[24]

Imperial officers who had lived in Canada had come to appreciate colonial nationalism. In politically appealing terms they could now call for transformation of the anachronistic Canadian militia into a modern "national army." In the process they raised the possibility of a national navy as well. A British army and navy committee, under Major-General Edward P. Leach of the Royal Engineers, met in Canada in 1897–8 to consider defence against the United States and to establish the basic elements of the national army program.

A central issue was naval command of the Great Lakes, on which success of land operations would ultimately depend. Maritime defence of the Great Lakes required special vessels, for ships of the oceanic fleet could quite obviously not traverse the St Lawrence canals. A Great Lakes fleet was an extremely costly commitment, which the Admiralty did not want. The Admiralty found a loophole in the fisheries protection service, the vessels of which were small enough to transit the canals. Yet even then their lordships acceded only grudgingly to the army's proposal that Canada raise its own naval force by mobilizing the fisheries service and organizing a substantial "naval militia" to man armed lake steamers.[25]

This was probably the source of the Toronto Navy League's proposal for a national naval militia, for the branch had been in touch with the Leach committee.[26] There was, however, one significant difference. The Torontonians conceived of the naval militia primarily as an oceanic force that would operate armed merchant cruisers together with British reserve warships on loan; the cruisers would operate against European sea raiders on the Atlantic. The Toronto branch had little direct influence on government, despite its publication program and its lobbying of the two major political parties. Yet it helped shape and give currency to seminal ideas that, often in fragmentary form, worked their way, by now untraceable paths, into the decision-making councils of government. Its ideas ultimately emerged in official policy. The group demonstrates that, on the naval question at least, leading Canadian imperialists were intensely nationalistic and unwilling to accept the dictates of British authorities.

Paradoxically, however, the Torontonians' greatest political impact was probably negative. French-Canadian nationalists had long since understood the need for an army to maintain internal order and to protect Canadian soil; in the light of Britain's vaunted maritime supremacy, the need for Canadian warships was much less clear. The Toronto origins of the idea for a national navy led Quebec nationalists to believe that any such scheme was but a thinly veiled commitment to imperial defence. Indeed the principles of imperial defence that the British government had published in 1896 confirmed the Quebec view and allayed any doubts that French-Canadian nationalists might have had on this score. As the chairman of the British government's defence committee had publicly declared:

The maintenance of sea supremacy has been assumed as the basis of the system of Imperial defence against attack from over the sea. This is the determining factor shaping the whole defensive policy of the Empire, and is fully recognized by the Admiralty, who have accepted the responsibility of protecting all British territory abroad against organized invasion from the sea. To fulfil this great charge they claim the absolute power of disposing of their forces in the manner they consider most certain to secure success, and object to limit the action of any part of them to the immediate neighbourhood of places which they consider may be more effectively protected by operations at a distance.[27]

In this light Britain had absolutely no need of local naval defences in the colonies; any vessels it might subsequently procure would be operated in remote waters – and under exclusively British control.

Wilfrid Laurier's Liberals had won the Canadian general election of June 1896. But Laurier, who led his party from 1887 to 1919, was no more inclined to take initiatives in defence than his Conservative predecessors. Certainly, his rejoinder to Chamberlain's bid for naval subsidies at the Colonial Conference of 1897 was reminiscent of Macdonald's response to British requests for military support in 1880. Thanks to friendly relations with the United States, Laurier now echoed, Canada had really no defence problem at all. Sea raiders formed the only external threat, easily met by measures improvised at the time of crisis.[28] This sense of enduring stability was more apparent than real.

Changing circumstances drew Laurier's government into military programs more ambitious than any previous ministry had attempted. The economic expansion and attendant growth of public revenue that began in the late 1890s made it impossible for Canadian politicians to plead their perennial excuse of poverty when responding to British recommendations for military reform. Even more, the Dominion's assertion of greater political autonomy – which for Laurier was the key to both Canada's future and that of the empire – implied fuller responsibility for self-defence.

But as revelations about the militia's decrepitude at the time of the political crisis in 1895–6 had shown, national defence was moribund. There was much to be done. Although neither the prime minister nor his minister of militia and defence, Frederick Borden, believed that defence against the United States was either possible or necessary, Laurier was able to carry out some of the modest improvements that British army officers had urged. In the fall of 1899, the minister of marine and fisheries, Louis Davies, began exploratory discussions with the first lord of the admiralty in London about the possibility of raising a naval militia.[29]

The South African War of 1899–1902 lent decisive impetus to further initiatives at military expansion in Canada. These initiatives focused primarily on the land militia but drew the proposed naval militia into their wake. Laurier had ceded to the pressures of pro-empire sentiment among English Canadians to send troops to South Africa but now faced a severe backlash in Quebec. Reaction in French Canada was sharp. Henri Bourassa, the brilliant Liberal member of Parliament, broke with his leader to champion anti-imperialism and French-Canadian "nationalisme" under the banner of the Nationalist League of which he was the mentor. He had been particularly suspicious of Davies's talks with Admiralty.[30]

Meanwhile in London, the colonial secretary, Chamberlain, appealed to the patriotic fervour among large sections of the populations in the dominions and urged them to promote permanent military union with Britain. In calling the Colonial Conference of 1902 he specifically aimed at extracting commitments of manpower and subsidies for the British services.

Laurier sought to master these conflicting pressures by further emphasizing national, as opposed to imperial, defence. Furious at Chamberlain, he prepared himself with papers on both the 1878 Russian cruiser scare and the Leach committee in order to remind the colonial secretary that the British services themselves had admitted their inability to provide adequate protection; they had in fact urged Canada to develop its own defences.[31] At the conference Laurier flatly rejected the British proposals as "an important departure from the principle of Colonial self-government."

Yet he had to admit that both he and his ministers "fully appreciate the duty of the Dominion as it advances in population and wealth, to make a more liberal outlay for those necessary preparations of self-defence which every country has to assume and bear."[32] The Dominion government might organize a naval militia on the sea coasts and also take greater responsibility for the land defence of Royal Navy establishments at Halifax and Esquimalt. Strengthening Canada's national defence would not only promote Canadian nationhood but also assist the imperial services by reducing their North American commitments. This was the policy Laurier proclaimed at the Colonial Conference of 1902.

Laurier and his colleagues intended to build the naval organization on the Fisheries Protection Service, precisely as Macdonald had contemplated. Once properly trained and equipped for the naval role, the service could provide instructors for naval militiamen recruited from the seafaring population. Responsible for the project was Raymond Préfontaine, whom Laurier appointed minister of marine and fisheries at the end of 1902. A former mayor of Montreal, Préfontaine had been one of the few prominent French Canadians to have endorsed the decision to send troops to South Africa. He eventually drafted the Naval Militia Bill of 1904 which Laurier had promised to introduce to Parliament.

What might have been an astute political appointment for gaining Quebec support for naval plans turned sour. Disregarding Laurier's warnings, Préfontaine embarrassed the government with speeches about the prospects for a substantial Canadian force that would work closely with the Royal Navy. Laurier never brought Préfontaine's bill before Parliament. Nothing more was achieved than the construction in 1903–4 of two steel vessels equipped with rapid-fire guns to replace the obsolete fisheries cruisers. One of the new vessels, the Canadian Government Ship (CGS) *Canada*, offered rudimentary naval training for fisheries service personnel.[33] The government was under no effective pressure to do more.

Robert Borden, who had in 1901 begun his almost twenty years as federal Conservative leader, publicly favoured the concept of a distinctly Canadian "naval militia." But because his party had to rebuild its position in Quebec, he was in no hurry to grasp the potentially inflammatory issue of imperial defence.[34] As a measure of the opposition he faced, even his Quebec lieutenant, F.D. Monk, was already stumping against imperial military centralization.[35] Indeed, imperialists ultimately complained that both parties were now pandering to French-Canadian nationalism. As one exasperated imperialist exclaimed in 1907: "The conservatives allege that the liberals have adopted the conservative platform [on imperial defence], and the liberals don't deny it. Why not ... split ... upon a serious issue as Imperialists or Parasites "[36]

Navalists did not manage to arouse public opinion on the question. A lecture tour by the secretary of the British Navy League, H.F. Wyatt, during the winter of 1902–3 provides one notable example. Sensitive to the doctrine that Canada should control its own forces, he embraced a mission. Having worked closely with Wickham, he promoted the program of the Toronto branch. Some press reports dismissed him out of hand as a presumptuous agent of imperial centralization who was trying to dictate policy to Canadians. Indeed, not even his sympathetic listeners could accept his jeremiads about

Britain's precarious international position in the naval race. On one occasion, for example, Sir Frederick Borden attended a meeting; he too had hoped that Canadian warships might "some day" assist the Royal Navy in an emergency. But unlike Wyatt he saw no imminent threat to British maritime supremacy. Nor did he foresee any danger that Canada might become an American protectorate, as Wyatt had warned.[37]

Yet unlike the actively hostile French-Canadian audiences, most listeners regarded a Canadian navy lukewarmly as simply "nice to have." The bishop of Nova Scotia held a not untypical view. As reported in a front-page article of the *Halifax Herald*: "[He] had little fear of French or Russian, or of German hostility, and he spoke of fear of the United States as something of a 'bogey.' He favoured the idea [of naval development], however, on general principles and also because it would be a good thing for our boys who would be much improved by the training."[38] At least nine new Canadian branches of the Navy League emerged in response to Wyatt's appeal, but few were active and most died out.[39]

New changes in British policy of great importance to Canada were in the offing. The Admiralty had argued during secret meetings of the Committee of Imperial Defence in London that Britain should concentrate its resources against increasingly powerful potential enemies closer to home. It was folly to dissipate British forces in anticipation of an unlikely war with the United States; in view of American military and naval expansion such a war would be unwinnable anyway. In December 1904 the Admiralty therefore effected a major reorganization of the fleet by virtually abandoning the Western Hemisphere; it did so in order to strengthen forces in European waters. Not only did the Pacific squadron disappear, but the force permanently based in the western Atlantic was reduced to a single cruiser and the dockyards at Halifax and Esquimalt were closed.

Canadian reaction to the Royal Navy's withdrawal was not wonder or dismay; it was confident and serene. British press reports, which were widely republished in Canada, gave every assurance that Canadian security had actually been increased by the fleet organization.[40] As the Halifax *Morning Chronicle* repeated: "A powerful flying squadron of armoured cruisers ... will visit Canadian waters time after time and show the flag, while Admiralty plans provide for battle squadrons to be in Canadian waters within a week of any development dangerous to the peace of the country."[41]

Nationalistic editors wondered if Canada really needed any Royal Navy support at all. Doubtless recalling Britain's recent sellout of

Canadian interests for the sake of Anglo-American friendship in the
Alaska boundary dispute, one Liberal newspaper asked: "When has
Canada ever been protected by the Motherland against American
aggression or American cheatery – which is all that the Dominion, so
far as its external relations are concerned, has to fear or contend
against?"[42] Yet, with a twist of logic, the paper turned vice into
virtue: whatever the difficulties encountered by the North American
neighbours in settling local disputes, Canada had a friend on whom
it could call when threatened by overseas powers.

The Conservative *Daily Star* of Montreal echoed this last theme
with prescient fervour: "American power will be exercised to protect
freedom and make possible the advance of progress. ... The day for
churlish criticism of the growth of the American navy is long past ...
Canada, as a British colony and a next-door neighbour of the United
States, should rejoice to see the growth alike of the friendly co-
operation and of its power to protect a joint world policy which,
whatever its faults, is the best at present offered to humanity by any
strong government."[43]

No one seems to have enquired what might happen if the United
States should remain neutral in any European conflict. Although
Americans would ultimately exercise their naval power to protect
Canadian interests, American neutrality until April 1917 would bear
serious consequences both for Great Britain and for the maritime
defence of Canada.

Laurier's informal offer in January 1905 to assume full responsibility
for the army garrisons and fortifications at Halifax and Esquimalt
had pleasantly surprised the British. They had, of course, been prepared to maintain the defences, particularly those at Halifax; Admiralty regarded defended ports as essential to the mobility of the
fleet, and the army had made a last-ditch appeal for a foothold
in Canada in the event of a conflict with the United States. The
departments in London had only dared hope that Canada would
accept an increased share of the defence of the bases.

Now, however, Laurier insisted on early and complete control of
the fortresses and rejected the alternative of subsidizing British soldiers there – even though their rates of pay were a fraction of those
paid to Canadian regulars. The Dominion government thus tripled
the size of the tiny militia permanent force, to provide over 1,000
regulars at Halifax and a maintenance detachment of 150 at Esquimalt. Largely for this reason, militia expenditures rocketed from $4.2
million in 1904 to $6.9 million in 1907.

Laurier's defence initiative thus focused on Canada's traditional
force – the land militia – to the virtual exclusion of a navy. If develop-

ment of a naval militia was slow, so the *Canadian Military Gazette* explained in June 1905, political realities were the cause: "We must never forget that there are people in Canada who look with no friendly eye" on defence expenditures. Indeed, any increases beyond those necessary for the fortresses might arouse "a great cry"; they would even raise the alarm "that militarism was getting rampant in Canada, and that soon we would be not better off ... than the 'down-trodden people of Europe'."[44]

The *Military Gazette* was closer to the mark than it perhaps knew. Laurier's quick and far-reaching action in taking over the fortresses was inspired by a broad range of political agreement. Nationalists were glad to see the last imperial troops depart Canada, and imperialists were pleased that Canada was finally relieving the Mother Country of an expensive burden. Troops to man forts on Canadian soil were one thing; naval forces, with their great mobility, were quite another.

Renewed speculation about Préfontaine's by then defunct naval militia bill percolated through the press in late 1904 and 1905.[45] It seems likely that the minister of marine and fisheries had himself inspired comments about the possibility that the government would soon act. Despite Laurier's warnings to avoid the whole subject, Préfontaine publicly waxed eloquent during a trip to London in December 1905; he enthused about a Canadian organization "that little by little will come to form a part of the great British navy, and be a power in defending the Empire wherever and whenever the occasion may arise."[46] Laurier may well have felt some relief when Préfontaine died in his sleep a few days later. He summoned L.P. Brodeur to succeed him. A long-time party loyalist, Brodeur was bound to the mainstream of French-Canadian nationalism by very close links.

Préfontaine had hoped that withdrawal of the British fleet to European waters would strengthen Canada's interest in having its own navy. The reverse, however, appears to have been true. At the very least, Admiralty's increased emphasis on the defence of European waters probably reinforced Canadian perceptions of naval defence as remote, irrelevant, and entwined with the worst evils of the Old World. One prominent proponent of French-Canadian nationalism associated with Bourassa characterized Canada's naval requirements as "juste assez de bateaux pour assurer la reproduction du petit poisson!"[47] Brodeur echoed this view at the Colonial Conference of 1907. Countering the claim that Canada spent nothing on naval defence, he argued that the Fisheries Protection Service carried out precisely the same kinds of duties as performed by British warships. And that, he added, was all the navy Canada needed.[48]

British authorities were none the less quite right not to attach any military significance to the Canadian fisheries service organization. When, in the winter of 1904–5, Préfontaine had asked if the recently completed CGS *Canada* could train with British warships exercising in the West Indies, the Admiralty had properly refused. British officers, they explained, had no legal power of discipline over the Canadians, and the level of training was so low that they could gain little from the manoeuvres. In any case, arguments ran, it would be dangerous for a ship "unfamiliar with Fleet work" to operate in close company with the Royal Navy squadron.[49]

Admittedly, the ex–Royal Navy officer who had headed the Fisheries Protection Service since 1893, Commander O.G.V. Spain, had done what little he could to raise professional standards in the force. Each year since 1901, for example, he had sent a half-dozen personnel to a gunnery course at the militia artillery school in Quebec. Yet even these modest advances were scuttled by long-standing difficulties of which his predecessors had complained. Most seamen were engaged for seasonal work only and received low wages. Politicians insisted on their rights of patronage and therefore controlled hirings. All this resulted in poor-quality crews; the better men left as soon as they had obtained some training. "Many of them," Spain wrote to his deputy minister, enlisted in "the United States Navy."[50] These problems persisted even after the training program on *Canada* had begun. An ex–Royal Navy seaman gunner was the most qualified instructor in the scheme.

British officials denounced Canada's Department of Marine and Fisheries as one of the worst-run ministries in a country they described as one not noted for efficient, principled public administration. They were convinced that nothing could be accomplished unless a first-class Royal Navy officer were sent to take charge. A major problem lay with Commander Spain, who had left the Royal Navy in the late 1880s with the junior rank of lieutenant; his professional knowledge was necessarily limited. And furthermore, as the governor-general wrote Laurier in 1907, Spain had retired "under a cloud which still makes it impossible for him to go on board a British man-of-war." Spain, he advised Laurier and Brodeur, simply had to go.[51]

Whether or not the allegations were true, they triggered grave questions about his conduct while employed by the Canadian government. A Royal Commission on the Civil Service, established in 1908 in response to Conservative scandal-mongering, singled out Marine and Fisheries for scathing criticism: "constant blundering and confusion ... no sign visible of ... an intelligent purpose, unless it be that of spending as much money as possible."[52] A subsequent investigation documented these charges, and Spain came in for his share of notoriety.[53]

Laurier and his minister, Brodeur, cleaned house in the department once the royal commission had reported, in the spring of 1908. G.J. Desbarats replaced an incompetent and aged deputy minister, whom Brodeur described as having been kept on simply because he knew too much.[54] A Quebec-born engineer, Desbarats had managed the government shipyard at Sorel, Quebec, with both probity and efficiency. Rear-Admiral Charles E. Kingsmill succeeded the maligned Commander Spain. Kingsmill was a Canadian who had entered the Royal Navy in 1869 at the age of fourteen. He had met Laurier a number of times before and had indicated his interest in retiring from the imperial service to start a new career in Canada.

The appointment of such a senior and experienced officer was an important step in Canadian development, but it brought no significant initiatives in its immediate wake. Indeed, Kingsmill was soon giving vent to frustrations at his own powerlessness to correct the very deficiencies that had plagued his predecessors.[55] Within months of his arrival, he informed a Conservative journalist that he was "frightfully sick of the way things are run" and leaked a story of inefficiency and corruption.[56]

Tenacious Australian lobbying was meanwhile effecting changes in imperial defence. In contrast to Brodeur's confident assertion at the 1907 Colonial Conference that the Fisheries Protection Service met all Canadian requirements, the Australians had been determined to procure their own warships. They had good reason. Britain's fleet reorganization in 1904–5 had reduced the number, size, and quality of Royal Navy vessels stationed in the Pacific. Moreover, the British withdrawals to European waters had inauspiciously coincided with the first full-scale sea battle of the century – Admiral Togo's annihilation of the Russian fleet at Tsushima in May 1905. The Japanese fleet now dominated the Western Pacific.

The Australians had little faith in the alliance that Britain had concluded with Japan in 1902 and found small comfort in Britain's assurances that the Royal Navy's centralized battle squadrons would intercept any raiding forces of more than two or three ships dispatched by other powers.[57] At the 1907 conference the Admiralty conceded that the dominions might build local defence forces but did not retreat from the doctrine of a single imperial fleet: "While the distribution of the fleet must be determined by strategical requirements of which the Admiralty [alone] are the judge, it would be of great assistance if the Colonial governments would undertake to provide for local service in the Imperial squadrons the smaller vessels

that are useful for defence against possible raids or for co-operation
with a squadron, and also to equip and maintain docks and fitting
establishments which can be used by His Majesty's ships."[58] Still, this
begrudging concession offered at least a glimpse of promise, for
Britain had in effect conceded that dominion forces were not necessarily a waste if they served purposes other than a mere manpower
pool for the British fleet.

The change in the Admiralty's attitude reflected the influence of
new technologies. The self-propelled torpedo had become a powerful
weapon since its invention in the 1860s; it enabled small, fast vessels
to destroy major warships. For that reason, second-rank navies – like
those of Germany and France – had favoured small torpedo craft as
an economical method of challenging Britain's maritime supremacy.
Although too small to operate effectively at sea, the craft had proved
themselves in coastal waters during the Russo-Japanese war. That
experience had emphasized the wisdom of expanding the British
torpedo force. Such a force could not only screen major warships but
also augment land fortifications, the most effective guns of which
could still fire only a few miles out to sea.[59]

By this time the Royal Navy had virtually abandoned local harbour
and coast defence to the army. Torpedo craft now enabled the navy
to return to these vital roles without dispersing the strength of the
main squadrons. The London newspaper the *Spectator* had covered
the public debate on "Torpedo Warfare" as early as March 1902
and published letters to the editor that the German Kaiser himself
ultimately read. Kaiser Wilhelm endorsed the new trend. As he noted
in the margin in English: "I think the Torpedoboats will have succeeded to sink half a dozen Ironclads! and blo up their pursuers into
the bargain!"[60]

Admiral Sir John Fisher was keenly aware of the new technology.
As first sea lord 1904–10, he had forced through the redeployments
of 1904–5 and had created the modern British battle fleet. Torpedo
boats would free his fleet for its proper offensive role; he was particularly excited about an entirely new prototype weapon: the torpedo-
firing submarine. The first operational versions had only recently
entered service. Although these craft were small and short-ranged,
the first sea lord believed that they had transformed maritime warfare
in coastal waters. With these virtually invisible ship-killers lurking off
Britain's harbours and shores, no substantial enemy force would dare
approach. They were the definitive answer to those politicians and
army officers who wanted to tie down the British battle-fleet for anti-
invasion duties.[61] Neither Fisher nor the Germans had yet foreseen
that submarines would one day become offensive weapons and would
almost thrust Britain to its knees.

In the mean time, Admiral Fisher turned to this new technology in order to resolve the difficulties created by the dominions' demands for their own navies. If the dominions would limit their forces to torpedo flotillas, they would help rather than hinder Admiralty control of the main British fleet. There would be much less chance of panic-stricken overseas governments demanding Royal Navy support in the face of minor threats. Should British squadrons ever have to mount major operations in the vicinity of one of the dominions, these local torpedo flotillas would also be useful in defending anchorages which the large warships would use.

The Australians were rewarded in 1908 for their unrelenting pressure when Admiralty completed a plan for a dominion force of nine submarines and six torpedo-boat destroyers. The latter were in fact large vessels, with quick-firing guns capable of attacking other torpedo craft and effecting torpedo-strikes against major warships.[62]

Canadian navalists were already urging their government to follow Australia's example. They were quick to interpret the implications of the shift in British policy, to which they ascribed a much greater significance than the Admiralty had intended. According to prominent Canadian commentators at the time, their lordships had admitted that the Royal Navy could not adequately defend the Dominion against an attack from overseas; for this reason, it seemed, Admiralty had therefore approved the very kind of local naval force that had always seemed best suited to Canadian needs. Certainly, this was the most likely navy to win political support.

Canadians may not have realized it, but these arguments questioned Arthur Thayer Mahan's doctrine of aggressive naval action by large fleet units. His epoch-making *The Influence of Sea Power upon History* (1890) had become the strategic and tactical bible of naval minds in Great Britain, the United States, and Germany.[63] The Kaiser himself had been enthralled by it. As he telegraphed to an American friend on 26 May 1894: "I am just now not reading but devouring Captain Mahan's book and am trying to learn it by heart."[64] Translated into German in 1894–5 at the urging of the Oberkommando der Marine, it became a core document in Admiral Tirpitz's popularization of German naval affairs. The American naval captain's works were "serialized in German journals, copies were placed on board every warship and some 8,000 copies were distributed by the Navy Office."[65]

Significantly, Mahan had sought his models in the past by analysing seventeenth- and eighteenth-century struggles for maritime supremacy. Accordingly, he argued that large-scale blockades and a concentration of battle fleets decided who controlled the sea lanes; he illustrated the crucial importance of strategically placed naval bases and of overseas colonies. He voiced a compelling principle: seapower alone guaranteed a nation's claim to world status.[66]

Mahanian principles thus underlay Germany's Dreadnought race against Britain and inspired many of the Kaiser's thoughts on naval prestige and power. The Kaiser had assumed personal command of his navy early in 1899, and had been busy awakening public enthusiasm for Germany's naval interests. The German press was as busy watching Britain as the British press was watching the Germans – for example, in October 1899, when the Kaiser visited Hamburg. Here Germany's "Supreme War Lord," as he liked to be known, made one of his many public speeches on the importance of a national fleet for the security of trade. It attracted the attention of *The Times* of London, which the Kaiser read.[67]

Announcing that "The British Empire is the gift of seapower," the article readily found a common ground. *The Times* explained that the Royal Navy embodied the British ethos of maritime strength on which international commerce depended; in this light it found the Kaiser's position "perfectly reasonable." With perhaps a touch of ironic mirth, the Kaiser acknowledged the flattery in the margin. As *The Times* observed, "The Emperor himself is intensely interested in naval affairs, and understands more about the conditions of sea power that the vast majority of his subjects, very many of whom have never seen the sea." The Kaiser marked these lines with approval and read on: "Germany can fairly claim to create a navy in proportion to her trade and her Imperial expansion, provided always that her people ... are not indisposed to pay the price."

The Kaiser saw to it that the price would be paid. Together with Grand Admiral Tirpitz, his state secretary of the navy, he entered an armaments race. But Germany's unwavering adherence to Mahanian principles created its own obstacles to sound tactical thinking. So convinced was Tirpitz of what had now become doctrine that in 1904 he "viciously attacked proponents of cruiser warfare" among his own naval leaders and refused to countenance the submarine as a serious engine of war. He "denounced submarines as only local and secondary weapons, and refused to create what he termed a 'museum of experiments' " by even entertaining the idea of underwater warfare.[68]

While Canadian navalists were urging a local fleet, British newspapers had been reporting the growing naval armaments race in Britain and Germany. In April 1906, for example, *The Times* reported on debates in the German Reichstag on the development of German maritime power. Tirpitz and the German Admiralty, the newspaper observed, were pressing for expansion under the pretext of following Mahanian principles. "The necessity of a navy," so *The Times* quoted

Mahan, "springs from the existence of a peaceful shipping." The Kaiser marked the passage and added in the margin: "That's [precisely] why we want one."[69]

The theme warmed up in the press as war approached. Thus in July 1908 the *Spectator* grasped the real bone of contention and wrote an article that the Kaiser angrily underlined in red: "[Britain's] ultimate object ... is not merely to secure the command of the sea, but to secure it in such a way that it shall be unchallenged, or, at any rate not subject to the kind of competition to which it is at this moment exposed owing to the action of Germany." The astonished Kaiser underscored this comment and bracketed it with bold exclamation marks.

But even more damning charges against Germany followed: "The capital evil of the present situation is that we are engaged in a competition with Germany for the command of the sea which is not only ruinous from the economic point of view, but is fraught with very great temptations and provocations to an outbreak of hostilities." This the Kaiser attacked as an "!!absolute farrango of nonsense!" It was nothing but the last word in "englische Angstphantasie."[70]

Widespread alarm in Britain about the relative decline of its own military position reinforced the conclusion that the Royal Navy was becoming less capable of containing hostile fleets. Sympathetic responses followed in Canada. Where British Columbians had long been echoing Australian warnings about the Japanese menace, the situation on the Atlantic coast looked more dangerous still. Britain had achieved diplomatic settlements with its traditional enemies France and Russia but was locked in a bitter and closely run naval race with Germany. Kaiser Wilhelm II already possessed the strongest army in Europe; now he was building a large fleet of powerful, fast warships, the only purpose of which could be to break British control over the ocean approaches to western Europe. He would deny the obvious, claiming instead a Mahanian view that fleets were simply a vital adjunct of international commerce. The contest had in any event triggered a series of panics in Britain: the islands might be invaded, their life-links with the Empire might be severed, or they could be starved into submission.

Britain had experienced many such alarms since at least the time of the Spanish Armada. But this latest one struck an unprecedented note of pessimism and hysteria. This derived in no small measure from skilful British propaganda.[71] In this, an emerging mass-circulation, sensationalist press played a crucial role. It proclaimed that the enemy, now stooping to fiendishly unscrupulous strategies, and most foully armed with weaponry born of a perverted science, could wreak mass destruction on a scale as yet unheralded in history. The press campaigns formed a critical foil in the national mood. They both reflected and influenced profound debates within official circles as to the adequacy of Britain's defences and the soundness of Admiral Fisher's naval reforms.[72]

Canadians could not remain aloof. Even the German chancellor, Theodore von Bethmann Hollweg, recognized that at the very least the dominions had to help ensure that Britain would emerge from the conflict unweakened.[73] The most acute Canadian analysis of national requirements came from the pen of C.F. Hamilton, a journalist on the staff of the pro-Empire Toronto *News*. Although rooted in the program of the Toronto Navy League, of which he was a member, Hamilton's writings made a fuller, more palatable case for political action. A Canadian coastal force, he argued, was now essential for both national and imperial defence. Schemes for manning larger vessels for distant operations – which the Toronto branch continued to promote – should await a later stage in naval development.

Hamilton had no doubts about the soundness of the Royal Navy's concentration in European waters; the next war would most likely start there with a "stiff fight for the mastery of the sea." Britain would have to defend its battleship squadrons with vast screens of cruisers and smaller vessels, leaving no margin of strength to send warships to defend colonial coasts. Here, he argued, was the Achilles' heel, where a small number of enemy cruisers or converted merchantmen could inflict grievous damage. They could ravage not only Canadian ports but also the North Atlantic food trade, which both the Canadian economy and British survival depended. (The Germans, as will be seen, had reached precisely the same conclusion.)

A force patterned after the Australian model, Hamilton explained, could fill "this chink in the Admiralty strategy." One need only concentrate on those choke-points which neither raiders nor friendly ships could avoid: the Strait of Belle Isle, the Cabot Strait, the Halifax approaches, and the Bay of Fundy. All these could be readily defended by modern torpedo craft.[74]

Hamilton was well connected with the Conservatives and had conceived what he called his "coastal defence idea" as a plank in the party's platform. He had decided to publish the proposal and thereby awaken wider public interest, only to learn at the end of August 1907 that Robert Borden had "been scared off it temporarily." One reason for Borden's nervousness, Hamilton reported in confidential correspondence, was that "a number of French [Canadian] Conservatives were greatly horrified."[75] In the event, neither federal party leader raised the naval issue during the general election of 1908, which returned Laurier and his Liberals to power.

When the Conservatives finally did address the question, on the opening of the new session of Parliament in January 1909, they did so along the lines that Hamilton had suggested. The Conservative resolution, which was debated on 29 March 1909, focused on the point that united both parties: charity in defence begins at home. George Foster, MP for Toronto North, argued the case and put the motion: "In view of her great and varied resources, of her geographical position and natural environment, and of that spirit of self-help and self-respect which alone befits a strong and growing people, Canada should no longer delay in assuming her proper share of the responsibility and financial burden incident to the suitable protection of her exposed coast line and great sea-ports."[76]

This was not a new initiative, Borden explained during the debate. His party was merely urging the Liberals to fulfil the commitment that they had made at the 1902 Colonial Conference to provide adequate national defences.[77] The Halifax and Esquimalt fortifications, Foster declared, could protect nothing beyond the range of their guns, while the fisheries protection vessels were "simply childrens' toys" against even a third-class cruiser. The darkening international scene and the pressure on the Royal Navy in British home waters made action urgent along the lines of the Australian model.[78] Laurier had been prepared to stand by his position that Canada already had all the maritime defence it needed in the Fisheries Protection Service. This reflected Brodeur's words of two years earlier. Yet a dramatic transformation of the naval issue changed his mind on the eve of Foster's address in the House. The dreadnought race had begun.[79]

The all-big-gun, fast, steam-turbine "Dreadnought" battleship had become the most important measure of strength in the Anglo-German naval race. Having stolen a march on the Germans by introducing the type in 1905–6, the Royal Navy had had a comfortable lead. But on 16 March 1909 the British government dropped what one Canadian commentator described as a "bomb shell." British prime minister H.H. Asquith and his first lord of the Admiralty revealed to Parliament the disturbing intelligence that Germany was accelerating its dreadnought construction program. The British government was therefore prepared to lay down eight dreadnoughts in 1909–10 instead of the four originally planned. The prospects of tipping the balance against Germany were not good, for, as Asquith admitted, by April 1912 the Germans could well have seventeen dreadnoughts to the Royal Navy's twenty. Opposition leader Arthur

Balfour charged that the situation was even much more desperate than that; according to his own figures, the ratio would be 21 to 20 in Germany's favour.

The revelations about Germany's rapidly growing naval strength triggered an outpouring of imperial fervour and anti-German hysteria in the dominions such as Macdonald had predicted in 1880 would happen. The question of Britain's very survival suddenly displaced all arguments about local defence against cruiser raids. New Zealand's prompt offer to pay for the construction of a dreadnought for the Royal Navy – and if necessary a second one as well – brought leading members of both parties in Canada to demand that Laurier do the same. A special "emergency gift" of money to the Admiralty, they argued, in no way equated with the annual "tribute" Britain had once tried to promote.[80]

Laurier quickly asserted control over his party during the March debate and responded to Foster's proposal with a plan of his own. Standing firm against hastily offering an emergency contribution, he agreed to press ahead with expansion of the fisheries service and to create a torpedo flotilla like the one Australia was building.[81] This the Conservatives readily accepted. Borden and Foster, who were already facing strong resistance from French-Canadian Conservatives on the torpedo-flotilla proposal, merely promised on 29 March 1909 to support the government if it chose to provide an emergency contribution. Admitting that the nature and extent of the international naval crisis was not clear, the opposition leader was content with Laurier's commitment to develop his naval program in consultation with the Admiralty. He was reassured that Laurier would not entirely rule out the possibility of an "emergency" contribution in the future. Within a single day of debate, the parties had apparently achieved unanimity. The consensus would be precarious and short-lived.

Laurier had left no doubt about his belief that an emergency contribution would never be necessary. The essence of British sea power, he pointed out during the debate, was a mature and global maritime economy built on centuries of endeavour. How could Germany, a land power with but limited and recent experience of maritime affairs, so suddenly pose a dire threat? Noting that the Admiralty had postponed acceptance of New Zealand's offer, he suggested to the House that Britain neither wanted nor needed emergency gifts.[82]

Laurier's instincts in this instance were right. British alarmists had designed their campaign for domestic consumption in Britain. They had thereby hoped to eradicate the influence of "radical" members of the Liberal government who were resisting further increases in naval spending.[83] The British government, in fact, felt more than equal to the German challenge and was embarrassed by New Zealand's patriotic gift. In the words of one senior British official: "As there appears to be a general feeling in this country that ships presented by the Colonies must not be treated as a grant-in-aid towards the reduction of the Naval estimates ... [Our] acceptance of such gifts not only does not relieve the naval estimates of expenditure, but throws on them the heavy annual cost of maintaining ships which they would not otherwise have to bear."[84] In short, the gifts did not help, and cost money besides.

The Canadian and Australian attitude had by this time long since convinced British officials and political leaders that the only hope for useful assistance lay in the development of national navies. The policy was already reaping dividends in the land militias. By the spring of 1909 this view finally prevailed over the Admiralty's insistence on the principle of a single imperial navy.[85] The controversy that had echoed in the Canadian Parliament over the dreadnought gift had also reverberated in the Australian government – and with similar results. Although eventually offering emergency aid after a change of government, Australia's new prime minister, Alfred Deakin, conceded that the countries of the Empire might better spend the money by establishing their own fleets.[86]

The British government seized the opportunity afforded by the excitement in the dominions to call a special Imperial Defence Conference in August 1909. Laurier was appalled at the idea. In endeavouring to appease Quebec "nationalistes" he had been emphasizing national, not imperial defence. But having cornered himself with his promise to consult the Admiralty, he sent his minister of militia and defence, Sir Frederick Borden, and his minister of marine and fisheries, L.P. Brodeur, to the gathering in London.[87]

Admiralty confirmed his suspicions when greeting the Canadian delegates with a radical proposal. The Admiralty now readily admitted the unsoundness of its recommendation of 1907 that dominions acquire torpedo flotillas; the craft possessed limited sea-keeping qualities and required highly specialized crew. The new solution lay in creation of full-scale dominion "fleet units." Each of these would be built around a dreadnought battle-cruiser; this class of vessel was a less heavily armoured, but swifter variant of the dreadnought battleship.[88]

British worries about the Pacific had prompted this change. Reassured by the Anglo-Japanese alliance of 1902, the Royal Navy had greatly reduced its forces in that ocean. But now the mood had changed, and the Royal Navy was facing the real possibility that Japan might not be friendly in 1911 when the treaty expired.[89] All three dominion fleet units – those of Canada, Australia, and New Zealand – would be stationed in the Pacific in order to counter Japan's powerful fleet. Thus relieved of its most burdensome overseas commitments, the Royal Navy could complete its concentration against Germany.

The scheme was of course irrelevant to Canada's situation, for it had been tailored to meet Australia's concerns. British Columbia, so their lordships reassured the delegates, was protected both by distance and the Monroe Doctrine from any but the most minor Japanese assaults. For that reason, the Admiralty intended to deploy Canada's fleet unit in wartime far from home, in the western reaches of the ocean. It was scarcely worth debating, for Laurier was quite convinced that friendship with Japan would endure.[90] And besides, Sir Frederick Borden insisted, a large portion of the Canadian force would have to be stationed on the Atlantic coast anyway so as not to disappoint voters in the heavily populated eastern provinces; the Admiralty replied that the British fleet in European waters provided Atlantic Canada with protection enough. In all, the Admiralty's advice confirmed Laurier's view that the Dominion was entirely safe from naval attack.

Consulting Laurier by cable, the Canadian delegates in London none the less came some distance in accommodating the British. Ruling out the battle-cruiser as too obviously intended for imperial service, the Canadians were willing to procure the other ships of the fleet unit within the maximum expenditure of $3 million per year. This prescription for the level of naval spending probably derived from Laurier's determination to win wide political support for the new service: it was precisely the amount Robert Borden had suggested during the debate of 29 March 1909. For that sum, the Admiralty advised, Canada could obtain four 4,800-ton Bristol-class cruisers and six destroyers.[91] Laurier adopted the plan.

The Canadian navy was born on 4 May 1910. In proclaiming the Naval Service Act that day, the government also created a Department of the Naval Service to administer the force. The coastal wireless stations, fisheries protection, and hydrographic services – the elements of Laurier's "nucleus navy" – were transferred to the new department from Marine and Fisheries. Louis Brodeur assumed the new portfolio while retaining responsibility for Marine and Fisheries; G.J. Desbarats was appointed deputy minister; and Admiral Kingsmill, as director of the Naval Service, became professional head of the navy while continuing in command of the Fisheries Protection Service. Thus the new navy had strong institutional links with its progenitor, the civilian marine department.[92] It remained to be seen how long this civilian and military bond would last.

Kingsmill had first foreseen the close linkage of civilian and military tasks in the wake of the defence debate of 29 March 1909 and had recommended acquisition of two older cruisers from the Royal Navy for naval training and fisheries patrol.[93] This decision reflected the government's determination to tie naval development as closely as possible to existing policy. Thus the Canadian government purchased the 3,400-ton HMCS *Rainbow* for the west coast and the much larger, 11,000-ton *Niobe* for the east, where the bulk of naval training was to be done. *Niobe* reached Halifax on Trafalgar Day, 21 October 1910, and *Rainbow* entered Esquimalt on 7 November, after delays in refitting the ships for Canadian service.[94]

Germany was looking on. Its diplomatic authorities had been reporting the Canadian political scene to the Reichskanzler, who passed the reports to the Imperial Naval Office. Whether Germans were amused or perplexed by the Canadian vacillations is not clear. By this time German warships had been scouting the Canadian and American coasts as a prelude to serious war plans. The splendid isolation in which Canadians lived would soon be broken.

– 2 –
German Designs on North America

Sea power and naval prestige underpinned Germany's national dream of empire before naval defence was ever widely discussed in Canada. They formed the pillars of imperial grandeur. "Imperial power means maritime power," a typical German naval historian had formulated the old theme in 1901. "This magnificent pronouncement of the Kaiser will have to be taken to heart by generations of good Germans."[1] The German fleet itself was actually a creation of empire. Unlike the German army, which stressed particularist values and the virtual independence of its many provincial corps, it was a symbol of national unity.[2]

Founded by General von Stosch's first plans for a national fleet in 1873, the fledgling naval service drew on the ships of the former Norddeutscher Bund and reached a pinnacle of naval power under Admiral von Tirpitz. Throughout the 1870s and 1880s Germany undertook surveys and explorations in distant waters, deployed the East Asia Cruiser Squadron, jostled for colonial possessions, and exercised gunboat diplomacy. Once-exotic territory like South and Central America, the Caribbean, the South Seas, China, and the Philippines became familiar to generations of German seamen.[3] All this maritime activity by a nation geographically bound to the European continent raised spectres in Britain and its colonies of an unprecedented 'German peril.'[4]

Each year the German navy exercised its Order of Battle in the Baltic and the North Sea under the Kaiser's doting eye. Operating in phalanx – squadrons, divisions, and subdivisions of cruisers, corvettes, and torpedo boats – they bore grand and stirring witness to time-honoured fleet tactics.[5] Parallel lines of huge ships firing broadsides steamed in close formation, while torpedo boats dashed among the columns like greyhounds. Tradition became firm doctrine, with little room for submarines or commerce warfare.[6] Thus a mock attack against Kiel harbour, not unlike the exercise at Halifax in 1881, demonstrated that victory could be won only by massive confrontation between fleets as the first stage of assault; "attack against coastal batteries is only possible for those whose naval forces ensure a considerable superiority at sea."[7]

Germany's rearmament, like that of Britain and the United States, hinged on the concept of the decisive big-ship naval battle. The annual fleet review sail-past offered a public display of national destiny. In the words of the *Tägliche Rundschau*, which witnessed one such scene with thousands of onlookers: "Ever onward as though guided by some spectral hand each colossus carves the wake of the ship next ahead; 300 meters from bridge to bridge; one giant follows another close aboard in a line 12 kilometers long. A magnificent pattern as the fleet slips past, a front of steel, and everywhere the most powerful guns staring into a bright sky."[8] The romanticism surrounding such impressive power would uphold the spirits of German navalists even when they were describing their losses in the Battle of Dogger Bank, or when wresting spiritual victory from actual defeat at Jutland in 1916.[9]

The first thrust of German naval strategy toward North America sprang from a German-American confrontation over colonial claims in Samoa in the 1880s which threatened to break into open hostilities. The crisis facing the German Admiralty in February 1889 posed two crucial questions: "How is war to be waged against North America, and what preparations must be made?"[10] The answer seemed deceptively clear. Ideally, victory should be seized in big-ship 'blue water' sea-battles: "annihilating the enemy battle-fleet, destroying the merchant marine and driving it from the seas, and finally through bombardment ... wreaking damage ashore and putting pressure on the populace." But the German Admiralty realized that its battle fleet was as yet too small to achieve these results. The alternative lay in cruiser warfare, a strategy that would endure through 1918, although by that time the means of carrying it out would have switched to submarines.

Cruiser warfare aimed at undermining an opponent's economic life in order to force it to sue for peace.[11] It was considered especially effective against opponents like Britain that depended on their sea-lines of communication for economic survival. Like full-scale blockade of an enemy coast, it was a form of commerce warfare that struck against an opponent's merchant shipping and against any neutrals that might carry its supplies.

Cruiser warfare, however, differed from blockade in two key

respects. It was not restricted to a specific geographic zone but encompassed broader activities: hit-and-run operations, attack by landing parties, bombardment of ports and other military targets, and destruction of communications and industrial facilities on the coasts. Trade blockade – such as Britain undertook against Germany in 1914 – was the tactic of the superior naval force that could effectively control a whole sea frontier; cruiser warfare had traditionally been the tactic of the weaker. It was sometimes deemed the weaker navy's principal, if not sole, means of waging war at sea.

The naval historian Erich Raeder, later Grand Admiral in the Third Reich, endorsed Mahan's tenet that such trade interdiction caused serious "harassment and distress"; but it remained at best "a most important secondary operation of naval war." Raeder accepted Mahan's caution that "as a primary and fundamental measure, sufficient in itself to crush an enemy, [cruiser warfare] is probably ... a most dangerous delusion when presented in the fascinating garb of cheapness to the representatives of a people. Especially is it misleading when the nation against whom it is to be directed possesses, as Great Britain did and does, the two requisites of a strong sea Power – a widespread healthy commerce and a powerful Navy."[12]

The Kaiser himself, as has been seen, embraced the Mahanian view. Had he and his advisers replaced "Great Britain" by "the United States" in the above quotation, they would have gained ample warning of the danger they courted. Indeed Raeder later explained that even before the outbreak of the Great War the German navy was becoming increasingly persuaded that "cruiser warfare by *surface warships* could only be of *decisive effect* if based on the superiority of one's own fleet."[13] The Germans, he added, "had no illusions that surface-vessel cruiser warfare alone could essentially influence the outcome of the war."

Although von Tirpitz recognized that submarines were an engine of war better suited to commerce warfare, he regarded them negatively as undermining his risk theory: "Thus he saw the new weapon as a threat to the battleship and himself, and his feeble efforts to integrate u-boats into the navy further betray these feelings, and go a long way to explain why von Tirpitz ignored u-boat research until 1900."[14] To his mind, the submarine was at best only an auxiliary to the battleship. Only with the unexpected success of the submarine as a commerce raider in 1915–18 did Germany – in the person of the Kaiser and his chief of the Imperial Naval Office, Admiral Henning von Holtzendorff – hope to make cruiser warfare a decisive strategy.

But in 1889, when the German Admiralty began wrestling with the problem of war against North America, the Samoan question had already crystallized key issues. As Germany's state secretary of the Foreign Office, Bernhard von Bülow, wrote in April that year, it had provided "new proof of the fact that overseas policies can only be carried out with sufficient fleet power." The Kaiser appropriately minuted von Bülow's brief: "That's the very thing I've been preaching to those dunderhead members of parliament every day for the past ten years."[15] For von Tirpitz, and to a lesser extent for von Bülow, building a gigantic battle fleet was clearly a matter of "world status or national decline" – Weltgeltung oder Niedergang – (on which Germany's survival hinged. Von Tirpitz called it a crucial survival question – Lebensfrage Deutschlands – in his initial speech to the *Reichstag* in support of the first naval bill (Flottengesetz) on 6 December 1897.[16] Failure to sustain maritime interests, he argued, would lead first to Germany's economic demise and ultimately to its political collapse. Von Bülow defended the bill with rousing rhetoric that rang of manifest destiny: "We want to put no one in the shadows, but we demand our place in the sun."[17]

The first naval bill (Flottengesetz), of 10 April 1898, edged Germany toward the powerful fleet to which its leaders aspired: Seventeen ships-of-the-line, eight coastal cruisers, nine heavy cruisers, and twenty-six light; these were to be backed up by a reserve of two ships-of-the-line and seven cruisers. The standardized ship-of-the-line, the German "Einheitslinienschiff," was a veritable monster warship at the turn of the century: 12–15,000 tons displacement, 120 metres in length, with a cruising range of 4–5,000 nautical miles; her 15,000-horse-power steam-engines thrust her at speeds of 18–20 knots. Armed with four heavy-calibre guns (24–33 centimetres) in two turrets, she could also deliver broadsides with 10–12 medium cannon in the 12.7-cm-to-16.7-cm range.

As imposing as the size and technical quality of these ships – which matched or exceeded those of the capital units of any major maritime power – was von Tirpitz's success in marshalling the enthusiastic support for naval expansion of an army-oriented, virtually land-locked populace.[18] This required a powerful public relations program. The German Navy League, which had been spreading the gospel of navalism and naval prestige, had by 1901 over 600,000 members and provided a broadly based and dynamic corps of converts through which von Tirpitz could sell his message. Britain's Navy League, by contrast, comprised only 15,000 members that year. But, as Marder explains, Germany was in need of conversion to the new faith and relied on mass enthusiasm; Britain, with its history of seafaring, only needed reminding of the truths it had all but forgotten.[19]

Immediately after assuming the position of state secretary of the

Imperial Navy Office, von Tirpitz had created the Press and Information Branch – Abteilung für Nachrichtenwesen und allgemeine Parlamentsangelegenheiten – which formed the nucleus of the later Naval Intelligence Service. Known as "N" (for Nachrichtenbüro), it co-ordinated preparation of parliamentary papers, promoted the naval bills, and published popular works on sea power for civilian consumption. Information published by the anonymous "N" developed into the periodical *Nauticus*, which argued the economic and political cause for the non-military reader. Marshalling a broad spectrum of officers, writers, and well-known academics to his banner, von Tirpitz launched the modern era of military propaganda.[20] The von Tirpitz "bandwagon provid[ed] a scaffold of cultural, economic political, military and vulgar Darwinistic timber for the new structure."[21]

Darwinism was thick in the air. Admiral Scheer defended Germany's aspirations for a world-class fleet by insisting that its "urge to burst out of the confines of the Fatherland was like a powerful natural instinct."[22] Darwinist solutions to international conflicts were of course no preserve of the Germans alone. Thus the British Empire's patriots saw emergence of a new and powerful supernational order in the close, but entirely voluntary relationship between self-governing colonies and the Mother Country. But where Germans saw North American democracy as regressive weakness, Americans argued its evolutionary strength. An article by an American naval captain that reached the desk of von Bülow in Berlin might have given him some cause for thought: "Every test goes to show that Americans, with [but] a few generations of free life in a free continent, are already, physically, intellectually and spiritually, a race of giants."[23] Canadian imperialists were convinced that these same North American qualities especially fitted the Dominion to lead the empire to new heights of glory. Such assertions were as unequivocal as a British position that argued for the innate superiority of the British tar because he had "salt in his veins" and could think for himself.

The books, periodicals, articles, and photo reports which von Tirpitz's staff produced for home consumption successfully promoted the concept of Germany as a seafaring nation with a vital need for a powerful navy.[24] By 1901 no fewer than eleven newspapers in Berlin and thirty-one in the provinces subscribed to the ready-made stories churned out for public consumption.[25] But despite all the support, lamented the official German publication on the fleet exercises, Germans still did not "think navy to the extent that Germany's vital interests require"; it none the less took solace in the fact that things would change. It was only a matter of time before Germans would overcome "the prejudice that their geography and history contradict the idea" of having a navy.[26] That same year the Kaiser presented all school children with a special glossy edition on Germany's naval heritage, illustrated by the famous naval artist Willy Stöwer.[27] With bold and stirring images, its text argued the theme of Seegeltung – naval prestige. Other books soon followed to encourage the affection of "mothers and children" for the navy.

Kapitänleutnant Karl Boy-Ed, whose espionage activities would later gain him some notoriety as naval attaché in Washington, began working for "N" in 1906. The profession of "literary pedlar," as he described his task in a personal letter to a colleague on the China Station, meant providing pulp fare for the public that did not stop short of distorting fact.[28] As Boy-Ed advised one of his press officers who was reporting on the fleet manoeuvres of August 1911: "The articles must contain nothing that allows specific conclusions about our military intentions or the real course of the manoeuvres. Use the sequence of military events just as a frame-work for describing interesting episodes – which can actually be invented anyway."[29]

The German fleet was actually an offensive weapon designed with England – and later North America – in mind. Germany justified it as a defensive force in the light of the then current risk concept of deterrence (Risikogedanke). "The military concept of the risk principle," as Admiral Hollweg wrote in reply to British reproaches that Germany was setting the pace in the naval armaments race, was "a cross between defence and offense."[30] To his mind it had been foisted on the German navy no less by political and parliamentary considerations than by financial restraint. Economic imperialism loomed large in German thinking, both as a cause of war and as a reason for its own fleet expansion.[31] International events had meanwhile shown German naval enthusiasts in no uncertain terms just how important a strong naval force was for any nation desiring a place in world politics and economic power: the Spanish-American War of 1898 during which the United States annexed Hawaii, the Philippines, Guam, and Puerto Rico; and the confrontation in Manila Bay in the summer of that year between USN Admiral Dewey and Vice-Admiral von Diederichs.[32]

In short, war planning reflected German nervousness not only about the Americans' increasing bellicosity against Spain but about their increasing attempts to gain influence in the Pacific, the Far East, and the Caribbean during the years 1893–1900. In the struggle for colonial possessions, Germany once more saw the United States emerge as a dangerous rival.[33]

Detailed planning for war against North America had an unprepossessing beginning in a "winter works" essay assignment written by a young naval lieutenant in 1898, just when the British Admiralty was abandoning consideration of the problem. These annual Winter-arbeiten quite typically covered a broad range of geopolitical and military topics, with a view to honing subordinate officers' skills in operational planning. Political and strategic relevance was not necessarily a criterion for such pedagogical exercises.

However, the topics assigned for 1897–8 were markedly different, focusing on urgent issues – Cuba, the Philippines, the Monroe Doctrine, Central America, and the United States as factors in German naval policy.[34] Nor did the study on operations against North America by Lieutenant (later admiral and naval historian) Eberhard von Mantey end as an academic exercise. Subsequent revisions made their way up to the highest-ranking front-line officer, until they emerged as Operation Plan OP III. Though ultimately dropped in 1906, the plan none the less sheds substantial light on German preoccupations, misconceptions, and occasional sheer foolishness with regard to a possible attack on North America.

Von Mantey disregarded the German Admiralty's earlier emphasis on cruiser warfare against North American trade and suggested instead military occupation of Norfolk, Hampton Roads, and Newport News, all in Virginia, by combined army and naval forces.[35] For the primary naval assault he selected the area between Portland (Maine) and Norfolk: "the heart (Kern) of the American country," where the Americans could be "struck at their most sensitive point and be most easily forced to accept peace." Subsequent operations could strike up Chesapeake Bay toward Washington and Baltimore. Von Mantey appended sketches of harbours and estuaries and listed distances to be run; but he virtually neglected the problem of re-supplying such an assault across over 3,000 miles of open sea.[36]

Nor was he daunted by the size of the population centres which the German forces of occupation were to control: Portsmouth, 10,000; Gloucester, 24,600; Portland, 47,000; Salem, 40,000; Baltimore, 434,000; Boston, 600,000; Philadelphia, 1,105,000; New York, 2,885,000. Von Mantey pondered the abject state of the US navy, with its niggardly budget and antiquated equipment. To his mind, democracy itself hampered the development of a strong navy, for "every free citizen can speak his own mind, and if his opinion is rejected he simply throws care to the winds and makes the loudest noise in the press." Von Mantey's criticism may have been shallow, but it was no exception. German observers of the American scene in subsequent years frequently picked up on the theme of the crippling effect of democracy in a volunteer force.[37] In short, von Mantey found US forces – from professional navy to "tinker-toy" militia – in a sorry state and therefore easy fare for superior German forces.

Von Mantey's patently impracticable scheme of 1898 was assessed by successive senior officers. First-level review granted it the typical sobriquet of "an industrious piece of work" and accepted the details at face value, simply because the reviewer confessed to having no means of checking them out.[38] He took exception to von Mantey's primary target and proposed instead the Delaware River, from which point he hoped to threaten both New York and Philadelphia simultaneously. Confessing ignorance of the Delaware's suitability as a landing site, he noted the need for transporting "suitable means" (i.e. landing craft) to get the troops ashore. For the rest, so he observed, von Mantey ought to have mentioned the US navy's serious defects. And here the reviewer trotted out the usual litany: the American service was unprepared, did not have a balanced fleet, and consisted of a higgledy-piggledy collection of troops whose officers were so old that they blocked promotion and forced younger, more promising types either to leave the service or become indifferent.

When von Mantey's paper reached the desk of the chief of the Baltic Naval Station, Admiral Hans von Koester, it received almost entirely favourable marks. Von Koester, as inspector-general designate of the German navy, was an officer of considerable influence. A genial-looking patriarch with white beard and moustache impeccably trimmed to a Vandyke point, he was known in navy circles as "the taskmaster of the German fleet"; he would press for technical and tactical reform that brought the Imperial Navy to an unprecedented level of combat readiness. Admiral von Koester accepted von Mantey's essay as "an industrious piece of work which in a panoramic way gives a general overview of the coastal conditions of the United States."[39] Significantly, he found it a timely and "therefore especially interesting" proposal. There is little doubt that some of Germany's leading naval officers were pondering the possibility of war with the United States.[40]

The German press was by this time reporting escalating tensions between Spain and the United States. Newspapers would have been an obvious and graphic source of information to von Mantey, had he been genuinely interested in the practicalities of strategic planning; they stressed the real difficulties of an actual confrontation, where he himself was only wrestling with speculative theory. Articles emphasized, for example, the great distance that Spanish warships had to cover in order to reach American and Central American waters; they highlighted the accompanying problems of replenishment and resupply; they spoke of the Americans' naval strength and flexibility in responding to threats.

None of this seems to have touched von Mantey. Had he looked closer, some press reports would have confirmed his bias against the

Americans' weakness and unpreparedness. Thus a story in May 1898 commented on the vulnerability of the US coastal states to naval attack. Americans themselves, according to these accounts, "feel how sensitive their coast is, how unprepared their defence institutions are, and how easy it would be for Spanish ships to lob some well-filled shot onto the coast or even to undertake a full-scale bombardment."[41] To be sure, the US fleet had at first repulsed the Spanish, but American "indecision, powerlessness and inactivity" in Manila seemed to be offering the Spanish a chance at ultimate victory. "The first genuine decision at sea," newspapers explained, "can bring this favourable situation to fruition or bring about a new change of scene."[42] Von Mantey would have felt justified by the contempt which the German press showed for both the US army and navy. If the "money-bag snob" Americans were having this much difficulty facing down the "impecunious Spaniards," to borrow epithets from the press, they would fall easy prey to a powerful German assault.

The Germans were not alone in their low assessment of US naval forces. An article in the *Scientific American* of March 1900 that reached the Kaiser's desk revealed prescient insight into the problem: "If we are in danger of falling behind Germany by the year 1900, where shall we stand at the close of the year 1920? To leave such an important matter as the authorization of the new warships to the caprice of the naval committees of each current year, while our competitors, with commendable far-sightedness, are establishing programmes that reach two full decades into the future, is to expose ourselves to the danger of being hopelessly outmatched at some future critical period in our foreign relations."[43]

The Kaiser underlined this last phrase – "being hopelessly outmatched at some future critical period in our foreign relations" – and commented in English: "I fervently hope so!" The Kaiser had no intention of relaxing the pressure to expand his fleet and watched with deep and often amused interest both British and American naval debates. British "navalism" and "expansionism" gave him ready marks by which to measure his own plans. Particularly salutary was the position taken by the secretary of the British Admiralty in a public address in October 1901. So crucial is a powerful navy to a nation's economic and political health, the secretary had asserted, that one can never rest on one's laurels and affirm that "all is well with the fleet." Political constellations, he insisted, are always shifting, "and the man who is content, who regards finality as obtained or obtainable, is a dangerous person, not to be trusted and not to be encouraged."[44] The Kaiser annotated his copy with the remark: "Good! that's my principle too!"

Von Mantey's second Winterarbeit, of 1899, none the less proved even bolder and more daring than his first effort the previous year. The key to German success, he reflected, lay in solving three vital problems: ample logistic preparations in peacetime, active planning for rapid transport of men and materials by sea to the US Atlantic coast, and, finally, execution of unexpected lightning strikes. He most clearly overreached himself by selecting as the principal target New York City, with its over two million inhabitants. But he stressed the importance of striking before the Americans could mobilize, lay protective mines, or even arm coastal batteries. With an eye to Germany's own unprepared naval base of Wilhelmshaven, von Mantey was convinced that the attacks would unleash sheer terror in New York and "the greatest panic at the mere thought of a bombardment."[45]

Von Mantey estimated that by 1900 the Americans would have seven ships-of-the-line, fourteen cruisers, and fourteen coastal cruisers; if that were so, then Germany required at least seventeen ships-of-the-line, thirty-three cruisers, and four auxiliary cruisers to carry out his proposed invasion. He anticipated the requirement for between 30 and 60 freighters to transport some 75,000 tons of coal but did not comment on further logistic support for sustained operations against the United States. As in all subsequent plans, defeat of the US navy in a decisive sea battle was a crucial precondition to invasion. Von Mantey and his study supervisor both knew, of course, that if the Americans refused to accept the challenge of a decisive encounter at sea, then the German attack would necessarily fail.

The chief of the First Battle Squadron, Vice-Admiral August Thomsen, readily recognized the merits of von Mantey's paper but saw its limitations as well. First, he wrote, American intelligence would have twigged to the intended assault; second, even a victorious German fleet would be too weakened by its encounter with the US navy to assault shore batteries effectively. Nor did Thomsen agree with the value of seizing Norfolk for a support base; he suggested instead a base that would in fact figure prominently in later war plans: the island of "Perteriko," as he called it.

Attacking Puerto Rico, he wrote, would be relatively easy. If successful in decoying elements of the American fleet into battle, the feint would force them to operate far from home, without support. Although Thomsen confessed his ignorance of American geography – "I'm not aware of its size ... but would like to think that none the less much would be achieved if the East of North America were in our hands" – he recognized the timeliness of the plan. "At the moment," he wrote, "every thinking German sea officer is occupied with the consequences of a belligerent conflict between Germany and the United States of North America."[46]

Two aspects of these proposals are striking: the very fact that senior officers even considered such a war an immediate possibility, and the blinkered parochialism of an officer corps that admirals von Tirpitz, von Trotha, and Scheer at various times touted as cosmopolitan and "open to the world." For, as Herwig and Trask have pointed out, "Vizeadmiral Thomsen was not even informed, or bothered to inform himself, of the size and the industrial-military capability of his potential opponent."[47]

Writing privately many years later, in 1929, Admiral Eberhard von Mantey excoriated the German navy of his early years that had talked so pretentiously of global maritime war while remaining both in thought and in action little more than an inbred and provincial army corps. Officer training was more concerned with caste-conscious social niceties than with realistic state-of-the-art warfare and had little vision of what was actually taking place outside coastal waters: "We, the navy, the Fleet and Fleet Staff, clung to our home ports and thought continentally. Only when we puffed ourselves up with Mahanian wisdom did we act as though we could survey the world. Under scrutiny, however, the Fleet was just as continental-European as the Army General Staff. We were a Prussion army corps planted in iron boxes."[48] German autobiography and historical fiction subsequently supported von Mantey's harsh view. Thus Friedrich Ruge, who served in four successive German navies, recalled his officer training prior to 1914: "We learned nothing about leadership, tactics, strategy or naval history."[49]

Organizational changes were meanwhile occurring at the highest level of the German navy. The year 1897 marked a crucial turning-point: "the appointment of new men to implement more efficaciously than before the Kaiser's personal rule, which saw the inauguration of a full-scale *Weltpolitik* and the beginnings of the battlefleet."[50] On 14 March 1899 the Kaiser personally assumed supreme command of the German navy by issuing an Allerhöchste Kabinettsordre that dissolved the previous supreme command structure. The constitution had of course already declared him the head of the armed forces, but the new order confirmed his personal relationship with the navy. A further "All-Highest Cabinet Order" of 30 March created the successor to the now defunct Admiralty; this was the Imperial Naval Office (Reichs-Marine-Amt) with its Naval Cabinet and Naval High Command (Oberkommando der Marine). As the highest imperial ministry, the Reichs-Marine-Amt was responsible for the organization, administration, and further development of the navy.

The administration of the navy was, of course, part of the entire imperial administration. As such it was subordinate to the imperial chancellor, though the latter had a permanent representative in the

state secretary of the Imperial Naval Office. In his relationship to
the Kaiser, the state secretary therefore served as the chancellor's
representative in naval matters; imperial orders were passed through
him to the chancellor, with copies to the Imperial Naval Office. Not
surprising, the staff structure fostered the germ of conflict.

Grand Admiral Alfred von Tirpitz, whose career had sky-rocketed
after early recognition by the Kaiser, held this highest naval office
during the crucial years 1897–1916. His principle – "the natural
mission of a fleet is strategic offensive" – guided his development of
German naval forces. He was succeeded by Admiral Eduard von
Capelle, who served until August 1918. Immediately subordinate to
them as chief of the Imperial Naval Office through the critical years
of the war was Admiral Henning von Holtzendorff. He was one of
the Kaiser's closest confidants. They communicated officially through
correspondence and the imperial briefings (Immediatvorträge), during which von Holtzendorff would put the navy's case and receive
instructions; shared aspirations, mutual respect, and friendship created a strong bond between them. Thus von Holtzendorff could, and
sometimes did, short-circuit the policy-making apparatus and – in
the case of submarine operations against North America in 1916–18 –
bypass the political wing of the imperial administration. He sometimes cut out von Tirpitz, von Jagow of the Foreign Office, Chancellor
von Bethmann Hollweg, or all three. The Kaiser's role as supreme
commander of the navy, in which he liked to involve himself in the
most minute details of tactics and officer discipline, was never openly
disputed until the undercurrents of revolution that forced his abdication on 9 November 1918.

Drawing on von Mantey's two essays, the newly reorganized Admiralty Staff soon formulated in 1899 the first detailed Marschplan
against the United States. The details need not concern us here.
Suffice it to say that they dropped Puerto Rico in favour of a staging
point in the Azores and support bases in Frenchman Bay (Maine)
and Long Bay (South Carolina); their primary aim was defeat of the
American fleet prior to attacking the eastern seaboard. Over the next
ten years the plan was altered only in matters of detail. Vice-Admiral
von Diederichs, who had overall responsibility for planning from the
time he was appointed chief of the Admiralty Staff in December 1899,
had experience not only with distant operations but in standing up
to the Americans. As commander of the East Asia Squadron, he had
seized the Chinese port of Kiachow and in 1898 had confronted
Admiral Dewey in Manila Bay. Von Diederichs's first assignment,
however, was not to refine secret plans but to supply political ammunition for increased naval estimates.

Von Tirpitz asked the new chief of staff for "a thorough elucidation" of the possible situation "in the event of war either with England or America" in order to convince the Reichstag's budget committee of the need for further fleet expansion.[51] He therefore wanted "not a scientific staff paper" but a report in layman's terms understandable to members of the budget committee; the paper should "prove convincingly how extraordinarily unfavourable if not desperate our situation in such a war would be." Von Tirpitz particularly wanted von Diederichs to demonstrate the German fleet's inability to cope with the United States. He thus determined the answer before the study was ever made.

Von Diederichs replied on 20 January 1900 that an "effective blockade of the American coast [was] not possible with the means [provided by] the Naval Bill of 1898."[52] Von Diederichs based his proposals on the assumption that Germany would never have initiated such action but would have been forced into war with the United States; under such circumstances, offensive operations offered "the sole means of resistance." From this he espoused a conventional maritime doctrine: first gain maritime supremacy (i.e. defeat the US fleet), and only then "commence operations against maritime commerce, enemy coasts and colonies." War with the United States called for combined army-navy operations on the eastern seaboard. Finally, "the acquisition of valuable coastal cities in the New England states would be the most effective means of wresting peace" from the enemy. In urging that the German fleet be doubled, to thirty-eight ships-of-the-line, twelve heavy cruisers, and thirty-two light cruisers – virtually the number approved by the second naval bill of 1900 – von Diederichs gave von Tirpitz what he wanted. Germany's confrontation with Britain over the latter's war in South Africa – with the Americans sympathetic to Britain – served as the catalyst for this second fleet expansion.

Von Tirpitz had meanwhile directed the naval attaché in Washington, Kapitänleutnant (later Admiral) von Rebeur-Paschwitz, to advise with some urgency "which points of the Atlantic and Gulf coast of the USA would be suitable for establishing support bases in the event of a combat mission."[53] The attaché replied on 26 January 1900 that once the Germans had destroyed the US fleet – to his mind, the "principal object" of the exercise – then the "only means left for forcing the opponent to accept peace is an energetic assault on the rich harbour towns of the north." He rejected attacks on Cuba and Puerto Rico as having no military value in the enterprise. Continental lodgements were what mattered. The attaché had personally inspected Cape Cod and Provincetown as possible support bases for an advance against Boston and recognized that city and New York as the key targets. In his view, it was pointless to thrust further inland to the "nominal capital city," Washington. Quite apart from the military difficulty of such a trek, the real wealth and power of the country lay in the commercial and industrial centres of the northeast.

Berlin continued to press the attaché for information on US coastal defences. No one in Berlin seems to have realized the enormous length of the American coast nor how difficult it was for one man based in Washington to visit it. Rebeur-Paschwitz seems to have relied entirely on the American press, whose official sources had now all but fallen silent. Frustrated no doubt by the failure of German naval planners to grasp the real magnitude of an attack on North America, he asked Berlin on 29 March 1901 to clarify the issue. Was the General Staff in fact genuinely convinced of the principle of an assault "against the trade centres Boston or New York?" The Army General Staff subsequently decided on Cape Cod. His (German) majesty's ship (Seiner Majestät Schiff) SMS *Vineta* therefore visited Boston in the summer of 1901, under the guise of a routine repair stop, and took the attaché aboard for a tour of the area.

Vice-Admiral von Diederichs had meanwhile secured the first step of an operational plan against the United States by issuing preparatory war orders on 1 February 1900 to his overseas cruisers. The cruiser squadron in East Asia was to adopt the usual offensive stance by securing German trade routes and "by seeking out as quickly as practicable enemy [i.e. American] naval forces near the Philippines." In such an emergency, those cruiser squadrons currently deployed in East Africa, western America, and Australia would be ordered to hasten to the aid of Germany's East Asia Squadron. The Kaiser initialled his agreement.

Von Diederichs first briefed the Kaiser in an Immediatvortrag on 26 February 1900 and recommended an offensive thrust against North America by the whole German fleet.[54] His overseas cruisers would support the main thrust by distracting the US navy. Rejecting the advice of the naval attaché in Washington, von Diederichs insisted on the old routes: coaling in the Azores, winter advance to the West Indies, and a direct run to the New England states in summer. As German naval forces were still too weak for such an undertaking, he refrained from formulating further plans, pending the anticipated second naval bill of 14 June 1900. As we have seen, this virtually doubled Germany's fleet. Further detailed planning followed. In fact the Kaiser's notation on the naval attaché's report of 26 January 1900 led to joint consultations between Vice-Admiral von Diederichs and Count Alfred von Schlieffen, chief of the General Staff; von Mantey's theoretical groundwork had to be turned into a practical mobilization plan.

Von Diederich's Immediatvortrag before the Kaiser over eight

months later, on 10 December 1900, again recommended Boston and
New York as targets, with a support base in Provincetown. Germany's
projected fleet advantage over the United States by 1901, he argued,
would give Germany the necessary offensive power and initiative.
The Kaiser was less optimistic and sought von Schlieffen's advice on
the number of troops necessary for an occupation of Cuba as a
staging point for ultimate thrusts against Boston and New York. Von
Schlieffen seems to have been unwilling to commit himself to paper
and responded in the vaguest terms.[55] When it came to hard figures,
he was more precise. Assuming Cuba were friendly to the United
States, the Germans must land 50,000 men, with a further 100,000
for the advance on Cape Cod. But, in the final analysis, "even this
number would in all likelihood be by no means sufficient for the
thrust into the continent." This analysis undercut von Diederichs's
plan completely. As Herwig and Trask explain: "Schlieffen's letter of
13 March 1901 formed a turning point in the formulation of the
operations plans against the United States ... It marked a return to
sober military strategy and a turning away from what can only be
termed the reckless offensive-oriented thinking that had characterized Admiralty Staff ... ever since Mantey's first Winterarbeit of
1898."[56]

Rivalry between von Tirpitz and von Diederichs forced the Kaiser
in 1902 to replace the latter by Vice-Admiral Wilhelm Büchsel. The
new chief of the Imperial Navy Office had been a close aide of von
Tirpitz and was a proponent of the grand admiral's expansionist
policy of creating a chain of maritime support bases in the Americas
and the Far East.[57] A resourceful, though sometimes undiplomatic
officer, with thirty-seven years of service in the navy, Büchsel had
scarcely taken up his new office when a major crisis flared up that
threatened to bring Germany and the United States into open conflict. Venezuela's default of loan payments to both the German and
the British governments provoked these two nations to blockade the
Venezuelan coast. "At the root of the worsening relations between
Berlin and Caracas lay Venezuela's inability (and unwillingness) to
honor mostly guaranteed interest and loan payments on several
major industrial undertakings financed by German entrepreneurs at
hefty rates."[58]

The Americans feared the combined power of the two navies. In
fact, however, the blockade threatened neither US security nor the
Monroe Doctrine. The combined tonnage of the blockading forces
(even including that of Italy, which later joined the blockade) constituted less than half that of Admiral George Dewey's Caribbean forces.
The blockade had none the less triggered serious misgivings in both

the German and American camps about the adequacy of their respective navies. This nervousness lent impetus to a further escalation of the arms race.

Important parallels and differences in the German and British attitude toward the United States suggest themselves at this point. As a result of the Anglo-American war scare over Venezuela between December 1895 and January 1896, the British services had begun making war plans that were very similar to the plans that the German fleet was evolving in 1898–1906. A certain Lieutenant-Colonel Foster of the British army was even sleuthing about the New England coast in search of likely landing sites and assault positions – much as Berlin would expect Rebeur-Paschwitz to do some three years later. The difference was, however, that the British recognized the full potential of us military expansion and wisely pursued a policy of rapprochement. One of the first results was the British policy of benevolent neutrality in supporting the United States in the Spanish-American war.

By contrast, the German fleet seems to have had no such sure sense of the Americans' awesome power and therefore fine-tuned its war plans in 1898–1906 – during precisely the period when the British Admiralty was succeeding in having the British government abandon the contingency of war with the United States. Canada, of course, had been well ahead of the British government, writing off the possibility of war with the Americans as early as 1880. The Royal Navy's sure grasp of strategy and deep sense of realism could come only with centuries of experience. Thus for all the lapses and instances of stupidity, for all the confusion over steam-power and new weapons, the Royal Navy of the late nineteenth and early twentieth centuries was the most experienced and professional navy in the world. It knew what it was doing and knew what was possible and what was fanciful. The Wilhelmine Germans lacked this grasp.

German plans none the less continued unabashed. Büchsel briefed the Kaiser in February 1903 on the roles of his foreign cruiser squadrons in the event of war.[59] Noting the reinforcement of the American East Asia Squadron, he argued for a thrust against the North American west coast in order to draw the Americans off; this would, he hoped, remove the us threat to German trade in the Orient and support Germany's principal attacks on the us east coast. Büchsel's Immediatvortrag before the Kaiser on 21 March 1903 presented a comprehensive plan entitled "War against the United States." He clarified the state of naval planning against the United States and – for the first time in German naval planning – concerned himself with political issues. In effect, he unwittingly offered the same reasons as the British Admiralty for refusing to plan a war with the United States: "The *necessary precondition* for a war of Germany against the u.s.a. is a *political situation in Europe*, which gives the German Empire a completely free hand extraterritorially (nach aussen). Any uncertainty in Europe would preclude the execution of a war against the u.s.a. We will therefore not seek such a war, but it can be thrust upon us."[60]

Comparison of fleet strengths suggested that Germany could still take advantage of a temporary superiority which the United States most certainly would overcome within three to five years. Büchsel therefore deemed it necessary to "bring about a decisive battle as soon as possible." Following the support-base strategy, he would first gain control of Puerto Rico and the neighbouring island of Culebra, thus establishing German supremacy in the Caribbean and over the Panama Canal. Staging northward to occupy Long Island and threaten New York, he hoped to achieve his principle war aims: "a firm position in the West Indies, a free hand in South America, and the [American] abandonment of the Monroe Doctrine."

The major thrust of Büchsel's arguments shifted from von Diederichs's concept of forcing the Americans to seek peace to a concept of naval offensive power in order to destroy us dominance in the Western Hemisphere. This in turn was designed as a first stage in German commercial and industrial exploitation of the occupied zones. Büchsel and his staff – with the Kaiser's approval – had shifted the focus of naval planning "from an offensive military to an offensive military-political campaign."[61]

Germany's views were no secret. By May 1903 the Kaiser was briefed on reports from the German naval attaché in Washington on us public opinion. The American press, he had written, even including "serious journals, says repeatedly that Germany is a threat to the Monroe Doctrine," which would lead to war.[62] Indeed, Admiral Dewey's "strong aversion to Germany and complete confidence in the American fleet [were] shared by the whole officer corps ... who expect war with Germany as a fait accompli." This largely explained the continued expansion of the us navy.

German warships were meanwhile cruising the areas of political concern. On 14 May 1903, for example, sms *Gazelle* was in Newport, sms *Falke* was in the West Indies with sailing plans for Central America, and sms *Panther* was on passage from St Thomas in the West Indies to Newport News.[63] The Kaiser also approved the exploratory voyage of sms *Falke* in April 1904 to "all the more important coastal points including the west coast of Canada."[64] German warships, as we shall see, continued their intelligence-gathering cruises; successive naval attachés reported on US fleet training and exercises, while German naval staff, keeping close tabs on the balance between the German and American fleets, honed their war plans.[65]

From 27 November 1903 onward, the von Mantey proposals for an assault on North America were known officially as Operationsplan III (OP III).[66] But within three years, European politics had shifted to Germany's disadvantage and forced reconsideration of its naval strategy. In the amendment to Plan OP III written by a former German naval attaché who had served in Washington since 1904: "A declaration of war by Germany against the USA is only possible if we have an alliance with England and if our flank facing France is covered by Austria, Italy and possibly even Russia as well."

Should such be the case, German assault forces would land in Canada and attack the United States by means of a territorial campaign across the border. In the light of political realities, this was at best sheer fantasy. Yet we might remind ourselves that even such a leading British advocate of rapprochement with the United States as Admiral Fisher still liked to fantasize about tackling a German-US alliance. But he had no doubts about reality. In May 1906 Germany's Admiral Büchsel was forced to admit that OP III was no longer specifically directed against what he called the "United States of Northamerica." This was precisely the time that the British Committee of Imperial Defence confirmed British policy that war with the United States was unthinkable.

Even though OP III had now been shelved and relegated to a theoretical exercise, German operational authorities still believed that naval warfare against North America was a distinct possibility. They acted accordingly. It was therefore imperative that German warships reconnoitre the coasts and harbours of potential enemies. The search for U-Plätze – "Unterstützungsplätze," or "U-places," where cruisers could hide at anchor unobserved and undetected – and the updating of the important *Cruiser Handbook* remained an essential undertaking until the beginning of hostilities in 1914.

To this end, the gunboat SMS *Panther* had in 1905–6 undertaken lengthy voyages in the Atlantic and Pacific oceans and along the east and west coasts of Canada and the United States in search of secret anchorages, in which cruisers could replenish with coal from friendly steamers and prepare for combat. She submitted a report from Seattle on 16 September 1905 covering her voyage along the BC coast to Alaska. She had located on the BC coast "a large number of hiding-places and protected harbours ... of special importance in the event of war against the United States and against Canada."[67] On 14 November 1906 she was 4,000 miles away, on Canada's Atlantic coast, charting and photographing in Saint John, New Brunswick. German ships had also reported on fortifications at Bremerton, Astoria, San Francisco, and San Diego. By March 1908 Admiral Büchsel had sufficient information on the west coast of North America to brief the Kaiser on sites for assault landings in Puget Sound and the Straits of Juan da Fuca: "For the timely landing of larger masses of troops outside gunnery range of the forts, the undefended Port Angeles [fifteen miles across the straits from Victoria, BC] seems the appropriate location."[68]

The east coast of North America, however, was more important in German planning. In June 1907 the chief of the Admiralty Staff sent secret, handwritten orders to the commanding officer of SMS *Bremen* to scout the harbours of Halifax and Quebec City. Noting that "the English navy" had given up Halifax as a fleet support base in 1905 and "had transferred the administration to Canada," he sought details of any changes. As all "available war charts" of the area were "sketchy and of older origin" he required the *Bremen* to update current navigational charts. He sought as well precise information on the progress of fortifications on the St Lawrence below Quebec and on their armament. It was a secret commission to be carried out "with the greatest circumspection."[69] The Kaiser himself expressed satisfaction with *Bremen*'s tour, particularly the sojourn in Montreal in September 1907, which had "helped secure the good repute of the German navy abroad."[70]

The carefully formulated report, written in the commanding officer's graceful long-hand from St Thomas, West Indies, on 10 October 1907, revealed intimate knowledge of Canadian defences.[71] SMS *Bremen* had scouted the areas, sent parties ashore in Quebec and Halifax, examined building sites for new batteries and the ruins of old forts, surveyed and photographed, and ultimately drawn sound conclusions.

The tour of the Quebec region revealed "that the Canadian government [did] not lay great store on an energetic defense of Quebec City." Halifax, examined in detail both from seaward and shore, presented a different picture. Starting from Sambro Island (where there were no defences at all), the crew of SMS *Bremen* noted the precise location and calibre of guns from seaward to the inner harbour and had briefly inspected the Eastern Passage, which seemed to offer cruisers quick passage through lightly defended waters. One local resident had even offered the intriguing disinformation that British cruisers had navigated it at night. (This detail would lead to a serious German survey the following year.)

The defences of Halifax seemed a strange mixture of run-down redoubts and promising new construction. The commanding officer found it difficult to explain the new construction – unless perhaps the Canadians were bracing themselves against an attack by England. For Canada, he reflected, defence of "the much too open and vulnerable border with the usa" should really have higher priority than naval development. England, he mused, could only have withdrawn its maritime forces in order to pressure Canada into contributing toward imperial defence. In fact, neither of these conclusions was true. Laurier was determined *not* to develop substantial defences against the United States, and Admiral Fisher was giving no thought whatever to Dominion contributions when reorganizing the fleet in 1906–7.

Understandably, the German commander had difficulty in grasping the subtleties of relations between members of the "North Atlantic Triangle" and of the domestic political compromise that was shaping Canadian defence policy. In one critical area, however, he showed both strategic and political insight: "Despite the great extent of coast, Canada has at present but one especially important gateway for world trade, the St Lawrence River. But even public opinion in Canada itself it divided about whether its defence is advisable. The present Liberal government only does so much so as not to expose itself to the reproach of letting everything fall to ruin."

Other German warships followed. The cruiser sms *Freya* found little had changed on her visit to Halifax in August 1908. Her crew discovered that the Eastern Passage was in fact unnavigable for large vessels, and the calibre of harbour defence guns – assessed by frequent German observation of firing practice and "conversations with Canadian artillery officers" – proved smaller than the Germans had anticipated.[72] From an intelligence perspective, her visit had been worth while despite her tragic entry.

Groping through thick fog banks near midnight on 9 August 1908 she had sliced through a schooner, killing nine Nova Scotians. The *Halifax Herald* spread the story across the front page, but with a restraint and deference it would quickly cast off once war had begun: "Captain Maas had never before been in Halifax, though he has been on the American coast. He is a typical sailor – one of those thorough kind who are assisting to build up a great navy for Germany."[73] The visit ended with a large church parade, crowned, according to the *Halifax Herald*, by an "excellent sermon on the visit of the Queen of Sheba to King Solomon."[74] The moral lay in the virtues of hospitality.

The visits to Canada by German trade missions next year met an ambivalent response; they raised the hopes of Canadian businessmen and the eyebrows of the military. The German government had in 1908 formed a German-Canadian Economic Association, under the chairmanship of Reichstag delegate Dr G. Stresemann, in order to explore possible expansion of trade between the two countries. Canada and Germany had been waging a tariff war since 1897. The economic struggle was fraught with serious political overtones, for many imperial-minded Britons viewed Germany's overtures as an attempt to undermine the colony's links with the Mother Country.[75]

"One of the most encouraging signs of the times," the *Ottawa Free Press* wrote on 6 August 1909, "is the movement on the part of Germany to end the commercial differences with Canada and to restore those business relations which have been hampered and impeded since 1898 by the discrimination against Canada by Germans and by the retaliatory surtax imposed by Canada."

Colonel Willoughby Gwatkin, a senior officer at the headquarters of the Department of Militia and Defence in Ottawa, was not entirely convinced. In March that year he had advised the chief of the General Staff in Ottawa, a post he himself would assume in 1913, that "in view of the situation in Europe German activity in Canada may have some [military] significance."[76] A moderate and cultured gentleman who read and wrote Greek poetry for relaxation, he was yet somewhat of an alarmist in the years 1909–14 as he worked to awaken the government to both the German and the Japanese threats. Only on the outbreak of war did Gwatkin try to cap anti-German hysteria; excessive security forces in response to public clamour would have interfered with dispatch of troops to Europe.

For the moment, however, Gwatkin's genuine concern about the naval race between Britain and Germany had made him highly suspicious of German attempts at economic rapprochement. Like many Canadian leaders, he viewed the German move as a Trojan horse. Two early press reports that he included with the note to his chief seemed to hint at enemy infiltration into the Canadian fabric: one story covered the trade delegation to Ottawa; the other revealed the proposal of the Trades and Labour Council of Berlin (later renamed Kitchener), Ontario, to build a German-style "public baths and gymnasium" where youths "could develop their body and mind." It could only be the thin edge of a subversive wedge.

Having accepted the view that us German-Americans were already hostile to British interests, Gwatkin observed: "It would be deplorable if Germans who settle in Canada were to be imbued with a similar spirit; yet it is not impossible that secret agents of the German Government are at the present moment working in that direction."[77] Where Gwatkin sensed the presence of hawks, the editor of the *Ottawa Free*

Press saw doves. As the editorial on the German economic initiatives concluded: "Any increase in commercial relations between Canada and Germany would be a factor for peace. The Germans are a practical people and they prefer the pursuit of peace to the art of war, and any extension of business ties would be so many steps away from war." British propagandists would later argue that Germany's pursuit of peace was a cynical means of grasping for power. Indeed they made it look as if German intellectuals had formulated Germany's ultimate military goals. Thus the prolific propagandist "Ajax" introduced his *The German Pirate and His Record* by quoting Friedrich Nietzsche: "Ye shall love peace as a means to new wars – and the short peace more than the long."[78] Gwatkin requested the assistant director of intelligence to gather any possible information on suspicious Germans in Canada.

It did not take long to dig clues out of the woodwork. Canada's military anti-insurgency organization net was staffed by "Saturday soldiers." Working as part-time sleuths, these militiamen wrote their confidential reports on the letterhead of the companies that employed them in civilian life. Trickles of information soon formed an intelligence pool. Early suspicions led to the discharge of a young German immigrant from the permanent force coast artillery at Halifax for fear that he might be in contact with German military authorities and would divulge details of the defence scheme.[79] Then a report from Quebec offered some eighteen-month-old information that had apparently just come to light: "When the German ship [SMS *Bremen*] was here they sent a boat's crew down the river to try and find out something about the new forts at Beaumont, but they failed to secure that for which they sought."[80] Of course, German scouting parties had discovered precisely what they had sought. And so a rather blurred, kaleidoscopic image of the threat emerged.

Gwatkin and his associates in the Department of the Interior and the Dominion Police were soon making inquiries across the country and in London in pursuit of possible agents. Gwatkin was particularly interested in "one Baron von Nettlebladt whom I and others have reason to suspect of being a secret agent of the German Government, in spite of the fact that he is received both by His Excellency [the governor-general] and the Minister" of the Department of Militia and Defence.[81]

The ubiquitous and ingratiating baron, "who floats about the Dominion with Toronto as a sort of headquarters," was a colourful character.[82] South African authorities believed that he had been head of the German secret service in that dominion; they suspected him of having attempted to join the British secret service after having fallen out with the Kaiser. In Gwatkin's words, he was a "pleasant inquisitive fellow, obviously a gentleman, spends money ... and is fond of [high] society." Press reports from Toronto described him as fronting large schemes to bring German capital and immigrants to (northern) "New Ontario"; other clues soon linked him with "a suspicious character" known as Baron Oswald von Brakel. These and other clues to covert activities quickly ran into the sand and are not substantiated by German records. Still, Canadian officials were deeply concerned. As Gwatkin explained: "I am not an alarmist, but it appears to me that the Germans are 'getting busy' in Canada."[83]

- 3 -

"Heart-breaking starvation time"

Bunting broke out over the whole length of HMCS *Niobe* on the morning of 22 October 1910 as her anchor cables rattled out the hawsepipes in Halifax harbour and volleys of naval gun salutes reverberated from her decks and re-echoed with replies from Citadel Hill. Just the previous day, on the anniversary of the Battle of Trafalgar, she had arrived off the harbour mouth after an easy passage from Britain and awaited the auspicious cermonial entrance designed to celebrate Canada's new naval era. Many hoped that it might perhaps even erase the stigma of the Admiralty's questionable gift of the corvette *Charybdis* some twenty-eight years earlier in 1882. Dressed over all, her escorts, CGS *Canada* and *Minto*, now stood by as Admiral C.E. Kingsmill hoisted his pennant aboard Canada's new cruiser. He became the first Canadian admiral to do so aboard a major warship.

A bevy of official guests and newsmen hastened on board with Kingsmill and the minister of the naval service, the Hon. L.P. Brodeur. Enthusiastic press reports extolled the ship and her crew. The skipper was "a fine sample of [a] Canadian." A native of Victoria, British Columbia, who had served long and well with the Royal Navy, he now returned home to play a leading role in a new national fleet. Captain W.B. Macdonald lacked none of the qualities so frequently extolled in exuberant navalist clichés. He was "a typical sailor, frank, open and honest, handsome and strong – just the kind of man one likes to see whether on shipboard or on land."[1]

Niobe's captain impressed the media with his sense of history, for he had brought along mementos of the grand tradition onto which Canada's navy would now be grafted. HMCS *Niobe* carried a piece of the fore-topsail of Nelson's HMS *Victory*, a collection of medals issued after the Battle of the Nile, and bits of a leading block from HMS *Royal George* mounted in a piece of wood from *Victory*'s main deck. She doubtless looked grand: 11,000 tons of fighting ship – about three-fifths the draught of a dreadnought – 435 feet in length, and boasting sixteen 6-inch guns, twelve 12-pounders, five 3-pounders, and two 18-inch torpedo tubes. Her wartime complement of some seven hundred could take her to speeds of 20.5 knots.

Accolades and the rhetoric of national destiny punctuated the ceremonies. Brodeur proclaimed *Niobe*'s arrival as "a dawning epoch of self-reliance"; Canada would now for the first time take into its own hands responsibility for maritime defence, he asserted, and become a full partner with the Mother Country in imperial naval policy. His bathos took flight: "Let us rise to the height that the event demands and give our heart and soul to the celebration of the arrival of the first vessel that is to begin the work that we have before us. Like the advent of the discoverer's ship in a new land, the Niobe comes to plant the standard of progress and true Canadian national greatness upon the virgin slopes of a glorious future that unrolls its splendid proportions before our vision today."

HMCS *Rainbow* reached Esquimalt, British Columbia, on 7 November 1910, to a similar gala reception. For the Victoria *Daily Colonist*, this was a "historic" occasion that marked Esquimalt's "recrudescence, the revival of its former glories."[2] With inept allusion to the biblical deluge, Victoria's *Times* reminded its readers that "the first rainbow was set in the sky as a promise of [good] things to come"; the armed *Rainbow* was therefore "the first fruits on this coast of the Canadian naval policy, the necessary forerunner of the larger vessels which will add dignity to our name and prestige to our actions."[3]

The Canadian navy had come of age. Or had it? There were some discordant voices amid the general euphoria of the press. Toronto's *Mail and Empire* described the *Niobe* as a Royal Navy discard that had been "on her way to the scrap heap when the Ottawa Government determined that we should have a navy of our own." The *Quebec Chronicle* also proclaimed her obsolescence, while the ultra-Tory *Bridgewater Bulletin* saw *Niobe*'s arrival as little more than a pompous occasion for Haligonians "to throw out their chests and strut around in gay uniforms"; Canada's "expensive toy" served little purpose except to provide a source of government graft "and the training of politicians' sons to wear natty uniforms at five o'clock teas." In less than five years the Admiralty itself would declare the long-since obsolete vessel "not fit for service as a fighting unit."[4] HMCS *Rainbow* on the west coast fared little better.

The vessels were manned by nucleus crews from Britain. A total of 600 personnel from the Royal Navy on two-year loan, and former members on three- and five-year engagements, they would operate the vessels and serve as instructors while Canadians were recruited and trained.[5] Canada received full title to the Halifax and Esquimalt dockyards when the ships arrived. Britain's generous terms obliged Canada only to allow the Royal Navy to use the ports.

Prime Minister Laurier had endeavoured to broaden the appeal of his policy by promising the Canadian navy modern cruisers and destroyers. All ten vessels were to be built in Canada, even though that would cost at least 30 per cent more than the $11.6 million estimated for their construction in British yards; the Conservatives themselves had emphasized the benefits to the Canadian shipbuilding industry when pressing the naval question in 1909. Because no suitable shipyards existed in Canada, the 1910 session of Parliament passed legislation which increased drydock subsidies in order to encourage private firms to develop the necessary facilities for both naval and advanced civilian work.[6] As would happen time and again in the twentieth century, the government marketed its defence policy by promising economic spinoffs.

These events did not pass unnoticed in Berlin, where the Kaiser was briefed on Canada's naval defence. Germany's Imperial Naval Office had found Laurier's statement of political independence from Britain particularly striking and quoted him approvingly to the Kaiser: "We should stand on a policy of being masters in our own house, of having a policy for our own purpose, and leaving to the Canadian Parliament, to the Canadian Government and to the Canadian People to take part in those wars – in which today they have no voice – only if they think fit to do so." To the Kaiser it seemed that Laurier might even be laying the foundations for colonial neutrality. Although the Imperial Naval Office observed that it would be unrealistic to expect a colony not to support the Mother Country, the Kaiser's briefing hung on Laurier's words that "it did not necessarily follow that Canada would take part in all the naval wars in which Great Britain might engage."[7]

Canadian policy, however, was by no means as confident as it might have seemed from a distance. The political consensus so carefully cobbled together by party leaders had long since begun to come apart. In particular, the compromise reached months earlier, on 29 March 1909, had manifestly failed to heal a growing rift within Conservative ranks; in the wake of the imperial defence conference in August of that year it became an open division. Prominent English-Canadian members of the party – notably the premiers of Ontario, Manitoba, and British Columbia, on whose support both the federal party organization and Borden's own position as leader depended –

denounced Laurier's decision for a "tin-pot" navy in the face of
Admiralty's advice that the empire really needed dreadnought battle-
cruisers.

Meanwhile Borden's Quebec lieutenant, F.D. Monk – now the
linchpin in an alliance the Conservatives were forging with Henri
Bourassa in order to break the Liberal stronghold in Quebec – cried
out against Laurier's "Imperial drunkeness."[8] Monk quoted official
British documents to good effect in proving that Laurier's scheme
was much more ambitious than the harbour defence torpedo flotillas
that the Admiralty had recommended in 1907 and which formed the
basis for the joint resolution of 29 March 1909.[9] The big Bristol
cruisers, he argued, could have no other purpose than the very high-
seas operations over which the Admiralty had always claimed the
right of "absolute" control. Laurier, in Monk's words, had therefore
abandoned the accepted policy of Dominion responsibility for local
defence only and instead intended to build a "war navy [for] active
participation in the defence of the Empire." That meant that Laurier
had in fact joined the "new movement towards a centralizing federation of British territory wherever situated."[10]

The German consul in Montreal reported these developments to
Reichskanzler von Bethmann Hollweg in considerable detail.[11] Diver-
gence of public opinion throughout the country and within political
parties, he explained, was causing the Canadian government "utmost
discomfiture." He reviewed the various proposals for ship construction and deployment and the arguments on emergency financial
contributions versus the founding of a Canadian fleet, and he reported the expected costs of the various options. The situation, the
consul reported, was mercurial and tense: "The subject is continually
in the centre of public discussion. On the one hand the officious
French-Canadian press lets not a day go by without parading before
its readers the advantages of their own Canadian fleet. The Imperialists are no less zealous in advocating the approval of an annual
contribution to England, and it is said that England is also involved
in this as best it can. And there are hints as well that [the United
States] has a certain interest in the Canadian fleet project." The
German naval attaché in Washington would later lend credence to
the consul's closing remark when reporting that some Americans
were alarmed by Canada's apparent attempts at joining arms with
"militarists" in Europe.

About two weeks later, on 7 January 1910, the German consul
reported on Laurier's address to "a political club in Toronto."[12]
Laurier had asserted Canadian nationhood; he had declared that
even though Canada stood "under the suzerainty of the King of

England," the king had no more rights here than the Canadian parliament granted him. The Kaiser underlined the phrase and penned a lusty "Donnerwetter!" in the margin. Laurier did not think Germany wanted war any more than any other nation, the consul wrote. Certainly "the German peril" was not imminent. If blood is thicker than water, the consul reported Laurier's words, it was doubtful that the German Kaiser intended to attack the royal family in England – nor indeed were the German people themselves contemplating such a thing. The Kaiser found this view "correct" and underlined the phrase. In the consul's concluding words, Laurier had thereby expressed views "rather the opposite from a year ago during debate on the naval question." This could only mean "that the government's requirement of enthusiasm for the navy was now considerably less than before."

The facts were rather different. The temperature of the controversy in Canada rose still higher when, following the government's introduction of the Naval Service Bill in the House of Commons on 12 January 1910, Borden unveiled a new Conservative policy. The opposition leader was now concerned primarily with bridging the yawning chasm between the Quebec "nationaliste" and imperialist wings of the party; he therefore offered something to both factions. As the powerful provincial premiers had long urged, Borden now unreservedly called for an emergency financial contribution to the Royal Navy sufficient to build two dreadnought-class battleships. He justified the shift by adopting the anti-German rhetoric of British panic-mongers: "The war [of construction] has already begun, and victory will be as decisive as in actual battle."[13] Where the naval race would reach a crisis "probably within three years," he declared, Laurier's erstwhile navy could not be made efficient in "less than ten [and probably not before] 15 or twenty years." Optimists like Laurier, he added, should remember what had befallen unprepared countries before at the hands of Prussian aggression: Denmark in 1864, Austria in 1866, and France in 1870.

Borden also charged Laurier with breaking the traditional ties with Britain; indeed he was "Empire smashing." The Naval Service Bill required that the Dominion government grant specific approval before Canadian ships could be placed under British command; this seemed to reveal the Liberals' intention of creating a separatist fleet. He evoked the humiliating picture of an enemy raider sinking British merchantmen under the silent guns of a Canadian cruiser that helplessly awaited passage of Ottawa's order-in-council that would allow her to offer aid.[14] The German ambassador in London, who summarized for the Reichskanzler the comprehensive reports of the Cana-

dian debate published in the British press, was not taken in by
Borden's histrionics. He attached little importance to these legalistic
arguments over the fine points of how far the important principle of
dominion control over dominion forces should extend. Canada, he
correctly concluded, would be at Britain's side in the event of war.[15]

Attempts to placate the Quebec "nationalistes" wove an intricate
counterpoint into this pro-empire theme. In a confidential policy
paper of November 1909 Borden had linked his switch to an emergency contribution with his commitment to scale down the fleet that
Laurier was proposing to build. The founding of the new naval
service, Borden insisted, should "proceed cautiously and by slow
beginnings."[16] Thus when he rose in the Commons, on 12 January
1910, to denounce the government's naval project as "too little for
immediate and effective aid" to Britain, he added that it was also "too
much for carrying out experiments in the organisation of a Canadian
Naval Service."[17] Yet no matter how draconian this view might have
seemed to some, the opposition leader had not gone far enough in
addressing the conviction of both Monk and Bourassa that Canada
should really have no navy at all. Borden had originally suggested
that he might make a symbolic gesture by demanding six months'
delay for the Naval Service Bill. But he had been dissuaded by anglophone supporters, who warned that such a negative stand would
undermine the credibility of his declaration about the gravity of the
German threat.[18] As it was, Monk openly contradicted and criticized
his leader in the House.[19]

Whatever satisfaction Laurier derived from Borden's discomfiture soon disappeared. In the Quebec by-election of Drummond-
Arthabaska on 3 November 1910, an obscure "nationaliste" candidate, supported by Bourassa and French-Canadian Conservatives,
made Laurier's imperialistic naval policy the main issue – and
defeated the Liberals. Ironically, this was not only the prime minister's hometown but had once been his own riding. The defeat followed only by a margin of days the arrival in Canada of HMCS *Niobe*
and *Rainbow*.

The German naval attaché in London took particular note of the
by-election. Laurier, he wrote to Reichskanzler von Bethmann Hollweg on 5 November 1910, showed "the greatest reticence of all the
Dominion prime ministers, and watched more jealously than the
other colonies over the independence of his soon to be created
fleet."[20] But Laurier could not count on full national support, for "a
part of Canadian public opinion holds the view that he has gone too
far in complying with British wishes." Although the attaché himself
drew no immediate conclusions, it is clear from German assessments

of the Canadian naval scene that the defeat was gratifying. In the attaché's words: "The nationalist opponent defeated the Liberal government's candidate by combating the creation of a Canadian fleet as useless and politically dangerous both for foreign relations as well as for Canadian autonomy." The German position was clear: the less support the colonies gave Britain, the better.

The initiative and impetus behind the Canadian naval program faded as the government turned to face the challenge of Quebec nationalism. Naval recruitment fizzled into the mere distribution of information at post offices, while essential improvements to the cramped and outdated Halifax dockyard died on paper. Nor would cabinet make a decision on whether to award contracts for the new cruisers and destroyers. As one British officer on loan to Canadian headquarters complained: "Items have been postponed, and again postponed, until at last a point approaching stagnation is being reached."[21] There was little the staff could do. The cautious deputy minister, Desbarats, had no inclination to question the will of cabinet and staunchly controlled all access to the minister – limiting even Admiral Kingsmill's personal contact with his political master. The government supported Desbarats's claim that the office of deputy minister took precedence over Admiral Kingsmill, despite tradition in the militia department, wherein the military head stood second only to the minister himself.[22] The military head had always been a British officer.

A marine accident after midnight on 31 July 1911 dashed Canada's hopes for big-ship training, when HMCS *Niobe* signalled she was ashore and "in grave peril." In the words of the *Halifax Herald*, "The Flagship of Canada's Navy was on the rocks off Cape Sable."[23] She was returning from Yarmouth, Nova Scotia, where she had been the main attraction in "a big old home week celebration," when she struck the vicious southwest ledges while trying to work her way to seaward in a heavy blow and fog. Evidence suggests that she did not have the proper navigation charts and that her navigator had lost his way.

Grounding is a traumatic experience for a commanding officer; he is responsible for whatever his ship might suffer. Even when the dust has settled on the reports of boards of inquiry, he alone really grasps the full significance of the event in a measure that exceeds the sum total of evidence, deduction, and surmise. The press was as sympathetic to *Niobe*'s Captain Macdonald as it had been to the captain of the German warship SMS *Freya* which had rammed a Canadian fishing vessel on approaching Halifax in the dark in 1908. Admiral Kingsmill journeyed from Ottawa to cast an eye on events but made little public comment on his officers when writing from *Niobe*. He did, however, praise the crew: "The discipline on the Niobe by the boys and young recruits was everything that one could wish. With the ship in the position she was, a gale of wind blowing and dense fog, the Canadian boys behaved fully up to the traditions of the British navy ... Of course, the ship's crew and officers displayed fine discipline, but I am speaking now of the Canadian boys and recruits."[24] He said not a word about competence, properly leaving that to the court martial, which reprimanded the officer-of-the-watch, severely reprimanded the navigation officer, and dismissed him from the ship. Towed to Halifax on 5 August, HMCS *Niobe* remained in dock under repair for some sixteen months, until December 1912. The accident proved a critical blow.

Although both political parties avoided the naval question during the Canadian general election of September 1911, it still contributed to the Laurier government's defeat. In Quebec, where the Liberals lost twenty seats, the nationalistes allied with the Conservatives and continued to hammer away at Laurier's naval imperialism. In Toronto, by contrast, disgust at the prime minister's narrowly nationalistic policy played a part in the defection of eighteen prominent Liberals to Conservative ranks.[25] Faced with this divided mandate, the new prime minister, Robert Borden, understandably left naval policy in abeyance. "It is infinitely better to be right than to be in a hurry," he responded, when pressed in the Commons. He hoped to unite his party by organizing a Canadian naval force rather different from that of Laurier; beginning on a small scale, as he had promised the Quebec nationalists, it would be more closely integrated into the Royal Navy. An ill-considered promise followed: he would repeal the Naval Service Act, which both wings of his party despised.[26] Borden's plans were soon overtaken by a fresh panic in Britain.

Early in 1912 Germany embarked on a further expansion of its "dreadnought" construction program. Its allies Italy and Austria had also begun to build the huge battleships. These developments were not the sole reasons for the subsequent change in British policy toward the dominions; growing resistance among the "Radical" members of Britain's governing Liberal party to further increases in naval spending, and the presence of an aggressive new first lord of the Admiralty, Winston S. Churchill, exerted a decisive influence.[27] Churchill considered the dominion fleet units scheme of 1909 a "thoroughly vicious" departure from the fundamental strategic principles of concentration and centralized British control.[28] When Robert Borden arrived in London in July 1912 to consult on naval policy, Churchill immediately asked him for an emergency contribution. In agreeing to provide $35 million – enough for three dreadnought-class battleships – Borden seriously underestimated the bitterness in Liberal ranks at home which he himself had recently provoked with the promise to revoke the Naval Service Act. As we shall see, the Conservatives' Naval Aid Bill would not pass the House until closure had terminated a prolonged filibuster – only to be rejected by the Liberal majority in the Senate on 30 May 1913.[29]

Never during the struggle for naval aid, however, did Borden waver from his long-standing conviction that gradual development of a small-warship Canadian force was the only "permanent policy" that could win widespread and enduring domestic support. This was the approach on which the parties had tacitly agreed since at least 1902 and which they had formally endorsed in the joint resolution of 29 March 1909. Laurier's error in 1910, Borden privately admitted, had been to attempt too much too quickly. Had the Liberals promptly followed through with the start they had made in 1902–3 in expanding and improving the Fisheries Protection Service, there would have been "little or none of the excitement or criticism which have developed."[30] Thus when Borden visited London in the summer of 1912 he raised the possibility of carrying out the torpedo flotilla proposal that had united the parties in March 1909. At his request, the Admiralty prepared a series of reports on local Canadian requirements.[31]

The British assessment asserted that because Japan had agreed to renew the alliance in 1911, Canada's defence priorities had now shifted to the Atlantic. The reports were striking for what they omitted; they specifically ruled out the possibility of submarine raids. The only threat on either seaboard was attack by "one or two" un-armoured cruisers or armed merchant vessels, which, in addition to their guns, might also be equipped to lay mines. The mouth of the St Lawrence River therefore required the most comprehensive floating defences: twelve torpedo boats, nine submarines, and a small cruiser. Another six torpedo boats and three submarines would suffice for Halifax, and a still smaller flotilla might eventually be needed on the west coast.

Significantly, Admiralty considered none of these "Harbour and Coast Defence" measures particularly pressing: "From the point of view of Imperial requirements taken as a whole, Canadian financial assistance towards naval development would be better applied to the construction of vessels suitable for the general service of the Empire than to that of vessels available only for local defence of a particular portion which might not be threatened at all."[32] Canadian action, it further argued, would be "most valuable" in the defence of the Atlantic trade routes between North America and Great Britain.

The proposals that followed called essentially for the very Atlantic

cruiser force that Laurier had intended to establish; and this despite
the Admiralty's objection during Laurier's day that Canadian cruisers
were not really needed at all. The Admiralty's reversal, and what
could only be described as a plea for help, departed markedly from
the usually dispassionate loftiness of imperial government documents. It is striking evidence of the anxiety caused by Germany's
increasing capacity for high-seas operations:

The trade of the Empire is essential to the existence of the Empire ... Any
prolonged interruption of the food imports by the action of hostile cruisers
would necessarily lead to the reduction of the Mother Country by famine,
with consequences to the Oversea Dominions which it is impossible to
foretell ...

   The required protection cannot be afforded by the unaided action of a
superior battle fleet ... [Faster] cruisers of our own are therefore necessary
to deal with those of the enemy which may succeed in evading our main
Fleets at the start ... Certain Foreign Powers openly claim the right to convert
their merchant steamers into cruisers at any time and in any place. Such
vessels ... would be well suited ... to destroy defenceless traders, and as large
numbers of them are always to be found under the German flag all over the
world ... and are believed on good authority to carry their armaments on
board permanently ready for use, they constitute a new and very extensive
menace demanding serious and constant attention.

Admiralty identified the North Atlantic as the decisive theatre. It was
over these sea routes that "a large portion of the food supplies"
reached Britain and over which "all Canadian trade with European
markets is carried on." Equally important, the vast commerce on the
North Atlantic could be "more quickly reached than any other by
a hostile cruiser starting from a European base."[33] Although the
Admiralty had made "special arrangements" for protecting North
Atlantic trade, "the construction and maintenance of the necessary
cruisers add considerable sums to the British Naval Estimates."
Indeed, Admiralty concluded, "any [financial] help from Canada
would be most valuable."

   The British officers worried with good reason, for the German
naval staff had reached identical conclusions about where imperial
trade was most vulnerable. As a briefing for the Kaiser explained:
"Cruiser warfare against England finds most targets in the Atlantic,
through which almost the total import of foodstuffs and raw material
[for Great Britain] passes. For this reason we must ... anticipate
English countermeasures here as well, for England sees the situation
correctly and fears cruiser warfare [here] in the Atlantic more than
on any other seas."[34]

Borden was willing to extend his navy project to include cruisers, as the Admiralty urged. But, with an eye to the bitter reaction Laurier's cruiser scheme had aroused in Quebec, he wanted the very smallest ships of this class so that they could be incorporated into the Fisheries Protection Service. Indeed, their primary purpose would lie in "defending our fisheries against poachers and marauders."[35] This idea was of course unrealistic, for even HMCS *Rainbow*, a ship scarcely two-thirds the size of the modern trade defence cruisers proposed in Laurier's program, had proved too large to chase down poachers in the shallow coastal waters where they most often fished.

Borden soon pressed his "permanent policy" into political service. In November 1912, his Quebec lieutenant, Monk, resigned from the cabinet over the Naval Aid Bill; by that time the prime minister had abandoned any hope of reaching accommodation with the most committed nationalistes. He was, however, able to reassure most members of his French-Canadian caucus by renewing the promise to repeal Laurier's Naval Service Act and by describing his scheme for the evolution of the Fisheries Protection Service into a local defence force.[36] Moreover, he planned to unveil the permanent policy when introducing the Naval Aid Bill in the House during December, with the expectation that the Liberals would be appeased by this firm commitment to a national fleet. In the event, he was dissuaded from taking such action only by advisers who urged the wisdom of not offering two hostages to fortune.[37]

A furious filibuster prolonged debate for month after month and left little doubt that Laurier would ultimately use his majority in the Senate to kill the Naval Aid Bill. This suspicion dictated a change in Borden's tactics. Borden had reason to suspect that there might be room for compromise, for the parliamentary fracas had created polarities that were much more extreme than the views of many members of both parties. Thus where some Conservatives harboured nationalistic doubts about the cash subsidy and would have preferred to procure and operate dreadnoughts as part of a substantial Canadian navy, so too a number of prominent anglophone Liberals believed that Canada must directly help Britain.[38] In April 1913 the prime minister was pleased to learn that the Liberal Senate leader, Sir George Ross – onetime premier of Ontario and a convinced contributionist – believed that accommodation could be reached if the Conservatives made an early and generous start in reviving Laurier's naval service. Perhaps the $35 million intended for Britain under the Naval Aid Bill could be reduced by a third and these funds applied to the Royal Canadian Navy.[39]

Although Borden would not let himself be drawn into a specific deal, he at least opened the door for an arrangement along these

lines. On 15 May 1913, the day the Naval Aid Bill finally passed in
the Commons, the prime minister rose to unveil the permanent
policy.[40] He described his plans for procuring torpedo craft and small
cruisers; his fleet would differ from the one planned by Laurier only
in its smaller scale and more gradual development. Indeed, he would
retain not only HMCS *Niobe* and *Rainbow* but also the shore organization the Liberals had established.[41]

    Borden did not withdraw his pledge to repeal the Naval Service Act;
this stubbornness was decisive. Laurier was by now deeply engaged in
a struggle with Bourassa for the allegiance of Quebec. In opposing the
Naval Aid Bill, Laurier had rooted his opposition in the fundamental
principle of Canada's soverign control of its own defence forces. As
Laurier declared, the Liberals would gladly agree to acquisition of
dreadnoughts under two conditions: the ships must form part of the
Royal Canadian Navy, and they must be protected against arbitrary
transfer to British command. The very legislation that his own government had set in place, he argued, had once safeguarded this
independence. Laurier instantly rejected the strong appeal for compromise urged upon him by his former finance minister, W.S. Fielding. As he wrote to Fielding, any departure from the Naval Service
Act "would discourage and perhaps disintegrate our party, especially
in Quebec, where at great sacrifice we [have] brought up our friends
to accept it."[42] In the end, Senator Ross had no choice but to lead the
Liberal Senate majority in rejecting the bill.

    A severe downturn in the Canadian economy, and the possibility
of an early election, deflected Borden's attention in the following
months from his schemes for circumventing or overcoming the Senate. In Britain, meanwhile, Churchill had made other arrangements
to finance the "Canadian" battleships: these were three "super-
dreadnoughts" of the *Queen Elizabeth* class that ultimately served
with distinction in both the First World War and the Second. The
enormous fifteen-inch guns of one of them, HMS *Warspite*, would
provide fire support for the First Canadian Army in 1944–5 as it
fought its way up the channel coast during the northwest Europe
campaign.[43]

German authorities kept in close touch not only with the naval debate
but with all aspects of Canadian maritime development. The German
consul in Montreal, Germany's constant watchdog on political and
military affairs in Canada, had reported to the Reichskanzler on
budget items for the maintenance of HMCS *Niobe* and *Rainbow*; he had
reported on plans for drydock facilities in the province of Quebec
and on strategic matters affecting the Canadian Pacific Railway's links

with Canada's far-flung harbours; he had informed his government on the development of wireless stations on the Pacific, on the Atlantic, and in the Gulf of St Lawrence.[44] Another consular officer had even journeyed to Victoria in order to research a report for von Bethmann Hollweg on plans for expanding Esquimalt harbour. He saw it as "a colossal project" that augured well for Canada's commercial and military development.[45] German intelligence services gleaned information from agents and the public press. German warships paid regular visits to Canadian ports for both military and political purposes.

SMS *Bremen* arrived in June 1911. Having drydocked in Newport News, and changed crew in Baltimore, she was to spend four months in Canadian waters, including visits to Halifax, Charlottetown, Sydney, Montreal, and Quebec. Admiral Büchsel briefed the Kaiser on all aspects of the tour: she was, among other things, to undertake full-calibre shoots and exercise the crew in cruiser warfare while in the Gulf of St Lawrence.[46] Although Canadian military authorities denied her request to send platoons ashore in Halifax to shoot on local rifle ranges, she did carry out firing practice in the Gulf.[47]

In response to a request from Naval Service Headquarters for investigation of disturbing rumours, militia intelligence learned that *Bremen* had bought lumber in Charlottetown for construction of four targets, had destroyed one of them by torpedo during firing practice out at sea, and had then sold the timber of the remaining three back to the lumberyard.[48] No one seems to have drawn any conclusions about her gunnery prowess. Her return to Canadian waters the following year to reconnoitre the Bay of Fundy and the new dock construction in Saint John would cause a greater stir. The public response in Canada was not untypical: local politicians and socialites glossed over political realities, while an inept press generally stumbled over itself – and discovered glimpses of the truth.

Germany meanwhile planned to deploy a squadron of the latest warships on a goodwill visit to the principal harbours of the North American coast.[49] American warships had visited Kiel in 1911, and the US ambassador in Berlin had invited the Kaiser to have his ships return the courtesy call. Anxious to impress their hosts, the Kaiser, Admiral von Tirpitz, and Admiral Georg von Müller initially planned to send the most formidable flotilla of ships that diplomatic propriety would allow. Unfortunately for their plans, other fleet commitments ultimately trimmed the squadron to the cruisers SMS *Moltke*, *Stettin*, and *Bremen*. The squadron commander was the former naval attaché in Washington, Kontreadmiral von Rebeur-Paschwitz. In close cooperation with US Secretary of the Navy von Lengerke-Meyer – a

German American whom the German ambassador, Count von Bernstorff, described as "completely friendly to Germany" – the ambassador organized the tour. "Since von Rebeur-Paschwitz knows the American scene," Bernstorff wrote to the Reichskanzler, "he will be prepared for ten days on the entertainment circuit and have braced himself for a strenuous life."[50] The ambassador stressed the importance of playing down his own role in order to give the impression that the receptions were really home-grown German-American hospitality. On conclusion of the American visit, sms *Bremen* would pay a courtesy call to Saint John.

Von Rebeur-Paschwitz judged the American visit a diplomatic success, even though the Americans were less awed by German naval power than the German sailors had been by American munificence and life-style.[51] The German ships anchored near two battleship divisions of the us Atlantic Fleet and were met by President William Howard Taft aboard the presidential yacht *Mayflower*. If von Rebeur-Paschwitz felt his cruisers dwarfed by the American battle squadrons, he did not report it to the Kaiser. But he did point out that Germany had sent larger ships before:

We repeatedly heard expressions of pride and joy about the 'huge' ship [the battleship *Von der Tann*, which had visited the previous year]; this confirmed the impressions received by your Majesty's Ship *Von der Tann*, that the assessment of the capacity of our fleet is essentially determined by the size of the ships we station abroad. Despite all contrary assertions there is not the slightest doubt that occasional visits of our ships and/or squadrons abroad constitute a powerful factor in fusing the German presence there together, in strengthening it, and thereby as circumstances permit, making it politically useful to us.

The Kaiser agreed.

Von Rebeur-Paschwitz toured widely with his hosts. He (and the Kaiser, who carefully read the admiral's reports) were impressed by the high standard of living in American ships and shore stations, by the modern facilities in the recently opened Naval College at Annapolis, and by the fact that Washington had become a vibrant national capital. While German officers were wined and dined by the president, by the Vanderbilts, by the Navy League Club, and by a host of others, German sailors indulged in the delights of Coney Island with their American confrères. After such a lavish, well-orchestrated visit, *Bremen*'s Canadian sojourn was a drab affair.

sms *Bremen* entered Saint John on 18 May 1912, having had to anchor offshore in thick and persistent fog. The ageing honorary

German consul had taken his instructions from the German naval attaché in London quite literally and had not forewarned the press; in fact he had not notified anyone. But, according to the commanding officer's report to the Kaiser, the mayor none the less found the occasion "an unexpected delight" and took his guest on an automobile tour of the harbour and the surrounding area.[52]

"Of special interest," the German skipper reported, "were the mayor's explanations of the planned comprehensive harbour improvements such as the deepening of Courtney Bay and [the construction of a] protective mole, large drydock and quay facilities." The mayor's gift of a special issue of Saint John's *Standard* for 19 February 1912 provided diagrams and a full description of the project. Ever the obliging host, the mayor had further promised to send "a precise copy of the original [harbour] plan through the offices of the German embassy in London." Amid receptions ashore and afloat, the Germans set about reconnoitring the region in more detail.

The reaction of the local press to the visit was divided. Whereas the *Saint John Globe* warmly endorsed the mayor's hospitality (including the reception at the Union Club) and was delighted to have the "well behaved" German sailors in town, the *Daily Telegraph* was openly hostile. Suspecting that *Bremen* had come to "learn of St John's [sic] Fortifications," its headlines hinted at skulduggery and the "Dark Designs of [the] Kaiser's Men." Rumour had it that "the visitors had made a very close study of St John [sic] and that hardly a street or hill remained unobserved by the Kaiser's seamen, while the harbour had also been very generously photographed and soundings taken ... At any rate it is easy to believe that if there was anything about St John's formidable fortifications that the Bremen's officers did not know before they arrived, they are possessed of the information now."[53]

In fact there were no modern defences at Saint John at all, only a collection of run-down earth-works dating from the mid-nineteenth century. The *Standard* revealed as much in a lampoon captioned "City Slept Calmly, Tho' in 'Great Peril'." As the spoof explained in part: "The Telegraph yesterday morning gravely informed its readers that German observation parties had so far abused the hospitality of the St John people as to photograph our 'defences.' This was fine, but the reporter forgot to take the public into its confidence to the extent of telling where the defences were. Perhaps he didn't know, but the Germans did."[54] Outraged by the article, "so contemptible that it is unworthy of further consideration," the mayor apologized to the German captain on behalf of "the whole populace."[55] The German skipper wrote an appreciative reply in impeccable English.

Soon afterward, in September 1912, SMS *Viktoria Louise* put into Halifax for two weeks. The scenario was routine: social visits, diplomatic eavesdropping, reconnoitring, observation of harbour installations and ship movements, followed by political-military evaluation.[56] As the *Halifax Herald* recalled, this was "not the first visit of this cruiser to Halifax, as she was in these waters last summer."[57] In fact, "some fourteen or more [such ships had visited] within the past ten years [and] it is pleasant to be able to say that during the stay of these ships not a word has appeared in the press or elsewhere to mar the relations existing between the two great countries." (The reporter had obviously not followed the Saint John newspapers.)

The commanding officer of *Viktoria Louise* found "the English society very cordial to [his] visit as in the previous year." The mayor of Halifax came aboard and "expressed the city's joy at once again seeing a German warship in the harbour"; such vessels, the mayor noted, had visited Halifax "about a dozen times in the past ten years, without the slightest difficulty" arising between citizens and crews. The commanding officer's attempts to contact German emigrés, however, were thwarted by an honorary consul, more interested in advancing his own social standing than in supporting German interests. The skipper eventually met "several well-situated German families in Halifax," whose primary cultural interest lay in preserving their language and literature. As will be seen, such families – suspected during the war years of being the "spy in our midst" – became the object of the *Halifax Herald*'s paranoia when German submarines struck offshore.

The captain of *Viktoria Louise* learned all he could about Canada's naval policy. As in other German assessments, Borden seemed extremely cautious and indecisive; Laurier, by contrast, was "youthfully vigorous despite his seventy years [as he] travelled the eastern provinces ... gaining adherents for the Liberal cause." Although nothing suggests that the captain ever met either Borden or Laurier, he cited at some length a speech by Borden at a political banquet in Montreal on 21 September in which he asserted Canada's will to participate fully in the defence of the British Empire. Germany's Imperial Naval Office found this especially noteworthy in light of concerns that the colonies could provide financial support to the Mother Country's already strained defence budget.

The German captain also reported "leaks in the press [that] Canada wanted to contribute three Dreadnoughts as defence against the German threat"; but he doubted that the Conservative government could survive if it pressed such an unpopular policy. "The realisation of the Dreadnought plan is in a sorry state," he concluded. So was the Canadian navy:

The huge cruiser *Niobe* has not left drydock for the past nine months ... The training of cadets has ground completely to a halt [and] as the Director of the Naval College told me, cadets find work ashore to 'earn dollars' as soon as they go on long leave. Officers complain openly of difficulties with the cadets' social education, for [the cadets] come from very divergent social circles. There are difficulties too with cadets of French-Canadian parents, who in political terms are not entirely sound. The officers themselves seemed generally not particularly enthusiastic about their duties [and] the English officer regards his Canadian comrade as 'colonial' and therefore inferior.

These observations caught the attention of Germany's Imperial Naval Office. German naval leaders had detected similar failings in the US navy at the turn of the century and still felt the United States to be weak. They doubtless found satisfaction in the politically unreliable personnel and militarily unprepared ships of another potential foe.

The German naval attaché in Washington, Captain Boy-Ed, reported on US reaction to Borden's Naval Aid Bill in December 1912. Particularly significant, and no doubt gratifying in his view, was "how unpleasant the strengthening of the link between Canada and England was for the USA in light of the pending [Anglo-American] controversy about [discrimination against British shipping in the] fees for the Panama Canal."[58] Clippings from the *Washington Post* that Boy-Ed forwarded to Tirpitz announced that Canada "Gives 3 Battleships" to Great Britain and that "Dreadnoughts are Canada's Share in Imperial Defence"; they commented on "Canada's Ugly Mood" and charged that Borden had timed introduction of the bill to strengthen Britain's hand in the matter of the Panama Canal fees.[59]

As might have been expected, the German-language *New-Yorker Staatszeitung* accused Canada of escalating "the armament race into infinity" and urged Borden be brought before the Hague Court. The German consul in Montreal had by this time reported Borden's change of heart on withdrawing the dreadnought scheme.[60] Boy-Ed neglected to mention this. The *New York Times*, on which he based much of his intelligence, was scarcely less inflammatory than the other American papers. Borden was "Reorganising the British Empire" and playing with fire: "The price that Canada pays is no less repugnant to settled ideas. With Canadian battleships in the line, the Dominion is thrown into the vortex of European militarism from which it has [now] recoiled as from a witches cauldron."

By contrast, a report from the German consul in Sydney, Australia, nicely encapsulated the nuances of Borden's policy. He summarized a speech by the Canadian minister of trade, George Foster, then on a trade mission to the Pacific dominion. Despite differences being aired in Parliament, Foster claimed, "none of the Canadian parties were absolutely opposed to supporting the British fleet." Whatever else one might think, the form of support that Canada had chosen should "not be construed as a permanent policy"; it was merely "the present view of the Canadian government."[61] The Reichskanzler underlined these pronouncements in red. Accurate as the statement was, it could scarcely have been better designed to baffle the Germans.

As always, Laurier's views seemed clearer, more vigorous, and sensible as viewed from Berlin. A report by *The Times* of the Liberal leader's speech during an October 1913 by-election in Ontario particularly delighted the Kaiser. Laurier's denunciation of "the present Administration in Ottawa [as] the lowest, the most retrograde, and the most reactionary which has ever sat in Canada from the days of the Family Compact of evil repute" drew a "bravo" from the German monarch. He then underlined it and wrote "good" beside a passage in which Laurier declared that Borden's Naval Aid Bill had been "conceived in iniquity and mendacity."[62] Equally gratifying was Laurier's reported assertion that Germany was not building a large navy for the purpose of attacking England.

Years of following the tortuous course of Canadian naval debates had awakened in some German quarters at least a glimmer of recognition of the underlying issues. This was evident in the German press reports on the defeat of the Naval Aid Bill in the spring of 1913. Of course, the German press took satisfaction in such "a severe moral and material loss for [Britain's] Imperial defence" and in the "very unpleasant disruption in Britain's concept of world empire and in Churchill's idea of an Imperial squadron." Yet it was quick to acknowledge that the most important question of all – "Will the British imperium be strengthened or weakened by the Canadian naval question?" – found no confident answer. Prescient indeed was the conclusion reached by the arch-conservative *Neue Preußische Kreuz-Zeitung*, which appealed to an influential circle of readers, including many at court: "However [naval] policies might change externally and [even] take favourable shape, the watchword remains – Germany be alert!"[63]

The commanding officer of the German heavy cruiser SMS *Hertha* observed the results of Canada's "great debate" when reporting his three-week visit in Halifax during September and October 1913:

As in the previous year naval policy forms the principal point of contention of the two major parties in Canada. However, the businessmen and industrialists I met judge the naval question by no means according to its significance for Canada or England, but regard it merely as an election slogan ... All the English sea officers aboard the *Niobe* are in some respect inferior – either physically or in regard to their professional competence ... The docks present a melancholy aspect. Fresh water cannot be brought aboard the ships as there is no barge ... The *Niobe*, with the breeches of all guns removed, is tied up alongside the dock as there are no maintenance personnel. English midshipmen from HMS *Cornwall* called the *Niobe* rotten, and a voyage aboard her as risky. [Older retired officers grumbled] bitterly that young people were listless and had lost the joy in work ... Nobody wanted to undertake tough demanding work of the Service or in business any more.[64]

There was more than a little truth in this report. The first three years of Conservative rule had indeed been what Captain Walter Hose later termed the navy's "heart-breaking starvation time."[65] He clearly recalled Admiral Kingsmill's "very depressed mood ... soon after the general election" of 1911. Ironically, it was about the time of Borden's victory that King George V approved the title "Royal Canadian Navy."[66] The new government had in January 1912 authorized estimates of $1,660,000 for fiscal year 1912–13 in order to maintain the existing organization "on a mark-time basis."[67] But by fiscal 1913–14, expenditures had dwindled to a mere $579,566. Loss of personnel was equally severe. From a peak of something more than eight hundred officers and ratings in late 1911, the service had declined to about three hundred and fifty by the late summer of 1913.

This attrition necessitated laying up *Niobe* – which explains the Germans' harsh critique – whose full complement was a crew of 705. Service on the harbour-bound ships, in the words of Deputy Minister Desbarats, had become "irksome and distasteful"; so much so, in fact, that he himself expressed sympathy with those who deserted.[68] Certainly, the government made no special effort to pursue or prosecute those who made off.[69]

That the naval service did not lapse into utter indiscipline and inertia was largely the result of the presence of some one hundred British ratings on five-year engagements and to a small group of British officers. Two of them – Walter Hose and Richard Stephens – played key roles throughout the war.

Walter Hose had been literally born to the sea. The son of the bishop of Singapore, he had come into the world aboard a P&O liner while it was on passage in the Indian Ocean. After joining the Royal Navy at the age of fourteen in 1890, he spent much of the next twenty-one years aboard ship. He served on anti-piracy patrols on the rivers of China, chased gun-runners in the Persian Gulf, and sailed in the British blockade of Venezuela when that country's government renounced debts to British firms.[70] He was second-in-command of a modern cruiser when, in the spring of 1909, he offered his services to Admiral Kingsmill. Hose already had ties with North America: his service in 1902–5 in charge of training the newly formed Newfoundland division of the Royal Naval Reserve and his marriage to a woman from St John's.

Kingsmill admitted quite frankly that prospects in the new Canadian service were limited and uncertain. Hose replied that he none the less had two good reasons for wanting to sign up: promotion in the imperial service was extremely slow, and the Canadian service offered new challenges. "The work of assisting to build up one of our Colonial Fleets," he explained to Kingsmill, "appeals to me as most attractive," particularly "as one is likely to see *results* from one's work in a far greater measure than in the Royal Navy, where one's work lies [merely] in keeping things up to the mark."[71] Although Kingsmill had nothing to offer, the two kept in touch. His chance came in June 1911, when the captain who had brought HMCS *Rainbow* to Esquimalt became "fed up" with the Canadian service and left. Hose assumed command.[72] The following year Hose took advantage of special inducements offered to low- and middle-grade officers to retire from the Royal Navy and transferred to the Royal Canadian Navy (RCN).

Hose's sharp-featured, clean-shaven face suggests a more aggressive and impatient personality than does Kingsmill's bearded, kindly visage; the record bears out this impression. Hose was never content merely to keep the west coast establishment efficient – itself no small task, considering sometimes crippling problems of morale. Indeed, in 1913–14 Hose exceeded his authority by fostering a group of Victoria citizens who had formed themselves into an unofficial naval reserve company. This initiative gathered further support from both the premier and the governor-general and finally compelled Prime Minister Borden – over objections of his French-Canadian caucus – to authorize in May 1914 creation of the Royal Naval Canadian Volunteer Reserve (RNCVR).[73] Both for this, and for his advocacy of reserves during the dismal wasteland years of the Depression, Hose has since become known as "Father of the Naval Reserve."

In the mean time, Lieutenant R.M. Stephens had become the central figure in the often confused military administration of the department at naval headquarters in Ottawa. A few months younger than Hose, he was one of three officers brought out from the United Kingdom in the fall of 1909 to help establish the new naval service. Senior British officers had strongly recommended him to Kingsmill because of his "good brains," his achievements as a gunnery officer, and his devotion to duty. Yet he had never been promoted – apparently because his ship had done poorly in an important firing practice. As one report put it, "he had only just come out of the sick list and got mixed up over the deflection somehow." Though having threatened to resign in 1911 over the deputy minister's arbitrary administrative methods, he transferred to the RCN the following year.

Like Hose, Stephens too took advantage of the special scheme for retirement from the imperial service. By that time he was acting as Admiral Kingsmill's chief of staff and had responsibility for naval intelligence in addition to his original appointment as director of naval gunnery. His memoranda and reports abound in departmental files from this period and leave no doubt about his sharp and incisive mind.[74] Certainly he deserves a large share of the credit for mobilization planning, the one area in which Canada's naval service made significant progress in the last years before the First World War.

War measures had preoccupied most governments and armed forces since the latter part of the nineteenth century. Revolutions in transportation technology and communications and in weaponry and tactics had greatly increased the danger of swift and unheralded attacks. Japan's devastating surprise attack on the Russian harbour of Port Arthur in 1904 without declaration of war had dramatically stressed the need for comprehensive plans for mobilization of coastal defence. The attack had stimulated more rigorous efforts in Britain and had highlighted the urgency of inter-service co-operation.

The new era affected dominion governments as well. They now had to prepare themselves so that, with a single brief telegram from London, the whole of the empire could instantly orchestrate precautionary measures at the first apprehension of war. In Canada this arrangement was fraught with problems. To be sure, the Department of Militia and Defence had endeavoured to act on the steady stream of memoranda from imperial authorities, but it lacked the authority and resources to co-operate in a whole spectrum of tasks vital to maritime defence: detention of enemy and neutral shipping, censorship of wireless and ocean cable communications, and control of merchant shipping entering defended ports. The Department of Marine and Fisheries proved reluctant to assist. This situation forced the conclusion that no harbour – Halifax, Esquimalt, or Quebec – was safe from the wiles of a disguised raider.[75]

With the beginnings of Canadian naval organization in 1909, the situation began to improve. Commander Stephens became the naval representative of the newly established interdepartmental committee on defence. He developed an informal, but close and effective relationship with Colonel Willoughby Gwatkin, who continued to serve on the committee even after becoming chief of the General Staff in

1913. Together, the two men co-ordinated coastal defence policy and a wide range of other inter-service questions until 1920. Like Stephens, Gwatkin was an intellectual officer. Further, the shy, efficient chief of the General Staff had not an ounce of pretension that would allow differences in service and rank to become a barrier.[76]

Stephens drafted the navy's war book, the secret government document which specified responsibility for every measure required on mobilization. He joined forces with the militia staff in pressing cabinet on the need for a government war book to co-ordinate all departments. When action finally began early in 1914, Stephens and a militia officer guided the work of the interdepartmental conferences and drafted most of the documents. It was an enormous task that had never been undertaken before.

The coastal defence of Canada was the single most important concern. Here both services made their greatest effort toward perfecting arrangements at Halifax, Canada's only well-defended port. On assuming responsibility for the fortress, the Dominion government had agreed to specific terms: consultation with imperial authorities and maintenance of a current mobilization scheme. There was little doubt that the harbour would again become a base for British warships in the event of war. In 1911 the navy began to take over from Marine and Fisheries all waterborne aspects of mobilization. The following year the navy became the sole authority for wartime control of traffic in the port.

One defence requirement on which Marine and Fisheries had never acted was maintenance of a "swept" channel in the harbour approaches to guard against enemy mines. At Stephens's instigation, two Fisheries Protection Service vessels carried out exercises with minesweeping gear in 1912 and 1913. In another exercise, the navy once again resorted to a Fisheries Protection Service vessel to provide a "harbour examination service." Exercising the vessel with shore batteries resulted in greatly improved arrangements for stopping and identifying merchant vessels at the entrance to the port.

By the spring of 1914 the first full naval defence scheme for Halifax had been completed. Yet it suffered from limited personnel and resources. Five Fisheries Protection Service vessels and nine other civil craft of potential military value were earmarked for these duties. The navy's role was quite obviously secondary to the militia's shore-based defences. These included seven modern batteries, over 1,000 regular troops, and as many as 2,000 part-time militiamen.[77] But Canada still needed a navy, for the forts could cover only the waters within the ten-mile range of their heaviest guns. As soon as it had become clear in 1913 that the government's naval policy had suffered a severe setback, the staffs of both services expressed concern at the growing danger from raids against other parts of the Atlantic coast.[78] Admiral Kingsmill finally persuaded the recalcitrant Borden to reconsider the torpedo-craft scheme which the Admiralty had given him in 1912. The Admiralty's proposal for torpedo boats, we might recall, had also included submarines for each coast.

The prime minister again sought the Admiralty's opinion. The British reply in May 1914 was even more pointed in stressing the priority of trade defence over coastal defence than had been the studies prepared for Borden during his London visit in 1912. Attacks on the Atlantic coast of North America were still unlikely. However, Admiralty warned that an enemy would "probably select" the waters south of Cape Race as an "excellent" area for raiding transatlantic trade; against that threat, their lordships explained, torpedo craft would be quite useless. Canada should therefore take a different tack. "Very necessary" now were cruisers to reinforce the "very limited number" that the Royal Navy "can allot to the North Atlantic in war." Britain needed not only Canadian ships but Canadian shore bases. The Dominion government should therefore improve the inadequate coaling facilities at Halifax and develop Sydney harbour as a secure fuelling base for cruiser operations by installing coastal artillery.[79] In June 1914 Borden informed Churchill that he hoped to be able to study the recommendations at the end of July.[80] By that time much larger events had intervened.

PART TWO
Whither America?
1914-1916

– 4 –

Britain's Lifeline

The "Guns of August" would change the face of Europe, destroy millions of young lives, and scar the surviving generation. They would thrust dominions into a new relationship with the Mother Country and forge new national identities. Germany declared war on France on 3 August 1914, invaded Belgium at dawn on the 4th, and provoked Britain's declaration of war against Germany on the 5th. The British declaration had automatically included the overseas dominions, and the government of Sir Robert Borden was determined to assist generously. On British advice, Canada concentrated on raising land forces rather than a navy. The first Canadian contingent, of 30,500 men, would reach England on 14 October. But for the citizens of Halifax, it seemed from the outset that their city was at the very centre of the European conflict.

Banner headlines in the Halifax *Morning Chronicle* of 7 August 1914 announced "Another Vindication of the Empire Port [as] Two Crack Liners Shelter under the Guns of Halifax." Not since HMS *Shannon* towed the American frigate *Chesapeake* in here one hundred and one years ago has there been such excitement over any local naval happening." But of course the two events were decidedly different. For this time the "monster" Cunard liner *Mauretania* and the White Star liner *Cedric* had been approaching Nova Scotia on scheduled transatlantic runs to New York when warnings of German raiders caused the British cruiser HMS *Essex* to divert them into the Canadian port. *Mauretania*, with her 31,000 tons and her 762-foot length, was one of the largest ships in the world; even the 21,000-ton *Cedric* was more impressive than anything the port had seen in years. Moved by the awesome sight of such huge vessels escorted by the British cruiser, the newspaper evoked Kipling's tribute to the city:

'At rest but ready' was the thought that unconsciously rose to the mind when

looking over the moonlit harbor ... At the mouth of the harbor the dull
colored warship slipping out as noiselessly as she had entered. Near at hand,
the brightly lighted *Cedric*, and still further up ... lay the *Mauretania*. For all
the time, this first call of the *Mauretania* will be remembered ... She meant to
Halifax the incontestable proof that this is the premier port of the New
World ...

In the years to come when the war will be a thing of the past ... Halifax
will remember last night – the luminous beauty of the full moon, the soft
summer air, the peace that almost deceived one into thinking that all was as
usual; the thrill of pride that she held securely in the embrace of her wonder-
ful harbor the two great ships ... and the proud uplift of her head at having
so soon done signal service for the Mother Country. Stirring times bring
stirring opportunities and these be great days for Halifax.[1]

Thousands of miles away, in Kiel and Wilhelmshaven, similarly
romantic sentiments were being expressed. Here too the commanding officer of his german majesty's cruiser SMS *Stralsund*, en route to
the North Sea through the Kaiser-Wilhelm Kanal, felt a surge of pride
in a promising destiny: "Midnight – neither moon nor any star in the
sky, mist hangs in the breeze, nary a lamp. While passing the Kaiser
Wilhelm Bridge a thousand-voiced invisible choir breaks through the
impenetrable darkness and bursts forth with the Deutschland-song,
the Kaiser-hymn, and unceasing hurrahs. The most magnificent
patriotic feelings well up from the deepest recesses of the heart,
awakening pride in everyone on board: to be the first cruiser summoned to take up the watch for the Homeland, and to be able to bear
the responsibility with joy."[2]

This was high melodrama – not least, in the Canadian case, because
reports of German raiders had been false. But the argument for the
greatly increased importance of Halifax was none the less sound.
Immediately on the outbreak of war, Halifax had once again become
what it had not been since the Napoleonic Wars: a front-line, strategically vital imperial port.

Of course, a great deal had changed in the intervening century.
But as the Admiralty had explained to Borden in 1912 and again in
early 1914, the expansion of Germany's high-seas cruiser forces had
underscored the potential importance of Canada's Atlantic ports as
bases for trade defence. Perhaps a sixth of the world's entire ocean
commerce plied the North Atlantic, whose short Great Circle route
from the Americas to northwestern Europe swept close by Nova
Scotia and past Newfoundland's Cape Race.

Indeed, it was no exaggeration to boast that this was Britain's
lifeline. By 1914 Canada and the United States were supplying nearly

45 per cent of Britain's grain and flour imports, large proportions of other foodstuffs, and substantial quantities of industrial raw materials.[3] Admittedly, much of this trade came from the United States. But while the US declaration of neutrality had still left American ports open to commerce, it had closed them sharply to Allied trade defence forces.

As it happened, a number of German and Allied cruisers had been patrolling the Caribbean at the outbreak of hostilities. They had been deployed to protect European nationals and interests in Mexico that were threatened there by civil war. In 1913 Britain's Admiralty had dispatched the Fourth Cruiser Squadron under Rear-Admiral Sir Christopher Cradock to the North America and West Indies Station while the French sent two cruisers. Two German cruisers were on station there in late July: *Dresden* and her recently arrived relief ship, *Karlsruhe*. News of European events disrupted *Karlsruhe*'s voyage to Mexico; having refuelled in Havana on 29 July, she now kept out of sight while awaiting further orders. *Dresden* had by this time refuelled at the Danish island of St Thomas on the outer edge of the West Indies; she was therefore in an excellent position to strike northward against the main transatlantic shipping routes in the event of war.

Reputable sources immediately confirmed Admiralty's fears that Germany was preparing to make a concerted assault on the northwest Atlantic. On 1 August the governor of Newfoundland relayed an intercepted radio report from the liner *Lusitania*, which had claimed to have sighted *Dresden* off New York. Two days later, the British consul at the French island of St Pierre, off the south coast of Newfoundland, reported that both *Dresden* and *Karlsruhe* were in the vicinity in order to strike at trade from the Gulf of St Lawrence. Press reports indicated that "a naval fight seems imminent in these waters."[4]

Nor was that the only danger. In accordance with their standing instructions for periods of apprehended war, some fifty-four vessels of the Central Powers were taking refuge in American ports in order to escape capture. Most of them, including large, fast liners that British naval intelligence had identified as potential armed merchant cruisers, had sheltered in New York. Such vessels could readily emerge and strike into the heart of the major focal area for British trade in the western Atlantic; indeed on the night of 3–4 August the Liner *Kronprinz Wilhelm* did just that. The liner *Vaterland* followed within twenty-four hours. Even the smaller vessels constituted a threat; they could conceivably slip out to refuel and supply the raiders and thereby overcome Germany's lack of bases, which was the principal impediment to sustained German operations on the North Atlantic. In fact *Kronprinz Wilhelm* and another liner, *Prinz Eitel Friedrich*, soon interned themselves in Newport News, as they were short of fuel and could not fight their way home through British patrols. Germany's Admiralty Staff concurred with the captains' action.[5]

Small cruisers like the *Karlsruhe*, *Emden*, and *Geier* would continue to perform sterling service for the Germans: always keeping the enemy off-balance, striking where least expected, causing the enemy to redeploy its major warships to its disadvantage, and disrupting lines of communication. The German popular press praised the achievement of cruiser warfare: "never since men have gone down to the sea in ships have a seafaring people more stolidly and joyously affirmed the old tenet 'navigare necesse est'."[6] Erich Raeder would later extol their achievements as textbook models of cruiser warfare. Indeed, he would class their tactical achievements among the best of big-ship chivalry and élan and regard the death throes of *Emden* and *Königsberg* in combat with superior British forces as worthy of the highest national honours accorded the "decisive battle" of the Falklands when *Gneisenau*, *Scnarnhorst*, *Leipzig*, and *Nürnberg* fell victim to British naval forces on 8 December 1914. But the very circumstances that caused Germany to resort to such modest vessels as *Emden* and *Geier*, Raeder argued in 1923, "bears unequivocal witness" to the fact that Germany had not been making long-range preparations for a war.[7] German records disprove his case.

Warned of the international crisis at the end of July, Cradock had assigned two of his five cruisers, *Essex* and *Lancaster*, to the northern route, in order to block any German raiders. The two British cruisers were in Bermuda at the time. Accompanied by the cruiser *Bristol*, he himself followed from the Caribbean in *Suffolk*.[8] The Admiralty had urged haste. Naval Service Headquarters in Ottawa had by now implemented such defence measures as were possible with the meagre resources at hand: ordering Fisheries Protection Service vessels to Halifax, recalling all personnel from leave, mobilizing censorship staffs, and monitoring movements of all Austrian, German, and Italian vessels in Canadian waters.[9] When Britain entered the war, at midnight on 4–5 August (German time), Admiralty warned Cradock that "trade form New York and the St Lawrence is seriously threatened."[10] Later on 5 August, Admiralty ordered the armoured cruiser HMS *Good Hope* and the old battleship HMS *Glory* to proceed directly to Halifax and arranged with French authorities for two French cruisers that were homeward bound from the Mexican patrol to put into Bermuda for operations under Cradock's command.[11]

Dramatic confirmation of the possibility that some German warships were operating in southern waters came on 6 August, when HMS

Suffolk and *Bristol* undertook searches in the direction of intercepted German radio messages while en route to Bermuda; they encountered *Karlsruhe*. Superior speed enabled the German cruiser to escape. Significantly, she ran due south. Cradock did not realize at the time that she had not been alone. The liner *Kronprinz Wilhelm* had been running in company in order to take on armament; she too had made off to the south. Cradock sent *Bristol* back to the West Indies and ordered the two French cruisers waiting at Bermuda to follow her. He thereby restored the Caribbean force to an adequate strength of four cruisers.[12]

The precise location of the German warships remained for the moment a purely academic matter. Their general presence underscored Britain's urgent and overriding need to secure the vital North Atlantic trade on which its war effort and very survival depended. Even if German forces at sea posed no immediate danger, British sea lanes still lay within easy reach from two directions: from the fast liners sheltered in neutral American ports and from warships based in a belligerent Germany. The latter threat loomed ominously through the war.

The commencement of hostilities in August 1914 had brought in its wake a radical shift in German strategy. Germany had indeed a powerful land army, but its navy was comparatively weak and unready. The Imperial German Navy could therefore not follow through on von Tirpitz dictum of strategic offensive. The German Admiralty suffered a further and double disadvantage. Its lack of an operations division prevented it from functioning as a naval war office; its lack of authority to act rendered it inadequately prepared for the difficult task of advising the Kaiser and the Commander-in-Chief Fleet in a naval war against the greatest sea power in the world and its allies.[13]

Even though the Royal Navy's principle battle fleet, or "Grand Fleet" as it was now called, contained the German High Seas Fleet within the North Sea, the apparent checkmate left no real margin for British confidence. By exploiting new technology – mines, submarines, surface torpedo craft, and long-range coast artillery – the Germans had virtually sealed off their coasts against marauding enemy forces and forced the Royal Navy to revise its traditional strategy of close blockade. British warships could no longer press close off German ports but had to operate and observe from a distance. With forces based in Britain, Royal Navy patrols swept the North Sea and maintained constant guard over the exits into the Atlantic.

These defensive sweeps were thinly spread over a vast expanse of ocean, and so German ships and squadrons could evade them. Even more important, British tactical weakness allowed the Germans to avoid any major fleet action by running for the cover of their coast defences. On the one occasion that the Grand Fleet managed to bring full strength to bear against Germany's High Seas Fleet, off Jutland in May 1916, the Germans were able to escape as night descended and reach the protection of mine-fields before dawn. Thus the decisive pitched battle on the high seas that Mahan had maintained would ultimately decide who held "command of the sea" – the very Entscheidungsschlacht on which von Tirpitz had based his constant pressure for battle-fleet expansion – became theoretically obsolete. In practice, however, the strategic threat remained strong. From a British perspective, Germany preserved an immensely powerful "fleet in being" until the final days of the war. Never could Admiralty disregard the danger that major German fleet units or raiders might slip into the North Atlantic and dash for the thinly protected western ocean.

Germany's destabilizing effect on high seas trade at the outbreak of war forced Britain to grapple with the immediate and pressing task of restoring confidence among panic-stricken shippers. Press reports datelined New York had been quick to announce "Shipping Men Fear Cruisers" and revealed that "Streamers [were] reluctant to leave the shelter of New York."[14] No matter how perfectly Britain might contain enemy raiders, the achievement was worth little if nervous ship owners and operators held their vessels in port.

Germany could wish for nothing better. In this respect, trade defence was much like the work of civilian police. The Royal Navy had to assure the merchant marine community that sea lanes were safe for commerce: the paralysis of shipping through fear could have a potentially much larger effect on Britain's transatlantic trade than the limited number of vessels the small German raiding forces might actually destroy. The Germans had to make shippers believe that the sea lanes were fraught with danger.

In August 1914 panic was the greatest menace in the northwest Atlantic. Shippers at New York were refusing to send their vessels to sea, and a veritable blizzard of reports about German raiders in Canadian waters delayed deployment of British patrols to reassure shipping at the American port. So grave was the apparent danger in the vicinity of Nova Scotia that, while HMS *Lancaster* steamed from Bermuda to the Cabot Strait to protect the Gulf of St Lawrence, HMS *Essex* cancelled her planned New York patrol in order to remain off Halifax, where she had just taken on coal.[15]

Not until Britain demonstrated its strength at the very entrance of the great port did trade begin to move from there. Cradock had rushed north to New York from Bermuda aboard HMS *Suffolk* and had signalled *Essex* to rendezvous with him. On 11 August he brought *Suffolk* close off the port and sent word through the British consul that two cruisers were arriving on station: shipping could now proceed safely.

Uninformed by Admiralty about the deployment of HMS *Lancaster* into the Gulf of St Lawrence, Naval Service Headquarters in Ottawa had meanwhile responded to the threat by stopping all Gulf shipping on the 10th. Indeed, the quiet arrival of HMS *Lancaster* off Cape Breton had triggered speculation that she was actually a German raider – possibly part of a force that was rumoured to be on its way to occupy St Pierre et Miquelon and turn them into an advance base.[16]

As so often happened in operational enterprises like this, the Admiralty went in one direction (without informing Canada), and an isolated Ottawa had to reach its own conclusions and act on its own. The Admiralty was of course annoyed at the Canadian action and seemed unable to appreciate that the perspective of Canadian authorities not privy to British information was necessarily different: "Admiralty know of no reason why this [closure of the Gulf] should be done, and His Majesty's Government are most anxious that trade should continue uninterrupted as far as possible ... When any trade route [proves] unsafe Admiralty will send warning."[17] This acerbic reassurance was often observed in the breach.

Further intelligence had meanwhile erased any doubt that German raiders were actually in southern waters. After putting into Halifax, Cradock therefore shifted his flag to the newly arrived cruiser HMS *Good Hope*; she was faster and more powerfully armed than the other cruisers on station. On 15 August he departed to hunt German raiders. As Cradock steamed south, reports reached Admiralty in London that confirmed suspicions: *Dresden*, and possibly a second raider, were attacking shipping off the coast of South America. Their lordships therefore dispatched reinforcements to the "South East Coast of America" station and placed them under Cradock's orders when he arrived off Pernambuco, Brazil, on 3 September.

The well-known events that followed require only a brief summary. It had quickly become clear that the gravest threat to the Atlantic came from Admiral Graf von Spee's powerful China squadron, which was now crossing the Pacific eastward, toward the southern tip of South America. Bravely, but foolishly, Cradock passed westward around the Horn to Chile and intercepted Spee, who handily destroyed the much inferior British squadron at Coronel on 1 November 1914. Here Canada registered her first naval losses of the war: four midshipmen, members of the first class of the Royal Naval College of Canada, went down with Cradock.[18] But once having broken into the Atlantic, Graf von Spee's force was in turn destroyed by a British battle-cruiser force on 8 December at the Falkland Islands. Vice-Admiral Sir David Beatty judged that "poor old Kit Cradock" and his ships had been unwittingly sacrificed by the Admiralty's incompetence.[19]

But despite miscalculations on the part of both the Admiralty and Cradock that led to the disaster at Coronel, the modest British forces available in the Western Hemisphere had quickly contained the German raider threat. Over the next five months, reinforced British cruiser squadrons in West Indies and South American waters tracked down the last of the independent raiders. Most important, the thinly stretched British force had secured the crucial North Atlantic routes and had restored the confidence of shippers within ten days of the outbreak of hostilities.

Cradock had left the cruisers *Essex*, *Lancaster*, and *Suffolk* in the Halifax area when he departed the Canadian port on 15 August. These ships formed the nucleus of the trade defence force that would operate from the Canadian base until the end of the war. Although *Essex* departed shortly for the West Indies, the battleship HMS *Glory* arrived thereafter, followed by the armed merchant cruiser *Caronia* on 14 September. *Caronia* brought Rear-Admiral R.S. Phipps-Hornby to succeed Cradock in command of the northern forces.[20] Phipps-Hornby was responsible for the defence of trade over a vast area: from the northern part of South America to the Arctic circle and out to forty degrees West in the central Atlantic, through a meridian running some five hundred miles east of Newfoundland. However, in terms of possible enemy action and confidence of the shipping community, the most important area lay in the approaches to New York. Thus maintaining a permanent patrol off that port remained the primary commitment of the Halifax force until the United States entered the war in April 1917.

Halifax itself was of course ideally located for trade defence operations. But it was an ill-equipped base because of the lethargic and desultory development of the Canadian navy. As Phipps-Hornby reported, the dockyard facilities and staff were in a sorry state: "[They had] been allowed to relapse to a state which only permits ... meeting the requirements of fishery protection vessels, etc., and no modern machinery has been installed. The Yard cannot effect more than minor repairs for H.M. ships, items of any magnitude being placed in the hands of the Halifax Graving Dock Company – a commercial concern over whose dock the Admiralty possess certain rights, but whose principal work is connected with merchant vessels. They do not necessarily give priority to naval work and their charges are extremely high."[21]

For this reason, most warships went to Bermuda for refits and major repairs. Unlike the old and cramped facilities at Halifax, the Bermuda dockyard had been expanded and thoroughly modernized at the turn of the century. Even when reducing its forces in the Western Hemisphere in 1904–5, Britain had kept the island base open. Well situated between Halifax and the main Caribbean operating base at Kingston, Jamaica, Bermuda served as headquarters of the North America and West Indies Station.

Increasingly, however, the activities of the admiral commanding centred on Halifax. As Rear-Admiral Phipps-Hornby explained:

One of the first questions I had to decide was whether Halifax or Bermuda should form the main base for ships of the Northern Division, and for the following reasons I unhesitatingly chose the former:–

(a) Its position flanks the trade routes from Canada and northern ports of the United States, and is approximately 100 miles nearer New York.

(b) It could be entered or left at anytime of the day or night by vessels of heavy draught [whereas the passage into Bermuda dockyard was notoriously treacherous].

(c) It possessed far better and more direct means of communications with the United Kingdom, Ottawa, and Diplomatic and Counsellor Officers, and other bases ...

(d) It would enable me to be in close touch with the Dominion Authorities.[22]

Canada's contribution to the security of the Western Hemisphere was at first limited. But the organizational and planning efforts of militia and naval staffs prior to the outbreak of hostilities had enabled Naval Service Headquarters in Ottawa to take prompt action on receiving the telegraphed warnings from London at the end of July and the beginning of August. Stephens's work in preparing the government war book came not a moment too soon. In fact, the war book committee had just gathered on 29 July to resolve some final details when the governor-general's military secretary telephoned to say that Canada had just received the executive message to carry out "precautionary stage" measures.[23]

By this time the committee had completed sufficient ground-work to ensure effective co-operation of other departments with both the navy and the militia. The naval and military schemes for Halifax had been thoroughly revised as recently as the spring of 1914, and the armed services could now bring coast defence schemes into force.

Provisions for the defence of Quebec City and Esquimalt were far less current and elaborate. They none the less provided an adequate basis for the mobilization that was already well in hand when Ottawa received the "war telegram" on the evening of 4 August 1914.

The Canadian navy carried out its harbour defence responsibilities as planned with some ten or eleven vessels. Most were government ships that continued their civilian work between "defence tours" at Halifax. Very lightly armed – and some not at all – they played roles already envisaged in peacetime harbour defence exercises with the navy. The ability to provide basic and essential defence services so quickly was significant: it reflected well on the naval staff's pre-war preparations and on the Naval Service Act's close integration of the RCN with other government vessels. Modest as it was, this achievement to some extent vindicated Macdonald and Laurier's long-standing contention that the whole of the government's marine resources was a potential defence force. Civilian vessels would be vital to the navy's success throughout the war.

Given the sad condition of the Canadian navy in 1913–14, not even an optimist might have expected that the RCN was capable of doing much more than merely implementing the port defence schemes. But significant developments did in fact follow. The most dramatic of them took place on the west coast, a lonely outpost left virtually to its own resources.[24] Once the Royal Navy had reduced its forces on the Pacific in order to reinforce European waters in 1904–5, no major warships lay any nearer to the BC coast than the cruisers assigned to the China Station. Thus, in sharp contrast to Atlantic ports during the anxious first three weeks of the war, Canada's meagre Pacific forces stood alone.

Britain's disbandment of the Pacific squadron in 1904 had left but two Esquimalt-based minor war vessels to carry out residual British responsibilities in the eastern part of the Pacific: the sloops HMS *Algerine* and *Shearwater*. Both ships were operating off the west coast of Mexico in the summer of 1914, protecting British interests, just as Admiral Cradock's squadron was doing on the eastern seaboard. The Admiralty had therefore asked Ottawa to commission HMCS *Rainbow* to carry out the annual British patrol of the Bering seal fisheries. Following these developments with great interest, the *Daily Colonist* proudly printed her photograph and announced her mission.[25] She was in fact just approaching readiness for the patrol in late July when the international crisis changed her task. But she was short of crew. Even with the addition of a detachment of Royal Navy personnel who had been sent from England, and another group from HMCS *Niobe* on the east coast, her numbers amounted to barely two-thirds of the full complement of 350 officers and men. Thus she took aboard 76 virtually untrained members of the RNCVR from the companies that Hose had recently organized in Victoria and Vancouver.

Germany's fast, light cruiser *Leipzig* had meanwhile been operating off the west coast of Mexico and began heading north at the end of July. According to the Victoria press: "The German cruiser *Leipzig* [had] naturally aroused considerable interest"[26] on the west coast. *Rainbow* was the only major warship Britain had to counter her. Therefore at the Admiralty's request *Rainbow* put to sea without fanfare under Commander Walter Hose during the early hours of 3 August in order to protect British shipping off the American west coast and to succour the vulnerable Royal Navy sloops as they worked their way home from Mexican waters.

Many British Columbians never expected to see *Rainbow* again and braced themselves instead for the appearance of enemy cruisers with guns blazing off Prince Rupert, Victoria, and Vancouver. This was precisely the nightmare British Columbians had envisioned when they vehemently protested withdrawal of the British squadron in 1904 and repeatedly lobbied the governments of Laurier and Borden to act on naval defence. The Conservative premier, Richard McBride, stood in the forefront of proponents for maritime defence. McBride was a man of unusual drive. Through contacts in Seattle he immediately purchased with provincial funds two submarines being built for Chile. Company crews brought them across the Straits of Juan da Fuca to Esquimalt on the morning of 5 August, hunted by a US cruiser in its vain attempt to enforce US neutrality laws that forbade the sale of arms to combatants.

A single broadsheet which the *Daily Colonist* released at noon on 5 August proclaimed McBride's political finesse: "On behalf of the Dominion Government and with their concurrence, Sir Richard McBride ... some days ago completed the purchase of two submarines, which are now lying at anchor in British waters ready for action under the command of Lieut Jones, R.N., submarine expert. Lt Jones is a recognized submarine expert, in fact his knowledge of submarine warfare is not excelled in the Empire. Every preparation for naval warfare is complete. The submarines are newly built and said to be of the most destructive class ... The vessels now form part of the national forces."

The facts were not quite as announced. Commissioned in the RCN as *CC 1* and *CC 2*, the submarines were crewed by RNCVR personnel under the command of retired British naval officers who happened to be living in Victoria. A grateful federal government ultimately reimbursed the BC treasury, and the crews quickly set about learning to operate their new craft. Of more immediate importance, by the last week of August, Allied cruisers were taking up position in the northeast Pacific.

As it turned out, *Leipzig* never did move north of San Francisco but instead ran far to the south to join Graf von Spee's squadron which was then making for South America. But another foreign visitor appeared whom few British Columbians would have expected. On 25 August, two days after Japan's entry into the war on the Allied side and one day after all the Allied armies on the Western Front had begun their humiliating retreat in the face of the swift, deep German thrusts through the Low Countries and into France, the large Japanese cruiser *Izumo* reached Esquimalt. McBride was doubtless surprised, for he had recently offered Borden and Churchill the sage warning that Japan would throw in its lot with Germany. Five days later, the modern British light cruiser HMS *Newcastle* arrived from the China Station. This concentration of warships at Esquimalt anticipated reports that Graf von Spee's squadron might head toward British Columbia. At the time of the German victory at the Battle of Coronel, when the danger to Canada had seemed greatest, further and much more powerful reinforcements – including the modern Australian battle-cruiser HMAS *Australia* – were already on their way toward the eastern Pacific. The rapid build-up was for nought. The destruction of the German squadron at the Falklands in December eliminated any but the most remote threat to the Canadian west coast.

Yet despite the happy outcome, Naval Service Headquarters had good reason for concern about events in British Columbia. Here, however, it was a question of internal politics and the rival claims of the Royal Navy and Canadian authority. At the outbreak of war, the Borden government had placed HMCS *Rainbow* and *Niobe* and the submarines at Admiralty's disposal, as provided for in Laurier's Naval Service Act. On his arrival in Esquimalt at the end of August, the commanding officer of HMS *Newcastle*, Captain F.A. Powlett, RN, immediately assumed control of all operations on the west coast. He outranked Commander Hose and therefore had every right to do so.

But Powlett, acting in concert with the anxious McBride, had in effect taken over Esquimalt dockyard as well and was freely using the resources of other government departments for what struck Ottawa as exaggerated precautions. For example, he mounted two guns on the shore of the treacherous Seymour Narrows, that surging race some 150 miles north of Victoria, beyond the northern reaches of the Strait of Georgia. He manned them with Militia and dispatched cgs *Newington* to the scene to lay a field of mines hastily contrived with local materials. All this imaginative activity aimed at preventing a cunning Graf von Spee from reaching Vancouver via the hazardous route around the northern tip of Vancouver Island and southward through Discovery Passage. The Canadian solution to this conflict between the Royal Navy and the rcn lay in an administrative gambit that created a senior west coast appointment.

Canada's army build-up was meanwhile continuing apace. Troops were preparing as far away from the front as Victoria. There, on 28 August 1914, crowds of well-wishers flocked to the Inner Harbour in straw boaters and long summer dresses to bid farewell to the city's first contingent, departing for Vancouver aboard *Princess Sophia*, en route to staging and training in Valcartier, Quebec. In the words of the *Daily Colonist*: "The crackle of musketry, the skirl of bagpipes, rousing and appropriate airs by bands and the shouts and cheers of the immense crowd assembled" created an air of festivity.[27]

Amid this outpouring of imperial patriotism, the efforts of Canadian naval bureaucracy to safeguard fine points of Canadian sovereignty understandably aroused little interest. The press scarcely noticed the appointment of Rear-Admiral W.O. Story as superintendent of Esquimalt Dockyard in October. A retired Royal Navy officer living in Guelph, Ontario, he had offered his services to the Canadian navy. Kingsmill instructed Story not to fly his flag or interfere with ship deployments but to use the full weight of his rank "in an advisory capacity" in order to curtail the excesses of Powlett and McBride.[28] Story soon established proper lines of communication. From the time of his arrival, the dockyard requested authority for action and refrained from its disturbing habit of presenting the government with faits accomplis.[29] He immediately dismantled the emergency defences on the defeat of Graf Spee in December.

Extraordinary efforts on the east coast had meanwhile readied hmcs *Niobe* by the beginning of September. The transfer of much of her crew to *Rainbow* on the west coast had reduced her personnel to seventeen officers and men, but over three hundred men soon volunteered to serve in her. Many of them were ex-Royal Navy seamen. Admiralty topped up the complement of 700 by transferring the crews from hms *Algerine* and *Shearwater*, which were by now laid up in Esquimalt, and adding a further 107 from the Newfoundland Royal Naval Reserve. Her new commanding officer was Captain Robert G. Corbett, rn. As senior British naval officer on the west coast, he had flown his pennant in *Algerine*.[30] *Niobe* was undoubtedly obsolescent and slow. But given the desperate shortage of cruisers in the

Royal Navy, she was a welcome addition to Admiral Phipps-Hornby's squadron. In early October she took her place in the New York patrol.[31]

Canada's contribution of the old cruiser was but one aspect of its immediate defence commitments. Even more important for the moment was the Dominion's essential role in supporting British naval communications and enhancing arrangements for command and control in the northwest Atlantic. Two revolutions in communications had permitted swift, efficient deployment of Cradock's handful of warships on the eve of hostilities over the whole of the North American seaboard and the Caribbean: undersea cables and ship-borne radio. The development of undersea cables for transoceanic communication had made major advances since the nineteenth century and for naval purposes provided greater security than transmission of signals between transatlantic radio stations. Advancements since 1900 in the production and maintenance of increasingly rugged ship-borne radio equipment permitted closer and more spontaneous tactical control. Serious problems remained: for instance, the short range of ship-to-shore and ship-to-ship equipment. Considering that Cradock received messages late and often garbled aboard HMCS *Suffolk*, his performance was all the more impressive.[32]

Eastern Canada formed the hub of imperial communications in the western Atlantic. Undersea cables to Britain, Bermuda, and the United States came ashore in Nova Scotia, where they connected with the extensive continental system of telegraph landlines which extended through the whole of the Americas. Then too the Canadian government's east coast wireless system – including stations in Newfoundland – provided a vital link with ships at sea. Shortly before the outbreak of war, the cabinet had approved reconstruction of the station at Cape Race, Newfoundland, in order to extend its transmitting range to the New York approaches. Cape Race was the "clearing house" for most traffic on North Atlantic sea lanes; work was completed in October 1914.[33] By this time Rear-Admiral Phipps-Hornby had realized the need for a direct link between Halifax and British warships operating off New York and southward toward Bermuda. On his recommendation, the department built a new high-powered station at Barrington Passage, near the southeast tip of Nova Scotia; landline linked the station directly to the dockyard when the wireless installation was completed in the spring of 1915.[34]

The commercial transatlantic station at Newcastle, New Brunswick, which the Universal Radio Syndicate had built shortly before the war, was in quite a different category. Although the government had closed down other commercial stations in order to prevent the broadcast of information useful to the enemy, it left Newcastle open on Admiralty advice;[35] the facility was brought under RCN control in order to intercept German signals. The station soon proved useful in monitoring messages transmitted by German diplomats and officials in the United States, whose sole means of broadcast lay through the Atlantic station at Sayville, Long Island.[36] As the British had seized control of ocean cables at the outbreak of war, the Germans were compelled to use this means of communication.[37]

Intelligence gathering was a natural offshoot of radiotelegraphy. With its excellent communication facilities, Halifax emerged as the logical centre to collect and disseminate information for the operations of British warships in the northwest Atlantic. Stephens, as part of his mobilization planning in 1911–13, had already made arrangements for the organization of an intelligence office at Halifax under Lieutenant Charles White, the unfortunate navigator of *Niobe* who had nevertheless proved to be a capable officer. On 18 August 1914 the "Imperial Senior Naval Officer," as he signed himself, informed Halifax dockyard that it had now become the intelligence centre for the northern area. Just who this senior officer was is no longer clear; he may have been the captain of HMS *Suffolk*, whom Cradock left in charge of the northern division, or Cradock himself, who is known to have put into Bermuda on that same day and dispatched instructions about northern operations.[38]

Lieutenant White had already been compiling reports from Ottawa, from Canadian customs officials, and from other sources, as required by the mobilization plan; the centre's new status triggered a rapid expansion of operations. White and his staff appear to have met the challenge for Admiral Phipps-Hornby reported to Admiralty shortly after his arrival the following month that "Halifax has performed duty well."[39] But seeds of tension between the navies had already been sown.

Radio intelligence is a case in point. While developing its links in the western Atlantic the Admiralty had decided that St John's, Newfoundland, rather than Halifax should be the Royal Navy's intelligence centre for the North Atlantic. With effect from 1 October 1914, British consuls at US Atlantic ports and other intelligence centres were now directed to report to St John's instead of Halifax. St John's was then to broadcast all information in code to any cruisers that were at sea in the northern area and to pass to Halifax all information for cruisers in that port. Ironically, Halifax was doing all of this anyway. Phipps-Hornby protested that the St John's centre was not needed and should at most remain an ancillary to Halifax. Admiralty would not demur.[40]

Shortly after these events, the director of the intelligence division at the Admiralty explained the series of apparent misunderstandings by asserting that Cradock had not informed him in August 1914 of the decision to use the Canadian intelligence centre at Halifax. That was undoubtedly true as far as it went, for the station commander had acted quickly and informally in those harried days of mobilization.

However, when organization in the western Atlantic again became a pressing concern in 1917, Admiralty's intelligence division gave a more candid account of the reasons for the decisions of 1914: "The Intelligence Centre at St John's was originally established there rather than at Halifax in order that Admiralty might retain control over it and avoid friction with Canadian naval authorities, though it has always been recognised that Halifax was the more suitable port for an intelligence centre in this part of the world."[41] Admiralty's reference to "friction with Canadian naval authorities" reveals more than at first appears. It reflects, on the one hand, British resistance to Canadian attempts to assume much more than a basic information-gathering role in the intelligence organization and, on the other, Canadian resistance to British exertion of control over the RCN establishment at Halifax. Naval Service Headquarters was frequently kept in the dark about much of this conflict.

In August 1914 Ottawa had learned of Halifax's designation as the intelligence centre for the British squadron only after the fact, in a telegram from dockyard. Cradock had supplied no notification or explanation whatever. It was merely a point of etiquette for the British to inform Ottawa, for the department had always intended that the intelligence centre should work with the British squadron. Initially, as with similar difficulties on the west coast, headquarters lent the necessary support and tried to settle matters locally, so as not to impede naval operations. Stephens needed only remind the Canadian naval officer in charge of the dockyard that imperial officers had no authority over Canadian shore establishments.[42]

A sense of grievance took hold of Naval Service Headquarters during the following months. The St John's intelligence centre, which Admiralty had promised would keep Ottawa informed, reported only sporadically, and the Halifax centre reported scarcely at all. "In reality," Stephens fumed, "Halifax has established a complete blockade."[43] Headquarters pursued the question with an unsympathetic Admiral Phipps-Hornby, who suggested that the department was demanding too much detailed, routine information. In a memorandum for Admiral Kingsmill, Stephens hotly disagreed and pointed to the lack of advice on such crucial matters as ship movements; nor was the Dominion government informed "as to what steps are being taken for the protection of Canadian trade and coasts." To his mind it was "quite indefensible, as actually occurred, that a squadron [of British warships] should concentrate in the Gulf of St Lawrence as a convoy to the Canadian Contingent [the Canadian Expeditionary Force sailing for England] without the Dominion Government being informed of their presence or movements." On the face of it, Phipps-Hornby was deliberately closing Ottawa out. "The whole idea," Stephens concluded, "of Officers in the Canadian Service being in possession of information they are not allowed to communicate to their Government is wrong in principle."[44]

Kingsmill appears to have realized that Stephens was placing too much blame on Phipps-Hornby's influence at Halifax.[45] The larger problem was the delays, confusion, and multiplication of work caused by employing St John's as the main intelligence centre. Reports from the United States and the Caribbean passed close by Halifax on their way to Newfoundland; then a large proportion of them had to be redispatched back because Halifax was the principal operating base and had the most pressing need for information. In January 1915 Kingsmill laid all of this before Admiralty.[46] But their lordships came less then half-way in addressing his concerns. St John's remained the "north Atlantic" centre, while Halifax became the principal centre for the "Atlantic coast of Canada."[47] The geographical dividing line between the two centres is no longer clear. But British consuls at US Atlantic ports eventually began reporting directly to Halifax once more during the winter of 1915–16. These were perhaps short-term gains.

The imperial authorities had been entirely unimpressed by Kingsmill's argument that centralization of intelligence at Halifax would give Naval Service Headquarters in Ottawa readier access to information that was urgently needed in Ottawa. In fact, the Canadian admiral's appeal landed him in a nest of vipers. This headquarters, he explained, had to keep in touch with developments throughout the Western Hemisphere and was already requesting and receiving information from British consuls as far away as South America on such matters as contraband trade with the Central Powers. This was startling news to the British foreign secretary, Sir Edward Grey, and it annoyed him. The Canadian naval service, he remonstrated, had broken proper lines of imperial communication and, without consultation, was imposing an additional burden on the British consular service. He therefore reminded the Canadian navy that all dealings with British officials in the United States and elsewhere should be through the governor-general in Ottawa.[48] As we shall see, many unnecessarily convoluted links in intelligence matters obscured and delayed issues that required rapid clarification, authentication, and action.

Understandably, imperial authorities regarded the RCN as fulfilling a minimal wartime role. After all, the service had no modern ships and few trained personnel other than the cadre of Royal Navy seamen who had been lent or transferred to Canada. The officers were all specialists in the sea-going branches and had been selected primarily to carry out training duties during initial organization of the force. Not a single Canadian officer, not even Kingsmill or Stephens, was a qualified staff officer. The Admiralty's reluctance to delegate important responsibilities to the department in Ottawa is therefore not surprising.

The Admiralty had in fact discouraged Canadian naval expansion under wartime conditions, for the sound reason that the Dominion service would need substantial assistance which the Royal Navy could ill afford to provide. When the outbreak of hostilities brought offers from prominent men across Canada to raise RNCVR companies, headquarters had to decline: the RCN had no personnel to spare for training duties, and Admiralty turned down at least two requests for the loan of British instructors.[49] In response to an appeal from Sir Richard McBride for expansion of the west coast RNCVR, Kingsmill declared that he did "not see that it is possible to do any more in British Columbia ... and I fear that in other parts of the Country it is impossible to do anything."[50]

Kingsmill undoubtedly knew that the Admiralty had emphatically advised the prime minister against naval expansion. The question had arisen during the fall of 1914 when the Canadian government was seriously considering calling a general election. Seeking to protect himself politically against any revival of the inflammatory naval issue in Canada, Borden had asked the Canadian high commissioner in the United Kingdom, Sir George Perley, to sound out Admiralty unofficially as to what "naval aid" to Britain their lordships might recommend now that war had broken out. The answer was unequivocal. "Admiralty inform me," Perley cabled on 10 October 1914, "[they] don't think anything effectual can now be done as ships take too long to build and advise [that] Canadian assistance be concentrated on army ... "[51] Churchill had intended this as a definitive injunction against any form of sizeable Canadian naval development.

Local defence of Canada's coastal waters was a more complicated issue, however, and in this area British expert advice was not monolithic. Not unnaturally, the Royal Navy admiral who commanded in the western Atlantic held a perspective often at odds with that of officials and senior officers in London, preoccupied as they were by the European theatre and global responsibilities. Canada relied on the British cruiser force for the protection of the Dominion's coast and trade; and the British admiral commanding the cruiser force relied on Canada's marine resources to maintain some adequate defence in the critically important northwest Atlantic area. Understandably, the admiral encouraged Canada to develop its maritime defences. This was advice that the Dominion government could ill afford to disregard. Although the British admiral had no formal responsibilities toward the Canadian government – and no authority over the RCN – his status and the interdependence of the two naval forces enhanced his authoritative voice.[52]

Phipps-Hornby's formal channel of communication with the Dominion government lay through the governor-general–titular commander-in-chief of Canadian forces. This in itself heightened the admiral's influence in Ottawa through an interplay of circumstances and personalities. Critical of Borden's failure to prepare more thoroughly for coastal defence, the Duke of Connaught did not hesitate to seek the British admiral's advice and to press it on both the Admiralty and the Canadian government. His dark view of the German menace to Canada received support from Sir Cecil Spring Rice, who, as British ambassador in Washington, represented Canada in the United States. Spring Rice was an alarmist; he feared the opportunities that US neutrality provided to anti-British elements and German agents for covert operations. Although most of his reports to Ottawa were little more than gossip and bar-room bravura, their very transmission in cypher lent a measure of credibility.

Then too, the minister of marine and fisheries, J.D. Hazen, seems to have left navy matters in the hands of his deputy minister, Desbarats, who continued to treat Kingsmill as a subordinate. A full-fledged Royal Navy flag officer may well have impressed the deputy more than the mild-mannered Kingsmill, who had never commanded anything more than a single warship while on active service with the imperial fleet: certainly, outbreak of war had done little to raise the profile of the vestigial Canadian staff within the Borden government.

In all this lay potential for bureaucratic struggle: the possibility that the British commander might supersede the Canadian staff as the government's principal source of advice was at least as serious a threat to the Canadian service's status as was extension of British control over Canadian shore establishments. But because a larger and more capable Canadian organization served the interests of the imperial commander, the matter of influence with the government did not become an issue until late in the war. Even then, it took the form of ill-feeling and tension rather than open dispute.

Phipps-Hornby tackled the question of local defence from the moment he arrived at Halifax in September 1914, when he discovered that Colonel Gwatkin, chief of the Canadian general staff, had ordered reductions in the garrison at the Halifax fortress. Over 2,500 troops were on duty there, and Gwatkin – who was determined to trim back excessive home defences that might interfere with the dispatch of troops to Europe, where they were really needed – declared that the Royal Navy's success in containing German raiders had made an attack on the fortress "remote in the extreme."[53] Phipps-Hornby protested Gwatkin's decision to the Admiralty, which in this instance cabled Ottawa in support of the admiral.[54] Gwatkin promptly rescinded the orders for cut-backs at Halifax.

The incident nevertheless confirmed the governor-general's worst suspicions about the Borden government's neglect of coastal defence, and he asked Phipps-Hornby to report on improvements that should be made at the Halifax fortress. Flatly contradicting Gwatkin, the admiral argued that the enemy might attempt to "rush" the port with cruisers, armed merchant cruisers, or even landing parties; such events loomed likely, "especially in later stages of the war," as part of a final, desperate assault against Britain's maritime supply lines. For this reason Phipps-Hornby encouraged projects already under way to improve coverage of the outer harbour by search-lights and quick-firing guns but warned that heavy Nova Scotia fogs frequently blinded shore batteries. A naval flotilla was therefore "much needed." He recommended two torpedo-carrying surface vessels and two submarines.[55]

One suitable craft was in fact available as a result of a peculiar chain of events that underscore the informal nature of Canada's naval organization in 1914. The flamboyant Montreal millionaire, yachtsman, and zealous patriot, J.K.L. "Jack" Ross, had been devastated by his medical rejection from service in the expeditionary force and therefore turned to the RCN. He sweetened his appeal for a commission by offering to buy the RCN a warship – which he would then command. Shortly after donating in 1914 to the navy his own yacht *Albacore* – too small for sustained duty in anything but harbour work – he set off for New York and with his own funds bought the Vanderbilts' fast, 24-knot yacht *Tarantula*. She was reportedly one of the first high-speed steam-turbine ships ever built.

Ross got her and took her to Halifax at some risk, for American neutrality laws prohibited the sale of vessels to combatant powers for the purpose of converting them into fighting ships. Renamed HMCS *Tuna* on her arrival at Halifax in September, she was fitted at Ross's expense with torpedo dropping gear and a small three-pounder gun. She entered service in December 1914 – with a contented Lieutenant

Ross, RNCVR, in command. *Tuna*'s long, narrow hull – 153 feet in length, but only 15 in beam – made her unsuitable for extended patrols in heavy seas. But she could dash out of port once warned of enemy vessels. That seemed a reasonable task.[56]

In mid-November the Admiralty itself warned all station commanders and dominion governments that the Royal Navy might not be able to prevent the escape from the North Sea of even very large mine-layers capable of transoceanic operations; efficient defences would therefore be needed to a distance of as much as forty miles off major ports.[57] Only a few weeks previously, the 17,000-ton liner *Berlin* had disguised herself as a British ship, and had evaded the blockade; she had sown a vast mine-field on the main shipping route off northern Ireland which had destroyed a merchant ship and, more seriously, the new super-dreadnought battleship HMS *Audacious*.[58] Advice from Admiralty and Phipps-Hornby linked up with reports from US ports that warned of German plots secretly to charter vessels and outfit them as mine-layers for operations in Canadian waters; together they spurred on efforts to improve the RCN flotilla.[59] Although Kingsmill did all he was asked to do, he felt that Phipps-Hornby was overreacting to the "remote" danger of a mine attack.[60]

What the director of the naval service wanted was proper warships that could take effective action against the enemy and which would secure the RCN's future by turning it into a proper fighting service. In both respects, jury-rigged auxiliary vessels and non-professional crews were a dubious investment. As we shall see, Kingsmill's war would become an ongoing struggle for acquisition of true warships, while circumstances forced him to create a large auxiliary fleet whose limitations he knew only too well.

The RCN's immediate hope for procuring warships lay in Phipps-Hornby's recommendation that Halifax have a strong flotilla to deal with marauding German cruisers. On 25 November 1914 Borden drew this proposal to Admiralty's attention. Canadian Vickers at Montreal, he reminded their lordships, was eager and able to undertake warship construction; the firm should therefore build the necessary destroyers and submarines for the RCN.[61] This too, as we shall see, was a lost cause.[61]

The prime minister was as concerned about unemployment in Montreal as about coastal defence. The outbreak of war had not only failed to alleviate the depression which had been gripping the Canadian economy since 1913 but had actually deepened it through dislocation of trade and finance. Montreal had been particularly hard hit, and the grim conditions helped to foment labour protests and political turmoil in the city.[63] Canadian Vickers had been established in 1910–11 in anticipation of contracts for construction for the RCN and since that time had persistently lobbied the government for orders. Borden, who had always declared that his naval policy would bring economic benefits at least equal to those promised by Laurier, helped to sustain the yard with civil government work. One notable contract was for the ice-breaker *J.D. Hazen*. Churchill soon disabused Borden of the hope that Halifax's requirements might justify naval work at Vickers.

In any event, Borden was not especially keen to spend large amounts of Canadian money on building warships. The Dominion government's finances were already strained by war expenditures, most of them to raise and equip the overseas expeditionary force. What he really wanted was British shipbuilding orders. As we have seen, from the moment Borden had adopted the policy of direct financial naval aid to Britain in 1910, he had argued that Canada must receive compensating economic benefit in the form of contracts for ship construction and repair in Canadian yards. Although naval aid had never come to pass, the Dominion was now supplying assistance in the form of land forces on a much larger and more costly scale. Yet Canadian firms were receiving precious few contracts for naval or military material. Infuriatingly, the business went to the more experienced and better financed industries in the United States.[64]

A number of delegations by frustrated and angry businessmen caused Borden to send a blistering message to London on 26 November 1914: "Not only the people of Canada as a whole but individuals are making sacrifices hitherto undreamed of to support the Empire in this war. A very painful and even bitter feeling is being aroused throughout the Dominion. Men are going without bread in Canada while those across the line are receiving good wages for work that could be done as efficiently and cheaply in this country ... Public opinion is being so seriously aroused as to most gravely affect our future action."[65]

Unknown to Borden, the British government was scheming with American firms during the fall of 1914 to have submarines prefabricated in the United States and assembled by Canadian Vickers in order to evade US neutrality laws. Churchill's consistent advice – that there was absolutely no scope for warship construction in Canada – seemed misleading at best and dishonest at worst when Borden belatedly learned the facts in January 1915. Indeed, Admiralty had not consulted the Canadian government during negotiations with Bethlehem Steel in the United States and Vickers in Montreal, even though its order caused "the arbitrary deferment of work [in the Montreal yard] of an important icebreaker [the *Hazen*] and the illegal employment of American technicians and supervisors."[66] More serious, the absence of consultation made a mockery of Borden's declarations that Canada was participating in the war, and generously offering its blood and treasure, not as a British colony but as a partner of the Mother Country.

Britain would need all the support it could get. German advances had indeed been stopped at terrible cost, but futile trench-warfare during the bitter battles of Ypres continued to drain the resources of all the belligerents alike. The Germans had launched the first battle along the whole front on 20 October, the second on 31 October, and the third – the so-called Massacre of the Innocents (Kindermord von Ypern) with inexperienced troops – on 11 November. The British Expeditionary Force lost 86,237 of its original 160,000; the French lost 213,444. In the last two weeks of October alone the Germans lost 134,315.[67]

From the German perspective, the stalemate between the battle fleets in the North Sea was an extension of the stalemate on land. Existing plans – and there were no alternates – were rooted in the pre-war assumption that the swift, victorious thrust by the army into France would draw the British fleet, in an act of desperation, into a battle off Heligoland and the Skagerrak, close in to German bases. There the High Seas Fleet would have the advantage of support from coastal forces whose torpedoes and mines would wear down the British margin of superiority. For his part, the Kaiser blamed the failure to achieve early success in the North Sea on the navy's leaders.

Shocked by shortcomings in tactical leadership that led to the loss of three light cruisers, a destroyer, and 700 men in a confrontation with British forces off Heligoland on 28 August 1914, the Kaiser took control of fleet units.[68] It remains disputed whether this action made any substantial difference, for his staff was already beginning to consider new concepts of naval warfare. As Admiral Scheer briefed the Kaiser, naval battles could not force Britain to accept peace. The only means at Germany's disposal lay in commerce warfare by attacking merchant shipping. As he later put it: "setting the submarine against English trade" offered the sole hope "for wearing down England's economic life."[69] Germany's naval leaders were gradually converted to this view.

Cruiser warfare in foreign waters, planned well in advance by German Admiralty staff and supported by coaling arrangements and agents in neutral harbours, threatened to cut Britain's lifelines by attacking merchant shipping. According to the prize rules of international law governing such tactics, warships could not attack without warning.[70] The rules defined the rights of belligerent governments to stop and search merchantmen for contraband; they specified the nature of different types of "absolute" and "conditional" contraband and permitted destruction or confiscation of vessels only if the attacker had secured the safety of passengers and crew.

But combatants, and the neutral American government, which often tried to adjudicate or intervene through diplomatic means, became entangled in legal controversy. Each side flayed the other verbally for its illegal acts. The German press denounced British despotism that arbitrarily changed the prize rules; Britain, it asserted, "bullied neutral trade, extended the war to trade relations with private interests, and raped international law."[71] The *Daily Telegraph*, for its part, dubbed Grand Admiral von Tirpitz "the master Pirate."[72] Strategic and tactical expediency, as will be seen in the case of u-53's attacks off Newport, frequently prevailed. Gripped by Britain's stranglehold on German trade, the German navy resorted to its back-up force – submarines and mines. It ultimately developed the submarine cruiser, a new engine of war without legal precedent in international law. Desperation triggered the so-called Tirpitz questions.

Ten weeks before German submarine warfare began, Admiral von Tirpitz had in December 1914 granted an unprecedented interview to the Berlin representative of United Press, during which he revealed his plans for unrestricted submarine warfare against Britain. (It would actually start on 1 February 1915.) As observers of the day later recalled, it evoked a "world sensation," which many suspected of being a "Tirpitz bluff."[73] The reporter had sent his scoop to New York by courier, fearing British censors if he sent it by cable. Thus it did not reach the North American press until 22 December 1914.

Certainly, von Tirpitz had startled many of his own countrymen, including the German foreign office and even the Reichskanzler himself, with the directness of his charge: "What will America say if we open u-boat warfare against all ships sailing to England, and starve it out?" And then he added, with a twist of the blade: "What will America do?" Von Tirpitz had unleashed the disturbing question without the Reichskanzler's knowledge and, in the latter's view, had forced Germany into the fateful first step toward a style of submarine warfare for which it was by no means ready. As von Bethmann Hollweg recalled: "Publicly the enemy were warned to brace themselves for a u-boat blockade, and publicly the German people's attention was drawn to their possession of an infallible weapon. From this point on, u-boat warfare could not be wrested from the nation's soul."[74]

The naval intelligence office – the Nachrichtenbüro, or N – informed von Tirpitz that the German press had greeted the interview with jubilation.[75] "N" reported public satisfaction in Germany "that any German statesman at all had finally taken a stand on these crucial questions, and then had done so with frank, vigorous language against England, and directed himself to the United States." The *New York Tribune* found von Tirpitz's tactics impossible; the *New York World* explained why: "The German Navy and the German merchant marine are both bottled up, and until British seapower is disposed of it is fantastic for any German to think about starving Great Britain by submarine raids."[76]

In fact, however, Germany found it unnecessary to dispose of the Royal Navy by fleet action. A new risk principle was emerging. As Admiral Hollweg explained: "The new Risk Principle is based on the energetic execution of submarine warfare against commerce. If events of the war cut the U-boat as a destroyer of trade out of the formula, if the English-American doctrine of pseudo-humanity is victorious, then the risk principle loses all justification for its existence. In that case we have to rethink and relearn."[77]

The new submarine technology, as will be seen, spawned new tactics that cut through the British blockade with a vengence. As submarine deployments widened their range deep into the Atlantic, the second of von Tirpitz's questions–"What will America do?" – dominated German strategic thought. Political realities had summersaulted earlier strategic plans which had once preoccupied a theorizing staff in drafting plans against North America. The purely military concept of a direct frontal attack on the east coast gave way to higher political wisdom: submarine attacks off the North American coast should stop just short of provoking the United States to declare war. The crucial question for German strategists was no longer how much punishment Britain could take; it hung on the more fragile thread of how much stress "America" might wish to bear.

– 5 –

Canadian Intelligence and Patrols

Two events in the bleak spring of 1915 brought home to Canada the horror that the European war of attrition had become both on land and at sea. In their first major action defending the Ypres salient at the end of April, soldiers of the 1st Canadian Division endured an attack by a new weapon of terror: clouds of poisonous chlorine gas overwhelmed them as the German assault forces advanced. Six thousand Canadian killed and wounded were lost within a few days of ferocious combat. Less than two weeks later, on 7 May 1915, the German submarine U-20 torpedoed the British liner *Lusitania* in the Irish Sea. The huge passenger liner sank almost immediately with the loss of 1,198 lives, including 170 Canadians. This disaster marked the climax of the German navy's first major submarine campaign against merchant shipping, an attempt to sever the maritime trade routes that were supplying the Allied armies. "All the waters surrounding Great Britain and Ireland," the German government had warned all Allied and neutral nations, "are hereby declared a war zone. From the 18th of February [1915] onwards every enemy merchant ship found within this war zone will be destroyed without its being always possible to avoid danger to the crews and passengers."[1]

Lusitania's loss so close to the Royal Navy's base at Queenstown in southern Ireland underscored Britain's apparent powerlessness to counter the new menace. It took no great leap of imagination to envision similar tragedies in Canada's unprotected waters. Such thoughts cast into doubt Admiralty's insistence that Canada would be wasting its resources by attempting to expand local naval defences. Yet neither the gravity of the threat, nor the character of defences needed to meet it, was particularly clear. As far as Canada was concerned, the Admiralty played its cards very close to its chest. Denied full or even clear advice, the Canadian naval staff could draw conclusions only from alarming reports uncovered by British and Canadian intelligence operations in the United States.

Intelligence-gathering was but one aspect of a covert struggle in the United States into which American neutrality had cast both Germany and the British Empire at the outbreak of war. Propaganda and disinformation formed another part of the undercover arsenal and, in the case of Germany, sabotage and the clandestine supply of fuel for warships.

The United States was by no means as "infested with spies" as strident press accounts of the day would have us believe, and it was certainly not a "poisonous German sore."[2] A few well-placed officials in the diplomatic community were responsible for most of what happened, and there can be no doubt that Britain was the more successful.

Canadian-born Sir Gilbert Parker, a popular romantic novelist employed by the British government to disseminate propaganda in the United States, advised the British cabinet in 1915: "In the eyes of the American people the quiet and subterranean nature of our work has the appearance of a purely private patriotism and enterprise."[3] This was important, for neither of the warring nations could afford to offend the US government. During the early years of the war, British propaganda aimed at fostering American goodwill in order to ensure a supply of loans, foodstuffs, and war materiel; it did not stop short of painting the darkest pictures of Germany's "barbarism" and cultural depravity.[4] Even prominent historians like Arnold J. Toynbee served as government hacks by churning out pulp-trade distortions like his *The German Terror in France* and *The German Terror in Belgium*. Britain's later propaganda sought to engage Americans as allies by turning isolationist sentiment into anti-German fervour through articles placed in leading American papers and journals. Parker was the principal operative, and Ambassador Spring Rice his aide.

Germany's hopes for ultimate victory depended on the United States remaining neutral. German diplomacy sought to preserve economic ties in the face of British mastery of the Atlantic, while protesting Britain's violation of international law in its increasingly rigorous enforcement of blockade. Even before hostilities had begun, German military and political authorities at the highest level had discussed the feasibility of using retired German officers in neutral countries as agents both in peace and in war.[5] The army had objected that doing so would remove the "agent" from his European war billet. Spying, moreover, was unworthy of a German officer.

Resourceful pro-German elements none the less worked as best they could. Thus one very active lieutenant who represented a German firm in the United States worked undercover in August 1914 arranging deliveries of coal and supplies for the German warship SMS *Leipzig* in North America (including in Mexico) and in South America.[6] Less successful were the few amateurish expatriates whom German officials managed to recruit in the United States.

Military and naval attachés were the key players in intelligence operations. They were also acutely aware that the United States had little patience with this aspect of the Old World's "great game." As early as 1903 the German naval attaché in Washington had advised Admiral von Tirpitz that "here in this country foreign attachés are regarded by the majority as tolerated spies."[7] That chilly atmosphere – and Washington's reputation among the European diplomatic community as a backwater far removed from great events – seems scarcely to have bothered Captain Karl Boy-Ed, who became the naval attaché in 1913. He was fortunate in his ambassador, the clever socialite Count Johann von Bernstorff, who stood in sharp contrast to Britain's brooding, hypersensitive Sir Cecil Spring Rice. And besides, the extrovert Boy-Ed relished the social whirl just as much as ferretting out information both from the Americans and from representatives of other nations as well. Soon he established effective links with what he called "extremely sensitive" sources in the US navy and with a "representative of the Newport News Shipbuilding Company."[8] He had obtained details of torpedo trials, ship design and tactics, and the results of experiments with new armour plating tested by the British Admiralty. Undercover work, he once wrote to the chief of the Admiralty Staff, was entirely justified – "short of infringing the international laws on neutrality."[9] His net would widen until the United States forced his recall for infringement of neutrality in 1916.

On the eve of hostilities, Boy-Ed described his counterparts for Admiral von Tirpitz in considerable detail.[10] The British naval attaché had been on post since 1912; he had arrived just before Boy-Ed and was therefore the senior member of the corps. Travelling frequently for both business and private reasons, he was to Boy-Ed's mind "your typical likeable battleship captain without any special technical preparation." Socially withdrawn and "constantly complaining of the high cost of living," he maintained "an automobile and two polo ponies," as well as a wife and five children. He was obviously of no use to the German cause and in any case apparently showed no "special interest in any topic of conversation" at all.

The twice-married Russian attaché was a different kettle of fish. "A social gad-fly of a loud blustering cast who indulges much time and interest in food and drink," he was on his second tour. He had fostered close associations not only with American shipbuilding but also with older Americans of social status and wealth. A man of apparently independent means, he had given up all interest in returning to sea – apparently in favour of a career of social pleasure. Boy-Ed found him of no value.

The "best informed attaché on American affairs" was the French representative, a former submarine commander who apparently could not wait for his next seagoing command. Perhaps because of his detailed naval knowledge he lay no great store on the US navy–an attitude shared by Boy-Ed since at least his arrival in Washington. Americans reportedly regarded the French officer as "slippery" because of his "exaggerated politeness." Boy-Ed found the man's social intrigues against him offensive and treated him "with great caution" militarily as well.

One member of the military coterie was a veritable outsider despite himself. The Japanese representative, with his typical "tooth-sucking Japanese civility," as Boy-Ed put it, had become an object of some mistrust in the United States. He was at best merely "tolerated" in the club-life and social rounds of the town. Boy-Ed recorded suspicions then current that this loner's primary source of information was "the Japanese cooks, servants and stewards employed by American naval officers."

Boy-Ed found only one real soul-mate in the lot: not surprisingly, the Austrian attaché. Here was "a colleague and friend, a high-minded officer in thought and action, and [one] reliable in every respect." He would support German espionage work.

Canada, with neither ambassadors nor military attachés, relied entirely on the British connection for information from this inner clique.

Yet Canada had important resources of its own. Watching the United States was of course an ancient and essential Canadian pastime. In countering the threat of invasion from the United States by Fenians during the late 1860s and early 1870s, the new Dominion government's chief commissioner of police had developed a widespread network of secret agents and hired detectives who gave timely warning of the Irish nationalists' every move.[11] The danger posed by American neutrality in 1914 was virtually identical to the earlier Fenian menace. Agents could foment raids or sabotage by sympathizers among the vast population of German, Austrian, and Irish descent in the United States and Canada.

Thus, within weeks of the outbreak of war, Colonel Sir Percy Sherwood, chief commissioner of police, had assembled an intelligence network similar to that of the 1860s. Amid the welter of rumours about German-American plots against Canada in August 1914, Sir Cecil Spring Rice belatedly admitted that the British embassy and consular service lacked the resources to maintain a proper watch. He urged the Dominion to put its own agents in the field. Sherwood was already passing regular reports to the prime minister. Their eyewitness evidence was already deflating the breathless tales then current about armed German-American "dens of insurrection" in US border towns.[12]

Colonel Willoughby Gwatkin, who as chief of the general staff was immediately responsible for military defence against invasion and subversion, fully supported Sherwood's work. Gwatkin, as we have seen, was determined not to let exaggerated home defence measures impede dispatch of troops to France. He quite rightly appreciated that the civilian police were the appropriate agency to deal with most of the minimal dangers Canada then faced. In order to avoid duplication, he recognized Sherwood as the principal intelligence authority. Sherwood had the best connections, embracing not only foreign sources but also provincial and municipal police. As in most other matters, Kingsmill and Stephens agreed with the chief of the general staff in this decision. Sherwood, Stephens, and Gwatkin worked closely on intelligence, sharing information and analysing it together.[13]

The Canadian officers were deluged with data. The rumours of August 1914 proved to be only the beginning of a flood of reports from both sides of the border: from British officials in the United States, from concerned citizens, from zealous agents, and from journalists (who immediately rushed into print). "Murderous plots" of the German military attaché Captain Franz von Papen and "the other ruthless underlings of Germany" like "the villainous von Bernstorff" included schemes to blow up railway bridges in Winnipeg and Saint John, destroy the locks of the Welland Canal, and sabotage port facilities on both the west and east coasts of Canada.[14] They revealed apparently widespread infiltration into both Canadian and American industry and the planned destruction of the House of Commons in Ottawa.

Thus on 24 March 1915 Admiral C.E. Kingsmill offered the chief of the Admiralty War Staff in London "details of the German designs" for industrial sabotage.[15] These implicated "two German naval reservists" who had "escaped from Canada towards the end of last year" and had made their way to New York. Kingsmill had engaged detectives to track them down—whether directly, because of the urgency of the case, or through Sherwood, is not clear—and received evidence of a wide-ranging undercover network. It allegedly embraced branches of the Swift Dressed Beef Co. and the Dupont Powder Co., both of which had large contracts with the Allies. Reports convinced Kingsmill that German agents were already infiltrating Canadian firms like the Canadian Explosives Co., the Dominion Powder Co., and the Ross Rifle Co.

Again in March, reports warned Ottawa that the interned German steamer ss *Saxonia* would attempt to break out of Seattle with torpedo warheads for Germany.[16] The British ambassador in Washington later informed Ottawa of rumours that "Germans employed by Dupont ... might tamper with Explosives manufactured for the Allies."[17] Over two months later, newspapers in Seattle and Tacoma revealed that "German spies" had managed to blow up fifteen tons of dynamite destined for Vladivostok as part of an illicit cargo of war supplies. The British vice-consul in Tacoma then broke with custom by wiring Naval Service Headquarters in Ottawa to warn directly of "German sabotage" on the west coast which had "dire consequences" for Canadian defence.[18] Just what these consequences were he did not elaborate.

But on 1 May 1915, the British secretary of state for the colonies had warned the Duke of Connaught of "a possible German raid on Canada."[19] By early June the British consul-general in New York sent a secret telegram confirming the imminent attack. The "German circle" he had been monitoring had now divulged that Germany would "break off relations with the United States on June 11th or 12th [1915], and that a raid on Canada will at once be made from the United States border."[20] Most disturbing of all, his sources had "stated that gas will be used." In the mean time a Canadian double-agent was negotiating with German diplomats in San Francisco to dynamite the rail lines of the Canadian Pacific Railway at Revelstoke, British Columbia.[21]

One investigation by Pinkerton's National Detective Agency of New York, which Sherwood employed to augment his own agents, typifies the quality of much of the information. The connection between the Canadian government and the American firm went back to the intelligence operations against the Fenians. Pinkerton's also had contracts with the British embassy and consulates and with the American government; no less a person than President Wilson's secretary had recommended its services to Canada.[22] As readers of detective fiction know, it was Pinkerton's whose "Private Eye" logo and blood-hound tactics soon generated a national pulp-trade mythology of sleuths, "gum shoes," and vigilante justice. The work of "Operative no. 68" on behalf of the Canadian government was in this rough-and-ready vein, albeit with a strong dose of ineptitude.

The detective convinced his boss that he had penetrated a suspected espionage ring. The trail had led from the Aschenbroedel Club in New York, through Loew's Theater, the Droste Café, and Meyer's restaurant, and to a certain saloon supposedly frequented by "German" workers from Swift's meat-packing; it had run from the docks of North German Lloyd and the Hamburg-Amerika Line in Hoboken, New Jersey, to Chicago's Kaiserhof Hotel. Like the gutsy Mike Hammer of those Mickey Spillane whodunits, long recognized as "the degenerative product of unsurpassable triviality,"[23] he struck home.

Operative no. 68 cracked the boarding-house run by one of the linchpins of the suspected ring: a certain Fräulein Seithen, in whom he seems to have developed a distinctly lascivious interest. With a fastidiousness redolent of good business and vicarious intrigue, he passed his flimsy reports to the Pinkerton's office in New York, which put them into Canadian hands: the chief commissioner of the Dominion Police in Ottawa, who then passed them to Commander Stephens in Naval Intelligence.

Stephens became restive at the paucity of hard information being derived from these ostensibly rich sources. Characteristic of a B-movie script, Pinkerton's ultimately agreed that the suspects were much too tight-lipped: "Unless they are under the influence of drink they never let much slip."[24] Operative no. 68 tested the theory. But despite having taken "some drinks up to the house and got Miss Seithen full," he at first elicited few clues. The first promising lead broke on 17 March 1915. Fräulein Seithen now revealed that "people working in the Canadian government and at Canadian ship companies" with direct contacts in the American shipbuilding and armament industries were passing intelligence on ship movements and cargoes to the German government. The latter "in turn communicated it to the authorities having charge of the submarines."

Pinkerton's surveillance continued through 1917, even though operative no. 68 had blown his cover by the end of April 1915 and had left the scene. By this time too the Dominion Police had informed Naval Intelligence that they had "practically dropped all this shadowing business and are content to keep in touch with the situation generally."[25]

In his pursuit of such far-fetched leads Sherwood showed no predisposition to believe them; quite the reverse. Only by debunking rumours could he – and Gwatkin – reassure the government and forestall wasteful expansion of the home defence garrisons. Only by spreading a wide net, moreover, could Canadian intelligence hope to detect those threats that really did exist, even if they proved much smaller than the government and public had feared. Early in 1915, for example, a German reserve officer was apprehended while attempting to blow up a major railway bridge across the border from Vanceboro, Maine, and confessed to being an agent of von Papen.[26] The confession proved true.

Later that month, the naval attaché Boy-Ed came in for his share of notoriety. From his private office in New York the German officer had been recruiting German émigrés to operate as spies and couriers. With assumed names and fraudulently obtained US passports, they passed back and forth on neutral vessels through high-seas war zones.

The *New York American* exposed Boy-Ed on 25 February 1915 by scooping the arrest of a key agent by American authorities. The spy had revealed the existence "in New York City [of] a most extraordinary organisation of German-Americans ready at all times to do secret work for their Fatherland."[27] The newspaper gave an accurate account of the evidence on which a US court ultimately convicted him. Accompanying the story were photographs of letters Boy-Ed had allegedly written to introduce his spies as legitimate businessmen to British commercial contacts, as well as the German text and English translation of an incriminating letter Boy-Ed had written the suspect.

The editors also printed photographs of the agent's fraudulent passport and of Boy-Ed himself in German naval uniform. No longer could he move about incognito in American society, a fact he subsequently lamented to his superiors. Sheltered by diplomatic immunity, Boy-Ed protested his innocence. However, other newspapers caught the line and blamed him for further feats of sleight-of-hand and skulduggery. Even in late 1916 the British House of Commons was reminded in debate of the now notorious Boy-Ed. He had been "the head of an organisation engaged in forgery, murder and arson in the United States," the assertion ran, and indeed was not "organising occasional U-boat operations off the American coast from Lübeck," Germany.[28]

Though much of this information was entirely specious, German records now confirm that Boy-Ed was in fact involved in the plot that the *New York American* had exposed. Boy-Ed was actually so upset by the story that he included the press clipping in a personal letter to Admiral von Tirpitz, state secretary of the Imperial Naval Office in Berlin, and had a courier take it the very next day aboard the neutral vessel ss *Rotterdam*.[29] The ingratiatingly apologetic letter confessed to a certain ineptitude in recruiting an expatriate whose "un-german" morals had betrayed him to American authorities. But the storm quickly blew over.

The Kaiser awarded Boy-Ed the Iron Cross, class ii. As Boy-Ed explained in a letter to the chief of the Admiralty Staff, the honour was diplomatically awkward in light of the charges in the American press.[30] Any public announcement of the award would be regarded as the Kaiser's direct approval of his clandestine activities. Boy-Ed therefore begged his superiors not to publicize the award.

Boy-Ed remained in New York long after the furore had subsided and continued to pursue clandestine schemes. As British decryption of diplomatic signals revealed, for example, he had attempted to supply arms to Sinn Fein Irish nationalists in support of the planned Easter rising of April 1916.[31] He later involved himself in a plot to embroil the United States with Mexico; in a prelude to the famous "Zimmermann telegram" which helped to precipitate American entry into the war, he negotiated with General Victoriano Huerto the abortive delivery of American weapons to Mexico by German submarine.[32]

Boy-Ed was of course not the only theatrical figure on the espionage scene. The exploits of the charlatan and confidence-man Max Meincke, alias Dr Armgaard Karl Graves, made equally saleable copy. His attempts at exploiting the visit of U-53 to Newport in 1916 would lead to his arrest on charges of espionage and blackmail.[33] He had, among other things, "threatened to expose and publish certain letters containing matter showing the infirmities and failings" of the German ambassador's wife. And then there was playboy and confidence-man Max Lynar Louden, alias Count Loudow, who travelled in high society among Ottawa, Toronto, and Washington and was suspected in many countries of being a freelance secret agent.[34]

The Canadian navy could not react to reports of maritime threats with the same calm assurance with which both the police and the militia addressed intelligence about insurgency and cross-border raids. Agents could immediately chase down the sources of rumours about land operations and had strong military forces standing by in border areas. Indeed, the government had decreed in the fall of 1914 that there always be at least 50,000 troops mobilized for home defence – despite Gwatkin's urgings for economy. The Admiralty, however, had severely curtailed the flow of maritime intelligence to Naval Service Headquarters in Ottawa, and Stephens did not have detailed information about enemy ship movements. Nor did he have other sources needed in order to assess reports emanating from the United States about German plans for seaborne strikes. More especially, the Admiralty had given no inkling of its success in breaking German radio codes, and not the slightest hint that intercepted messages were fast becoming the main source of reliable intelligence. That aside, Canada was utterly dependent upon the British fleet for defence. But in the spring of 1915 it had every reason to doubt the capacity of that protection. Canada had no local forces of its own to fill the breach.

In late May 1915 the British consul-general in New York cabled Admiralty concerning "rumours" that German submarines might shortly be expected in the northwest Atlantic in order to attack British shipping; Germans might even establish supply bases in Newfoundland, Labrador, or St Pierre.[35] The Colonial Office then warned Canada to take the danger seriously.[36]

Naval Service Headquarters readily recognized that the more likely targets lay off Halifax and along the shipping routes of the St Lawrence River and Gulf. This hunch explains the importance attached to the anonymous tip that "A. Britisher" in New York sent to Canada's commissioner of police.[37] He warned of a German-owned sailing vessel loading in New York "for a place in Canada to supply a wireless station and a submarine base"; this was "to be held by English speaking Germans [in order] to attack the troopships as they leave Canada."

The anonymous lead was the first of many reports throughout the war suggesting that Germany controlled supply bases in Canadian territory. Diplomatic intelligence, often scarcely more substantial than the variety of Pinkerton's clues, patriotic gossip-mongering, and hearsay, would corroborate the threat. Canadian naval intelligence took "A. Britisher" rather seriously. On 23 June 1915 it advised Halifax by cipher that the plot could have but a single purpose: "establishing [a] submarine base in [the] Gulf of St Lawrence." Indeed, as the cipher explained, "the rough plan points to Mingan Islands." These lay to the north of Anticosti Island in the Mingan Passage.

This natural choke-point on the troopship route from Quebec City to Great Britain via the Strait of Belle Isle and the open Atlantic was an entirely plausible place in which to attack. It was remote from any significant settlement, was the narrowest waterway through which the troopships passed after entering the Gulf from the St Lawrence River, and was not normally patrolled by Fisheries or other Canadian government vessels. Nor did the navy frequent the zone. With an insufficient number of ships, and without hope of British support, Canada was on its own.

In fact, by the end of July 1915 this uncontested u-boat threat would force the RCN to divert scheduled departures of troopships from St Lawrence ports to Halifax.[38] In May 1915 the commander-in-chief, North America and West Indies Station, based at the time in Halifax, had warned Canadian authorities that in the event of attack he could offer no defence. "It should be clearly understood," he had insisted, "that should enemy submarines appear off the Canadian Coasts, my cruisers are no protection to Transports against submarine attacks."[39] Admiralty had not yet informed Canada that u-boat attacks in Canadian waters were unlikely at best.

British leaders were meanwhile grappling with more immediate and much larger concerns.[40] Lack of public and official confidence in the Admiralty resulting from the failure of the navy to break through Turkish defences at the Dardanelles, despite repeated efforts since February lay at the centre of the British government's crisis of May 1915. A crescendo of litanies soon forced Liberal Prime Minister Herbert Henry Asquith to save his government by forming a coalition with the Conservative opposition, while German submarines were tightening their attempted stranglehold on British home waters.

Winston Churchill and Admiral Sir John Fisher, whom Churchill had brought out of retirement as first sea lord at the outbreak of war, had fallen out, and Fisher had resigned on 15 May; Churchill was replaced by Arthur Balfour as first lord in the new government, with Admiral Sir Henry Jackson as first sea lord. These circumstances help to explain the incomplete, contradictory, and insulting replies that Borden received to his appeals for shipbuilding orders during the first half of 1915.[41] Small wonder, then, that Vice-Admiral Kingsmill's distant voice crying for British assistance in the wilderness of Canada found no response.

Diplomatic intelligence filled a vacuum. It sharpened Canadian fears of German submarine aggression in North American waters and added fuel to the flames already licking at Kingsmill's heels in his frustrated attempts at establishing a St Lawrence patrol. He had no choice but to assume that the u-boat threat was patently real. On 5 June 1915 the British Foreign Office sent a cipher telegram to the British ambassador in Washington for onward transmission to all British "consular officers, Atlantic coast." The message enjoined his majesty's consuls to exercise vigilant supervision of maritime trade; "suspicious sales and shipments of liquid fuel" would betray German plans to establish oil supply bases in thinly populated areas of the coast.

Four days later, Bonar Law, recently appointed secretary of state for the colonies in Asquith's new coalition government, sent a disturbing cipher telegram to both the governor-general of Canada and the governor of Newfoundland.[42] Undisclosed sources, he explained, had convinced the British consul-general in New York that "Germany intends to send to the Atlantic coast one or two submarines"; in Admiralty's view the latest type had a maximum range of 3,000 miles – insufficient for a return trip. But if u-boats could overcome the "probably not insuperable difficulty of supply and communication in neutral countries and on uninhabited coasts," they could constitute a real threat.

That was as far as the telegram went, though it was abundantly clear to Bonar Law that Germany was limited only by its ability to establish supply bases in North America. His suspicions were fuelled next day by a cable from the British consul-general in New York: "A most reliable source ... close to the German Ambassador [had now revealed] that Germany plans to send over one and possibly two of her latest submarines to the Atlantic Coast, where, at some point, a base will be prepared for them."[43] Germany, it seemed, "proposed to send them over under convoy, or in company with some Scandinavian vessel." There is no doubt that Canada's prime minister took these warnings extremely seriously. His testy note of 16 June to the acting minister for the navy suggested that the department had been slow to respond to the threat. Borden wanted prompt, vigilant, and energetic action "for the purpose of patrolling our coast in order to prevent the Germans from establishing a base for submarines."[44]

Intercepted radio signals between German diplomatic posts in the United States and Germany seemed to confirm the danger. The Canadian wireless station at Newcastle, New Brunswick, had for some months been monitoring radio signals passed between the German embassy's transmitter in Sayville, New York, and the Germans' powerful station at Nauen, just outside Berlin. Beefed up to 100 kilowatts, the Sayville station could, by British assessment, "communicate with Nauen in all static conditions."[45] American neutrality required that such messages be sent en clair, but simple codes enabled messages about covert operations to masquerade as commercial traffic. Using one such system, Berlin could advise its embassy: "Bloomfield advises that Thos. Hadley should arrange funds through Steven Lawson. Request that John Childs discuss arrangements with Flammigere. sgd Gary." Its meaning: "Reichsbank advises that the German front commercial office of Amsinck & Co, New York, seek financing through the Royal Bank of Canada; Boy-Ed to coordinate deal with Bethlehem Steel."

On 5 June 1915, Newcastle radio intercepted a telegram which seemed to substantiate the arrival of German submarines.[46] Six days later, corroborative information from an agent in New York known as "Condie" reached Naval Intelligence: four submarines had left Cuxhaven ten days earlier for the United States.[47] If defence against U-boats were impossible, Kingsmill reasoned, he could at least remove their targets. He therefore sought the Admiralty's opinion on his only real alternative: closing the Strait of Belle Isle to commercial shipping "in view of possible submarine activity." (Twenty-eight years later, in 1942, the Canadian war cabinet faced a similar decision when U-boat penetrations actually forced closure of the Gulf of St Lawrence.)

But closing the Strait of Belle Isle was not a practical proposition in 1915. The Admiralty rejected the idea and cautioned Naval Service Headquarters about overreacting. On 25 June their lordships sent a signal that suggested measures the Canadian service should undertake now that it was faced with "the possibility of German submarines operating in Canadian waters." The first recommendation – "to patrol coast by small craft obtained locally in order to prevent unfrequented harbours being used as a base of operation," – was clear enough. The second was decidedly different: "Arrangements should be made for rapidly increasing this patrol service so as to deal with any submarines which may reach Canadian waters."[48] This was not only vague, but alarming: Canada might have to face at least the initial stages of a U-boat assault without British assistance. Canada needed well-armed ships and had none. Kingsmill had no resources with which to comply with this clear encouragement to expand the Canadian fleet.

More detailed advice reached Ottawa about this time through the governor-general; it came from Vice-Admiral Sir George Patey, who had recently succeeded Phipps-Hornby in command of the North America and West Indies Station. Earnest as always about his nominal position as commander-in-chief of the Canadian forces, the Duke of Connaught had visited the admiral while the latter was at Halifax in his flagship HMS *Leviathan*. Like her sister ship HMS *Good Hope*, which had been lost in the Battle of Coronel, she exemplified the imposing strength of iron-clad sea power. Built in 1899 at a cost of some £1 million sterling, she was a fine, if ageing, 14,100-ton armour-belted cruiser capable of 23 knots and carrying a crew of 900 men. Her main armament, consisting of two 9.2-inch and sixteen 6-inch guns, reflected the principles of outdated fleet tactics: a high volume of fire-power at moderate range. But maritime warfare was changing, and she was useless against the submarine.

Patey was deeply alarmed about the U-boat threat.[49] The ocean routes to the north and east of Newfoundland, by which U-boats could readily penetrate the North American shipping lanes without much risk of detection, were now clear of ice and free from winter's ferocious weather; so too was the Gulf of St Lawrence. What could he do? Patey's conclusions, telegraphed to the Admiralty, were discouraging: "It will obviously be the duty of my comparatively large and slow cruisers to keep out of [the U-boats'] way, if possible; and a number of smaller and faster vessels will be required."[50]

Clearly, he remembered only too well the fate of the aged Bacchanti-class cruisers HMS *Aboukir*, *Cressy*, and *Hogue*, vessels similar to those of his own force that had been sunk within an hour by a single U-boat in September 1914. The Bacchantis had been carrying out a standing patrol off the Dutch coast – much like Patey's force off New York – and the parallel did not escape him. So vulnerable and tempting a target were his warships, he claimed, that the Germans might well sacrifice a submarine in a one-way mission to destroy his squadron and then surrender to internment by the Americans at New York.

The admiral therefore rewrote his squadron's orders: cruisers would no longer hover close to the edge of territorial waters where they could easily be located but would pull out further to sea and make only "occasional, irregular appearances off New York."[51] Patey was not as ambiguous as the Admiralty in his advice to the governor-general about Canadian anti-submarine defences. Canada needed "suitable vessels of good speed, armed with guns sufficient to destroy a submarine [for the] patrol of Belle Isle and Cabot Straits and the Gulf of St Lawrence."[52]

Kingsmill had needed no prompting from Admiralty about expansion of the Canadian flotilla, but the cautionary note of 25 June 1915 hastened his deliberations.[53] In fact, he had a proposal ready the very next day. He had recognized that the isolated nature of much of the Canadian seaboard presented special defence problems. Thus, in order to prevent the Germans from hiding a submerged cache of U-boat supplies "in one of the unfrequented harbours of Newfoundland and Canada," he required "an organised system of coast watching in connection with a coastal patrol of small but numerous vehicles."

This view seemed vindicated by his receipt of an Admiralty cipher a couple of days later, on 28 June 1915. It instructed him to have authorities closely observe "any Germans or foreigners coming to Coast Settlements"; it also assured him that the "Director of Intelligence Division of the War Office [was] sending [him] sketches [of] submarines for distribution to local authorities, fishermen, and coasting vessels." (These sketches were a forerunner of the U-boat identification kits provided to mayors, parish priests, and coast watchers along the St Lawrence shores in 1942.)

Kingsmill had a stop-gap solution in a plan for chartering or comandeering locally "a large number of motor fishing vessels, say 250 to start with."[54] His ambitions for a "Motor Craft Reserve" were soon trimmed. Charterers were not very forthcoming, and vessels were difficult to find. Nonetheless, two motor boats were on station off the southwest coast of Newfoundland in early September, and ten more had been chartered by the end of that month.[55]

These little twenty-foot launches were never intended to provide anything more than detailed local coverage of bays and inlets behind sea patrols by steamers. Kingsmill proposed to expand the navy's existing scheme, whereby one or two of the larger vessels of the Halifax flotilla kept an "outer patrol" off the harbour and one or two others covered the vicinity of the Cabot Strait. He now wanted to establish eight patrol zones. These he identified according to "salient points" along the Atlantic coast, such as trade-route junctions and arrival ports, which would be "favourite spots for submarine operations." The great changes lay in the number and type of ships. Commander Stephens had conceded that modest craft had perhaps been satisfactory up to now for the navy's principal mission of minesweeping; but with the new possibility of actively hunting German submarines, the RCN needed ships of 175 to 225 feet in length, with a speed of 15 knots.[56] Nor was that all. They should be adequately armed and commissioned into the navy, so that their crew, as members of the RCN, could be properly trained and disciplined for combat.

On receiving Kingsmill's proposals, the government continued to press for quick action. George Desbarats's diary gives some sense of the mood in Ottawa. On 29 June, Acting Minister Crothers was "anxious to have action taken immediately and gave instructions to have [additional patrol] vessels obtained immediately." Two days later Navy Minister "Hazen is back – finds we are not going fast enough in obtaining patrol vessels though [we] have telegraphed advertisements to the papers" for suitable ships. Attending a meeting of cabinet on 14 July, he found "cabinet alarmed at rumoured submarine operations in St Lawrence [and] tried to allay their fears without much success."[57] Two weeks later, another spate of submarine rumours found Sir George Foster, minister of trade and commerce and the government's most senior member, brooding: "We are defenceless [and] can only watch and wait."[58]

Under these circumstances, one might have expected the government to have issued the navy a blank cheque. But that was not the case. Department files leave little doubt that the need for economy governed key decisions.[59] The exasperated Stephens even penned a whimsical note to a memo reminding his superiors how much they could save by not bothering to arm the vessels at all. Fortunately the navy had friends. Acquisition of civilian yachts proved a short-term response to long-term problems.

As early as August 1914 the Canadian millionaire John Eaton had offered his 166-foot family yacht *Florence* to Sir Sam Hughes, minister of militia and defence, and had been refused.[60] But the German threat to Canadian waters had now become much more acute, and on 15 June 1915 Kingsmill suggested that Eaton renew the proposal. Eaton generously offered his yacht to the government for one dollar, and his vessel was commissioned in Toronto on 19 July. She was the only Canadian yacht to join the navy.

Meanwhile the department availed itself once again of Jack Ross's American connections.[61] He resigned command of *Tuna* in June and slipped down to New York, where he purchased the yacht *Winchester*, a larger, more successful version of *Tuna*'s design. Two hundred and two feet long, with a beam of eighteen feet, she could make 32 knots. She was commissioned as HMCS *Grilse* under Ross's command on her arrival at Halifax that July. The following month she received two twelve-pounder guns and a fourteen-inch torpedo tube. Ross himself bore the rather considerable expense of spiriting her out of American waters but was forced by his own financial problems to accept the department's reimbursement of the $100,000 purchase price.

By 6 July 1915 the department was in direct contact with American yacht brokers. Officially at least, Ross had been acting independently on his buying trips to the United States. But because the navy now wanted to buy directly, it was necessary to find a civilian intermediary in order to circumvent US neutrality laws. Kingsmill turned to the ebullient and aggressive Toronto financier Aemilius Jarvis, who could scarcely sate his appetite for all things naval by his membership in the Royal Canadian Yacht Club. At the outbreak of war he had assembled Royal Navy reservists who lived in southern Ontario and arranged for their transport overseas, and he had offered to form a company of RNCVR. Harnessing his enthusiasm and business flair, the Canadian government undertook covert operations to acquire other yachts from the United States. At the end of July 1915 – after Kingsmill had persuaded the government that prices for American yachts were lower than any Canadian alternatives – Jarvis purchased the Morgan yacht *Waturus* (HMCS *Hochelaga*) and the Ladew yacht *Columbia* (HMCS *Stadacona*) in New York, with departmental funds. Their substantial size and good sea-keeping qualities made them among the most useful of the Canadian patrol vessels until the war's end.[62]

Increased anxiety about German designs against North America coalesced and intensified a number of Canadian grievances against the

British Admiralty. Shipbuilding contracts were notable among them. Encouraged by Canadian Vickers of Montreal making much more rapid progress in constructing h-class submarines for Britain than expected, Borden stepped up his campaign for more British warship orders in April 1915. He argued that Vickers's achievement had removed any doubt that the firm deserved a "reasonable share" of British contracts and laid bare the injustice of Admiralty's failure to consider Canadian industry when initially placing the h-boat contract in 1914.[63] Failure to place follow-up orders would now put over two thousand men out of work in Montreal, with no alternative employment.

Churchill's response – that Vickers was merely assembling parts that had been prefabricated in the United States – only added fat to the fire. At that very moment the Canadian government was investigating German charges that Britain was violating us neutrality by sending prefabricated submarines to Montreal; it found that Vickers was actually building a large proportion of the structure of each boat from basic raw materials. Churchill nevertheless maintained that follow-up orders were not necessary, as the Royal Navy now had an abundance of submarines.

This reply seemed to open the way for Canadian action.[64] If Britain indeed had so many, Kingsmill argued, it surely did not require all those under construction in Montreal. Two of them ought to be spared for Halifax, where the RCN could man them with personnel trained on CC-1 and CC-2 at Esquimalt, with no assistance from the imperial service. Borden's proposal was still stronger. Canada would order its own pair of h-boats from Vickers, as a follow-up order to Britain's contract, and therefore required only the temporary loan of two British h-boats.

The Admiralty remained adamant. It could spare none of the Montreal h-boats, not even for temporary duty, and there was no need for submarines at Halifax anyway. This position drew a sharp response from the governor-general: the Admiralty was contradicting its own commander-in-chief in Halifax and had utterly failed to appreciate "the danger to which ... Eastern Canadian ports are exposed from raiding cruisers." This aroused Admiralty's caution to Admiral Patey in Halifax, with whom the governor-general had been consulting; Patey was to toe the official line from London and recognize "that additional floating defences at Halifax [are] not urgent."[65]

Of course, the Admiralty could not object to Canada's placing its own order for submarines. But the Canadian naval staff itself was already harbouring doubts about the wisdom of building the small h-class for the RCN. Certainly the h-class submarines were fully adequate for the defence of coastal waters, as Commander Stephens admitted; but were they really worth a major investment by the Canadian government? What might happen if the government should wish Canadian naval forces to go overseas later in the war? In that case a larger and more modern type of submarine would be needed. "Naval affairs are in such a state of flux," he concluded, "that the policy of yesterday is by no means necessarily suitable for today."[66] In his view, the government should really assess its whole position. Kingsmill agreed but commented acidly that there was no use in even raising such questions until the government showed "any serious indication of formulating a Naval Policy."[67] In the event, Borden killed the H-boat scheme on learning in June of Vickers's "very high" bid of $650,000 per vessel.[68]

Meanwhile Borden had seized on news of the Royal Navy's shortage of cruisers and destroyers and urged the Admiralty to help both itself and Canada by building them at Montreal. He sharpened his appeal by citing Churchill's advice of 1914 that Canada concentrate on raising land forces. Canada had done that, and well. Borden's oblique reference to his country's generous commitment would have left the British officials with no doubt about what was on his mind: the 1st Canadian Division's recent and terrible losses in its heroic defence of the Ypres Salient and provision of a second Canadian infantry division which was already arriving in Britain.

Yet once again, in early July, Admiralty rejected the Canadian shipbuilding bid – but this time at least with the courtesy of a reasoned explanation. British experience with the H-class submarine had demonstrated that warship construction in North America cost double what it did in the United Kingdom. As it was, British shipyards were producing with greatly increased speed, and the necessity of supplying the required special machinery for production in Canada of such ships as destroyers could only hinder work in the United Kingdom.[69] And there the matter lay.

On paper, the St Lawrence patrol came into being on 15 July, when HMCS *Margaret* joined the still-unarmed chartered steamer *Sable I* in the Cabot Strait.[70] Soon afterward, the fisheries protection ship *Gulnare* took up station on Quebec's north shore. HMCS *Canada* and Ross's *Grilse* escorted two troop ships through the Gulf, but both vessels required repairs after the long run and confirmed Kingsmill's view that the RCN could not escort high-value ships on the St Lawrence route.[71] The organization of the east coast patrols did not stabilize until the last of the new ships had completed their refits in September. The commissioned ships HMCS *Grilse*, *Premier*, and *Tuna* and nine non-commissioned civilian vessels could then be assigned to the port defence of Halifax and to patrols along the Nova Scotia coast. By this time a wire-cable anti-submarine net had strengthened defences across Halifax harbour. This situation allowed the navy to commit the seven remaining commissioned ships – *Canada*, *Florence*, *Hochelaga*, *Margaret*, *Sable I*, *Sinmac*, and *Stadacona* – to the Gulf Patrol.[72] The twelve chartered motor boats kept isolated sections of the Canadian and Newfoundland shores under closer surveillance than was possible with the sea patrol vessels.

Kingsmill organized the Gulf Patrol steamers and motor boats as a separate command. His decision not to subordinate the patrol to Halifax was doubtless influenced by the presence of the influential Vice-Admiral Patey at the base; certainly, Kingsmill feared that the British admiral would exercise de facto control over Gulf operations, with little reference to Canadian needs and priorities. There being no qualified Canadian available, Kingsmill applied to Admiralty for an officer to command the patrol directly under Naval Service Headquarters. A good candidate was available. Captain Fred C.C. Pasco, RN, who had been serving in Australia at the outbreak of war, had retired there in the hopes of going to the front with the Australian expeditionary forces. Age and seniority had prevented him; but he quickly accepted the Canadian offer.[73] He arrived in Sydney, Cape Breton, on 5 September 1915.

The captain of *Margaret*, acting senior officer of the patrols, must have breathed a sigh of relief. Deluged by correspondence and telegrams from both Ottawa and Halifax that could be handled only while his ship was in harbour, he had sought transfer ashore simply to cope with the paper work. Headquarters had refused but then criticized him for not being at sea often enough when he stayed in port to run the office.[74]

Pasco could not have been overawed by his new command: base facilities included one-half of a commercial pier and some rented accommodation on the waterfront. He none the less continued in command of the St Lawrence force until early 1917, when expansion of the flotilla began, and accepted the new appointment of senior naval officer, Sydney. In this capacity he directed the greatly increased activities at the port until the war's end.

The recollections of a former RCN junior officer who had served under Pasco shed light on the relationship between the young Canadians and the retired British officers who then held so many of the senior appointments during the First World War. Insisting that his crew be "pusser" and correct according to the standards of discipline and deportment prescribed for the Royal Navy, he knew when to relax strict standards and to foster relations with his men. As one of the rare accounts puts it, "Captain Pasco R.N. was a gruff old fellow who's [sic] specialty was finding fault; nevertheless he had a humane side in his make up."[75]

Like Nelson, Pasco could also put a blind eye to the telescope when it served good purpose. As the former subordinate recalled: "During this period prohibition was in force in Halifax and deliveries of evil spirits came via the underground route, the beer in bottles from the Dartmouth Brewery being packed in barrels stenciled 'Sugar.' [One day] one of these barrels was waiting until Captain Pasco went ashore before being unpacked. There was a sigh of relief when [he finally] walked down the gangway. Immediately [our pals] went into action. [But] apparently the old man had forgot something and backtracked and caught them red-handed. [When told it was only sugar] the old man whispered 'Don't forget to send some of that sugar to my cabin too.' " Fraternal complicity with one's subordinates has always been a mainstay of naval leaders.

As could only have been expected, the flotilla over which Pasco assumed command in 1915 was in many respects a fighting force in name only. Even by transferring all personnel who could be spared from Esquimalt, the RCN could do no more than supply each vessel with a couple of officers and a handful of ratings. Fortunately, most of the civilian crew of the newly commissioned ships proved willing to enrol in the RNCVR.[76] Kingsmill wisely enjoined his officers to "remember that the men with whom they have to deal are totally unaccustomed to discipline, and that great tact will be necessary."[77] Of the seven ships in the St Lawrence patrol, the tug *Sinmac* and the yacht *Florence* proved unseaworthy in any but the most moderate weather. Living conditions aboard the larger *Sable I* were so foul that nine ratings deserted rather than face a patrol; senior officers must have been sympathetic, for they awarded a rather lenient punishment of ninety days' detention.[78]

Kingsmill had wanted ten dependable and reasonably well-armed vessels for the sea patrol, but in fact only four could meet these standards: *Canada*, *Grilse*, *Hochelaga*, and *Margaret*. Although *Grilse* was a fast and formidably armed craft, her narrow hull, like that of *Tuna*, did not take the open seas well. Both ships were in any event better employed as a strike force ready to dash out from Halifax and provide some semblance of advanced defence against German surface raiders.[79]

Modest as expansion of the Canadian flotilla turned out to be, it soon encountered opposition from the Admiralty – and quite unexpectedly, even from Canada's prime minister, Sir Robert Borden,

who had come to share Admiralty's views during a trip to London in
July.

Kingsmill found the ground being eaten from under his feet almost
immediately, as he endeavoured to develop and execute the plans he
had proposed at the end of June. The first hint of trouble came on
14 July, when both the acting prime minister and the minister of
the naval service sent fresh appeals to Admiralty for anti-submarine
vessels. Borden chided his colleagues for inconveniencing British
officials with the duplicate telegrams and thrust his point home.
Britain had "no light craft available" and did "not regard the situation
as serious." Indeed Admiralty "think one or two of your vessels should
be furnished with light guns capable of sinking submarines."[80]

Borden now suggested that the "swift type used by Jack Ross"
would be especially suitable; he was referring, of course, to the 30-
knot HMCS *Grilse*, the Glasgow-built 202-foot yacht (ex-*Winchester*)
that Lieutenant J.K.L. Ross, RNCVR, had brought from the United
States in June 1915. This rebuff flew in the face of all the intimations,
warnings, and advice that Kingsmill had received to date. No reply
from Kingsmill is extant. But one can imagine what it might have
been, for Admiralty's advice made no sense: "one or two" armed
vessels would be virtually useless for hunting submarines off the vast
coasts of Canada and Newfoundland. Nor were they much help in
escorting transports "out some considerable distance to sea."[81]

Admiralty clarified its position somewhat on 17 July, when it
rejected Kingsmill's proposal that troop-transports should sail from
Halifax, rather than through the vulnerable St Lawrence route. It
was "not of the opinion that the probability of German Submarines
operating in Canadian waters in the near future is great"; it merely
stressed "the desirability of taking steps to patrol the coast with small
craft in order to have an organization ready" in order to deal with
any German submarines violating Canadian waters.[82] Rooted at the
core of this message, as indeed of every message on the subject
dispatched since early June, was the assumption that Canadians could
quickly expand their organization in the event of an actual attack.
But as Admiral Patey reminded their lordships, Canada's vessels
might be "useful in gaining intelligence of hostile submarines [but]
are not sufficient to run them down or destroy them."[83] Of one other
thing he was certain: "There is no doubt whatever that, should the
war continue, [U-boats] will cross the Atlantic next year."

Diplomatic intelligence and U-boat scares had shaped Canadian
patrol schemes. Reported sightings of periscopes off the northeast
coast of Newfoundland at the end of July provided Kingsmill with a
graphic example of the Canadian navy's inadequacy. The combina-

tion of incipient threat and meagre response virtually phased out troop transports on the St Lawrence after patrol vessels scrambling belatedly to the distant scene left a troopship to fend for herself.[84] The ss *Caledonia* had departed Montreal carrying the 38th Battalion, only to disembark the troops at Quebec City when faced with a u-boat threat. She then proceeded in ballast through threatened waters while her troops crossed overland by rail and met her in Halifax.

The fact that the u-boat alarm proved false did nothing to soften Kingsmill's fury over his inability to take any but the most desperate precautions.

The only way to provide effective anti-submarine protection to troop transports as they passed through Canada's vulnerable coastal waters was by escorting them. And for that duty the RCN needed at least four ships that could sustain 20 knots and carry substantial armament. Any delay in providing these vessels, Kingsmill exploded in early August, "is next to criminal."[85] In response to Desbarats's request for clarification of the background of this issue, Stephens and Kingsmill gathered the many warning telegrams received from both Admiralty and the Colonial Office and showed that the initiative for creating the RCN flotilla had in fact come from Britain.[86] But they also showed that Britain's failure to provide support – or even full and complete advice – had condemned Canada to squandering its precious finances on second-rate ships barely adequate for the minimal role of coastal observation. It was "not unreasonable to suppose," Kingsmill charged, "that the Admiralty, well aware of the difficulties attendant upon the raising of an efficient Naval Force in this Country, propose to trust to luck in getting overseas our troops and munitions from here and the United States."[87]

The question of Canadian naval policy had meanwhile arisen from quite a different matter. During his trip to England, Borden had arranged with the Admiralty to exchange the worn-out *Niobe* for the somewhat newer and more powerful cruiser HMS *Sutlej*. She was one of the Bacchanti-class cruisers that had proven so vulnerable to u-boat attack in European waters.[88] Still clinging to the concept of naval power in terms of big warships, Borden was shocked when his own department rejected the scheme in early August. But the Canadian rationale did make sense. The 333 Canadian members of *Niobe*'s crews were urgently needed to complete the manning of the St Lawrence flotilla, while the cruiser's hulk could provide accommodation for naval personnel at Halifax, where barrack space was in desparately short supply.

Vice-Admiral Patey heartily endorsed the Canadian staff's priority of anti-submarine defence. Glad of the Canadian naval staff's offer to

release the 400 British and Newfoundland members of *Niobe*'s crews
for service in other Royal Navy ships, the Admiralty went along with
Ottawa's proposal. In doing so, it issued an abbreviated policy note
containing a strong warning about overreaction to the u-boat threat:
"It may not be clearly enough recognized that the submarine danger
on the Canadian coast is potential, not actual. Exaggerated measures
of precaution are to be deprecated."[89]

This much Kingsmill could accept. In this light he withdrew his
standing recommendation that the St Lawrence be closed to troopships.[90] But when he received the full text in September his blood
boiled. Having once played down the threat, their lordships now
explained that because of the shortage of destroyers for "urgent and
pressing" anti-submarine duties in European waters, none could be
dispatched to Canada until after u-boat attacks had actually taken
place. They nevertheless repeated the comfortable fallacy that the
RCN could extemporize adequate defences at the moment of crisis.
The time had come, Kingsmill warned, for Canada to start building
its own fast anti-submarine vessels.[91]

But Canada's minister for the navy had other concerns. Latching
onto Kingsmill's statement that u-boat attacks were unlikely in winter,
Hazen saw a way to save money. In the interests of economy, the
flotilla should be cut back as quickly and as substantially as possible.[92]
When the St Lawrence began to freeze up in November and the Gulf
force returned to Halifax, three of the chartered sea patrol ships and
all the motor boats were returned to their owners.[93] There was one
positive note in this dreary exercise of trimming already inadequate
forces. The hulk HMCS *Niobe*, which had been permanently tied up in
Halifax dockyard in September, helped to stabilize the organization.
Soon she was carrying 800 personnel on her books – 500 for the
patrol flotilla and others for the expanded services that supported
merchant shipping and Allied warships.[94]

Still it was a frustrating existence for those posted to the ship for
maintenance and dockyard duties; the constant round of chipping,
painting, and cleaning interrupted now and again with ceremonial
duties that gave them their "bellies full of being left behind." As one
member of the lower deck recalled: "We were used to act as guards
of honour and to keep the crowds back everytime a fist full of soldiers
were sent overseas. This sat on our dignities. Why should we, members of the senior service, present arms with fixed bayonets to those
monkeys? And when we were on our way back to the dockyard, which
was a good two miles march, we were the victims of much booing and
name calling such as: 'home guards and slackers, when are you going
over with the real men?' "[95]

One thing the RCN could not do as it consolidated the east coast organization after the trying 1915 season was bask in the plaudits of a grateful nation. In the nation's eye the army was far more important and captured all the exciting news. The populace could read of the grim battles in Europe, of the struggles between increasingly powerful technologies – flame-throwers, machine-guns, bombs, and poison gas. They could perhaps only guess at the losses at the battles of Champagne, Artois, and Loos – all for some 8,000 yards of blasted moonscape: 48,237 British lost at Loos, 143,567 French at Champagne, 178,000 Germans at Champagne and Artois.[96]

Shortly after the opening of the 1916 spring session of Parliament, the Liberal member for Pictou, Nova Scotia, launched a slashing and detailed attack on all aspects of Canada's naval effort. Why had Canada provided no significant numbers of personnel for overseas service in the Royal Navy while the tiny colony of Newfoundland had sent one thousand? Was it not a disgrace that Canada had to rely on Japanese and Australian warships for defence against surface raiders? Why had *Niobe* been laid up in Halifax, where by local accounts she merely served as a hostel for dockside loafers? He recapitulated accurate reports concerning rumours about transatlantic U-boat operations which the New York press, and then the Canadian papers, had begun publishing the previous July. How could it be that a nation of Canada's strength depended for anti-submarine defence on yachts given as gifts by Sir John Eaton and Jack Ross? Why had the government paid high prices for American yachts which, according to local reports, spent much of their time alongside because they were in such poor repair? Why, when the British government had recognized the efficiency of the Vickers works in Montreal by ordering submarines from the company, did the Canadian government not order destroyers and submarines from the plant? Why were RNCVR personnel being brought from Esquimalt to Halifax, while no organized effort was being made to recruit the maritime provinces' many well-qualified seamen?[97] The Liberal member for South Cape Breton joined in with a pathetic picture of motor-boat patrols in the Gulf that "were not able to cross [the Cabot Strait] to Newfoundland under their own steam, but were taken [back and forth on three occasions] on the little ship Margaret."

J.D. Hazen responded at length by producing much of the correspondence from the early part of the war in which Admiralty had refused Canadian offers to recruit naval personnel. Quite properly, he emphasized the large role that the RCN was playing in organizing the transport of men and materiel to Britain and Europe; he revealed

that there were not just two or three steamers available for local
defence, but eighteen. He was in a frustrating situation, unable to
play his strongest cards – the fact that Britain's Admiralty had actually
discouraged a larger anti-submarine effort and had refused to place
additional orders with Vickers.

The debate dragged on well past midnight and quickly disinte-
grated into an exchange of bitter recriminations about who had been
responsible for the collapse of naval policy in the years 1911–13. Like
the pre-war naval debates, this too featured its share of less than
illuminating repartée:

Mr. Pugsley: I beg my hon. friend's pardon, the right hon. leader of the
   Opposition never made that statement.
Mr. Hazen: I beg my hon. friend's pardon, he did.
Mr. Pugsley: I say he did not.
Mr. Hazen: I say he did.
Mr. Pugsley: I say he did not.

Parliament had perhaps already aired too much of its washing in
public. Certainly, the Colonial Office in London subsequently complained to Prime Minister Borden that the Canadian Parliament had
exposed too much information of potential value to the enemy.[98]

One thing was clear: Canada was no closer to having a naval policy
than in August 1914.

The soaring demands of the land war in Europe were settling the
matter by default. In January 1916 Borden had promised to increase
the number of men under arms to half a million and at Britain's
request had committed the recently raised third and fourth divisions
of the Canadian Corps to the Western front.[99] Yet despite Canada's
gesture, the Admiralty discouraged yet another bid by the Canadian
naval staff – a bid supported by Connaught, Patey, and now the
Newfoundland government as well – to undertake large-scale
improvements in local anti-submarine defences. Strapped for funds
and vessels, Newfoundland could do no more in 1916 than in 1915 –
precious little. But its government was now painfully aware of its
vulnerability to U-boat attack and of its dependence on Canada. It
therefore proposed that Canadians expand their anti-submarine sea
patrols out to the eastern edge of the Grand Banks.

Kingsmill supported the proposal. In March 1916 the Canadian
naval staff so advised Admiralty and requested assistance. Four vessels
would meet the minimum requirements for patrolling the Banks.
"The growth in the transport of munitions and troops from Canada

has been so enormous during the past nine months," the Canadian dispatch warned, "that it appears to the Department ... that the enemy is more likely to attempt attack by submarines on this side of the Atlantic this year than was the case last year."[100] Encouraged by the governor-general, Vice-Admiral Patey had already said much the same thing to the Admiralty a few weeks before. Kingsmill pushed the point further at the end of March: the Admiralty should recognize that the time had now come for the Dominion to build destroyers and submarines for the RCN.[101]

Senior officers at the Admiralty still remained convinced, however, that U-boats could reach North American waters only if accompanied by a supply ship; such a vessel would have to shelter in Canadian or Newfoundland coastal inlets where it would be vulnerable to existing defences both ashore and afloat. Canada should therefore feel secure. The Admiralty offered a further reason why a Grand Banks patrol was unnecessary: if U-boats struck that far out to sea, Admiralty would deny them targets by re-routing shipping to avoid them. This argued for the status quo: concentration of defences at the focal points of maritime trade close off Halifax and in the Gulf of St Lawrence.

But the mood had changed, for the Admiralty no longer charged the Canadians with over-reaction. The chief of staff in London, Admiral H.F. Oliver, found it quite "satisfactory" that Patey was sounding warnings without making specific proposals that would drain off British resources; the result would be to "induce the [Canadian] government to provide more and better patrol vessels from its own resources."[102] The Admiralty itself advised the Canadians that "in the event of Submarines operating off the Newfoundland and Canadian Coasts, they are likely to be well armed vessels of the latest types, and it is improbable that any lighter guns than a 12 pounder will be able to put them out of action." However "their Lordships regret[ed]" that no British vessels were available.[103]

Kingsmill correctly understood that the Admiralty did not expect an early attack. But the ominous warnings about the future worried him deeply. He therefore pressed the issue of building destroyers. Admiralty repeated the response of July 1915: construction in Canada would be too slow and require too much help from Britain.[104] And Britain, it had meanwhile transpired, now wanted naval help from Canada. While effectively setting low limits on RCN expansion during the first half of 1916, the Admiralty reversed itself on the recruitment of Canadians for the Royal Navy. Coastal patrols against enemy submarines, light craft and mines in British waters, the Mediterranean, and other theatres had created an unexpected need for hundreds of small vessels – and crews to man them.

Unknown at first to the Canadian government, Canadian industry had made an early and large contribution to the Royal Navy's expansion of European operations. Borden had been furious to learn in the fall of 1915 – shortly after he had received British apologies for not informing him about the assembly of H-class submarines at Montreal – that the Admiralty had secretly arranged for St Lawrence boat yards to assemble five hundred and fifty 75- and 80-foot fast motor launches with components from the Electric Boat Co. in the United States.[105] Despite its chagrin, the government responded quickly in early 1916 to Admiralty's request for men experienced in yachting and combustion engines. Canada recruited 376 men for the Royal Naval Auxiliary Motor Boat Patrol Service and sent them overseas immediately.[106]

This example of loyalty to the Mother Country Hazen cited when defending himself against his critics in the House of Commons in March 1916. He also announced that he had renewed his department's offer to recruit even larger numbers of unqualified men for training and service overseas in the Royal Navy.[107] This offer the Admiralty accepted almost immediately. At the end of May 1916, Captain the Honourable Rupert Guinness, a British MP and a prominent RNVR officer with Canadian connections, arrived to assist. He soon encountered difficulties. After two years of war, there were few patriots left in Canada who would volunteer for the British services, now that the Canadian forces were offering substantially higher rates of pay. Further, because of the RCN's limited role, no national recruiting system existed. The first problem was solved by creating an "overseas division" of the Royal Naval Canadian Volunteer Reserve wherein personnel would receive Canadian rates – paid by the Canadian government – while serving overseas in the RNVR. The second problem was solved with the assistance of enthusiastic, prominent citizens across the country—with the ubiquitous Aemilius Jarvis of Toronto taking a leading part. Progress was rapid once recruiting was launched in the fall of 1916. By March 1917, over eleven hundred men would be sent to Britain, nearly a quarter of the program's target of 5,000 men.[108]

After two-and-a-half years of war, dint of circumstance seemed to have finally defined the RCN's role: minimal patrol forces in Canadian home waters and provision to Britain of substantial numbers of Canadian seamen.

It rapidly became clear, however, that Canada and the Admiralty had failed to take proper account of Germany's ambitions.

– 6 –

Three German Visitors

The operational use of the modern submarine at the beginning of the Great War had provoked irrevocable changes not only in naval warfare but in international law. It had raised questions about tactics and challenged traditional interpretations of what actually constituted a belligerent vessel. The law concerning surface or "supermarine" vessels was already complex and subject to disputed judgments in international courts; the law concerning underwater or sub-marine ships was developing by trial and error in response to specific cases whose notoriety captured the public imagination.[1] Germany precipitated an entirely unprecedented phase of submarine warfare when deploying *U-Deutschland*, *U-Bremen*, and u-53 to North America. The visits had a profound effect on American neutrality laws, on us-British relations, and on the Canadian submarine industry and coastal defence.

The British naval blockade of Europe had by the spring of 1915 thrust Germany into an increasingly untenable position. As Germany's Imperial Naval Office observed in an internal note, "The intensification of English economic warfare against us requires reexamination of our arrangements for submarine warfare."[2] Recognizing that neutral nations (including the United States) would not "offer serious opposition to this new English rape," the note argued that Germany stood virtually on its own. As the German Foreign Office informed the American ambassador in Berlin: "Under silent or protesting suffrance of the neutrals, Germany is as good as cut off from overseas supply ... Such being the case, after six months of patience and waiting, Germany is pressed to respond with sharp measures against England's murderous measures of waging war at sea."[3]

Britain would indeed succeed, in the German naval view, if Germany did not "react against the shortage of commercial cargo space with corresponding countermeasures."[4] This assessment clearly called for intensification of what Germans called the "retribution principle" of submarine warfare. They pondered the extremity of waging unlimited warfare by tacitly revoking the prize rules and attacking without warning all civilian vessels serving British interests.

Time was of the essence. By all German assessments, their anticipated victory over Britain still lay at least many months away despite the obvious successes of the Central Powers in the land campaigns. As the Imperial Naval Office readily recognized, only a major decisive German victory on land could avert the necessity of aggravated attacks by submarines at sea. But Germany's war effort was consuming more resources than it could either produce or import. Severe shortages of foodstuffs and of vital industrial materials like nickel and rubber threatened to cripple its capacity to fight.[5] It was therefore necessary to break the British blockade.

Submarines provided the only really effective means. "The only reservations [we have] against carrying out submarine warfare against shipping," German Admiralty recognized as early as spring 1915, "are political." On that score, however, reintroduction of unrestricted submarine warfare was fraught with danger. Harsh retribution by Germany could alienate the neutral nations of Europe and provoke the United States to war. American lives and property had of course already fallen victim to u-boats, despite German precautions, and had been the subject of an often sharp exchange of notes between the two governments between February 1915 and May 1916.[6]

One of many notes of the American ambassador in Berlin had protested the sinking of the British vessels *Lusitania* and *Falaba* with the loss of American lives and the sinking of the American ships *Cushing* and *Gulflight*.[7] These attacks constituted, in the ambassador's words, "a series of events which the government of the United States has observed with growing concern, distress and amazement." The Kaiser and the Reichskanzler pondered the significance of these cases as well. The Kaiser commanded both von Tirpitz and the chancellor to collaborate on a reply to the American government. So sharp were divisions between the naval and political arms of the German government that von Tirpitz threatened to resign over the issue.[8]

The American notes challenged German interpretations of "the accepted principles of law and humanity."[9] Germany retorted that Britain was the prime offender; from the very beginning Britain had led the way by "extending this dreadful war to [include] the life and property of neutrals and noncombatants." Indeed, it had done so "with disdain for all internationally agreed upon legal standards."[10] Not least, Britain had applied starvation tactics against innocent non-combatants – the naval blockade of Germany – which had provoked Germany's counsel of despair.

The American position hardened against these pronouncements. In the words of the American ambassador in Berlin: "Illegal and inhuman acts, however justifiable they may be thought to be against an enemy who is believed to have acted in contravention of law and humanity, are manifestly indefensible when they deprive neutrals of their acknowledged rights ... If persisted in it would in such circumstances constitute an unpardonable offence against the sovereignty of neutral nations affected."[11]

Sharp notes like this underscored the danger of provoking Germany's powerful trading partner, the United States. Germany could not afford to alienate it. It was a delicate balance, for Germany was becoming increasingly convinced that the United States bore a "biased, ill-willed neutrality toward Germany" and actually favoured Britain.[12] The imagination and money of German entrepreneurs provided a peaceful solution. If one could not cut Britain's stranglehold by military power, one could at least slip through it with a fleet of commercial submarines.[13]

This "Deutschland solution" coalesced under the leadership of Alfred Lohmann, chairman of Lohmann & Co., Export-Import, and president of Bremen's Chamber of Commerce. The concept had of course suggested itself in shipping circles as early as 1914. The immediate thought, to which the Kaiser had been party, had been to employ combat submarines in transporting urgently needed cargoes of nickel and rubber. Entry into neutral harbours with warships for such purposes would infringe on international law, however; technical problems prevented the u-boats from transshipping the goods from neutral freighters on the high seas.

More important, in 1914 the capacity of submarines to make transatlantic voyages had seemed doubtful. That changed during the following year, when combat submarines remained at sea in excess of thirty days without replenishment and demonstrated their seaworthiness on extended missions from Wilhelmshaven to Constantinople without touching harbour.[14] Technically and politically, therefore, in the words of a secret letter to the chief of the naval cabinet, "Pursuit of this basic concept led necessarily and with compelling logic to the construction of special submarine freighters which, lacking all armament whatever, would have to be regarded and treated exclusively as merchantmen by even the least disposed neutrals."[15]

Lohmann could now act. Early in September 1915 he had proposed his idea to the state secretary of the interior and offered his services, provided the German Reich covered the venture financially. The state secretary readily assented, but with the clear understanding that the government would keep the project at arm's length; from the outset it must have all the appearances of a purely private venture. The chief of the Admiralty Staff stressed this point again almost a year later: it was "absolutely essential that any connection between the submarine shipping line and the Reich be kept secret for fear of causing difficulties for the [undersea] freighters in their neutral ports of call."[16]

Lohmann and the state secretary quickly sketched the new firm's financial basis: a limited company, with capital of two million marks secured by three partners: Lohmann, North German Lloyd, and Deutsche Bank. The new submarine freighting firm would contract construction of the vessel and oversee acquisition of goods on both sides of the Atlantic. The Reich would guarantee the partners their capital investment plus a 5 per cent return, while the partners agreed to return to the Reich all profits over and above that amount. These plans were known only to a select few. In fact not even Admiral von Müller, chief of the naval cabinet, would learn about it until July 1916 – five weeks after the first U-freighter had departed on her maiden voyage – even though the Imperial Naval Office had been party to discussions since October 1915.

Lohmann took the Bremen shipbuilding firm Weser A.G. into his confidence to explore the possibility of constructing submersible freighters. By 3 October Weser A.G. had completed its plans for a vessel of approximately five hundred tons' carrying capacity. However, the need to design and build special engines pushed the expected delivery date of the completed vessel forward almost eleven months, to September 1916. Time was pressing, and Lohmann sought other options.

Friedrich Krupp's Germania Werft in Kiel had meanwhile taken its own independent initiatives and had approached the Imperial Naval Office with proposals. Krupp wished to offer the Reich a submersible freighter as a gift, on the sole condition that it be used to transport supplies of nickel from the United States. By the beginning of October 1915 his firm had commenced design of a prototype submersible freighter with a carrying capacity of 700 tons, which it hoped would enter service in seven months' time, in April 1916. Krupp may have been drawing more heavily on American designs than most German records are prepared to admit. Meanwhile, yet a third company, the Vulcan-Werft in Stettin, had somehow caught wind of the freighter scheme and on 5 October 1915 offered to build four transport submarines for the Imperial Naval Office modelled on a minelayer design.

A series of events, no longer traceable in any detail, brought the players together, on 15 October 1915, to form a consortium, but with the exclusion of Stettin. Early plans had envisaged Krupp's Germania Werft in Kiel building the *U-Deutschland* while Weser A.G. in Bremen built the smaller *U-Bremen*. Now it was obvious that Krupp's Germania Werft could build two freight-boats with a 600-ton cargo capacity faster than either of the other two firms. Krupp would therefore build one of them on its own account and another on that of Lohmann's new submarine shipping company.

By the time the new shipping line, Deutsche Ozean-Rhederei, was legally constituted under the chairmanship of Alfred Lohmann on 8 November 1915, the keels of both U-boats had already been laid.[17] The director of North German Lloyd had become executive director of the new shipping line, which he managed from his own offices, in addition to his primary responsibilities. Two other businessmen, one from North German Lloyd and another from Deutsche Bank, completed the board of directors. All worked without stipend or salary.

Successful sea trials convinced the Imperial Naval Office of the freighters' potentially crucial importance for long-term naval strategy. The navy ordered six such vessels in the fall of 1916. During all this time the Baltimore firm of A. Schumacher and Co., American agents of North German Lloyd, had begun stockpiling bulk rubber for shipment across the Atlantic. By July 1916 some 1,200 tons of rubber, enough for three trips, awaited the U-freighter at Baltimore. As Germany's state secretary for the interior explained, "The construction costs for the [next] six submarine freighters are more than substantially covered by the net proceeds of the first trip."[18]

Builders speeded up construction of the U-boats by using already proved and readily available commercial components.[19] Thus, for example, non-reversible diesel generators ordered for the battleship *Sachsen* and the battle-cruiser *Gneisenau* became the submarines' main propulsion; this meant that U-freighters could go astern only by using the electro-motors originally built for submarine minelayers. Far more problematic was fully using the submersibles' cargo-carrying capacity. Here the space-to-weight ratio was crucial. The reduced size of the propulsion machinery and elimination of armament already made the U-boats lighter than the original design. In fact, when carrying a full load of rubber in interior spaces they would be too buoyant to dive unless the relatively light cargo were counterbalanced by transporting an increased shipment of heavy metal. Designers solved the problem by arranging for stowage of a considerable amount of rubber in the flooded spaces outside the pressure hull.[20]

Once completed, Krupp's submarine freighter was the largest of its type ever built: 65 metres long, 8.9 metres wide, and 5.8 metres in pressure hull diameter. She displaced 1,558 tons surfaced and 1,860 tons submerged and had a range of 14,000 nautical miles at a speed of 9.6 knots. In theory, consumption of fuel and provisions on the outbound voyage would reduce her weight and, as she would not replenish in the United States, enable her to carry up to 740 tons of cargo when homeward bound. She would in fact exceed this theoretical figure. In round figures, she carried 340 tons of heavy cargo and 170 tons of rubber in the holds and a further 230 tons of rubber between the pressure hull and outer skin. *U-Deutschland* was launched on 28 March 1916, five months after she had been ordered. Long before, Lohmann had begun hiring and training his sea-going personnel.

Captain Paul König commanded *U-Deutschland* and her crew of twenty-seven on two commercial trips to the United States in 1916. These were unprecedented journeys in an unprecedented class of underwater craft. Press reports exuded confidence in her daring technology. Behind the smooth public relations façade, however, lurked great risks: a hastily built prototype vessel was hurriedly being pressed to the limits of her capabilities. *U-Deutschland* courted danger, possibly disaster, at several turns in the necessarily imperfect meshing of venturesome pioneers in a new machine. On one occasion her uncontrolled dive in the North Sea may have presaged the mechanical failure that destroyed her sister ship *U-Bremen* on her maiden voyage to the United States that same year.[21]

U-Deutschland's forty-nine-year-old captain, Paul König, had in civilian life commanded the North German Lloyd liner *Schleswig*. A naval reservist, he had transferred to SMS *Brandenburg* in 1914.[22] Alfred Lohmann then chose him to command the flagship of the Deutsche Ozean-Rhederei. Through his service with the Baltimore line of North German Lloyd, König certainly knew the waters off Chesapeake Bay, where he would be operating. But he had no submarine experience whatsoever. Nor indeed did a number of his hand-picked merchant mariners, among them six of his former ratings from *Schleswig*, whom he managed to have transferred from the ill-fated *U-Bremen*.

The crew of *U-Deutschland* was trained by a diving instructor recognized and admired for his rare grasp of the profession: thirty-one-year-old Kapitänleutnant Hans Rose. Later that same year Rose would take the smaller combat submarine U-53 to the United States.

Rose, who ultimately joined the Nazi party in the 1930s and reached the rank of ss Untersturmführer in 1937, had entered the Kaiserliche Marine in 1903, at eighteen years of age.[23] He was appointed commanding officer of the submarine Seiner Majestät Unterseeboot smu-2 in 1914, and on 22 April 1916 he accepted smu-53 from Krupp's Germania Werft in Kiel. He remained with his u-boat until July 1918 – an almost unprecedented length of uninterrupted service with a single submarine. He covered over 70,000 miles in eighteen combat operations during which he sank eighty-seven ships of 217,508 tons. Awarded the "Pour le Mérite" in December 1917, he stood fourth in the precedence of u-boat aces, after Arnauld de la Perière, Walter Forstmann, and Max Valentiner.

Training under such a talented submariner, Paul König of U-Deutschland exploited every opportunity to exercise diving manoeuvres under all possible conditions. Whatever hesitations early volunteers for the commercial submarine service might have had about the new venture seem to have been allayed by a distinct economic advantage over the German navy's surface fleet. In addition to the then fairly handsome monthly wage of 200 Reichsmarks, each rating earned "diving allowance" (Tauchgeld) of one and one-half marks for each dive.

U-Deutschland departed Wilhelmshaven on 14 June 1916, bearing dye-stuffs, chemicals, and pharmaceuticals for the United States on her twenty-seven-day crossing of the Atlantic. The long-distance shake-down cruise revealed the often-galling problems of life in an inhospitable and sometimes threatening environment. As veterans recalled, "life could be hell." Even experienced sailors became wretchedly ill with the thrashing and bobbing of their exceptionally buoyant vessel. Engine-room personnel had to work in temperatures reportedly as high as 53 degrees centigrade; diesels sucked in most of the external air from the intakes, leaving a fetid, oily atmosphere that the fans whipped throughout the boat. An oily film lay everywhere: on clothing, equipment, food, and drinking water. Bodies sweated profusely, and off-watch personnel tossed on their bunks and felt completely baked in the heat. The routines of watch-on and watch-off, relieved only occasionally by brief visits to the upper deck, marked the slow passage of time.

Diving U-Deutschland proved an uncomfortable and sometimes precarious operation. For this reason, König resorted to camouflage in order to reduce the need for submerging until absolutely necessary. He attached a dummy funnel of canvas to the periscope so that it could be raised and lowered like a window-blind and made the conning tower look like the deck-works of a freighter. Smudge-pots of oil-soaked rags lent a touch of authenticity to what he hoped passing vessels would regard as a low-lying tramp. The disguise proved less than satisfactory. In fact, it attracted the attention of at least one inquisitive merchant ship, whose curiosity forced the submarine to dive.

On approaching American shores, König briefed his crew on their expected deportment ashore. They were above all to remain silent about the harsh living conditions aboard and about seasickness and technical difficulties. *U-Deutschland* picked up the light of Cape Henry during the evening of 8 July 1916, twenty-four days out of Wilhelms-haven. For the first time since leaving German waters, she switched on her navigation lights. She was met by a pilot boat and the Lloyd tug *Timmins*, commanded by Captain Hans F. Hinsch, whose North German Lloyd steamer *Neckar* had been bottled up in Baltimore since the beginning of the war. Together they entered Chesapeake Bay. As König recalled: "All the neutral vessels, Americans and others, that met us welcomed us with three blasts on the horn or siren. Only an english [sic] steamer sailed past us in poisonous silence."[24]

Rumours about the *U-Deutschland* had preceded her arrival, despite the secrecy surrounding her planning and construction. Over two months earlier, on 25 May 1916, while she was undergoing sea-trials in the Kieler Bucht, the German-language newspaper *New-Yorker Staatszeitung* had published a report about "the first submarine freighter." Though it sounded at the time like a chapter from Jules Verne's *Twenty-Thousand Leagues under the Sea*, the article insisted that she would actually attempt to cross the Atlantic from Hamburg to New York. Speculation included the possibility of an underwater passenger service at $5,000 per trip. One traveller had reportedly shown the *Staatszeitung* some photos of the experimental vessel, which he alleged to be over 450 feet long (more than twice her actual length of 65 metres); he had asserted that four more such freighters would be in service by 8 August 1916. These, so it was claimed, would transport mail, chemicals, and jewels on the outbound voyage.

As it turned out, this was a fairly accurate reflection of the Reichs-marine's intentions and suggests that the "traveller" who provided the report had been more than a casual observer of Kiel harbour. Picking up the story, the London *Daily News* then touched what would be a vital nerve in Anglo-American relations. Even if armed for self-defence, the British newspaper pointed out, these submarine boats were really not warships at all, but merchant vessels. As such, they could legally enter US ports like the surface merchantmen of other nations. Equally important, the *Daily News* correctly explained, inter-

national law forbade British warships from attacking them without
warning – unless, of course, they were to submerge in order to evade
a legal search.

Nevertheless, when *U-Deutschland* entered Baltimore, Great Britain
protested to the US government that the submarine should be
interned. The demand rested on the argument that submarine vessels
were not by law entitled to the treatment given "supermarine"
(i.e. surface) vessels entering neutral ports. Britain had taken a similar line in protesting the presence of German U-boats in the territorial
waters of Sweden, Norway, and Spain. The difficulty lay in applying
old laws to a radically new maritime technology. Germany's Admiral
von Tirpitz maintained, for example, that the innovation of submarines had overtaken all legal agreements and definitions: "U-boat
warfare [was] something entirely new and had been mentioned neither in the Hague Conference nor in consultations on the occasion
of the London Declaration, [simply] because the possibility of a submarine war had not yet obtained."[25] In *Deutschland*'s case, Britain
held that by virtue of the submarine's ability to disappear beneath
the surface of the sea she could pretend to leave American territorial
waters as an armed merchantman while in fact remaining a combat
vessel for the expressed purpose of carrying out hostile acts.[26]

The American government did not agree with Britain's conten-
tions. The debate concerning the legal status of German commercial
submarines turned not on what actions they might conceivably wish
to undertake, but on the specific purpose of their design and their
actual use. When *U-Deutschland* arrived in Baltimore, the US State
Department arranged for a team of three naval officers to conduct a
thorough examination of her construction and equipment. The team
found the completely unarmed *U-Deutschland* "not constructed with
a view to conversion into a war vessel" and ruled "that its voyage was
purely a commercial venture."[27]

Events would prove these findings wrong, for on 10 February 1917
the Germans would rename her U-155 and commence her transformation into a heavily armed and powerful submarine cruiser. But
after examination in 1916 she was granted the usual privileges
accorded belligerent merchant vessels visiting neutral ports: she
could remain in Baltimore to unload and reload cargo and then
depart once she was ready. From an international perspective, "the
question thus presented was unique and without precedent." The
German press naturally acclaimed the American action.[28] But as Reuters Agency correctly concluded from State Department interviews,
however, the American government regarded its decision as setting

no legal precedent whatever. Any similar cases in future, Reuters reported, would be judged according to their own particular circumstances.

U-Deutschland's visit triggered another dispute with equally intriguing ramifications. Although not apparent at the time, the points of contention were only the tip of a multinational armament iceberg. On the face of it, and as filtered to the German press through foreign sources, the Lake Torpedo Boat Co. of Bridgeport, Connecticut, intended to sue the vessel's shipping line, Deutsche Ozean-Rhederei, for infringement of patent.[29] The American firm allegedly held American patents on some of *Deutschland*'s equipment.

As might be expected, some French and British officials deemed the mere threat of a legal suit sufficient reason to intern the German submarine. One British newspaper story datelined Rotterdam explained with some element of truth that the Lake Torpedo Boat Co. and the New York representative of Krupp Works had long since founded a us company to construct huge "diving boats" displacing some 3,000 tons. To this end the two companies had allegedly agreed to share German and American patents.

U-Deutschland's arrival in Baltimore in July 1916 was a grand public relations and social event. Showered with congratulatory telegrams and invitations, and fêted by patriotic German-American associations, Captain König was welcomed as Germany's hero.[30] The mayor of Baltimore gave an official dinner in honour of both König and Count von Bernstorff, the German ambassador to Washington. As König recalled, it was a political event. After-dinner speeches celebrated the importance of the *U-Deutschland* for German-American trade relations; the civic band reportedly played the stirring strains of the patriotic *Die Wacht am Rhein* and the American anthem as the two national flags intertwined.

The scene, in König's words, was "a lovely symbol of friendship and understanding [for both countries] both of whom lay great store on the freedom of the seas."[31] This last comment was not merely a case of euphoria. Freedom of the seas had indeed been a guiding principle since the trade agreement between Prussia and the United States of 10 September 1785. In an exchange of notes with the American ambassador in Berlin in 1915, the German Foreign Office had evoked the old principle of this still-operative treaty when referring to links forged by Frederick the Great, John Adams, Benjamin Franklin, and Thomas Jefferson.[32]

König's words in Baltimore cast "England" in the role of the real high-seas pirate who offended against international law with its blockade of Germany and, of course, its cruiser patrols off American ports.

The Germans were cast in the role of injured humanitarian. For obvious reasons, both König and his American hosts conveniently forgot the years 1861–5, when the US navy blockaded Confederate ports and denied Britain neutral rights to trade with the South.

A humanitarian image was precisely what the Germans wanted and needed. A commemorative autographed photo of the *U-Deutschland* underscored the point. Captioned in honour of "the first transatlantic voyage of the submarine liner *Deutschland*," it was distributed to raise funds for German prisoners-of-war in Siberia.

Count von Bernstorff wrote a jubilant report to von Bethmann Hollweg: "The arrival of the submarine 'Deutschland' was the first event of the war whose repercussions on America can be regarded with complete satisfaction. The attitude of the government was entirely correct, and public opinion acclaimed us with admiration in rich measure ... It really seemed that the last two years of hate and bitterness [against us] had been forgotten."[33] The more sceptical chancellor rejected his ambassador's optimistic conclusions.

Had Germans designed the voyage of *U-Deutschland* in order to dispel the myth of the "marauding and merciless Hun," they could scarcely have offered the American press a better package. The Germans themselves put the event to good use. Lohmann himself wrote anonymous editorials for the *Berliner Zeitung* and the *Voßische Zeitung*.[34]

Once *U-Deutschland* had arrived safely in Baltimore, the German Naval Information and Intelligence Office, code-named "N," fed a great deal of material to the German press in order to boost morale on the home front. Thus the *Berliner Tageblatt* for 11 July 1916 announced the "America voyage of a German Mercantile Submarine," and in subsequent issues it followed the various political and strategic speculations about *U-Deutschland*'s arrival in Baltimore.[35] Twice-daily issues from 11 to 19 July covered retrospectives on the journey; they described the formidable impression she allegedly made on neutral nations and highlighted "England's protests" against the German achievement. In the words of the widely published congratulatory telegram from Alfred Lohmann to Captain König, "German technology and German daring celebrate a pioneering triumph."[36]

The Times of London promptly countered the claim by pointing out that H-class submarines built in Montreal had actually crossed the Atlantic much earlier. The point was well taken. The first six Canadian-built submarines from Vickers had left Halifax for Britain on 22 July 1915 – the first submarines to cross the Atlantic under their own power.[37] The remaining four Canadian boats had soon followed, en route for the Dardanelles. Dismissed out of hand by a jingoistic column in the German press, the Canadian achievement was again belittled in 1937, when Captain König, writing his memoirs in support both of the Wilhelmine naval traditions and the new German rearmament under Hitler, was singing a new propaganda tune.[38]

British Admiralty had been following the visit of *U-Deutschland* with keen interest. In addition to the ten H-class submarines that had been assembled in Montreal, Admiralty had ordered another batch of ten boats of the same type from American yards. The US government had invoked the Neutrality Laws and forbidden delivery of this second group to the Royal Navy. American acceptance of *U-Deutschland* as a submersible freighter now seemed to provide a way around this ruling.[39]

An Admiralty minute of 30 June 1916 suggested that the ten submarines "should be completed without armament fittings, mercantile crews arranged for, some cargo put on board [and] should sail to Halifax as merchant ships and be armed on arrival there or in England."[40] Admiralty's commodore (submarines) knew the risks involved and added that "America won't like this."

The Foreign Office cabled Ambassador Spring Rice the proposal in cypher and instructed him to approach the US government while *U-Deutschland*'s status was still being reviewed:

Ask whether, if we remove torpedo tubes, guns and all armament fittings [from the ten H-class submarines on order], and reduce them to the exact condition in which the German mercantile submarine visits New York [sic], we should be allowed to bring these boats, flying the British mercantile flag, over to this country. If this request is put in immediately after the corresponding request is made by the Germans, and before an answer is given, the State Department would be placed in the position of either refusing to give the Germans something which *they* want, or agreeing to give us something which *we* want. In either case we stand to gain.[41]

The ambassador sought further clarification from Admiralty despite the pressure of time and was finally informed of the crux of the matter. Delivery of the H-class boats would be only a consolation prize. What the British government really wanted was to force the Americans to admit that all submarines, including the Deutschland class of freighter, were ships of war.[42]

Britain's attempts to obtain the submarines it had ordered did not end with American refusal to permit their export. Scant clues suggest that some senior British official envisaged covert operations involving agents in New York, New Jersey, and Ottawa who would arrange for an American citizen to purchase the submarines, operate them briefly as commercial vessels under the American flag, and then transfer ownership to a British national. Admiralty rejected the notion, "since the use of such indirect methods would involve disguises and fictions which it is important to avoid in a matter which has already formed the subject of a frank private communication to the United States' government."[43] Admiralty simply let the matter lie until the United States entered the war.

U-Deutschland completed loading her cargo by the end of July 1916. She carried 350 tons of rubber, 343 tons of nickel, 83 tons of tin, and half a ton of jute sacks for the trenches. The fact that some of the nickel had come from Sudbury, Ontario, caused no stir on this trip; the second shipment of Canadian nickel would cause political embarrassment on the next trip, four months later.

In the late afternoon of 2 August the vessel slipped her lines for the twenty-two-day return voyage to Bremen. König had calculated his departure so as to be off Cape Henry by nightfall. The United States had declined his request for an escort of "one or more American war ships" into international waters, and he now found it necessary to rely on the unarmed North German Lloyd tug *Timmins*.[44] Submerged toward dusk, König counted eight British vessels searching the waters for him and a number of American fishing vessels that he suspected the British of having chartered to lay a mine barrage. His response was characteristic: "How often I have thought, as the eight cruisers lay off Cape Henry, if one or two of our u-boats were to blow a few of them out of the water – that would shift the whole mood in our favour."[45] Just how he thought such an attack would ameliorate German-American relations, or shake British resolve, is by no means clear.

For the moment, the unarmed submarine had no option but to run the gauntlet. Cruising blind at night, with the aid of depth gauge and gyro compass, *U-Deutschland* slipped through British cruiser patrols into the open sea. Twelve days out of home port she picked up the first signals from the German wireless station at Nauen, outside Berlin. Shortly thereafter, and just before her rendezvous with an aircraft and an escort of ten patrol boats, a German u-boat passed her the latest information on mine-fields. At 3 p.m. on 23 August she anchored in the mouth of the Weser River before commencing her ceremonial entrance into Bremerhaven. Within four hours the *Weserzeitung* had broken the news with a one-page broadsheet that reportedly triggered national euphoria. Five hours later, a disgruntled

Kaiser, whom the Reichskanzler had neglected to inform until eight that night, sent a congratulatory telegram.[46]

The German press, from illustrated magazines to serious newspapers, proclaimed her "happy return home" and squeezed the fullest possible propaganda effect from the event.[47] Articles could now tell selected pieces of the story of *U-Deutschland*'s origins, of the founding of Deutsche Ozean-Rhederei, and of the "epic" of German technology and courage in the face of uncountable odds. The Bremen Stock Exchange opened next day with speeches extolling the voyage's economic significance; Kaiser Wilhelm himself sent the Bremen Senate an effusive though benign congratulatory telegram. The Deutscher Flotten-Verein, roughly equivalent to Britain's Navy League, issued commemorative coloured prints of her arrival.[48] Even the US ambassador in Berlin, James W. Gerard, expressed praise during an interview with the *Münchener Zeitung*; but he did so in diplomatic language whose necessary niceties revealed little of the deeper implications of the vessel's journey: "The American people are convinced by nothing so much as by success."[49]

The homecoming had all the trappings of a national celebration; flags and bunting, ships' sirens, and bands in pubs and restaurants playing the uplifting strains of *Deutschland, Deutschland über Alles*. As the submarine slipped along the quays lined by throngs of onlookers, she was welcomed by a bevy of representatives from business and state: Alfred Lohmann, the grand duke of Oldenburg, and the ageing Graf Zeppelin, whose hopes of flying his own dirigibles to America had been dashed by the outbreak of war.

Hotel Hillmann treated the crew to breakfast; the press received luncheon and stories; and Bremen's Senate gave a formal reception to the crew and prominent guests in the Hansa city's famous city hall. Lohmann received an honorary doctorate in political science from the University of Kiel – the full title of which he would subsequently use when signing letters and telegrams – and Captain König an honorary doctorate of medicine from Halle. In the words of the medical faculty's testimonial, König "as bold captain of the first mercantile submarine [had] broken the enemy blockade and enabled science and the medical-chemical industry to regain its world position in times of duress." *U-Deutschland* reportedly paid for herself out of the proceeds of this first transatlantic trip and had supplied the German army's requirement of raw rubber for six months. In just seven weeks, both König and *U-Deutschland* would return to the United States.

Germany needed all the supplies it could get. The British blockade had cut off its imports, and the severe pressures of the land war on both the Eastern and Western fronts had turned the tide against any genuine hope of victory. The German army had "failed in [its] great attempt to break through the French front at Verdun, and the Allies in the battles of the Somme took such toll of the German army that it never fought as well again."[50] Germany was losing despite its use of the deadliest weaponry: phosgene gas attacks on 19 May and 20 June. The toll from 21 February to 20 December, in the protracted battles of Verdun alone, amounted to 362,000 French and 336,831 German.

The German navy dared make only four sorties: a cruiser force to Hull (England) on 6 March in order to lure Britain's Harwich force into combat; shore bombardment of Yarmouth, Lowestoft, Lincoln, and Harwich, led by eight battle-cruisers on 24 April; the Battle of Jutland on 31 May; and a bombardment raid on Sunderland on 14 July. Significantly, Admiral Scheer aborted the Sunderland mission without having reached his target, for fear of encountering Royal Navy opposition and having to face a second Jutland. Under the circumstances, submarines offered Germany the only hope of sustaining its waning strength. When Hindenburg arrived at Cambrai on 16 September 1916 to launch construction of the eighty-five-mile-long "Hindenburg Line," his supplies were short – and the combat strength of the German field armies was huge: 2,850,000 on the Western Front, and 1,730,000 in the East.[51]

The departure of *U-Bremen* on 25 August 1916 was perhaps quite rightly overshadowed by the homecoming celebrations for *U-Deutschland*. It was in any event crucial to keep her departure secret, as Britain had now ample warning of Germany's intention of maintaining mercantile submarine links with the United States. Confident that she could reach New London, Connecticut, unmolested, by 15 September, she departed in the early hours – never to be seen again. It is no longer certain what cargo she carried, apart from 32,500 doses of salvarsan.[52] German announcements reached the press after she was thought to be safely in mid-ocean. Long after she was hopelessly overdue, her name continued to flit through speculative newspaper accounts, suggesting possible journeys as far as South America and back.[53] Some of these reports had been released by "N." The submarine's spectral existence was for a brief time perhaps as strategically important as if she had actually been en route to a US port. The mere likelihood of her unscheduled appearance kept the Allies off-balance.

More important, *U-Bremen* was followed three weeks later by the combat submarine U-53. *U-Deutschland*'s experience had led the Germans to anticipate a concentration of British patrols off the American coast. U-53's principal mission was to protect the *Bremen* in her attempt to break through the British cordon after having unloaded and reloaded cargo in New London. For reasons of logistics, it was essential for U-53 to follow rather than accompany *U-Bremen* on the outward voyage. As we shall see, it was just barely possible to increase U-53's capacity for fuel and provisions sufficiently for a two-way trans-atlantic trip, and she had no extra margin to linger off the US coast while *U-Bremen* discharged her cargo. Nor could she put into a US port for more than twenty-four hours or request more fuel and provisions than necessary for a direct passage home. That would leave her no seatime for operations against British warships and merchantmen.

Intriguingly, in view of previous alarms in Canada and the United States about secret U-boat refuelling bases, the Germans had given no thought whatever to such covert attempts to resupply the boat. The limited range of ship-borne wireless made the more logical alter-native – arranging a rendezvous with a supply ship – too cumbersome and uncertain. But in light of *U-Bremen*'s importance and vulnerabil-ity, one wonders why the Reichsmarine delayed so long in providing her the necessary escort; the record leaves little doubt that there was no time for elaborate schemes and that the German navy's decision to use U-53 as back-up support was hasty and unplanned. Even more important, deployment of a combat submarine to hunt in American waters appears to have been the personal enterprise of the chief of Admiralty Staff, von Holtzendorff, who, despite the profound diplo-matic implications of the venture, proceeded without authorization from – and possibly in defiance of – senior government authorities.

Admiral Henning von Holtzendorff had given the Allies an unprec-edented glimpse of himself in a press interview early in 1916. In the words of the United Press Staff correspondent in Berlin:

The admiral is a small, plump, energetic man, with thick, white whiskers and a hearty handshake. He greets you smiling, with a military bow, a firm grip and word of greeting which comes so suddenly that you forget you are in the presence of one of the kaiser's most trusted officials. . . . He has watched the official relations between the United States and Germany grow friendlier . . . The admiral is a doer, not a talker, as evidenced by the things he has accomplished, and by the fact that this is the first time he ever talked for publication . . . Asked how long he thought the war would last [he replied] 'Until we are victorious.'[54]

Von Holtzendorff had long been advocating unlimited submarine warfare and had pursued military goals to the virtual exclusion of their political implications. However, he was by no means politically naive. As he briefed the Kaiser on the day of *U-Deutschland*'s arrival in Baltimore, it was necessary to adopt all the measures the enemy had done, short of provoking "a breach with America."[55] In August he had addressed a top-level meeting with von Bethmann Hollweg, State Secretary of the Imperial Naval Office Admiral von Capelle (von Tirpitz's successor), General von Ludendorff, and Minister of War Wild von Hohenborn.[56] Germany, von Holtzendorff explained, was now caught "in a difficult defensive war on all fronts against the increasing superiority of her old and new enemies." Britain's "mastery of the sea and America's unneutral attitude" permitted continuation of this "war of attrition until Germany is exhausted." Britain must be prevented from doing this "by all means available."

Much to von Holtzendorff's consternation, the meeting reached no practical conclusions whatever but petered out with a militarily useless resolution: "The total situation, particularly the military one," necessitated postponing any decision in the matter. Von Holtzendorff therefore proceeded on his own in preparing orders for commencement of unrestricted submarine warfare effective 18 October – some three and a half months earlier than the date his government was contemplating.[57]

The chancellor learned of these plans on 2 October, six days before U-53 commenced operations off Newport, and took extreme exception to von Holtzendorff's having gone so far without a definite decision sanctioned by the Kaiser.[58] In his telegram to von Hindenburg, chief of the supreme Military Command, the Reichskanzler explained his position: "We have promised America to conduct submarine warfare only according to the Prize Rules." Von Bethmann Hollweg apparently did not yet know that the plans entailed deploying a combat submarine off Newport.

However, Admiral Scheer, chief of the High Seas Fleet, had known about the U-53 scheme and telegraphed von Holtzendorff on 9 September that deployment should first be approved by the Military War Office. Scheer deeply feared "that deploying U-53 might bring about war with America."[59] The whole mission, he emphasized in his following letter, was completely out of harmony with decisions taken at the most senior levels and should not be undertaken until fully considered and approved by a plenary of the country's political and military leadership.

As will be seen, von Holtzendorff rejected that view. On 6 October 1916 he briefed the Kaiser on the use of submarines, only to be told that the total situation excluded immediate commencement of unrestricted submarine warfare. By this time von Holtzendorff had already dispatched U-53 to Newport, apparently without consultation with his political masters. In the words of his uncompromising reply to Admiral Scheer on 11 September: "The order [for U-53] takes account of the sensitivity of the neutral American government. I do not share the reservations of the Imperial Command [of the High Seas Fleet, i.e. Scheer] regarding the impact of the mission. I have refrained from communicating with the political agencies of the Reich since it is purely a military matter whose planned execution complies with the His Imperial Majesty's expression of intent."[60] No documents support this interpretation of the Kaiser's will. Indeed, the Kaiser had declared in an "All Highest Cabinet Order" of 1915: "U-Boat trade war is not an end itself," but a means to a political goal.[61]

Admiral von Holtzendorff's high-handed insistence on the primacy of military considerations over politics was, as Scheer had rightly pointed out, potentially disastrous. Apparently unknown to any of the military players was a German peace mission to the United States. On 25 September 1916, two weeks after von Holtzendorff had issued the orders to U-53, and twelve days before her arrival in Newport, the German ambassador in Washington had received personal directions from the Kaiser to ask President Wilson to intercede with Britain on behalf of Germany.[62] According to Germany's political scheme, the president could give the impression of independent overtures to Britain while passing on predetermined terms acceptable to Germany; according to this scenario, he would thereby ingratiate himself with Americans in the forthcoming presidential election and help Germany to save face.

Whether the Kaiser really knew that he now had two irons in the fire – one clasped by a hawk, the other by a dove – is not clear. By the time his orders reached the ambassador in Washington, his chief of Naval Staff had long since set critical events in motion. Toward the end of August 1916, just two days after U-Bremen's departure from home port, Kapitänleutnant Hans Rose of U-53 faced an unusual and unexpected challenge. The chief of Submarine Forces, Commodore Hermann Bauer (Führer der Unterseeboote), had summoned him to enquire how confident he was both in himself and in his U-boat about undertaking a daring mission to the United States. Bauer recognized that the task could easily lead to unforeseeable military or political situations, since a U-boat commander might need to make swift and independent decisions, with far-reaching consequences. Hans Rose struck him as the right choice for such a job.[63]

Rose, of course, had no doubts about himself either. But u-53 was a less certain choice. She was, after all, a 750-ton combat submarine designed and built for operations in European waters. With a crew of thirty-six and a range of 5,600 miles, she would be hard pressed to handle the journey without modifications for increased stores and fuel. At the very best, her range would have to be extended by another 2,000 miles. Rose took a day to consider the mission and to consult with the builders. He then accepted with a will. Bauer granted him no more than two weeks to effect the necessary modifications to the boat and to be in all respects ready for sea.[64]

In the days that followed, the crew joined dockyard staff in the major task of converting half the capacity of the u-boat's buoyancy tanks into fuel storage. This change caused a wide range of buoyancy and stability problems which revealed themselves only when the once-lively and responsive u-53 wallowed sluggishly in the troughs of stormy seas. Nevertheless, she now had the range for what turned out to be a 7,550-mile tour for raiding operations off the us coast and a ceremonial visit to Newport. For tactical reasons she would run only one hundred of these miles submerged. The trip stretched the boat to her limits, however, and she ultimately had to break off the successful blockade because of shortages of provisions and fuel.

The operational orders issued to u-53 by von Holtzendorff on 11 September 1916, the day he rejected Scheer's views on the matter, had both tactical and political objectives. The ship was to screen the departure of the unarmed mercantile submarine *U-Bremen* from New London; once outside the American three-mile limit of jurisdiction, she was to sink belligerent vessels and any neutrals carrying contraband. Also, she was to visit Newport to show the neutral Americans the state of German submarine technology.

Unaware of *U-Bremen*'s loss, the German Admiralty still expected the freighter to arrive in New London, Connecticut, by 15 September. They also assumed that enemy forces, especially the British, would patrol the eastern approaches to Long Island Sound in order to prevent her departure. u-53's immediate priority was to attack these ships. But she was to do so only "insofar as they are met outside [American] territorial waters, and outside a line drawn from Montauk Point Light (eastern corner of Long Island) to South East Light on Block Island, and [across to] Gay Head." The orders specifically cautioned Captain Rose that the Americans considered the area inside this line as inland waters and would therefore insist on exercising jurisdiction.

Once her primary attack mission was completed – or should she find the enemy either absent or within American territorial waters –

U-53 was to enter Newport. The visit had a twofold purpose: to provide US naval authorities an opportunity to visit the submarine and to have the Americans intern any prisoners she might have taken from British ships. Her orders required her to exercise "due regard for the enemy who cannot be assumed with certainty to observe American neutrality at all." Nor was she to assume that the British would refrain from encroaching into US inland waters in pursuit of an enemy warship.

Whatever the preliminary action prior to entering Newport, the visit had to be brief. The orders required U-53 to depart "at most after a few hours so that [American] authorities do not have time to find pretexts for holding the U-boat." Once having cleared harbour, she was clear to "wage mercantile war according to the Prize Ordinance," but only "in so far as this is possible without endangering the U-Boat." She could expect to rendezvous with another U-boat between the Faroes and the Hebrides, at which point she would once again communicate in cipher, on the 800-metre band, through the naval radio station at Nauen.

Captain Rose found his orders very promising. Indeed they struck him as especially significant in light of Commodore Bauer's almost casual remark about the mission's strategic significance: the Naval War Office was counting on the fact that U-53's appearance in the United States about the beginning of October would coincide almost precisely with the German invasion of Romania. These simultaneous events, it was felt, would sweep aside the restrictions that up till then had prevented full development of the submarines' war on Allied commerce.

The voyage of U-53 would also raise new and important questions of international law.[65] Already well established was the right of belligerent surface warships to enter neutral ports and remain there for a limited period. Article 9 of the Hague Convention (1907) prescribed certain rules that such vessels had to observe in such ports but in no way restricted the right of neutral governments to refuse entry if they deemed that such vessels failed in any way to conform to neutrality regulations. Belligerent warships could not, for example, take on fuel, provisions, or ammunition. To do so would in effect constitute use of the neutral harbour as a base of operations. Neutral countries were required by international law to forbid such use.

What was not quite so clear, however, was the obligation of neutral governments with regard to belligerent submarines. Should the rules applicable to belligerent surface vessels apply also to ships that navigate beneath the surface? *U-Deutschland*, an unarmed mercantile sub-

marine of a belligerent nation, had stretched the interpretation of
international law during her stay in neutral American waters. Significantly, however, neutral governments did not interpret the rule
uniformly.

This inconsistency proved advantageous to the Allies and moved
Britain and France to lobby for an embargo on German u-boats. The
latter two countries had sent a memorandum to all neutral countries
in August 1916 urging prohibition from their national territories of
all "belligerent submarines, whatever their purpose." Significantly,
North American newspapers like the *Ottawa Evening Journal*, the
Manitoba Free Press, and the *New York Times* would publish the text of
the memorandum on 10 October 1916, just three days after the
combat submarine u-53 had entered Newport. New submarine technology, the memorandum argued, now meant that "the application
of the principles of the law of nations is affected by special and novel
conditions: first, by the fact that these vessels can navigate and remain
at sea submerged and can escape all control and observation; second,
by the fact that it is impossible to identify them and establish their
national character, whether neutral or belligerent, combatant or non-
combatant, and to remove the capacity for harm inherent in the
nature of such vessels."[66] Submarines, it was further stated, should
be excluded from privileges accorded to belligerent surface vessels;
any such submarine entering a neutral port should therefore be
detained.

u-53 departed Wilhelmshaven on 15 September 1916 – her destination: the staging point Heligoland. Wretchedly heavy weather prevented her onward journey from Heligoland until the 17th, when
u-53 once again braved open waters in the face of an unseasonably
sudden onrush of a North Atlantic low-pressure area which tossed
the seas in awesome confusion. Secured to the conning tower by steel
cables, the upper-deck watch rode through the storm that threatened
at any moment to swamp the deeply laden u-boat. As Rose noted in
his log, the submarine was too heavy to take the huge stern-seas
comfortably; breakers rolled over the bridge, filling the tower and
threatening to wash the watch overboard as the u-boat clawed her
way from Heligoland to the Shetlands. Loss of her antennae mast
prevented further contact with Nauen.[67]

At times the u-boat struggled with powerful structural stresses that
caused her skipper grave concern: "In heavy weather the u-boat
would slam into the sea with powerful headlong thrusts; the shaft
and drive gear of the forward horizontal rudders, which pounded
the ocean like huge outstretched hands, would groan – enough to

fill you with horror. For hours on end Chief Engineer [C.] Moeller and I would sit in the forward compartments, expecting at any moment some disastrous catastrophe. Nothing could calm us but confidence in the material – and thank God we were justified in that." Had the weather not eased by 24 September, Rose would have cancelled the mission.

As it was, fourteen storm-tossed days strained the crew to the limit of their endurance. Living conditions were harsh and barely tolerable. Dampness seeped everywhere. Those in the forward compartments slept in constantly soaked hammocks and woollen blankets that were not even dry on the U-boat's return to Germany. The aft compartments, perhaps because nearer the engines, fared somewhat better. In the course of time the crew fell victim to feelings of debilitating lethargy occasioned by lack of movement, exercise, and fresh air, by the cramped living quarters, and by the constantly throbbing machinery and the churning of their submarine. Brief visits to the upper deck were rare: not until after fourteen days on the outbound leg, and not at all during the return. Energy, victuals, and fresh water were used sparingly: one washed the kitchen and eating utensils in salt water, drank controlled amounts of boiled fresh water, saved unconsumed tea and coffee – and did not bathe. Yet illness struck only once.

Rose finally dived to escape the full brunt of the low front, working wearily northward until he had reached the northern tip of the Shetlands and could break into the open Atlantic. The weather had taken its toll. The buoyancy tanks which had been converted into bunkers were leaking oil, the deck gun's watertight seal had broken, engines were labouring, stores had torn loose from their stowage, and the compass and repeaters no longer registered true. Hasty repairs began once the storm had abated.

Apart from brief interludes, the stormy weather covered the route from Rockall Bank to Newfoundland's Grand Bank. Astronomical navigation was frequently impossible. U-53 ran largely by dead reckoning until the skies had cleared or the first landfall had been reached. Only when Rose had first reached open water did he share his orders with his crew. Despite their fatigue, they found the news exhilarating. The cook, who claimed to have visited the United States, now regaled his shipmates with yarns of the New World: skyscrapers, easy money, automobiles, fast living – and space. Their captain further reminded them that this was also the land of James Fennimore Cooper's *Leatherstocking Tales*. The book was still popular in German schoolboy circles of the day.

Rose's orders called for reaching his destination within twenty days of his departure from Germany. That meant 7 October at the latest. He could just manage it with a daily run of 185 nautical miles, if only the weather would improve. On 24 September, nine days after having left Wilhelmshaven, Rose expressed concern in his log about his slow advance in heavy weather. Any additional delays would force him to abort operations. Lack of news about *U-Bremen* continued to cause him concern. By now she should have long since reached the United States, and radio broadcasts should have been announcing her arrival. But radio news services remained silent. By 28 September the weather had eased sufficiently to allow the crew to bathe on deck under a jury-rigged shower. This was the day U-53 received her last signal from radio station Nauen, near Berlin. The garbled message led Rose to construe it as a relayed arrival signal from *U-Bremen* in New London. This was wishful thinking.

U-53 reached the Newfoundland Bank in fog and light drizzle on 2 October and dived to avoid detection by Canadian forces. When five days out of Newport she picked up her first piece of spurious news of *U-Bremen*. As recorded in her log, an unidentified American station announced that a "submarine named Bremen is captured by the Allies and a third [U-boat] of the same name is now on the way to the United States." No matter what had actually happened, Rose concluded, he could no longer expect his sister ship alongside in New London – "unless of course the signal is the irresponsible chatter of some shipboard wireless." The sports news that followed confirmed a shore station.

The loss of *U-Bremen* would in his words have "no impact on the execution of our task." That, at any rate, was Rose's first recorded reaction to the situation. His tactical summary at the end of the mission suggests, however, that it had really given him serious pause. Indeed it had caused him to consider giving up the planned journey to Long Island Sound altogether, "in order to seek military success off Halifax." It was fear not of the Canadians that made him hold his course but of the Nova Scotia fog. Besides, his summary concluded, "the absurdities of the radio news were so unreliable" that no departure from the original mission was justified.

The "magnificent sunshine" that Rose recorded in his log on approaching the American coast facilitated the much-needed upper-deck work in preparation for the U-boat's ceremonial visit. She soon picked up the Sankaty Light and headed for Muskaget Bay, where Rose suspected the anchorage of "enemy cruisers waiting" for *U-Bremen*. "Ciphered wireless traffic" suggested the presence of British ships. U-53 remained anchored in fog about four hours just south of Martha's Vineyard until "the amplitude of enemy wireless suggested a [seaborne] transmitter in the immediate vicinity" and prompted her to weigh and proceed toward the western side of the entrance to Long Island Sound.

u-53 cruised off the entrance to New London throughout the night of 7 October without sighting anything suspicious. She entered Block Island Sound at dawn, passed around Block Island in the direction of Gay Head, and by noon was well inside American inland waters. Rose described the scene twenty years later in a bravura passage written especially for a propaganda publication. As one of his sailors boasted: "We've come over here to show the Americans our teeth, let's give 'em something to remember."[68]

u-53's grand entry into harbour after accepting an escort by the American submarine d-2 countered the principal argument put forward in the British and French memorandum of 16 August. In no way could it now be claimed that u-53 was trying to "escape all control and observation" to which surface vessels were normally subject. Nor indeed was it difficult for the neutral Americans to "identify [her] and establish [her] national character, whether neutral or belligerent, combatant, or non-combatant."

The aide to Admiral Austin C. Knight, commander of Newport Naval District, was the first American to board the submarine. He was soon followed by an officer representing Admiral Albert Gleaves, commander, Destroyer Force, in uss *Birmingham*. Captain Rose then responded with protocol visits to both senior American officers.

In an extract of his preliminary report to us naval authorities, which he released to the press on 10 October, Admiral Knight commented:

At 3 p.m. the commanding officer of the u-53, Lieutenant Hans Rose, came on shore in a boat furnished by the uss *Birmingham* and called on me officially. He was in the uniform of a Lieutenant of the German navy, wearing the Iron Cross, and stated, apparently with pride, that his vessel was a man-of-war, armed with guns and torpedoes. He stated that he had no object in entering the port except to pay his respects; that he needed no supplies or assistance, and that he hoped to go to sea at six o'clock. He stated that he left Wilhelmshaven seventeen days ago, touching at Heligoland.

The freedom with which [the German] officers and crew conversed with [their American] visitors, and their willingness to show all parts of the ship were very surprising. They stated that they were willing to tell all they knew and to show all that they had – this to officers and civilians alike.[69]

Rose's report of proceedings provides the other perspective:

Except when dealing with responsible officers representing official views, the u-boat's reception was quite warm. Younger [American] officers frequently took our watch-officers aside to encourage them to sink British cruisers; many expressed the sincere wish for our success. From many quarters – naval and civilian alike – my officers were repeatedly invited for tea or dinner, and questions as to how they might offer us kindnesses did not cease. The u-boat was always surrounded by a swarm of rowboats and motorboats; the nautical and technical achievement of the ocean passage received full praise.

Much to Rose's surprise, Admiral Gleaves arrived alongside at 4:30 p.m. with his wife and daughter. By both their accounts the German u-boat commander and the American admiral got on well from the start. Rose emphasized the importance of this personal visit both in his log and in his memoirs. Certainly he took special pleasure in receiving a senior officer who took a keen and experienced professional interest in the vessel. Gleaves later filed detailed and perceptive reports on the u-boat's equipment and on the deportment of her crew.[70] In the words of Rose's log: "I took him [Gleaves] through the whole boat just as I had done several younger officers previously. The diesel engines awakened in all of them envious enthusiasm. Then followed a great many officers with their ladies, civilians, reporters and photographers. The crew received all kinds of small gifts." The Germans were particularly interested in receiving American newspapers.

Rose sensed a changed atmosphere as soon as Gleaves had departed. Admiral Knight's office now requested that Rose forbid further visits pending quarantine clearance, a formality in fact long since completed. But by this time Rose had gained the uncomfortable feeling that Washington had become involved. Perhaps, he mused, American neutrality was at best only apparent; perhaps it was even an incompletely muted animosity toward German interests. No American records corroborate his suspicions. He was in any event about to leave. After only two and one-half hours in port, as his log records, u-53's visit had already "achieved the intended effect in the United States." u-53 therefore weighed anchor, cleared harbour, executed a test dive, and set course for the Nantucket light-ship. In the words of Admiral Knight, "He steamed out to sea and entered upon the work of destroying enemy commerce as a thoroughly accredited man-of-war."[71]

The cruiser warfare that u-53 had been waging according to prize rules would soon hazard any public-relations points the ceremonial visit had made. Within a few hours, Americans would awaken to what had happened once the Germans had reached the open sea. According to press reports, Newport had been "Aroused by [the] u-boat's Raid." In the words of the New York Times: "No one had thought of the long gray visitor as a destroyer of shipping and perhaps of lives."[72] The Kaiser, however, would express his pleasure in a personal letter to Kapitänleutnant Rose.[73]

- 7 -

The "Piracy" of U-53

Operational Intelligence had faced a virtual blackout of wireless intercepts during U-53's voyage and was taken completely by surprise. The North American intelligence community now took the slenderest of threads and wove a pattern of enticing intricacy. Captain Rose's suspicions about Washington's involvement had of course been correct. However, the network of information and disinformation stretched beyond the internal links of the US navy and the American government. On 7 October 1916 the ill-informed British ambassador in Washington, Sir Cecil Spring Rice, cabled the governor-general of Canada, the Duke of Connaught, sending him a skimpy and inaccurate cipher that misconstrued the most obvious: the skipper's name and the U-boat's armament.[1] It had been abundantly clear, in the words of US Admiral Austin M. Knight, that U-53 carried not one gun (as Spring Rice had reported) but "two guns in a conspicuous position."[2] Spring Rice had also neglected to mention features that had attracted visitors' special attention: her four torpedo tubes, her ten torpedoes, and her powerful diesel engines.

In the event, diplomatic, naval, and undercover reports that reached Vice-Admiral Kingsmill provided less information than the American public could read in its daily newspapers. One wonders why the ambassador had not simply sent along copies of the *New York Times*. Certainly, the German naval attaché had supplied the state secretary of the Imperial Naval Office not only with a full report on the public impact of the visit but also with a bundle of rather revealing newspaper clippings as well.[3]

Within hours of sending the first cipher – which took four days to reach the Canadian navy, via the Duke of Connaught and the undersecretary of state – the British ambassador wired the governor-general even leaner amplification: "Press agency informs me that

German submarine left Newport at 5:17 p.m. after landing des-
patches for German Ambassador. An appointment has been arranged
by him with the [US] President for October 9th."[4]

This and other British diplomatic messages failed to explain what
newspapers had already correctly reported: that the German ambassador had made this appointment with the president a week earlier
in order to discuss the thorny issue of Polish relief. Admittedly, the
appointment now gave the president an opportunity to respond to
U-53's visit, but, as newspapers had pointed out, the meeting had not
been triggered by the new turn of events. British diplomats none the
less continued to give advice to Canadian authorities with seemingly
no reference whatever to information readily available publicly. As a
result, the secrecy of official communications – based on "reliable
sources" within a supposedly covert net – lent misplaced credence to
what recipients could only construe as higher intelligence sources.[5]

Shortly thereafter the commander-in-chief, North America and
West Indies Station, advised Naval Service Headquarters that U-53
could be expected off Halifax on the night of 8 October.[6] He had in
all likelihood simply assessed the submarine's speed of advance and
stepped off the distances on a nautical chart in order to estimate her
radius of action; this was a perfectly logical step for a navigator with
even a modest tactical sense.

On 10 October Ambassador Spring Rice again communicated by
cipher with Connaught. Like the traditional saw, the ambassador's
message contained both good news and bad. The good news hinted
at the economic advantage that U-boat warfare in American waters
would bring to Canada: "A friend suggests that Canadian papers
should welcome operations of German Submarines off New York on
the grounds that allies will now use Canadian ports exclusively, which
will have a great [adverse] effect here [in the United States] in shipping circles."

Canadian newspapers did not share the ambassador's view. The
Manitoba Free Press, for example, thought the reverse effect more
likely: shippers would turn away from Canada in favour of southern
US ports in order to escape the blockade. The bad news from Washington raised the spectre of attack, for the ambassador's "friend" had
heard "from German sources that [a] mine-laying Submarine has
been sent to [the] mouth of [the] Bay of Fundy and St Lawrence
River."[7] The naval radio station at Camperdown, near Halifax, next
intercepted a cipher from the British naval attaché in New York to
Admiralty in London reporting a serious German escalation: "Apparently good sources at Newport say [that] German submarines U-53,
54, and 61 are all on this coast."[8]

St John's radio then intercepted a cable from the British consul-general in Boston that a submarine had actually been sighted in Boston Bay.[9] The sighting was of course false. Indeed, as the German newspaper *Weser-Zeitung* would later explain: "With all the fear spread abroad, excited people will believe they have seen one more u-boat in every empty butter crate drifting at sea."[10] The attaché's "good sources" were equally unreliable; they turned out in fact to be rather speculative and public. Before long, newspapers throughout Germany and as far removed from the action as Salzburg, Geneva, and Stockholm had drawn on "reliable New York sources" in announcing that u-53, "u-48," and u-61 were engaged in covert operations off the North American coast.[11]

Anticipating an attack on the St Lawrence River, the British consul in New York sent a plain-language warning to Admiral Kingsmill, via the Great North Western Telegraph Co. Couched in the often-transparent language of espionage, it warned "Kingsmill Villa, Ottawa [of a] Big Fish ranging up stream." It then urged the view that "extra large nets quick will make big haul below Montreal." Of course, Canada's anti-submarine nets – the only ones in service – offered no protection whatever to St Lawrence waters "below Montreal," some hundreds of miles from the open sea. They were solidly in place, deep inside the approaches to Halifax harbour, on the Atlantic coast of Nova Scotia. Nor had Kingsmill any means of finding "extra large nets" anywhere – and certainly no means of installing them quickly. If the term *nets* were a code for "anti-submarine patrols" it was equally misplaced, for there was no possibility of Canada's few and ill-equipped patrol vessels sealing off the St Lawrence River and Gulf.

Confirmation of the threat to Canadian waters came from other sources. On 12 October the chief commissioner of the Dominion Police in Ottawa passed to Kingsmill a detailed report from Pinkerton's agent no. 4 in Newport: "u-53 was going to get after some of the troop ships leaving Halifax and other Canadian Ports for France and England."[12] Two days later, the British consul in New York sent Kingsmill a curious urgent cipher: "I learn from something vague that shipping in St Lawrence River is to be attacked by German Submarines." Operations would "commence almost at once."[13] By this time the us navy had gathered detailed technical information on u-53 and her armament, crew, and mission.[14]

Kingsmill immediately stepped up precautions on the east coast. Naval wireless stations began to listen on the frequency normally used by the German fleet, while officers in the dockyard "telephone[d] fishing centres along the coast warning [them] of [the] proximity of [the] submarine and instructing them to keep a lookout" and recruited trustworthy civilians to serve as coast-watchers.[15] Anticipating instructions from Admiralty in London, Kingsmill had war warnings broadcast to merchant ships at sea, telling them to "take every precaution [because a] possible armed German Submarine may be off the Canadian coast."[16] He cautioned outbound vessels to depart only after dark or else in poor visibility, in order to obtain as good an offing as possible before daylight, and to extinguish all their lights on leaving harbour.[17]

By 9 October the militia chief of the general staff, Major-General W. Gwatkin, had committed eight companies of the Ninety-fourth Regiment, consisting of twenty-one officers and 338 other ranks, for guard duties in Cape Breton. Quite unnecessarily, he reminded Kingsmill of the possible need to defend "Sydney and other defended points [as the] Submarine carries a gun."[18] (The American public knew she actually carried two). Gwatkin instructed the military district commander at Halifax to co-operate with the captain superintendent of Halifax; he should also assist "civil authorities in giving effect to [the] wishes of Naval Commander-in-Chief [Vice-Admiral M.E. Browning, who had succeeded Vice-Admiral Patey in the station flagship, HMS *Leviathan*, only weeks earlier] regarding lights and other defensive arrangements at Halifax."[19] In all things, the army was to "avoid alarm, but look out for possible submarine attack." In his directions to the army, he clearly envisaged the traditional cruiser-style warfare of shore bombardment.

Vice-Admiral Browning's response to the anticipated attacks on 8 October was extreme under the circumstances. But it was entirely consistent with the fears that Patey had expressed in 1915 about the vulnerability of the rather elderly and slow cruisers on the North American station. Browning withdrew his entire squadron into the safety of Bedford Basin and extinguished the inner leading lights on both George Island and the Dartmouth shore. The outer reaches he left to a single patrol vessel from the harbour Examination Service.

Browning further requested that the Canadian government consider extinguishing all coastal navigation lights, according to the practice at British defended ports. Kingsmill's assessment of this proposal for Hazen, minister for the naval service, was astute and sound. Indeed, he anticipated the decision taken twenty-three years later at the onset of the Second World War: "Halifax is not merely a Defended Port as are those spoken of as Defended Ports in the United Kingdom[;] Halifax [is] one of our important shipping ports and Harbours of Refuge, and it seems to me that by a short notice of extinguishing coast lights leading to the approaches to Halifax, we might lose more shipping and tonnage than submarines could account for than even taking into consideration the possibility and probability of there being several of them on this side of the Atlantic."[20] The lights remained on.

Canada still faced the pressing problem of utterly inadequate anti-submarine patrols.[21] Understandably, some Nova Scotians were by this time openly alarmed at the weakness of the coastal defences. In the words of one mayor, "There is considerable unrest amongst the people of Pictou during the recent presence of submarines on the Atlantic coast."[22] He wondered "if the protection of Pictou Harbour, and the Steel plant was receiving consideration" by naval authorities. Desbarats, deputy minister for the navy, responded with assurances that "the defence of Atlantic sea ports is continually kept in mind and all possible action [is being] taken with ships available."[23] His letter said everything and nothing. Defence was obviously on everybody's mind, and the tiny service was indeed doing everything it could, but that was very little.

The RCN patrol scheme was, of course, designed to give the best general coverage of the sea approaches allowed by the flotilla's very limited capabilities. However, the slow and small patrol craft could not, as Kingsmill had so insistently warned in 1915, directly protect high-value ships by escorting them to a safe distance of 200 miles or more from the coast. Now, in light of the Admiralty's repeated discouragement of Canadian acquisition of fast anti-submarine escort warships, Kingsmill had no choice but to declare that "overseas transport is in the hands of Admiralty" in London.[24] He so advised both Admiralty and Browning. The latter, who was alongside at Halifax in HMS *Leviathan*, offered an interim solution: "Every effort should be made to protect His Majesty's Ships and transports in approaches to the port of Halifax" until at least the end of October 1916, "and all patrol vessels armed with 12 pounder guns and above should concentrate here accordingly."[25] The British admiral's decision to redeploy the Gulf patrol to Halifax was a desperate measure that underscored the vulnerability of Canadian waters.

It was still quite incomprehensible to both professional sailors and the public that attack submarines could really operate so far from home without local logistical support. Like many other North American newspapers, the *Halifax Herald* speculated that the Germans were constructing huge supply boats. It even seemed possible that the "Deutschland was built as [a] Supply Ship for Hun Subs."[26] Indeed it was "evident to anyone," a submarine expert was quoted from Paris, "that the submarine as a cargo carrier is not a commercial proposition." It must therefore be a mother-ship. For this reason, Browning proposed that one of his own ships search "Saint Pierre and Newfoundland Great Bank ... for the enemy's submarine supply ship." Any patrol vessels that Kingsmill found unsuitable for work off Halifax, he added, would of course be most welcome to join the hunting groups.

Evasive routing of commercial vessels was the only other defensive option. In fact, tightening of naval control of shipping in 1916 was an empire-wide policy. The RCN's contribution, through its expanded "Transport" staffs at Halifax, Saint John, Sydney, Quebec, and Montreal, was both major and important. Among other things, it enabled Canadians to support the convoy system in 1917. The necessary instructions were passed to merchantmen through the port Examination Service at Halifax and customs officers at other ports. Vessels leaving Canadian ports received a departure course and a terminal break-off point, whence they would sail independent of naval control. They would depart after nightfall in order to minimize the chance of being caught by u-boats lurking in the close approaches to ports, where shipping was easier prey; ships would then "clear the land by 200 miles and take unusual courses" to their destination.[27] To secure North American coastal trade against the immediate threat, Kingsmill advised "ships proceeding to neutral ports [to] make land some distance from their destination and keep inside territorial waters." In addition, Kingsmill arranged for naval wireless stations to broadcast suspected positions of u-boats on a commercial shipping frequency. A rash of possible u-boat sightings underscored the urgency and importance of these measures.

By engaging American naval officers and civilians at Newport with his "ostentatious frankness," Captain Hans Rose of u-53 had learned that enemy warships frequently patrolled near the lightships of Nantucket Shoals and Ambrose Channel; they could even be met off Block Island.[28] Some civilians had informed him further that he would always find either a British or a French cruiser lying off New York with the express mission of preventing the departure from New York of German vessels from the major shipping lines.

Since their institution in August 1914, these British patrols had been an irritant to Anglo-American relations. Many leading American officials and politicians bitterly resented this virtual blockade. The German ambassador to Washington supported the American view. In March 1916, for example, Count von Bernstorff complained to US Secretary of State Robert Lansing about Britain's "systematically escalated rape of neutrals according to the principle 'might is right'."[29]

Periodic American protest notes were no secret. Lansing's most recent note was published in the *New York Times* on 9 October 1916, one day after the departure of U-53. The US government, it emphasized, "has always regarded the practice of belligerent cruisers patrolling American coast on close proximity to the territorial waters of the United States and making the neighborhood a station for their observations as inconsistent with the treatment to be expected from the naval vessels of a friendly power in time of war[,] and has maintained that the consequent menace to the freedom of American commerce is vexatious and uncourteous to the United States."[30]

The British had complied under duress by withdrawing the cruisers HMS *Essex* and *Cumberland* from the New York patrol. The French cruiser *Corida* and two other British cruisers had taken up distant patrols to the south and the north respectively. The American press would soon remind its government how hypothetical the official interpretation of "cruiser warfare" really was. For it quickly became clear that U-53, having enjoyed American hospitality, was no less involved in "belligerent cruiser patrols" than British warships. U-53 proved itself far more belligerent than the Allied cruisers by actually sinking ships.

Aboard U-53, Captain Rose was unaware of these ramifications – or was unconcerned about them – and was weighing his chances of intercepting enemy warships near the Ambrose Channel lightship. By now he was worried about having lost all element of surprise; he was equally concerned that the thirty-metre depths off New York were too shallow for submarine attacks against merchant vessels. The Nantucket Shoals lightship, by contrast, offered two distinct advantages: the possibility even now of catching warships doggedly awaiting the overdue *U-Bremen* and "the swarm of steamships that tends to depart American harbours on Saturdays and might still be picked off here."[31] Five vessels would fall victim to her attacks while seventeen neutral American destroyers looked on.[32]

At 5:35 a.m. on 8 October 1916, on an almost cloudless, calm morning some two miles off the Nantucket Shoals lightship, U-53 fired a shot across the bows of the American vessel ss *Kansan*, bound from New York to Genoa via Boston. Riding low in the dawn light, the surfaced U-boat was at first almost invisible to the merchantman, whose skipper immediately radioed the Nantucket lightship of her plight. He thus sounded the first warning of the submarine attacks. Rose remained confident to the end that he had "successfully jammed her radio signals." He was mistaken.

Intercepted and retransmitted in cipher by communicators aboard the Nantucket Shoals lightship, all radio transmissions of the day got through to American authorities, though not without occasional editing.[33] A presidential order of 1914 prohibited all "radio stations within the jurisdiction of the United States . . . from transmitting or receiving for delivery messages of an unneutral nature, and from in any way rendering unneutral service."[34] Thus the Marconi station at Siasconett refused *Kansan*'s call that she had been stopped and searched by a German submarine and advised the ship to "omit word 'German' as it was unneutral" and retransmit.[35] SOS messages none the less reached as far as Ottawa by direct maritime radio link.[36]

U-53 herself maintained radio silence throughout. This certainly prevented Operational Intelligence from tracking her. While *Kansan* sought advice from the incredulous lightship, which claimed no knowledge of any German submarine in the vicinity, U-53 ordered her by flashing light to deliver her papers for inspection. The skipper proved to Rose's satisfaction that his ship belonged to the American-Hawaiian Line, with a cargo of soda for Genoa. (Subsequent American reports claimed she carried steel for the Italian government.) Rose allowed her to proceed at 6:15 a.m. Heading now in a southwesternly direction, Rose considered his options. As he wrote in his war diary, he did not want to "attack a larger passenger steamer because of the difficulty of rescuing passengers." In the event, circumstances would cause him to sink one anyway. For the moment, however, he sought only cargo ships.

At 6:53 a.m. he sighted the 4,321-ton Glasgow-registered steamer SS *Strathdene*, en route to Bordeaux under charter to the French Line. Several shots across the bow, followed by the light signal in English "Bring your papers," brought the vessel to a stop. Recognizing her as British, U-53 signalled for the crew to abandon ship. Two boats set out from *Strathdene*; according to Rose's log, they held a motley crew, "consisting of a few whites and mainly Chinese and Negroes." Realizing perhaps that his vessel would be destroyed anyway, Captain Wilson of *Strathdene* did not offer his papers to Rose. Once given their course to the Nantucket lightship, the lifeboats quickly set sail. Rose had little fear of their losing their way, for he could easily follow them by sight. At 7:43 a.m., almost an hour after having stopped her victim, U-53 fired a single torpedo with a three-metre depth-setting into her after hold. Her stern sagged low in the water; she nevertheless remained afloat while a new target drew U-53 away.

At 8:30 a.m., U-53 signalled the 3,878-ton Norwegian vessel *Christian Knudsen* to heave to. As one survivor recalled, the warning consisted of "three shots across the bow [with] a signal for our Captain to go aboard the submarine with the ship's papers."[37] She was carrying petroleum from New York to London and was therefore subject to capture. Rose now quickly issued a series of orders to the captain of *Christian Knudsen*. *Knudsen* should follow him back to the stricken *Strathdene*, abandon ship, and then stand by in boats while U-53 finished off *Strathdene*, sank *Knudsen*, and then towed all the lifeboats to the safety of the lightship. In the words of Rose's log, "The captain [of the merchantman] is happily surprised by this news."

With *Christian Knudsen* following, U-53 dashed ahead and at 9:52 a.m. sank the abandoned and drifting *Strathdene* by gun-fire. The crew of *Christian Knudsen* had meanwhile sailed off in its seaboats without awaiting the submarine's return. One of the boats was eventually picked up by the American destroyer USS *Drayton*.[38] U-53 now fired a torpedo with a four-metre depth-setting into the Norwegian vessel's stern. But she too refused to sink on the first shot. Raking her hull along the water-line with gun-fire brought the Germans no closer to success, for the heavy oil pouring out of the shell holes simply made the vessel ride higher on her increased buoyancy. At 10:54 a.m. Rose finished her off with a second torpedo. He then turned his attention to a third vessel approaching from the east.

U-53 stopped the inbound 3,847-ton British freighter *West Point* at 11:30 a.m. with shots across the bow and a flag signal ordering her to abandon ship. *West Point*'s repeated wireless signals broadcast her imminent danger and triggered U-53's hostile action even before the merchant crew had gotten into the boats: failing to jam her radio signals, the submarine silenced them by firing into the wireless cabin on the after deck. The signals had already gotten through – not only to Newport, but also to Boston, Halifax, and St John's. The latter advised Naval Service Headquarters in Ottawa.

While radio operators aboard the Nantucket Shoals lightship busily encoded and retransmitted traffic, ships at sea were relaying SOS signals according to maritime practice.[39] Thus SS *Philadelphia* in the western Atlantic intercepted *West Point*'s call and relayed it to St John's, giving the precise position of the attack; SS *Kansan*, now en route to Boston, notified Boston Navy Yard and reversed her course in order to retrace the approximately fifty-five miles to *West Point*'s aid.[40] The US governments radio station at Newport advised Rear-Admiral Albert Gleaves, commander of the Destroyer Force, who in turn ordered his ships to sea. This, however, took some time, as many members of the flotilla's crews were on Sunday leave.

West Point's determined signalling had aroused Rose's suspicion that she was actually a submarine decoy "Q-ship." Approaching his victim cautiously, he fired along the hull and upper deck to assure himself that she was not carrying concealed guns. The British had by now taken to the boats, and Rose ordered them to stand by while he sent his prize crew aboard to set the scuttling charges that eventually sank her at 12:35 p.m. Rose now feared the likelihood of having to face unfriendly warships. While *West Point*'s boats stood by, U-53 executed a test dive in order to prepare herself for the worst. Once submerged, Rose informed his crew that he would head for home just as soon as he had delivered the British steamer's crew to the Nantucket Shoals lightship.

It was not to be. When towing the boats two hours later through the wreckage of *Christian Knudsen* to within four miles of the lightship, Rose sighted a new target: the vessel seemed like a tanker outbound from New York but suddenly turned in her tracks as though warned of the submarine's presence. U-53 cast off the lines of the boats and set off in pursuit. A neutral vessel carrying grain to Norway, the Norwegian SS *Kapana* was eventually allowed to proceed.

Rose had by this time grown concerned about those survivors of *Christian Knudsen* who had disobeyed his instructions and sailed away without awaiting his return from sinking *Strathdene*. Not until 4:15 p.m. did he finally sight them. Drawing alongside, he gave their captain a stern lecture on the delays his intransigence had caused the U-boat. By now the considerable wireless activity along the coast that U-53 had been intercepting all afternoon had forced Rose to the unsettling conclusion that ships' wireless had managed to sound the alarm, despite his best efforts to silence them.

Indeed, it would have been no comfort to Rose to know that the news media had also gotten wind of the submarine's activities and were telegraphing the Nantucket Shoals lightship, offering to remunerate the radio operators for information. The lightship received radiograms from the Boston *Globe*, the New York *Sun* and *Herald*, and from the wire service of Associated Press. When the operators refused to accede or even reply, the *Herald* sent a schooner with a reporter from New Bedford. Despite the official clamp on information, survivors gave interviews which other "informed sources" corroborated.

At 4:55 p.m., U-53 stopped the 4,880-ton Holland-Amerika Line vessel *Blomersdijk*, outbound from New York to Rotterdam, and ordered her to deliver her papers by boat.[41] Before her captain, John H. Gunther-Mohr, could comply, Rose sighted a destroyer and dived. Satisfied that the warship was "only" an American heading for the Nantucket Shoals lightship, Rose surfaced at 5:30 p.m. The "intruder" was in fact USS *Drayton*, the first of eighteen destroyers deployed by Admiral Gleaves in Newport.[42] As the *New York Times* reported: "The departure of the destroyers was a spectacle that brought thousands of men, women and children to points of vantage on the shore or to small craft of all sorts, in which they kept as close to the warships as they could."[43]

Rose logged the German perspective: "At irregular intervals a rather large number of destroyers approached from Newport; the first of these to arrive at the lightship seems to pick up the crews of the vessels sunk this morning." The most difficult decision on sighting the first destroyer, Rose recalled, was whether to remain submerged or to surface: "By surfacing, we nurtured the possibility of direct belligerent conflict with the United States; but remaining submerged would have cost us all success in the operation. We therefore surfaced, and I can do nothing other than pay highest respects to the commanding officers of the destroyers for their completely neutral conduct."[44] Actually, the fact that USS *Drayton* and other destroyers picked up survivors left Americans open to charges of collusion, for the action had freed U-53 from her prize rules responsibilities and left her clear to destroy additional merchant ships.

U-53 once again ordered *Blomersdijk* to deliver her papers. Before her boat could manoeuvre alongside the submarine, yet another target approached from the east. Rose had by this time almost too much to handle – and he wanted both ships. He therefore fired a long-range warning shot in the direction of his newest target in order to prevent the vessel's closer approach. Obedient to international law, the ship hove to and awaited inspection. She was a passenger ship; her arrival on the scene caused the very confrontation that Rose had once hoped to avoid. In the sharp exchange of notes between the German and American governments the previous year, the American ambassador in Berlin had insisted that "the sinking of passenger ships involves principles of humanity which throw into the background any special circumstances of detail."[45]

The British-registered *Stephano*, of the Red Cross Line, had for the past five years been on her regular run between New York, Halifax, and St John's. Her company's latest and most modern vessel, she was this time bound for New York from Halifax, with 164 passengers and crew. Built with an ice-breaker hull for work in the ice of far northern waters, she had served with the Newfoundland sealing fleet and was completing one of her last trips on the triangle run before being delivered to her new Russian owners in Archangel.

As the *Halifax Herald* would announce at *Stephano*'s loss, "she was a splendid ship," of the most modern design: she was "fitted up with the Marconi system of wireless telegraphy, and bilge keels to prevent rolling[,] and a set of submarine signals [i.e. echo sounder] which told of the proximity of land or of sunken reefs."[46] Her sinking would trigger jubilation in the German newspaper *Kölnische Zeitung* that "German U-Boats have taken up the sea war off the Canadian coast."[47]

Captain Clifton Smith had been on *Stephano*'s bridge when she approached within four miles of the Nantucket lightship and sighted U-53. As he told reporters: "She fired a shot across our bows, and I slowed down. There were four shots by her altogether, about two minutes apart. None of them hit us. There were two American destroyers nearby at the time."[48]

Rose, in U-53, had not realized of course that Captain Smith had given the order to abandon ship as soon as *Stephano* had stopped. The reason for such unexpected haste is not clear. In his concern for passenger safety, he had complied to a fault with international law, neither running from the U-boat nor apparently even contemplating such an act. His passengers were at dinner and had time to gather coats and wraps before disembarking quietly in six of the eight available boats. They could have awaited U-53's disposition in greater safety and comfort aboard their vessel. Given Rose's concern about the safety of passengers, which of course no one aboard *Stephano* could possibly have appreciated, the vessel would in any case have been released.

Blomersdijk's papers had meanwhile proven incriminating. As Rose's log recorded, the ship was "fully loaded with both absolute and conditional contraband for ports in Holland." Absolute contraband, according to the London Declaration on the Law of the Sea of 1909, which the belligerents had never ratified, was easy to judge. It consisted of weapons and military supplies used exclusively for war purposes. Relative, or conditional contraband was more difficult to interpret and was subject to unilateral changes in definition. An early German definition explained it as "those goods and materials expressly declared as such by the German Empire."[49]

Perhaps even more serious, however, both the health certificate and American port certificate revealed her first port of call as Kirkwall, Scotland. The ship's officer later stated under oath that he had informed the Germans "that we only intended to touch Kirkwall in order to be examined by the British authorities"; he had shown his manifest and explained that the cargo "was meant for and [was] the property of the Netherland Government ... and that there were on board no cargo meant for any belligerent country." Crucial in German prize law was whether a vessel interrupted her journey (in this case in a belligerent port) and for whom the majority of cargo was destined.[50] Rose was caught on the horns of a dilemma as to which articles and codicils he should apply. It was also an open question, despite the certification of the Dutch consul-general in New York, whether the vessel were subject to confiscation.

In short, one set of rules permitted him to capture the vessel, the other to release it. Rose's juridical problem was heightened by the fact that German authorities – Ministry of Justice, Imperial Naval Office, and Ministry of the Interior – were constantly amending and reissuing prize rules in response to shifting strategic and political considerations. U-Boat captains needed a handy reference guide – one indeed that could stand up to the weather on an open bridge.[51]

The U-boat captain could not weigh the problem at leisure as a lawyer might have done. As his log records:

Under normal circumstances I would have inclined toward the milder view [of releasing the vessel]. But the circumstances here were such that, in order to spare American feelings, I [also] wanted to let the passenger vessel [*Stephano*] proceed unhindered after examining her papers; the growing darkness had until now prevented my ascertaining her citizenship. [But I also] had to take serious care not to awaken in all participants the impression that the presence of the American destroyers was urging me to yield meekly and renounce my rights. I therefore decided to be harsh and [when] 500 meters away from the *Blomersdijk* ordered her by flaghoist to abandon ship.

By 5:45 p.m., sixteen destroyers had converged on the area in which U-53 had been operating with impunity. A megaphone message from USS *Drayton* to USS *Fanning* provides a further example of US neutrality: "Do not interfere with German submarine and her legitimate prey or send out any message regarding location or movement of submarine. There are thirty survivors still on the lightship, who can come to you in their own boats. We have sixty-eight on board."[52]

Manoeuvring room sometimes became tight. In fact, as U-53 towed *Blomersdijk*'s messenger boat back to its ship in order to pick up other crew still aboard the vessel, the close approach of USS *Ericsson* forced the submarine to reverse engines in order to avoid collision. The vessels passed within fifty metres of one another.[53] Rose had granted the vessel twenty-five minutes to abandon ship – until 6:30 p.m. She was to haul down her flaghoist when cleared and ready for destruction.

Rose now turned his attention to the passenger ship *Stephano*. Finding her already abandoned and her passengers taken aboard the destroyers, he had time to reflect. As the destroyers' search-lights swept across the vessel, Rose identified her for the first time and confirmed it against Lloyd's Register. His report of proceedings would later note with some satisfaction that both *Stephano* and *West*

Point were cited in the "British List of Vessels [dated 29 June 1916] whose movements are treated as confidential at the request of their respective owners." This seems to have vindicated his action against them.

But as U-53's log explains: "After I had passed between the steamer [*Stephano*] and the destroyers I ran back to the *Blomersdijk* which the crew had meanwhile left without hauling down the flaghoist. By sounding my siren and calling through my megaphone, I ascertained that no one was on board. A destroyer [USS *Porter*] lying very close to the vessel was asked by morse to withdraw a bit so that the ship could be sunk. She acceded to this request immediately." A torpedo fired at 7:50 p.m. with a depth-setting of four metres struck *Blomersdijk* abaft the beam in the fourth cargo hold, causing her to sag markedly aft, but failing to sink her. A second torpedo exploded in the third hold at 8:20 p.m. Forty minutes later the ship slipped beneath the sea.

American destroyers passed through the vicinity of the wreckage, and most of them gradually dispersed toward Newport. USS *Benham* stood by the drifting and abandoned vessel after picking up survivors and was asked by U-53 to stand clear. While USS *McDougall* picked up another boatload, USS *Ericsson* (senior officer present) and USS *Drayton* followed U-53 back to *Stephano*.

Rose now sent his prize crew aboard her in order to set scuttling charges. One of his men took time to investigate the dining saloon and "saw resplendent on the tables the delights of both the Indies."[54] He filled bedsheets with provisions such as the Germans had not enjoyed for months; bananas, pineapple, grapes, grapefruit, duck, roast chicken, ham, and lobster. A combination of fate and poor maintenance decided otherwise. U-53's leaky boat began to sink as the prize crew rowed back, obliging the Germans to toss the bounty overboard in order to reach the safety of their submarine.

Though the prize crew had done its job, the exploding scuttling charges failed to sink the ship. *Stephano* next withstood artillery fire before succumbing to a torpedo shot at 10:30 p.m. The Amsterdam *Telegraaf* dubbed the sinking "a new act of piracy."[55] Her work completed, U-53 now headed eastward while the destroyers turned about and steamed west. Throughout the night, Rose tried in vain to report events by wireless to the German ambassador in Washington. The uneventful twenty-day voyage home was marked by violent seas that kept all hands below deck and by only occasional sightings.

If Rose's recollections some twenty years after the voyage were correct, the crew must have been exhilarated by the tonnage sunk off Newport. This certainly seems to have inspired them to sing patriotic songs, salty ballads, and the rousing verse of a "Pirate Song" that Rose would have us believe characterized the spirit of his crew throughout the war:

We thrust upon the enemy ships
Like an arrow shot from the bow;
The musket cracks, the cannon roar
The boarding axe lays 'em low.
The enemy falls, and heaven-ward lifts
Our jubilant cry at sea:
Long live the eternal ocean wide,
Long live our piracy.[56]

On that day, 10 October 1916, *U-Deutschland* slipped secretly out of Bremerhaven alone for her second voyage to the United States. Many observers were persuaded that German submarines had undermined the unwritten laws of humanity. In the words of a British propagandist working in the United States, the "brotherhood of the sea was a fine, manly freemasonry, and demanded from its members those qualities of courage, honour, and chivalry which are the true seaman's heritage." The rules had now changed: "Not until the coming of the German submarine commander was the Brotherhood of the Sea destroyed."[57]

News of U-53's visit and "piracy" hit the American press almost immediately. Blaring headlines, large photographs, eye-witness reports and "official" leaks, and pages of commentary told all there was to tell.[58] The *New York Times* announced on 9 October 1916: "German Submarines Sink 6 to 9 Ships off Nantucket; One a Liner with Many Americans ... Washington Sees Grave Perils in Raids off Our Coast." Stories tenaciously suggested that U-53 had not been alone but was accompanied by a mother ship or tender and by at least one other combat U-boat. These views had been corroborated to the press by the masters of *Stephano* and *Blomersdijk*. They were confirmed by crews of the US destroyers, "who said positively they had recognized two different boats, one painted white, and a little more than 200 feet long, presumably U-53, and another about two-thirds its length and painted gray."[59]

Journalists speculated about Britain's intentions after U-53's "day's work of havoc" beyond the three-mile limit. One report from Nantucket explained that three cruisers had already reached the lightship by 2:40 a.m. HMS *Essex* and *Cumberland*, then patrolling "in the vicinity of Currituck Inlet[, had] proceeded northward immediately." A report from Boston claimed "that British cruisers and patrol boats were already hurrying from Halifax." This was patently false. Indeed a "British naval reserve officer who was in New York" allegedly explained to the press that there were "no destroyers in Halifax Harbor that would be of use in the present emergency." However dubious the source, the statement was correct. The source was none the less curiously optimistic about Canadian capabilities: Halifax had "several powerboats that ... could be armed with three or four-inch guns and be very serviceable in chasing U-boats."

Assurances from "official sources in Washington" that strict neutrality would be maintained were widely reported. Even if the US government should "learn of the number and location of the submarines, it will not disclose anything which might be of assistance to the allied cruisers which will be sweeping the coast for them."[60] That in fact proved to be the case, but the press was virtually unanimous that U-53 had destabilized American neutrality. The U-boat had shown that "distance has been annihilated by new inventions."

By operating with such impunity, she had thrust an obvious warning and challenge in the face of US pacifists, who had long insisted "that everybody who is [militarily] formidable is thousands of miles away, and that the oceans are impregnable fortresses." Another commentator accused the Wilson administration of an inexcusable "failure through the last three years to prepare for the new conditions which modern inventions have developed." Both the *Boston Herald* and the *Journal* of Rhode Island pointed out that "the European war has been transferred to our shores"; this created for the *Public Ledger* of Philadelphia a situation whose "gravity can hardly be exaggerated." This "Prussian blockade [had] grossly violated" American neutrality. It was therefore "the highest duty" of the US government "to go to any length to put an end to this Prussian warfare in American waters without delay."[61]

US neutrality was now precarious at best, as New York's *Journal of Commerce* quite rightly asserted. In simply standing by to rescue the victims of U-53, the destroyers had now been "forced into partnership with the assailant"; American rescue operations had therefore removed all obstacles to U-53's commerce raids by effectively shielding her from the moral and legally binding obligation under international law to ensure the safety of her victims. But, in the words of an expert legal witness, American warships had no other option: they had "the absolute right to save life, but could not interfere in any attack."[62] This was also the view of Franklin Delano Roosevelt, at the time assistant secretary of the navy: the navy did not "violate their duty of neutrality" but acted in "absolute accordance with international law and the dictates of humanity."[63]

The German ambassador was elated. Broader U-boat operations in the western Atlantic required "a good working basis" with the Americans if the Germans were not to be burdened by responsibilities imposed by the prize rules. "We now have created a basis that smoothes the road for our submarine activity on this side of the ocean," he wrote to a colleague. The welcome "precedent guarantees that American ships will not hesitate to rescue passengers and crew of sunken ships."[64]

This tactic of drawing the United States into tacit co-operation was short-lived. Apparently leaked to the press, the incriminating letter betrayed Count von Bernstorff's expectations in the *Providence Journal*. German intelligence recognized the newspaper as one that had "uncovered many earlier German plots." By this time other papers had picked up the theme in a gradual turning of public opinion against neutrality. The *Pall Mall* of London insisted that this breach of international law by a German warship required Britain to set up counter patrols and "destroy the pirates" at every chance.[65]

American commentators focused primarily on the legal issues involved in the visit of U-53. Questions of military might, of defence preparedness, and of expediency were clearly secondary. If U-53 had indeed remained in the international waters and had in fact obeyed the prize rules on cruiser warfare, so arguments ran, then the United States would have no legal grounds whatever for protesting even the mere presence of the submarine. Where some voices insisted without evidence that U-53 had complied with international law, other voices argued the opposite view. Some indeed claimed that U-53 had "initiated a revival of [that] relentless [unrestricted] U-boat warfare" that in 1915 had almost led to a break in relations between Germany and the United States. In this light, debate about legalities was merely academic. In the words of the *New York Herald*: "Whatever the technical rules may be that a submarine is able to evade, it cannot indulge in performances of this kind without doing outrageous damage to neutral trade."

More serious to the Allies than the actual loss of ships to U-53 was the blow her mission dealt to the confidence of the shipping and commercial communities. Stock markets fluctuated uneasily, marine insurance rates increased as much as 400 per cent, and some ports temporarily suspended war-risk coverage on cargoes. Cotton prices fell drastically, a serious blow to a major industry. The cumulative

effect of these shifts, many feared, would slow down shipping between
New York and European ports. The famous firm of Furness Withy
and Co., owners of *West Point*, which had fallen victim to u-53, had
already announced temporary suspension of further sailings of company ships. Other lines quickly followed suit.

The International Mercantile Marine had advised its agents in
Boston, Baltimore, Philadelphia, Portland, and Montreal to hold
back in their respective ports all vessels under British flag. In the
United States this action stopped the sailings of Atlantic Transport,
Dominion, Leyland, Red Star and White Star Line; in Canada it
prevented ships of Dominion and White Star from departing Montreal and Quebec in the St Lawrence River. This "new phase of u-boat
warfare," German newspapers explained in notes datelined Montreal, had closed down Canadian ports.[66] Until such times as Britain
could restore lost confidence, only fast, armed merchant ships and
liners dared leave North American ports.

Cunard Lines ships, with their speed and four-inch guns, ran the
gauntlet. So too did Italian Lines, whose ships carried two three-
inch guns aft. *Dante Alighieri* had already sailed from New York on
8 October, the day of u-53's attacks; the armed freighter *San Guglielmo*
had followed in her wake. Passenger lines continued to maintain
regular advertised schedules between Europe and North American
ports.[67] On 11 November 1916, for example, no fewer than four huge
liners departed New York independently for Liverpool, Bordeaux,
and Naples. Galling as it was to the Germans, Cunard's *Carpathia*
carried Canadian soldiers from the supposedly neutral port of New
York. As one observer noted: "Persons who went to the piers along
the North River ... to see the four liners sail for Europe with well-
filled cabins found it difficult to realize that a war was waging on the
other side of the Atlantic."[68]

Within three days of the attacks, the British government was mus-
tering an official protest to Washington about the American handling
of the crisis. The Foreign Office forwarded a litany of complaints to
Spring Rice: the Americans had requested British warships not to
hover or patrol in the very waters in which u-53 had now operated
with such impunity; they had pressured Britain not to arm merchant
ships visiting us ports, thus rendering the vessels virtually defenceless; and they had refused to discuss the propriety of allowing belligerent submarines to visit American ports and, in this case, had even
allowed the Germans to obtain information regarding clearances and
arrivals of merchant ships.[69]

While the Foreign Office discussed its complaints with the American ambassador in London, and awaited the results of Spring Rice's

discussions in Washington, the latter hesitated. "We should keep silence so far as possible in [the] submarine question," he explained, "and leave [the] issue to the United States Government and people."[70] He suggested that it would be better to reduce dependence on American ports by using tugs and barges to transport goods to Nova Scotian ports for transshipment to Britain. He apparently did not inform the Foreign Office of the "dire warnings" of U-boat threat that he had sent to the Canadians. At any rate he seems to have been unaware that Admiralty had already, in the spring of 1915, rejected a proposal for diverting traffic from New York to Halifax because of "inadequate railway and port facilities at [the] latter place, and disastrous delays which might in consequence result."[71] The Foreign Office now advised the ambassador of Admiralty's view. No evidence suggests that Canadians had ever been informed of this assessment.[72]

On 13 October 1916 Spring Rice sent a nine-page report to the Foreign Office in which he surveyed the historical background of submarine warfare and political relations between Britain and the United States; he examined selected aspects of the visits of *U-Deutschland* and U-53 and reviewed the American government's attitude to submarine warfare and armed merchantmen. American attitudes toward Germany were becoming much less friendly, he reported. This was caused in no small part by "Sir Gilbert Parker's admirable organisation," whose covert propaganda efforts had been helping to sway American public opinion in support of British war aims.[73]

Spring Rice confirmed that U-53's attacks had sent insurance rates sky-rocketing, had bottled up shipping in the harbours, and had caused rail congestion. He emphasized the overriding importance of the forthcoming presidential election, "when public sentiment and the demand addressed to the Government from the mass of the people" would decide on whose side the United States would fight. However, until the Americans had actually made their decision to enter the war, he concluded, the allies could not fight German submarines in American waters: "The United States Government has already warned the allied governments that if they sink a United States submarine by mistake for a German submarine they will be held responsible, in fact that war would be the result. Their hands are therefore tied as these waters are continually traversed by American submarines and the United States naval authorities have repeatedly refused to give any pledge whatever as to the movements of the ships of their navy." The British had to stand clear until the United States was on the brink of entering the war in April 1917.

Reports about U-53 that reached Berlin via New York, Boston, Bern, and London triggered long and enthusiastic commentary in

the German press. Her arrival and operations of Newport seem to
have taken German reporters by surprise. Headlines now announced
no less than "3 German U-boats off the American coast." Particularly
gratifying, German technical achievements could send a combat submarine to the United States and back without taking advantage of
the right accorded by international law of provisioning in neutral
ports. Quite apart from serious flaws in the reporters' grasp of international law, the voyage of U-53 meant that Germany had "breached
the wall of England's concept of sovereignty on the seas."[74] On
11 October Berlin newspapers reproduced sensational cables from
Washington and other US cities about submarine operations in the
western Atlantic. In one important respect at least, the German perspective was as clear as it was correct: U-53 had complied meticulously
with the rules governing cruiser warfare. This was crucial, for the
Reichstag, as widely reported at the time, had been addressing a
subject that was causing much agitation in Germany: unrestricted
U-boat warfare. This extreme measure seemed to offer the only means
of bringing about a swift and victorious peace with Great Britain.

Canadians were reading American news by 9 October. Trumpeting
"The War Is at Our Doors," the *Halifax Herald* retold selected American bulletins in its usual inflammatory style. The people of Halifax
had been "rudely awakened at last," it editorialized; the "havoc
wrought by the subs" so near Nova Scotia had finally shaken Nova
Scotians out of their apathy. Their own *Stephano* had been "smitten
by the Hun." Haligonians would not rest until "the piratical craft or
crafts has either been destroyed or left this coast."

Stories about the "Submarine Hun Commerce Raider" highlighted
the pages of Canadian newspapers for days. The press churned out
reruns and recapitulations from foreign correspondents; it fired off
speculative commentaries on the number of submarines involved and
on the impact of the German "blockade" of North America. It queried
the legality of the attacks by the "Hun pirates" and suggested that
"Hun supply bases" lay somewhere along the Atlantic coast.

The *Manitoba Free Press* provided the most even-handed coverage.
Yet it too depended almost entirely on American releases. Its editorial
none the less introduced a Canadian perspective – the only newspaper to do so at the time. The appearance of German U-boats on the
North American coast, it pointed out, had been an inevitable event
which defence planners ought to have foreseen: "This development
of the submarine warfare puts new responsibilities upon the Canadian Government. Care must be taken to see that the activities of
German submarines along the Canadian coast are dangerous to

themselves and profitless. If we had a fleet of fast cruisers the task would not be so difficult."[75]

Typically, the editor revealed little grasp of Canada's naval resources or of maritime defence – hardly surprising, given the low priority and even lower profile of naval affairs in Canada's contribution to the Great War. Indeed, for most Canadian commentators, U-53 was the centre of an essentially British or American concern. Thus an editorial in the *Ottawa Evening Journal* traced President Wilson's diplomatic exchanges with Germany regarding U-boat warfare and speculated on whether he would now end the rhetoric and dare to redress a grievous wrong.[76]

Press reports could provide the enemy with vital information. In 1915, for example, the Canadian government had received from Britain "several urgent remonstrances" – from both the secretary of state for the colonies and the Army Council – because the press had published news on troop movements overseas. At that stage of the war the Canadians doubtless felt strict censorship too draconian a measure; they had proposed "remedying the evil complained of" by requesting publishers to kindly exercise their own "vigilant discretion in regard to the publication of war news."[77]

U-53 had now changed matters. In fact, the chief press censor for Canada had entered the lists on 8 October, the day of the submarine attacks. In a cable to all news services throughout the country he forbade all original Canadian stories. He quite rightly saw no advantage in restricting publication of American news about enemy warships in American waters but urged "particular care [in preventing] any leakage of news from Canada referring to precautions taken to meet the present situation."[78] In a further telegram, he advised regional censors of the assessment of "senior experts" that "the submarine activity off the Atlantic coast [was] designed more for the moral effect upon ship owners and shippers than for the actual naval object accomplished by the destruction of ships."[79] He therefore reminded his colleagues that "the press can assist to defeat the object of the enemy by exerting its powerful steadying influence."

As in the past, official channels were producing stories that were more alarming than any journalistic embellishment. Undercover intelligence and diplomatic scuttlebutt prickled with tantalizing leads. The British consul-general in San Francisco, as Spring Rice cabled in cipher to Ottawa on 27 October, had learned "on direct authority from [an] officer [in] U-53 that if she arrives [in] Germany safely, six other submarines will return and work on [the] Maine coast from a secluded bay in which [a] supply ship would lie." He was also quite specific about the German intention: the submarines planned "to work up northwards into [the] Gulf of St Lawrence and intercept ships from Canadian ports."[80]

Like program notes for a comic opera, Naval Intelligence records reveal that the ambassador's report originated with a certain Joe E. Miller of Victoria, who had chanced upon a letter that his landlady had received from an old friend in San Francisco. Miller had a patriotic turn of mind and was perhaps equally intrigued by the vicarious pleasure of clandestine matters. He forwarded the letter to the private address of a Captain H.H. Pegler of Victoria, who, he trusted, would know what to do. (How or why the information got back to San Francisco and into the hands of the British consul-general there remains a mystery.)

Miller's covering letter to Pegler explained the origin of the incriminating evidence. It had been purloined by a vigilant janitor in a San Francisco boarding-house allegedly frequented by German immigrants, one of whom had received the letter in question from the engineer of U-53. The engineer himself had claimed, in Joe Miller's words, "that as soon as the excitement had blown over they were going up the St Lawrence to sink as many grain ships as possible."[81] Naval Service Headquarters circulated the information to its commanders. Capping as it did the other nerve-wracking reports arising from U-53's voyage, Spring Rice's warning made Canada's navy minister, J.D. Hazen, once again lose patience with Britain's neglect of the northwest Atlantic. On 3 November 1916 he strongly urged Admiralty "that in view of all that has happened, torpedo boat destroyers should be sent to Canada to protect trade routes from Halifax and St John."[82]

U-53 had meanwhile arrived home to a hero's welcome on 28 October 1916 after a forty-two day mission. By now, the mercantile submarine *U-Deutschland* lay three days out of New London, Connecticut, on her second solo voyage to the United States. She had departed Bremen on 10 October 1916, two days after news of U-53's "piracy" had flashed through the Allied press.

SMS *Panther*, which undertook reconnaissance missions off Canada's Pacific and Atlantic coasts, 1905 (Horst Bredow, U-Boot-Archiv)

"Well, here it is: the Canadian Navy's Pioneer Band . . . taken aboard the [auxiliary patrol vessel HMCS] *Lady Evelyn* . . . in Sydney, N.S., 1918." Under the "x": A.H. Wickens, the RNCVR rating whose reminiscences of service at Halifax are included in chapter 5. (DHIST, DND, no negative number)

Three of the steel anti-submarine trawlers built in Canada under Admiralty contract and allocated to the RCN's Atlantic coast patrol, at Quebec City shortly after the armistice (Maritime Command Museum, DND negative, no number)

SC 242. One of the six 110-foot wooden American submarine chasers that operated under RCN control May–November 1918, *SC 242* was part of the division that ran fast escort missions from Sydney, Nova Scotia. In addition to a stern depth-charge chute, she carried a "y" gun, which can be seen clearly on the quarter deck, to fire charges off both beams. Forward is a six-pounder quick-firing gun. (DHIST, DND, negative CN 3280)

HMS *Niobe* arriving at Halifax on 21 October 1910. The larger cruiser had been purchased by the Canadian government as a training ship for the newly organized Naval Service. (DHIST, DND, no negative number)

HMCS *Festubert*, one of the 130-foot steel "battle"-class trawlers. Forward is a twelve-pounder quick-firing gun. She was commissioned in November 1917. (Maritime Command Museum, DND, negative CN-5078)

HMCS *Lansdowne*, the name given to the rented waterfront facilities that served as the RCN patrol base at Sydney in the 1918 season. Among the vessels at the wharf are the drifter *CD 73*, one of the New England trawler-minesweepers (called "PV's" in RCN service), and the Admiralty trawler *TR 33*. (Maritime Command Museum, DND negative, no number)

PART THREE
Unrestricted
U-Boat Warfare
1917-1918

– 8 –

Defending the Convoys

Germany's increasingly parlous military position in Europe throughout 1916 had underscored the dangers it courted of provoking a
break with the United States. Its war at sea was therefore a campaign
of half-measures.[1] The Imperial Naval Office had long since recognized that the war at sea was fraught with political implications
unknown to the armies in Europe. As Admiral von Holtzendorff
wrote Hindenburg in March 1917: "The naval theater of war cannot
be separated from the tracks of peaceful commerce. The aims of
commerce warfare are such that at every step they touch and cut
across the interests of the Neutrals and of neutral maritime traffic ...
The fact of the matter is that naval war is *impeded* in its success unless
politics run parallel to it."[2]

This close connection had not often been the case in Germany,
where the conduct of politics and the naval war had frequently been
at odds. The reversals of strategy and the anxious tactical shifts in
submarine warfare up to early 1917 revealed the divisions between
Germany's political and naval leadership.[3] Nor was the navy without
its own internal conflicts. Some senior German naval officers argued
in the post-war years that Germany had never really understood
naval warfare at all and had predicated its global strategy on irrelevant army models.[4]

Admiral von Holtzendorff's most persistent opponent in the drive
toward unrestricted submarine operations was Reichskanzler von
Bethmann Hollweg. As late as March 1916 von Bethmann had written
to the Kaiser rejecting unrestricted submarine warfare until such
time as Germany could clarify whether it would be possible to do so
"while avoiding a break with America."[5] Such arguments had always
raised the old shibboleth of offending American neutrality. Even von
Holtzendorff was gradually forced to recognize the danger, despite

his military instinct to use all measures at his disposal to defeat the Allies. Von Bethmann's refusal to authorize the drastic military measure of unrestricted submarine warfare ultimately contributed to his political downfall on 13 July 1917 and left von Holtzendorff virtually unopposed in his naval plans.[6]

By early June 1916 von Holtzendorff had advised the Kaiser to imitate the British blockade of Germany by interpreting international law according to the demands of his own national strategy. This self-interest was what he called the "English way" of doing business. But Germany should stop just short of "coming to a break with America."[7] As he wrote some six months later, on 22 December 1916, a breach with the United States, whether merely diplomatic or a declaration of war, was a serious matter Germany should make every effort to avoid. Nonetheless, "uneasiness about a breach must not [make Germany] shrink back in the decisive moment from using the weapon which promises us success."[8] As von Holtzendorff had explained to a meeting of state secretaries the previous August, he saw *Finis Germaniae* [not] in the deployment of the very weapon that could paralyze England and her allies, but in the refusal to use it."[9]

Von Holtzendorff felt that constant exchange of diplomatic notes with the United States served no purpose whatever.[10] Nor should one be overly sensitive to the Americans' diplomatic clamourings, as they were little more than foot-dragging and bluff. As Count von Bernstorff had written to the skipper of *U-Deutschland* during her first visit to Baltimore in July 1916, the Americans' first "principle is to act only after some intervention in their rights has occurred, and never to prevent it by taking avoiding action."[11]

Von Holtzendorff was convinced that the United States would ultimately enter the war on the side of England – but only after considerable delay. Everything seemed to point Germany toward taking the bit in its teeth. It took the step on 1 February 1917 by declaring unrestricted submarine warfare. The United States replied by breaking diplomatic relations on the 3rd and ultimately by declaring war on Germany, on 6 April 1917. These two events – the all-out push by the u-boats and American belligerency – transformed the war in the Atlantic with profound implications for Canada's navy.

U-Deutschland's second commercial voyage, in October and November 1916, was therefore the final maritime act in Germany's peaceful relations with the United States. Arriving on 1 November, she carried some ten million dollars' worth of cargo: nine million dollars in securities to bolster Germany's credit rating in American industry and a further million dollars' worth of chemicals, pharmaceuticals, and precious stones.[12] She would return to Germany with ten "wagon loads" of raw rubber, nine of nickel, three of chrome, and one of banadium.[13] It caused Canada's prime minister some concern that the nickel had come from the International Nickel Co. of Sudbury, Ontario.[14]

Nobody, it was later publicly reported, had known of *U-Deutschland*'s intended arrival which now caught the press entirely by surprise. The facts were different. The Admiralty's Operational Intelligence had known precisely what the submarine was about, a fact which makes the British failure to apprehend her all the more striking. The British naval attaché in Washington had even leaked her time of arrival to a reporter from *The Times* of London.

Despite all attempts at secrecy, the submarine immediately became "the talk of the town."[15] Captain Hinsch of the blockaded North German Lloyd steamer *Neckar*, who had now become director of the Eastern Forwarding Co., the front firm for the Deutsche Ozean-Rhederei, had prohibited public access to the submarine. One press account quipped that Hinsch had refused "permission even to look at the *Deutschland*, which, however, may be accomplished by climbing a fifteen-foot board fence with six feet of barbed wire entanglements on top of it."[16] American businessmen applauded her as a fitting augury of steadily improving trade relations with Germany, while naval officers from New London's submarine base examined her for compliance with neutrality and authorities on both sides of the Atlantic quietly negotiated a contract for her to carry US mail.[17]

U-Deutschland's skipper had cut a dashing figure with American journalists during the first voyage, and he sought out reporters once again. The Deutsche Ozean-Rhederei, he announced, intended to establish regular freight service between Bremen and New London, with sailings every forty days. He himself intended to leave in a fortnight and return to the United States just as soon as practicable. König also let slip that the combat submarine U-57 – which Operational Intelligence in London, England, knew to have departed Bremen just three days after *U-Deutschland* – would in all likelihood arrive off the US coast in time to escort him home.

This "leak" was most certainly a ruse, for König must have realized that the German navy had no plans whatever to cover his withdrawal: all combat boats were fully committed in European waters, and the government had no wish to further destabilize US neutrality. Unease about the possibility of British cruiser patrols lurking outside the three-mile limit must have led König to have suggested such a thing.

In any event, *U-Deutschland* departed on the bright afternoon of 21 November 1916 without military escort and reached the Weser estuary on 10 December.[18]

The freighter's quiet departure might have signalled a temporary respite in the danger of German submarine thrusts into the western Atlantic had shipping agents not received word of two more impending forays by combat boats. One of them would apparently focus on the Nantucket lightship, where u-53 had struck, and the other off Sable Island, Nova Scotia, in order to attack troop ships from Halifax. Whatever the source of these reports – no longer traceable – they demanded some reassurances that British sovereignty on the seas remained unchallenged. Shipping agents might have taken some comfort from at least one such public assurance, on 26 November 1916. The British admiral then temporarily at Halifax, commander-in-chief, North America and West Indies Station, had allegedly "taken every precaution to protect the shipping by patrolling the lanes with swift destroyers and light cruisers."[19]

The reality was radically different. Naval forces in Halifax had of course no such resources at all. The admiral's best effort under the circumstances had been to warn inbound shipping of the potential danger in the vicinity of Sable Island and Nantucket Shoals. The *Halifax Herald* meanwhile indulged its fantasies on the "submarine menace on our coasts."[20] But as we have seen, Canada's naval masters in Britain saw no real need to encourage home defence in Canada and now, six months after the Battle of Jutland, were undertaking recruitment of 5,000 young Canadians to serve with the Royal Navy abroad.[21]

Paradoxically, the governor of Newfoundland's expression of entire confidence in the modest defence measures previously recommended by the Admiralty drew their lordships' attention to the increased defences needed for Canada. Despite u-53's dramatic evidence, the governor of Newfoundland still persisted in the view that no submarine could yet undertake a prolonged transatlantic voyage without a refuelling base in some sheltered bay. Maritime defence was for him therefore quite simple: the locals would immediately report any suspicious activities along the coast, to which the military garrison and patrol vessels would respond.

But in Admiralty's understated response of 7 November 1916, Newfoundland's governor had "not fully realized the powers and radius of action of a modern submarine." Nor indeed would "any competent submarine officer ... be deterred by existing preparations" in the Canadian northwest Atlantic. With dismaying reversal of the advice given only months before, Admiralty now urged Canada and Newfoundland to make haste in greatly expanding their patrol flotillas. "Should Germany decide to make a serious submarine attack on trade in these waters, the present twelve vessels would be insufficient to provide a reasonable measure of defence"; [22] the "suitable patrol" should include thirty-six seagoing steamers.

Admiralty's blunt and untimely advice angered Robert Borden and his minister of the navy.[23] As Borden noted in his diary, the Admiralty had "always said they could take care of everything on [the] ocean." Both men protested by cable – and were ignored. On 28 December 1916 the prime minister tackled Admiralty once again, by letter. During the early months of the war, Borden again pointed out, the Admiralty had discouraged Canada's offer "to supplement [the] naval defence of Empire" in Canadian waters and had insisted that it concentrate instead on providing soldiers for the British army in Europe. The Admiralty, Borden continued, had repeatedly and steadfastly rejected Canada's recommendations that Canadian Vickers in Montreal (which had built submarines for the Royal Navy) build submarines and destroyers for Canadian use.

By insisting that Canada now turn about and suddenly expand its naval forces, Admiralty was implicitly criticizing Canada for wilful neglect of its own home defence. From a Canadian perspective, the British position was galling in the extreme: "Under these circumstances the Admiralty's intimation that we must provide against danger of submarines on our coast is very serious especially as many boats suitable for patrol work were acquired by [the British] War Office in Canada [for use overseas] in September last [,] and recruiting for overseas forces in Canada has denuded this country of most of the suitable men for such purpose, and every available gun has been sent to the British Government."[24]

This was strong medicine. By the beginning of January 1917 at least one official in Admiralty found it "necessary to show sympathy to the Canadian Government in this matter"; to him at least it did "not appear that the question [had] been very adroitly handled" by the Royal Navy. He drily understated the case in a marginal note to the docket: Admiralty's discouragement of Canadian proposals for "building destroyers evidently rankles."[25]

For the moment, however, sympathy was all that the Admiralty had to give.[26] By mid-January 1917 Canada knew where it stood: Admiralty could spare no anti-submarine craft from European waters and recommended that the Dominion find hulls among its fisheries fleet. Admiral Kingsmill bit the bullet and changed his approach. Whatever the differences with the British on the course of past policy, he recognized, Canada had no choice but to do its utmost to protect its own shores and those of Newfoundland as well.

This situation was particularly serious, as Canada was about to accept an additional burden. Since the arrival of u-53 in Newport, Admiralty had been considering the wisdom of rerouting transport of munitions from North America. It had therefore inquired into the quantity of Canadian-produced munitions now transported by rail across American territory for shipment either through Canadian or us ports and whether it would be practicable to ship all munitions by rail through Canadian territory to Canadian harbours. In the latter case it would insist on a trade-off: in exchange for rerouting explosives through Canada, all commercial cargoes would pass through the United States.[27]

Vice-Admiral Kingsmill had been discussing the matter informally with Ambassador Spring Rice in Washington. Admiralty pressed the point on 29 January 1917 by asking Kingsmill directly "whether it would be possible during the summer months to send munitions produced in the United States of America from the Chicago area by water to Montreal for shipment in Transports or Canadian Liners."[28] This would further strain the resources of the already-strapped St Lawrence Patrols.

Three days later, on 1 February 1917, the Kaiser announced unrestricted submarine warfare in special message to the German forces: "In the forthcoming decisive battle the task devolves upon My Navy to turn against our most spiteful and stubborn enemy England and her allies the very war of starvation which she has been using in order to crush the German people, and to combat their maritime trade with all means at our disposal. At the forefront will stand our submarines."[29]

u-53's report of proceedings provided the Germans with vital information as to how the new campaign could be pressed into North American waters and had proved "how effective u-boats can be [when] operating [even at very long range] at the confluence of enemy trade routes." However, the extra fuel load required for the long voyage had greatly impaired the u-boat's seakeeping qualities, and the slow speeds necessary to reduce fuel consumption prevented high-speed pursuit and attack. Together these problems deprived the submarine of its otherwise powerful tactical advantage. Such long-range missions therefore required "larger boats that offer a firm platform for a 15-cm [5.9-inch] gun even in moderate seas and in which habitability for officers and men has been significantly improved." The answer was perhaps all too obvious to Kapitänleutnant Rose's enquiring and enterprising mind. His consultations with

Krupp's Germania Werft convinced him that all requirements "can be met without difficulty by u-boats of the Deutschland-class."[30]

German Admiralty, as will be seen, had long since been working on plans for new classes of boats. One project envisaged a 1,950-ton submarine with two 15-cm (5.9-in) guns, twelve torpedoes, and a range at 10 knots of 12,000 miles; another proposed a 3,800-ton submarine with four 15-cm guns, sixteen torpedoes, and a range at 10 knots of 13,200 miles. Within seven months the Kaiser would be briefed about construction details for a 4,000-ton u-cruiser carrying four 15-cm and two 8.8-cm guns and twenty-six torpedoes and with a range of 26–28,000 miles.[31]

Thus began a new chapter in u-boat warfare. On 10 February 1917, nine days after Germany had begun unrestricted submarine warfare, and seven days after the United States had broken off diplomatic relations, *U-Deutschland* was renamed u-155. On 19 February the huge commercial submarine, which according to American inspection teams could not be converted to military use, commenced the refit that turned her into a submarine cruiser.

Canada's response was necessarily minimal: eleven naval vessels were in commission on the Atlantic coast, of which only five were seagoing. The remaining six were small and could only operate close inshore as minesweepers and on harbour entrance patrols. Naval department officials were hustling together additional vessels of varying quality, including the 15-knot postal service steamer *Lady Evelyn*, two slow survey ships from the hydrographic service, and seven wooden trawlers, through a quiet deal with us civilian shipowners. Finding nothing more available, the department issued contracts for six steel trawlers from Vickers of Montreal and an equal number from Polson's Iron Works in Toronto, in the vain hope of their being ready by summer. Named for actions fought by the Canadian Corps in France and Belgium – *Arleux, Armentières, Givenchy, Ypres,* and so forth – these "battle-class" trawlers were modest craft, of 320 to 357 tons displacement, 130-foot length, 10-knot speed, and armament of one 12-pounder gun and a crew of about eighteen. Only two-thirds of the projected fleet could operate on the high seas.[32]

At this same time, the global shortage of Allied shipping forced the British government to reverse itself on the matter of building ships in Canada. It ordered merchant ships and, in the Admiralty's case, anti-submarine vessels.[33] Initially, Admiralty's order of February 1917 called for thirty-six steel trawlers similar to the Canadian "battle class" and a hundred wooden "drifters," a type of fishing vessel that had proved useful in anti-submarine work in British waters. Eighty-four feet in length, with a best speed of 9 knots, drifters carried a crew of eleven and an armament of a single six-pounder. Admiralty placed a second order for an additional twenty-four steel trawlers in July. Unnamed, the trawlers bore the designations *TR 1* through *TR 60*, and the Canadian-built drifters *CD 1* through *CD 100*.

Admiralty paid for the vessels, thereby reserving the right to deploy them as it wished in response to the parry and thrust of anti-submarine warfare. Their lordships hinted at the possibility of using some or even all of them in Canadian waters but offered nothing definite. Of course, this refusal to make a commitment made good strategic sense, but, as we shall see, it burdened the RCN with yet one more imponderable as it struggled to grasp the rapidly evolving demands and techniques of anti-submarine defence.[34]

The British orders could not have come at a more difficult time. Canadian industrial resources had long since been committed to the British War Office's enormous demands for ammunition; workers with specialized skills in marine construction had been lost to the armed forces and to US firms. Most serious, there was not a single mill in Canada that could roll steel plate and manufacture other key structural components for ships. This meant ordering from the United States, in competition with the large American demand, which increased still more when that country entered the war in April 1917.[35] Substandard work and late delivery of the vessels from the eight hastily expanded yards on the St Lawrence and on the Great Lakes would cause the RCN no end of trouble. That most of the craft were actually available during the summer of 1918, when they were most desperately needed, was an accomplishment indeed.

The navy also urgently required trained, experienced personnel. Though recruiting for the overseas division of the RNCVR had ceased by February 1917, some 1,200 Canadians had already been dispatched to Britain. Provincial recruiting offices now sought men for Canada's own Atlantic division, and the Admiralty approved Kingsmill's only interim solution: lay up HMCS *Rainbow* on the west coast and transfer her crew east. Danger of attacks on the Pacific had by this time virtually disappeared, and she was due for a major refit anyway. *Rainbow* therefore suffered the same fate that HMCS *Niobe* had met in 1915.[36]

The cruise of U-53 to Newport in October 1916 had particularly worried the British commander-in-chief at Halifax, Vice-Admiral Sir Montague E. Browning. Later characterized by Walter Hose as "the hardest nut in the Royal Navy," Browning knew that a U-boat standing well outside the existing anti-submarine nets ranging on either side of George's Island could fire torpedoes deep into the main anchorage.[37] An "outer" net, closer to the harbour entrance, was imperative.

Browning had other worries as well. Admiralty advised him in April 1917 that one or two minelaying submarines were crossing the Atlantic.[38] This warning may have derived from cryptographic intelligence about the maiden cruise of the converted u-cruiser u-155 (ex *U-Deutschland*), though in the event she confined her operations to mid-ocean. She none the less underlined the increased threat to North American waters only a matter of days after the United States had declared war on Germany. In the light of German successes with deep mines off Britain, Browning demanded that the Halifax mine-sweeper force be increased from four to ten vessels. Nor was that all. Browning agreed with the Canadian naval and militia staffs that Sydney now needed proper defences. As the ice would not clear from the St Lawrence until May or June, Sydney could wait, but the commander-in-chief demanded immediate action at Halifax.

Appalled at Canada's byzantine administrative procedures, which often required cabinet approval for even trivial matters, Browning confronted an equally frustrated Kingsmill, who was only too familiar with the situation. Kingsmill explained his difficulties in carrying out Browning's recommendations for Halifax – lack of skilled tradesmen and industrial materials, overburdened railways – but was less convincing in his assurances that Ottawa's close and direct control had not stifled initiative at Halifax.[39] Browning took his complaints about the slow progress to the first lord of the Admiralty, Sir Arthur Balfour, who was then in North America to arrange co-operation with the United States.

When visiting Ottawa, the two men confronted Kingsmill in J.D. Hazen's presence in a scene that did little to improve already strained relations between the military and civilian authorities within the department.[40] Hazen and Desbarats blamed the naval staff for the shortcomings in defence arrangements. No record of Kingsmill's reaction has come to light, but it can well be imagined. Since 1910 he had been subjected to Desbarats's close control while politicians allowed partisanship to strangle the naval service. Now, overnight, he was expected to abandon restraint and undertake rapid expansion.

In the event, the new anti-submarine nets at both Sydney and Halifax were completed in July. The militia installed 4.7-inch guns at each of the Sydney headlands, and all seven of the wooden us trawlers (designated PVS I to VII in Canadian service) were converted to mine-sweepers. But a series of mishaps scuttled any substantial reinforcement of the port defence flotilla in 1917. *Tuna*, for example, left service because of irreparable wear to her engines; the Halifax minesweeper *Deliverance* was run down by a Dutch freighter; and another minesweeper, *Premier*, wrecked herself by running aground while steaming without proper navigation charts.

Not until the end of 1917, when the first new construction trawlers began to arrive belatedly on the east coast, could the navy carry out the full port defence schemes that Browning had demanded in the spring.[41] During the summer and fall Canada's sea patrol of nine ships had been scarcely larger than that of 1916. *Grilse* remained at Halifax to escort high-value ships through the harbour approaches, and the remaining eight seagoing vessels – supported by twelve chartered motor launches – operated in the Gulf of St Lawrence.[42] Newfoundland chartered five small steamers for local patrol and placed light guns on four coasting steamers that plied between Newfoundland and Labrador ports.[43]

Admiralty itself had to shoulder some of the blame for problems in laying plans for a larger sea patrol. To command and oversee expansion of the St Lawrence force, their lordships had offered, and Canada had accepted, the loan of an officer senior to Captain Pasco. The choice of retired Vice-Admiral Sir Charles Coke, who accepted the lower temporary rank of commodore so that he could return to active employment, proved singularly unfortunate. The man was certainly tactless and probably inept. There are even suggestions that Admiralty already had its doubts about him. As commander-in-chief, Irish Coast, he had borne part of the responsibility for the *Lusitania* disaster of 1915.[44] He had failed to warn the liner about the u-boat danger, even though he had been aware of u-20's presence in the area for some days; Admiralty had relieved him of his command.

Kingsmill suspected from the very beginning that by sending such a senior officer Admiralty was attempting "to create a separate [British] command" on the Canadian coast under the direct control of the commander-in-chief, North America and West Indies Station.[45] To do so, in his words, would have shown "an utter want of appreciation of the work done by this Department since the outbreak of war." For that reason, Kingsmill insisted that the appointee be the servant of the Canadian government, not of the British. The Admiralty acceded and so informed Coke.[46] But interpersonal problems may have intruded. Coke seems to have been unable to accept the fact that he was subordinate to Kingsmill. Coke had, after all, achieved the rank of vice-admiral on active service, whereas Kingsmill had been a captain while serving in the Royal Navy and had risen to flag rank on the retired list.

Whatever his motivations, Coke attended to everything in Halifax except the very task he was hired to do: organize the sea patrol.

Instead, he virtually took charge of Halifax, challenged the authority of the dockyard superintendent over the Halifax flotilla, and decided to keep his headquarters in Halifax year-round rather than shifting to Sydney during the Gulf navigation season. He had helped foment the imbroglio between Kingsmill and the commander-in-chief, North America and West Indies Station, regarding Halifax's defences; he interfered with the shipbuilding program and never drafted orders for the new construction trawler and drifters; and he hindered head-quarters' employment of two technical officers whom the Admiralty had seconded to the Canadian government, but whom Coke claimed were his personal staff. Only on direct order did he arrange for the required Gulf deployments.

Within less than four weeks, Vice-Admiral Kingsmill sent a strong, but by no means unfriendly, warning to his commodore.[47] Two weeks later, on 30 April 1917, Kingsmill sent a formal memorandum "by command." Such sharp directives were rare in the service. Kingsmill set forth his department's position, and thrust home: "It will be noted that your services ... were accepted on condition that you become an Officer of the Department. It is not considered possible that at any moment there was an idea prevalent that the whole question of our Defence should be in the hands of an Officer acting on his own responsibility."[48] Kingsmill was visibly relieved when the Admiralty offered to recall Coke.[49] Admiralty had at first been convinced "that his experience on the Irish coast during the war qualified him for the post" in Canada but had now come to realize "that his advancing age has seriously told on him." The oblique reference to Coke's infirmities remains unclear.

Reflecting on Coke's failures, Kingsmill commented that Coke had tried to impose Royal Navy methods when "what is done in England need not necessarily be suitable here."[50] This statement clearly referred to Coke's and Browning's criticism of excessive centraliza-tion of authority in the hands of headquarters in Ottawa. Here Kings-mill was wrong in insisting that he could co-ordinate seagoing operations more effectively than either of the commands at Sydney or Halifax; Coke had been right about the need for a senior naval officer to exercise broad command of the increasingly complex opera-tions on the east coast.

The experience with Coke, however, not only confirmed Kingsmill in his unwillingness to invest such broad authority in any single officer but now made him determined to reserve the Sydney command for "an officer conversant with the customs and manning of the Canadian Naval Service."[51] After an awkward interregnum of muddled commu-nications between London and Ottawa, Kingsmill appointed an officer of whom he had a very high opinion: Acting Captain Walter Hose, RCN. Like Coke and Pasco before him, Hose's authority was limited strictly to the St Lawrence patrol; the ships and establishments at Halifax continued as an entirely separate command. This was not the last time a Canadian service would persist in inefficient practices for the sake of national control.

By the time Hose took up his new command, in August 1917, Britain and Canada had been approaching the United States independently for naval support. The American response was a crucial element of imperial defence and derived not least of all from pre-war American strategic assumptions and cautious distrust toward the new allies.

The US navy's blueprint for war with Germany – the Black Plan, first drafted in 1913 – had envisioned a major German expedition consisting of the High Seas Fleet and some 25,000 troops to seize operating bases in the Caribbean, with Britain remaining neutral. It called for the American battle fleet standing alone in the western Atlantic against the full might of the German High Seas Fleet. Revised only in matters of detail, the Black Plan remained in force until 1917. It had in fact divined the general intention of Germany's plan for war against the United States – OP III, developed from 1898 to 1906.

The Germans had long since shelved their old plan, and the American response was by now equally out of date. Nonetheless, the Allies' repeated setbacks in the European land war still seemed to augur German victory; in that case the Black Plan scenario could yet become reality. Paradoxically, therefore, the course of the war from August 1914 to March 1917 had strengthened rather than weakened the old determinants of American naval policy: confidence in the battleship as the ultimate arbiter of sea power and the isolationist tradition in foreign policy.[52]

American attitudes toward the belligerents had been ambivalent. Certainly, both U-boat warfare and the disturbing number of subversive German plots alleged to have occurred in the United States had confirmed the dark view of Germany. Yet many Americans regarded Britain's "high-handed" disregard of American neutral rights at sea and the "shady" secret diplomacy that held the Triple Entente between Britain, France, and Russia together as but a less blood-drenched manifestation of Europe's "evil corruption."

American leaders had also distrusted Britain's alliance with Japan, the most likely enemy after Germany. In defiance of American interests, Japan had seized the opportunities afforded by the war to expand its hegemony both in China and on the Pacific. American planners could not rule out the possibility of an Anglo-Japanese combination against the United States nor the danger of a coalition between a triumphant Germany and a Japan that broke with a defeated England. When the United States finally did enter the war, it did so not as a full member of the Alliance but as an "associated power." The Americans were prepared neither for anti-submarine operations nor for alliance warfare.

US naval policy had looked not to early belligerency but rather to its avoidance through longer-term development of a fleet "second-to-none." The fleet was intended to project American determination to uphold neutral rights during the present war and to reflect readiness to counter aggression single-handedly in the more distant future, from either Japan or a victorious Germany. Thus the main feature of the 1916 naval expansion program was construction of fourteen "superdreadnought" battleships and battle-cruisers, vessels that could not be completed for some years.

In the interim, President Wilson was determined to undertake no provocative measures that might lay him open to charges of having led his country into war. Supported by the strength of isolationist sentiment, especially within his own Democratic party, his administration either neglected or studiously ignored some basic preparations for possible mobilization: augmentation of personnel, requisition and conversion of civilian vessels, and establishment of direct communication between the American and Allied armed forces. The absence of close contact with the Allies proved a major impediment to swift and effective action once the United States finally entered the war, for the Navy Department had not the slightest inkling of the full gravity of the U-boat crisis. The British government had distorted published information in order to maintain the confidence of neutral shippers, whose vessels sustained the Allied supply lines.[53]

From the very moment that President Wilson broke off diplomatic relations with Germany on 3 February 1917, the US navy sorely felt its lack of anti-submarine resources.[54] The Atlantic fleet, stationed at the time without anti-submarine defences of any kind at Guantanamo, Cuba, hastily withdrew to the less exposed anchorage of Guacanayabo, in the face of unverifiable press reports of U-boat activity in the Gulf of Mexico. There it remained until March 1917, when it could shift to the security of Hampton Roads, Virginia, behind new nets strung across Chesapeake Bay.

Shortage of destroyers created another problem. The navy boasted at the time only fifty-one modern seagoing types – an inadequate screen for its thirty-three battleships.[55] The Royal Navy's Grand Fleet,

by comparison, comprised forty-four capital ships and 139 destroyers, with over a hundred other modern and older types assigned to
coastal and trade defence duties.[56] Shortly after the declaration of
war on 6 April 1917, the Americans had assigned two-thirds of the
destroyers to a newly organized "Patrol Force" for defence of trade
off ports on the Atlantic coast and in the Gulf of Mexico; this left only
eighteen destroyers for operations with the fifteen most modern
and battle-ready battleships of the Atlantic Fleet. Even this single
remaining destroyer flotilla would have been scattered to the winds
had the fleet's commander-in-chief, Rear-Admiral H.T. Mayo, not
dug in his heels against its redeployment.

The exigencies of war soon overshadowed disputes about proper
deployment of destroyers in American waters. The British Admiralty
had been eyeing the vessels and insisted that the war's outcome
depended on their early dispatch to European waters. By April 1917,
Britain had managed to concentrate some seventy destroyers and
several times that number of smaller craft in the southwestern
approaches to the United Kingdom, where sinkings were heaviest.
However, even that had done little to reduce the soaring rate of
merchant ship losses.[57] As Admiral Jellicoe wired to the British naval
attaché in Washington on 9 April, "We require at least another 100
destroyers, and at least twice as many patrols craft ... as we have at
present."[58]

Vice-Admiral Browning pressed the same point in Washington
on 11 April 1917 when he discussed possible Anglo-American co-
operation with Secretary of the Navy Josephus Daniels and his staff.
Daniels found the British admiral as forceful a personality as the
Canadians had. Convinced by Browning's arguments, he wrote in his
diary: "O for more destroyers! I wish we could trade the money
in dreadnoughts for destroyers already built."[59] Daniels agreed to
dispatch six destroyers despite the reluctance of the ultra-nationalistic
chief of naval operations, Rear-Admiral W.S. Benson, and others to
weaken the home defences or even contemplate hasty division of
American naval strength.[60] Franklin Delano Roosevelt, assistant secretary of the navy and a long-time advocate of early American entry
into the war, had meanwhile whispered in Browning's ear that additional destroyers would almost certainly follow soon. Thus Browning
witnessed at first hand divisions within the Navy Department that
would continue to influence American policy until the armistice in
November 1918.[61]

The successful overseas forays of German raiders disguised as merchant ships had meanwhile awakened the Allies to a new and widen-
ing danger.[62] The Admiralty had therefore instructed Admiral

Browning to elicit American support for the thinly stretched Allied cruiser forces. The Americans agreed to provide a squadron for South American waters; should enemy units break out the North Sea, the Americans would have another squadron "immediately ready" to work with Allied warships between the parallels running through Cape Sable, Nova Scotia, in the north and the Windward Passage, between Cuba and Haiti, in the south.

In light of Admiralty's insistence that European waters held top priority for anti-submarine resources, it is not surprising that Browning seems not to have pressed the issue that most worried Canada at home: defence against u-boats in the western part of the ocean. He accepted as sufficient the Americans' tentative commitment: "If and when enemy submarines appear, [they would] attempt to send several [of their own] submarines to the Canadian coast."[63] But he recognized that the Americans would quite naturally lay greater emphasis on defence of their own waters when faced with imminent threat. Canada would therefore have to look to itself.

Canada was already making its mark in Europe. On 9 and 10 April 1917 – with one artillery piece every twenty-nine yards to provide cover – Canadians captured Vimy Ridge. In a battle that signals a turning-point in Canadian national consciousness, Canadians seized and held one of the major German bastions on the Western Front. Conditions had been appalling, casualties heavy. The British Third Army lost 8,238 troops, and the Canadian Corps 9,937. "No overall hero emerged from the Canadian Corps – no Wellington, Cromwell, no Washington ... The real heroes were the masses of ordinary soldiers who fought and died in the belief they were making the world a better place, and their inventive leaders who stubbornly refused to follow the old rules of war."[64] It was a world much different, more urgent, and terrifying than back home.

Within days of Vice-Admiral's Browning's visit to Washington on 10–12 April 1917, Admiral W.S. Sims, USN, fully endorsed Admiralty's bid for anti-submarine craft. Sim's activities form a crucial chapter in Anglo-American wartime relations. While the United States had still been at peace with Germany in March 1917, Sims had been sent to London incognito in an "eleventh-hour" mission "to study the naval situation and learn how we could best and most quickly cooperate in the naval war."[65] He assumed command of all American naval forces in Europe soon after the American declaration of war and from the beginning worked very effectively with Jellicoe. The two were already fast friends, having gotten on well since their first acquaintanceship in China in 1901.[66]

A highly intelligent officer, prominent among the reformers who had brought the US navy into the twentieth century, Sims had been an inspired choice for the London mission, despite – or rather because of – a background that made him suspect to American officers of Benson's ilk.[67] Jellicoe praised "his attractive personality, charm of manner, keen sense of humour, and quick and accurate grasp of any problem with which he was confronted."[68] Sims had been born in Port Hope, Ontario, of a Canadian mother and never concealed his admiration for Britain, its empire, and the Royal Navy. Sims's determination to have the United States send all possible aid to Britain became nothing less than a crusade from the moment he first shared Jellicoe's insights into the Atlantic war. In particular, he had been shaken to learn from secret documents shown to him by the British admiral that Allied shipping "losses were three and four times as large as those ... published in the press."[69]

Sims's first cable home on 14 April 1917 adumbrated the same strategic principles that Admiralty had been pressing on the Canadian government: "The issue is and must inevitably be decided at the focus of all lines of communications in the Eastern Atlantic."[70] Everything argued against Germany's shifting its focus to North American waters: the meagre number of available U-boats, their difficulties in sustaining transoceanic operations, and the wide dispersion of shipping in the western Atlantic as compared to the close concentration of targets in the British approaches.

Sims conceded that raids by submarine minelayers in North American waters remained "very likely" but insisted that such operations would have little strategic importance. Indeed, their aim would be "to divert attention and to keep our forces from the critical areas in the Eastern Atlantic through effect upon public opinion." American retention of an inflated anti-submarine force, Sims argued, was tantamount to playing into the enemy's hands. The day after Sims dispatched this message, Admiral Benson informed Daniels that German U-boats were already lurking off the American coast.[71]

It was about this time that Admiralty let Sims in on the work of "Room 40," the code-breaking organization that decrypted Germany's diplomatic and naval codes.[72] This eavesdropping into Germany's wireless traffic permitted the timeliest warning of enemy action. That would be especially useful in providing early information about any intended raid on the North American coast; the departure signals of a long-range U-cruiser would necessarily anticipate its arrival in the western Atlantic by at least ten days. The US navy, Sims advised his department, could therefore trim anti-submarine forces in home waters to modest levels with confidence that these could be concentrated wherever and whenever an attack was most likely.

Sims's early cables helped considerably in preparing the way for the arrival in Washington of the first lord of the Admiralty, Sir Arthur Balfour, and his mission on 24 April 1917. As Sims recalled: "It was the seriousness of the situation that soon afterward sent Mr. Balfour and the British Commission to the United States. The world does not yet understand what a dark moment that was in the history of the Allied cause."[73] Balfour later confided in Sims: "Things were dark when I took that trip to America. The submarines were constantly on my mind. I could think of nothing but the number of ships which they were sinking. At that time it certainly looked as though we were going to lose the war."[74]

Balfour's personal appeal, all the more powerful because of his elegant restraint and because of the very specific measures recommended by his naval adviser, Admiral Sir Dudley R. deChair, crystallized the Navy Department's dawning realization that Britain's very survival depended on early and generous assistance. By the end of July, a total of forty destroyers had crossed the Atlantic to Britain.[75] Balfour's mission also helped shift priorities in the American shipbuilding program: anti-submarine craft and merchant ships now took precedence over capital ships. Early in October 1917 the us cabinet agreed to build 150 destroyers beyond the 111 it had already authorized.[76]

Yet these advances had by no means transformed American policy. Suspicions that Britain stood on the brink of defeat, and unconfirmed but disturbing reports about a major offensive in the western Atlantic by some twenty *Deutschland*-class u-cruisers,[77] lent weight to the traditional policy of maintaining a large, balanced fleet, including a full complement of anti-submarine craft, in home waters.[78] It was therefore not until a year later, in 1918, that large numbers of American vessels arrived overseas.[79] From his London perspective, Admiral Sims was both irked and amused by his country's recalcitrance. "It would be very funny, if it were not so tragic," he mused to a friend; just imagine "the spectacle of many dozens of ships, destroyers, yachts and so forth parading up and down the American coast three thousand miles away from where the vital battle of the war is going on."[80]

The British had conducted their discussions with the Americans in April 1917 without involving the Canadians or even advising them. Only in May did the RCN learn about the meetings, and then by accident. During casual conversation with Captain Martin, superintendent of Halifax dockyard, Vice-Admiral Browning happened to mention that the us navy had agreed to extend patrols as far north as Cape Sable; that being so, Browning suggested, Canada could therefore reduce the forces assigned to defence of commerce off

Halifax. This was the first any Canadian naval authority had heard about the arrangements Browning had made in Washington. Only after puzzled inquiries from Naval Service Headquarters in Ottawa did the British commander-in-chief provide the text of the agreement. A few days later, on 17 May, Browning sent further good news: the United States would also patrol the Bay of Fundy.[81] As we shall see, this was not precisely the case.

The staff in Ottawa decided that it was high time for direct discussions with the Americans. This decision coincided with an invitation from the US Navy Department – passed via the British embassy in Washington. Encouraged no doubt by Browning's information, Commander Stephens went to Washington with proposals for the United States to assume responsibility for anti-submarine patrols beyond the three-mile limit of Canadian territorial waters, as far east as Cape Sable, and including the Bay of Fundy.[82]

Stephens's proposals quickly foundered on basic misunderstandings. Canadian naval headquarters had not the foggiest notion of American naval organization, and Browning had failed to explain the arrangements he had made. Assistance with "sea patrol," as the Americans had promised, had a specific meaning in US navy parlance. The term, Stephens learned, referred to operations by major naval vessels – in this case, the cruisers the United States had committed to anti-surface raider defence off southern Nova Scotia – twenty miles or more from shore. "Coastal patrol" – within twenty miles of shore – fell to smaller warships and auxiliary craft operated by the naval districts into which the American seaboard was divided. The Americans had given no thought whatever to extending the responsibility of the First Naval District, headquartered in Boston, into Canadian waters. "As regards the Bay of Fundy," Stephens discovered, "United States ships might occasionally be found there, say once in 3 months."[83]

Before returning to Ottawa, Stephens made some arrangements for the exchange of intelligence between the two services and for the use of common signal codes by American and Canadian warships. There the question of US assistance in Canadian coastal waters rested for the next ten months. It was a sharp lesson in alliance warfare.

German submarine attacks were meanwhile inflicting severe losses on Allied shipping in European waters. In the words of Admiral Henning von Holtzendorff, "The war of starvation, this fantastic crime against humanity had been turned against its originator"; [84] Germans were convinced that "England" was now getting its own back. Indeed Germany's minister for the interior informed the nation "that the technical results of U-boat warfare [had] exceeded the navy's expectations."[85] German analysts predicted a U-boat victory by August 1917, a date not far off British estimates that anticipated critical curtailment of supplies from overseas by October. Despite increased Allied deployment of anti-submarine craft in European waters, merchant ship losses from the end of December 1916 until April 1917 alone reached the staggering level of 335 ships. The vast Allied anti-submarine forces had retaliated by sinking a mere two submarines, far less than the number of new U-boats entering service that month.

Nowhere was the magnitude of the disaster clearer, nor the bankruptcy of existing anti-submarine methods more striking, than on the southwestern approaches to Britain. There converged the routes for most of Britain's vital overseas trade. Losses in this area jumped from twenty-eight merchantmen in March to fifty-eight in April; many of them were large, ocean-going vessels, the most desperately needed ships in the Allied inventory. In this critical area, not a single German submarine was sunk.[86] Hundreds of trawlers and other light craft constantly patrolled the sea lanes, but even this large number of vessels was thinly stretched over the broad ocean approaches and could be easily evaded by the submarines. Hunting groups of destroyers and other fast warships responded quickly to radio, sighting, and other intelligence, but the few hours it took them to reach the scene allowed the U-boat ample time to escape.

The sheer magnitude of the disaster forced the British Admiralty to reconsider an ancient method that had encountered insuperable objections since the late nineteenth century: introduction of convoys. Most objections to convoys lay rooted in untried assumptions, such as the belief that groups of merchantmen steaming together would merely provide enemy submarines with more convenient targets, unless there were at least two fast escorts for every ship in convoy. Modern trade was so vast and complex, ran another adage, that a general convoy system would be an impossible administrative task; the long delays it imposed on shipping would cripple trade.

Experience and analysis proved otherwise. Coal ships that plied the dangerous Channel waters between England and France had begun to enjoy virtual immunity from attack when in February 1917 they started to sail in loosely organized, modestly protected convoys. The U-boats had much more difficulty locating a single group of ships than in finding a stream of vessels sailing independently and funnelling into constricted approach routes. U-boats proved reluctant to attack even a weakly escorted group. If a boat did attack, then the prompt countermeasures of the escorts ensured that it could fire only one or two spreads of torpedoes before running for cover.

Statistical analysis by both the Ministry of Shipping and the Admiralty's recently created Anti-Submarine Division revealed a startling insight: the number of ships in the vital ocean-going trade was actually far smaller than suspected. Customs reports, on which Admiralty trade statistics were based until April 1917, showed over 3,000 ships entering and leaving British ports per week, but only 120 to 140 of these proved actually to be deep-sea vessels. The small number of ships that formed Britain's overseas lifeline at once underscored the gravity of the situation. If April's loss rate in the western approaches persisted, one out of every four deep-sea vessels departing British ports would not return. But it also revealed the solution. Convoys were clearly a practical proposition. A total force of seventy to ninety ocean-going destroyers, of which as many as thirty were already available and would soon be augmented by the United States, could supply adequate anti-submarine escorts.

Never was there any doubt that convoys from North America would constitute the predominant and most essential part of the convoy system. Canada and the United States had always been the largest overseas suppliers of goods for the war economy and were becoming still more important. To make more efficient use of shipping in the face of the heavy losses of early 1917, the British government had begun to place an increasing proportion of overseas orders in North America; it thereby allowed redeployment of merchant ships from the Pacific and other long-distance trade routes to the shorter Atlantic run.[87] In 1914 North America had supplied a quarter (by value) of all British imports; the proportion had grown to 37 per cent by 1916. In 1917–18 it would rise to nearly half, with Canada, despite its small population and economy compared to the United States, providing fully a quarter of the supplies from North America.[88]

Old prejudices delayed the adoption of a general convoy system until two months after Admiralty had approved the concept. Senior officers schooled in the principles of high-seas battles between major fleets clung to the view that convoys were a desperate defensive measure of last resort.[89] Indeed adoption of convoys confirmed suspicions in the us Navy Department that the Royal Navy had actually retreated into a defeatist strategy. President Wilson shared the view and encouraged his admirals' crusade to convert the British to grasp offensive initiatives instead.[90]

Only after merchant convoys from Gibraltar and Hampton Roads had made safe and timely passages in May and June while independently sailed merchantmen continued to suffer enormous losses did the organization of a comprehensive system begin. "HH" convoys (Homeward from Hampton Roads) commenced sailing for Britain at four-day intervals on 2 July. "HS" convoys (Homeward from Sydney, Nova Scotia) commenced eight-day cycles on 10 July. "HN" convoys (Homeward from New York) began eight-day cycles on 14 July. The "HX" (Homeward from Halifax) troop-ship convoys began on 21 August 1917 and also accepted all merchant ships from American and Canadian ports capable of 12.5 knots or more. Though at first limited in size by fears of presenting too large a target, convoys grew from fewer than twenty vessels to a peak of forty-eight merchantmen in the largest convoy sailing from Sydney in October 1918.[91]

Fine-tuned in the ensuing months to ensure minimum delays for shipping, convoys proved the key to Allied victory. The convoy not only secured merchantmen from attack but – contrary to expectations – in some instances actually speeded up the flow of ocean commerce. Previously, the mere suspected presence of a U-boat sufficed to close a port for many hours, perhaps for several days; when shipping finally sailed, it had to follow long and inefficient evasive routes. Now merchantmen invariably sailed on schedule and by the shortest, most direct route.

Nova Scotia, strategically placed on the Great Circle route to Europe, and with commodious harbours at Halifax and Sydney, played a crucial role in the success of convoys. Experience soon showed that "slow" vessels from all ports north of Hampton Roads saved days by running to Sydney (or Halifax in winter) to join convoys rather than having to go south to Virginia and then backtrack to the Great Circle. Faster vessels that missed a New York convoy could run to Halifax and, with little lost time, join a convoy there rather than wait as many as eight days for the next New York sailing.[92] It is a credit to the Canadian navy's control of shipping organization that it accommodated the Royal Navy's convoy system with only minor changes.[93]

Normally a cruiser or armed merchant-cruiser escorted each convoy through its whole passage to guard against the ever-present danger of breakouts by German surface raiders. Given the shortage of destroyers, however, transoceanic anti-submarine escort was not possible. Fortunately it was not necessary: U-boats hunted in coastal waters, where shipping could most easily be located. For this reason, British and American destroyers, and other fast seagoing anti-submarine types, concentrated at Irish ports, and a group of six to eight of them rendezvoused with each convoy as it neared the danger zone in the western approaches to the British Isles.

Local forces – and this was a serious Canadian concern – were responsible for providing convoy protection as convoys formed and departed from North American ports. As will be seen, efforts to expand and improve the Canadian Atlantic patrols from the late summer and early fall of 1917 hinged on the grave problems of providing adequate support for convoys.

Smoothly as the system worked, naval headquarters in Ottawa remained wary as ever that centralized Admiralty direction of the convoys might bring in its wake British control over the Canadian organization. These suspicions surfaced at the onset of the St Lawrence freeze-up in November 1917, when the British "Port Convoy Officer" at Sydney, who had only just arrived on 3 August 1917, moved with his staff to Halifax, the winter port for the "HS" (Home from Sydney) convoys.

Like his counterparts at American ports, Rear-Admiral B.M. Chambers, RN, came directly under Admiralty orders.[94] When the Admiralty next proposed that Chambers should now be titled "Senior Naval Officer Afloat, Halifax," it caused a flurry of alarm in Ottawa, despite Admiralty's assurances that Chambers would not meddle with Canadian shore establishments and warships. As Admiral Kingsmill wrote, "It is most undesirable to have an Officer coming from England to take charge over the heads of our Officers."[95] Chambers in fact outranked every Canadian officer on the Atlantic coast.

Kingsmill solved the immediate problem by having the dockyard superintendents in Esquimalt and Halifax swap posts. Vice-Admiral W.O. Story in Esquimalt had been promoted on the Royal Navy retired list and now outranked every British officer in the western Atlantic except for the commander-in-chief, North America and West Indies Station, himself.[95]

While the navy's memorandum-war continued, the Canadian army had been pressing home attacks against stubbornly entrenched German forces on the Western Front. The campaigns of autumn 1917 – Ypres, Broodseinde, and Passchendaele – gripped the soldiers in rain, mud, and intolerable suffering. The first Battle of Passchendaele began on 12 October, the second on the 26th. That day the Canadian Corps led the attack under appalling conditions but gained nearly all the objectives that Field-Marshal Sir Douglas Haig had wanted for his winter line. It was not without cost. From 31 July to 10 November, the British lost 244,897 troops.[97] By 1 January 1918 Haig would have fewer than 607,403 trained men available, excluding dominion troops. Supply lines and troop movements to Europe were critical.

Back in Canada another dispute with Admiralty had intensified headquarters' sensitivity to the Chambers problem in October and November 1917. It concerned control of the intelligence centre in Halifax. Their lordships in London had been preparing to close down the British centre at St John's and concentrate intelligence functions at the Halifax centre, which had assumed greatly increased importance since the introduction of convoys.[98] Canadian naval headquarters readily agreed to the change as it merely formalized the arrangements developed since the summer.

Then came the twist. The Admiralty proposed that the Halifax centre should logically come under London's direct control. It provoked not entirely unfounded nationalist objections in Ottawa, to which Commander Stephens gave incisive expression. As he wrote to Kingsmill, the whole question of "Admiralty control in Canada [was a] continuous process ... very derogatory" to the Canadian navy. Indeed, it was "the cause of difficulty and dissatisfaction amongst officers." It undermined national autonomy and smacked of opportunism: "Little was heard of [the proposal] whilst the war and its effects were more distant from Canada than now, but as operations extend [westward toward Canada] so does the Admiralty move ... The Admiralty has, of course, full command on the high seas; but in Canadian waters it is necessary that the [Canadian] Department should be supreme in all circumstances if [it] is to be anything but a name only."[99]

Canadians won their case at least partially by dint of efficiency, for successive commanders-in-chief had always been satisfied with the way the RCN had operated the facility. It was not the last occasion on which the navy pursued a quest for autonomy.[100]

The Halifax explosion of 6 December 1917 dwarfed all the political in-fighting. Caused by friendly vessels navigating in confined waters, the world's greatest man-made explosion before Hiroshima savaged Canada's principal Atlantic port.[101]

That morning the outbound Belgian relief ship *Imo* committed a fundamental error in rules of the road and collided with the incoming French munitions ship *Mont Blanc*, igniting benzol stored on the French vessel's upper deck and detonating over 2,700 tons of picric acid, TNT, and gun cotton in her hold. The blast and the resultant tidal wave and fires levelled over two and one-half square kilometres of the city's industrial section in the north end and obliterated the railway station and freight yards, ships, homes, and factories. Out of a population of 50,000, over 1,600 died, 9,000 were wounded, and 6,000 were left homeless. Fire that threatened the main dockyard magazine forced citizens to evacuate the city in appalling weather conditions.

The event marked a new datum in Canada's consciousness. In the perceptive account of novelist Hugh MacLennan: "The people huddled together on the trucks and carts looked miserable and hungry, and this was not a vision transported from France or Serbia or some country that was never immune to such things, but an actual occurrence in Halifax ... The snow fell invisibly in the darkest night anyone in Halifax could remember ... The ships in the Basin were still awaiting convoy and the storm hid most of them. In the dawn the harbour was bleak and steel-coloured, extending into the whitened land like a scimitar with broken edges, stained by fragments of debris drifting with the tide."[102]

Although adjacent to the convulsive explosion, the naval dockyard and commercial piers had escaped complete destruction; most buildings and docks, though severely damaged, remained standing. HMCS *Niobe*, her decks virtually stripped, suffered heavy casualties. No warship was sunk, however. Within days, convoys were once again sailing from the city, and the routine of defensive patrols was scarcely interrupted. Hasty repairs kept the dockyard functioning, even if at reduced efficiency.

The explosion turned public opinion against the Canadian navy. The disaster aroused suspicions that the RCN was not only utterly inadequate in strength but criminally inept. Responsible for traffic control in wartime, the navy was blamed for the collision. Indeed, local authorities charged the navy's chief examining officer with manslaughter.[103] Though he was quickly acquitted, public hostility toward the navy – and utter lack of confidence in it – continued to smoulder. It would soon flare up once again when German u-cruisers struck in the western Atlantic.

The German navy had meanwhile been struggling with a different kind of identity crisis. One aspect hinged on social and political conflicts within the organization itself; the other on strategic and tactical considerations in its gradual transition from a battle-fleet navy to a submarine force. The sailors' strike of August 1917 which led to the naval court martial and judicial murder of two seamen implicated in the Enlisted Mens' Movement marked the overt beginnings of revolutionary forces that would eventually help topple the Germany navy in the November Revolution of 1918.

Admiral Scheer was no less responsible than the officers of the court for the rampant disregard of due process of law; nor did he stop short of whitewashing the officers' record by blaming events on socialist infiltration of the naval service. Despite official attempts at suppressing any news of turmoil in the fleet, internal political machinations within both the navy and the Reichstag led to public disclosure of the navy's autocracy, caste-conscious militarism, and disdain for its subordinates. Indeed the ensuing Reichstag debate on 9 October 1917 brought "irreparable harm to Germany and the navy" by giving wide publicity to these events of such national and international importance.[104]

The British press quickly sensed the destructive undercurrents of dissolution in Germany. In the words of the *Manchester Guardian* of 11 October: "Without a doubt this mutiny is the most serious political event in Germany since the outbreak of the war, and indeed, since [the revolution of] 1848." In fact, however, it was no mutiny at all but a disorganized appeal by frustrated, angry, and neglected sailors for urgently needed social reform.

The navy's leadership responded with repression. "What the navy so effectively hid was the simple fact that its own officers through their bungling, incompetence, and abdication of responsibility were to blame for the navy's inglorious end and that there was virtually no Bolshevik influence in the rebellion that overthrew them and spread revolution in Germany."[105] Movements for reform would be held in check only for a year, until the autumn of 1918, when sailors mutinied against their superiors, and when the superiors themselves rebelled against their government.

Believing that they held revolutionary forces fully in check, German naval authorities turned their attention to what they regarded as a purely military concern. In doing so they experienced a strategic identity crisis. Even during the ascendancy of submarine warfare, Scheer had doggedly clung to supposedly inviolate principles of naval warfare which advocated the primacy of decisive battles by capital ships. He had again evoked his grand vision of the importance of a High Seas Fleet for national credibility and authority when signalling to his fleet the Kaiser's orders for unrestricted u-boat warfare on 31 January 1917.

A stirring mixture of patriotic fervour, blood and thunder, and wishful thinking, Scheer's signal from his flagship, sms *Kaiser Wilhelm II*, advised that all naval units were to subordinate themselves to the submarine war next day. Yet he hearkened back to his old Mahanian theme: "The maritime prestige of a state is [ultimately] borne by a combat-ready High Seas Fleet."[106] Indeed he had concluded his announcement with a flourish that revealed how much he still clung to the old dream: "The peace we aim to force through with submarines must become the second birthday of the German High Seas Fleet."[107] But events had gradually weaned some officers, and pried others, away from this classical strategic thinking toward the proved superior value of submarines. A hybrid "monster" seemed to accommodate the two schools: the u-cruiser.

Against both military and political opposition, Admiral von Holt-zendorff had been urging the primacy of submarines and unrest-ricted submarines warfare since first taking office as chief of the Admiralty Staff. Pressured by von Tirpitz, Scheer, and the Kaiser himself, he had shifted from adamant insistence on the priority of military expedience over political aims to the conviction that the naval war was not an end in itself. By June 1917 he was viewing with concern the "constantly increasing military support afforded to our enemies" from North America and anticipated "combat with American naval forces."[106]

Increasing US involvement in the war necessitated "an effective thrust against America" – but in the new style. As von Holtzendorff anxiously counselled the state secretary of the Imperial Naval Office: "We must even carry the war into American waters. But we lack the effective means to do so as long as our u-cruisers are not at our disposal. This fact compels me to renew my urgent request to Your Excellency to use all available means to hasten the delivery of the u-cruisers that are already delayed beyond schedule."

u-155 (ex *U-Deutschland*) had of course commenced operations against commerce in May 1917; she was only an intimation of what von Holtzendorff wanted to deliver. Nothing would have pleased him more than to advise the Kaiser that "u-cruiser construction was proceeding apace." Planning and construction gathered momentum in the closing months of 1917.[109] In the event, the Kaiser took per-sonal interest in accelerated production and on 22 December 1917 issued an "All-Highest Cabinet Order" creating the new u-Cruiser Squadron. The new organization was directly responsible to the chief of the Admiralty Staff, von Holtzendorff, but with all command appointments made by the Kaiser himself.[110]

Germany, as von Holtzendorff had written to the German chancel-lor in May 1917, was now caught up in a crucial "decisive phase for the very existence of the Fatherland" that would endure for many months.[111] It was a case of "Sein oder Nichtsein unseres Vaterlan-des." This conscious quotation of Hamlet's famous phrase "To be or not to be," which had been common coinage in the German language since the eighteenth century, reflected von Holtzendorff's ever deep-ening quandary: "Whether 'tis nobler in the mind to suffer / The slings and arrows of outrageous fortune, / Or to take arms against a sea of troubles, / And by opposing end them?"[112] His u-cruiser deployments off the North American coast proved a desperate gam-ble that marked the beginning of the end.

- 9 -

Long-Range U-Boats

The autumn of 1917 and the winter and spring of 1918 were a time of frustration for German and Canadian naval staffs alike. While Canadians were preoccupied with mobilization and organization of patrols, Germans struggled with problems of blockade. As Allied defences tightened in European waters, German officers looked to operations on the North American coast to restore U-boat success rates. But delays in completion of additional long-range submarines and reluctance of political leaders to sanction a full-blooded transatlantic offensive threatened seriously to diminish that initiative. From both German and British standpoints, it was only a matter of time before the offensive in North American waters would begin. Distracted by upheavals within its own senior ranks and by the demands of intense operations in other theatres, Britain passed its threat assessment only belatedly to Ottawa and provided often unhelpful advice.

Unaware of Admiral Kingsmill's decision to appoint Captain Walter Hose in charge of East Coast Patrols on the recall from Halifax of the ill-starred Commodore Coke in August 1917, Admiralty had sent a replacement to gather up the pieces that Coke had left. He was Captain Joseph Hatcher. All too soon, Kingsmill and Deputy Minister Desbarats began to doubt that the British officer's previous experience in the Mediterranean enabled him to grasp the quite different situation in the northwest Atlantic. Nor had they any confidence in his ability or inclination to defend the interests of the Canadian service.

Hatcher had in any event swallowed his disappointment at not receiving command of the patrols and had agreed to serve as an expert adviser in Ottawa; he set about drafting an operational plan for the expanded east coast flotilla. He agreed with Vice-Admiral Browning, commander-in-chief, North America and West Indies Station, that enemy mines posed the greatest danger. As experience in European waters had proved, submarine and surface minelayers could lay minefields within the 100-fathom line off Halifax or Sydney; the shelf stretched to seaward up to 37 miles from Sydney and 130 miles from Halifax. Hatcher therefore proposed outfitting a large proportion of the existing fleet and vessels then being completed with minesweeping equipment; this would not only improve coverage off ports but permit regular sweeps of the shipping lanes within the 100-fathom line. At his urging, the department also ordered depth charges from Britain, thus enabling patrol vessels to attack u-boats after they had submerged.[1]

Scarcely had Hatcher drafted the main body of his proposals when Admiralty unexpectedly laid claim to the complete first run of hulls being built in Canada on British account. This meant that the first twenty trawlers and fifty drifters off the ways would now be deployed in European rather than Canadian waters.[2] The decision turned Hatcher's plan into a paper exercise which he attempted to redeem with some last-minute amendments in the concluding pages of the final version of 3 October 1917. The result was incongruous. He had written the first sections of the paper when anticipating Admiralty's withdrawal of only a small number of those vessels then building in Canada under imperial contract; this let him insist upon 144 vessels as the very least number needed to carry out essential operations. But his conclusion now stressed the unlikelihood of enemy incursions into the remote and hazardous waters off the Canadian coast and argued that 113 vessels – the largest number that might be available after the seventy trawlers and drifters had departed overseas – would actually suffice.[3]

On seeing Hatcher's paper, Hose immediately launched himself into a verbal sparring match with the British officer over the utility of drifters. In European waters these vessels were employed in a passive role, drifting with indicator nets down in the approach channels to ports to catch a u-boat attempting a submerged entry. Hose insisted that even fifty of the little vessels – the maximum that the RCN could now expect – would be of no value whatever in Canadian waters. It would be much better, he advised, to allow the Royal Navy to take all one hundred drifters in exchange for an increased allocation to the RCN of the larger trawlers building in Canada on imperial account. This suggestion touched off a technical argument about the tactical employment of drifters, with Admiral Browning supporting Hatcher while Admiral Kingsmill backed Hose.[4]

Kingsmill recognized the dispute as symptomatic of larger difficulties that could be settled only if the Admiralty itself made a firm and reasoned allocation of vessels to Canadian waters. To his mind it was entirely unacceptable that Admiralty leave Canada only those few that were not immediately required for overseas duty. On 22 November 1917 Kingsmill telegraphed Admiralty over the minister's signature and asked three pointed questions. What was the precise scale of attack that Canada faced? What defences were required? And what assistance might Canada expect from the Royal Navy? Kingsmill followed the telegram with a lengthy memorandum that documented the difficulties that Admiralty's erratic advice had caused since 1916. Indeed he suggested that Admiralty's sudden allocation of the twenty trawlers and fifty drifters to European waters had repeated an already too-familiar pattern of half-baked and misleading advice. His communications set the stage for a Canadian mission to London; personal contact was the key to ensuring that Canadian requirements were properly addressed. Captain E.H. Martin, RCN, went to London at the end of November as the principal delegate; he was accompanied by Captain Hatcher, whom Kingsmill contrived not to have reposted to Canada.[5]

Martin's consultations at Admiralty soon established a disturbing fact: Canadian and British authorities in the western Atlantic were entirely out of touch concerning the potential threat to North American waters. Admiralty had in fact failed to pass even the most basic information, let alone any appreciations of the submarine threat;[6] this even though decryptions of German wireless traffic and other sources had enabled Admiralty to follow the German long-range U-cruiser program in considerable detail.[7]

Admiralty's failure to inform either Canadian naval headquarters in Ottawa or the commander-in-chief, North America and West Indies Station, in Halifax and Bermuda is particularly striking in light of Britain's close liaison with the US navy. Admiral William Sims, USN, had already been working in close touch with Operational Intelligence in London since May 1917. In September of that year Admiral H.T. Mayo, USN, commander-in-chief, Atlantic Fleet, had received specific warnings from Admiralty during his visit to London. He learned that the Germans had now converted five mercantile submarines in addition to *U-Deutschland* and therefore had the capacity for sustained mid-ocean patrols; there they could attack convoys well beyond the limit of existing escort by destroyers. The grim fact, Admiralty informed Mayo, was that Britain had no available warships with which to extend the destroyer escort of convoys into the central and western Atlantic.[8] Only as a result of Kingsmill's pressure and Captain Martin's visit did Canadian authorities finally learn of this danger at the end of the year; the most serious threat during the coming season was not hit-and-run raids by minelayers but direct attacks on shipping by long-range u-boats that would probably linger offshore for some weeks at a time.

By January 1918 the first purpose-built u-cruisers were nearing completion and the Admiralty in London had become still more concerned about the Germans' increasing capacity to sustain long-range operations. These huge combat submarines were sturdier than their commercial predecessors and could press home tenacious attacks. Admiralty did not advise the Canadian government of this danger until an appreciation of 3 January 1918, the essential elements of which were already some months old:

The introduction of the Convoy System has provided a strong incentive to the enemy to send submarines across the Atlantic and attack the Convoys at the ports of departure.[9]

... It is considered very probable that an attack by one of the new submarine cruisers may be expected at any time after March, but the prevalence of drift ice may act to a certain extent as a deterrent; but where the convoys can go, there the submarine can also go, and an attack on shipping issuing from Halifax or other ports on the Atlantic seaboard is to be contemplated ... [One must assume] that at any moment one submarine may be in a position to attack every outgoing convoy. In this connection, the probable tactics of the submarine cruiser must be considered. She will doubtless carry a large supply of torpedoes, but to compensate for such a long voyage and such an extended absence from her port, she is more likely to rely on her gun power and a large outfit of ammunition.[10]

Admiralty considered the threat of a submarine minelayer unlikely, though it allowed the possibility of a "hit-and-run" visit by a minelaying surface raider in the broad approaches to Canadian ports. Even then, it argued, the elaborate minesweeping schemes of Hatcher and Hose were unnecessary.

The primary and most pressing concern for Canada, Admiralty insisted, was direct defence of convoys against submarine attack. Experience in European waters had left little doubt that the u-boats would strike in the approaches to ports, where convoys were easiest to locate. Merchant ships were especially vulnerable during the first hours of passage, when they emerged single file through anti-submarine nets and lumbered into sailing formation. Preoccupied during this critical phase with establishing convoy organization and discipline, escorts could easily be caught off guard by a snap attack. The Admiralty therefore recommended a force of six trawlers and twelve drifters at both Halifax and Sydney in order to reinforce convoy escorts "until dark hours of first day out," or at least until the convoy had properly formed up. These forces should patrol harbour approaches between convoys in order to guard against lurking u-boats.

But where Admiralty's earlier advice had played down the threat to the Gulf of St Lawrence, this latest appreciation thrust it once more to front-stage. There seemed little doubt that German submariners might penetrate these inland waterways in order to strike the heavy traffic from Montreal and Quebec. Eighteen patrol vessels – virtually the whole of the existing Canadian force – should therefore continue to operate in the Gulf with a reinforcement of nine trawlers. Admiralty regarded this strong flotilla as a "striking force"; with its main strength concentrated in the Cabot Strait, it could quickly respond to u-boat reports in the Gulf, on the Atlantic route south of Newfoundland, or along the seaward approaches to Nova Scotia.

Admiralty recommended minesweeping forces similar to those proposed by Admiral Browning in 1917: ten trawler-sweepers at Halifax and six at Sydney. Most of these were already available. In addition, Admiralty called for a reserve of twelve sweep-equipped drifters to deal with any minefields laid beyond the defended port approaches to which the trawlers must be strictly confined.

As Kingsmill had hoped, Admiralty supported this advice with a generous and definite allocation to the RCN of the drifters and trawlers then under construction in Canada on British account. The first of the imperial-contract vessels to be completed – thirty-seven drifters and three trawlers – had arrived in Halifax for final outfitting during the fall of 1917 prior to the St Lawrence freeze-up; a thirty-eighth was damaged en route and put into Charlottetown for the winter. By January 1918 fifteen of the drifters had already left Canada for service with the Royal Navy; four of these had gone to New York and Hampton Roads in support of British convoy operations there, while the other eleven crossed to Bermuda prior to sailing for European waters via the short run to the Azores. Admiralty now cancelled sailing orders for the remaining twenty-three drifters at Halifax (and Charlottetown) and promised the RCN the next thirteen drifters that entered service from Canadian yards; the total number of drifters therefore stood at thirty-six. The three Admiralty trawlers were also to remain with the RCN, as would the next twenty-seven to come down the ways. This made a total of thirty.[11]

The Canadian defence problem remained unresolved despite even this most welcome decision. The additional drifters and, more important, the urgently needed trawlers could not leave the builders' yards in the St Lawrence until the spring thaw in 1918 – by which time the first u-boat might have arrived. Further, and more fundamental, because of the very nature of the expanded patrol flotilla, its complement of some ninety-six minor war vessels could fulfil only subordinate roles.

The first line of defence – and Admiralty emphasized the point – could be provided only by fast anti-submarine warships. The Admiralty recommended a total of twelve vessels: six destroyers or sloops and six "fast trawlers." Sloops carried armament similar to that of a destroyer but, with a maximum speed of 20 knots, were slower; "fast trawlers" were essentially "emergency construction sloops" with the characteristics of that class. As Admiralty explained, such a force could provide at least two fast escorts for each convoy for the fist twenty-four hours of passage (roughly a distance of 200–300 miles) and ensure the availability of at least two escorts to form the van of the Gulf striking force.

Significantly, Admiralty deemed two destroyers (or comparable fast warships) as the bare minimum that could confidently engage a single u-cruiser. Here Admiralty made what Canadians took as a specific commitment: "My Lords are approaching the us Naval Authorities and will later communicate to you information as to whether six us Destroyers can be provided by the 1st April 1918. By the same date My Lords anticipate that they will be in a position to send over to Canada six Fast Trawlers, should the situation make it desirable to do so."[12]

Captain Hose's reaction to this Admiralty appreciation of 3 January 1918 typified the Canadian service's response. Outgunned and outmanoeuvred by the new German undersea raiders, his force "would be practically at the mercy" of the u-cruisers. Three months earlier he had been led to believe that mines were the most serious threat; that was why he had sought only additional trawlers. Now that Admiralty had changed tack he wanted the latest, high-power four-inch guns for every vessel that could carry them. He wanted eight of the guns fitted on HMCS *Rainbow* and urged that she be recommissioned and brought around from the west coast; he pressed for immediate, emergency construction of a class of large trawler armed with the four-inch gun. He called for an anti-submarine patrol of five seaplanes and an airship based in Halifax. He appealed to headquarters to "get seven modern Torpedo Boat Destroyers out here" as quickly as possible.[13]

His exasperated cry was in vain. By the time Admiralty's appreciation of 3 January 1918 reached Ottawa, the promise to find fast escorts for Canada had already been shelved. Indeed, the appreciation had been written at a moment of upheaval in the Admiralty resulting from the dismissal of Admiral Jellicoe as first sea lord and the appointment, on 27 December 1917, of his successor, Admiral Sir Rosslyn Weymss.[14] Subsequent events leave little doubt that even if Wemyss had seen the Canadian appreciation before it was sent, he had not considered its implications. Senior officers in London appear to have given no further thought to Canadian requirements until the end of February 1918, when the newly appointed commander-in-chief, North America and West Indies, Vice-Admiral Sir William Lowther Grant, raised the thorny question once more.

Grant had arrived in Bermuda to assume his command on 10 February and was alarmed to discover that the Admiralty had done absolutely nothing about the destroyers and fast trawlers for the western Atlantic. Consultation later that month with Canadian naval officers in Halifax revealed how limited Canada's resources actually were. Convinced that the Canadian navy was doing everything it could, Grant warned Admiralty by telegraph of "the very grave risks" to Allied merchant and troop ships if "every effort" were not made to help the Canadians.[15] By this time, however, Admiralty had recognized that delays in Britain's fast-escort building program precluded dispatch of any Royal Navy vessels to Canada.

Wemyss refused to follow up on Admiralty's promise to make a direct appeal to the United States to provide Canada with American destroyers. Quite the contrary happened. Admiralty washed its hands of the matter by instructing Admiral Grant to seek assistance for the Canadian navy himself.[16] As Grant complained in his response of 8 March 1918, this directive thrust him into a question of basic policy.

Up till then Admiralty had insisted that the Americans send every available major anti-submarine vessel overseas. Grant wondered, therefore, whether their lordships in London should not inform the authorities in Washington directly that the u-cruiser threat now justified retention of destroyers in the western Atlantic. Admiralty's cryptic reply – that there had been "no intention to propose any alteration in policy" – still left Grant in some doubt. Admiralty's "conflicting" signals, as he called them, suggested that the threat was really not as grave as he supposed and that he should perhaps ask the Americans to allocate no more than a very small number of fast escorts to Canadian waters. Significantly, Grant had not grasped Admiralty's hidden agenda. He had not understood – and he had no reason to understand – that Admiralty wanted no major anti-submarine craft assigned to Canada at all.[17]

As ineffectively as Admiralty had communicated its intentions to Grant, it was none the less right in not wishing to be seen by the

Americans as having stepped back from its strategy of placing European waters first in priority. A watershed in Anglo-American relations had been crossed as recently as December 1917, when the chief of US naval operations, Admiral Benson, finally became convinced during a visit to London that sending as many warships as possible to Britain was the only solution to the German submarine peril.[18]

The US navy's plan of February 1918 for the defence of American waters against U-cruisers clearly reflected this change. Fully accepting Admiralty's contention that the risk to shipping in North American coastal waters was a slight and acceptable trade-off against victory in Europe, the American staff pared home waters' requirements to the bone. Thus it planned to retain only nine modern destroyers for the whole of the American seaboard.[19]

Grant was caught in a dilemma. As he explained to Admiralty, he was forced to "concur in the view generally expressed this side [of the Atlantic] that we are very open to a sudden attack and sinkings possibly of large troop transports." Such occurrences "would very probably cause great popular commotion in Canada and the United States."[20]

On 18 March Grant dispatched the bad news to Ottawa: no fast craft would be available from Britain for at least "some months," and no deal had yet been worked out with the Americans. When pressed by Grant as to how far he could reduce his demands for American assistance, Kingsmill and his staff responded with a request for five fast escorts instead of the twelve that Admiralty's appreciation of 3 January had laid down.[21] Grant accepted the number as a "maximum" that he could ask without undermining Admiralty's policy of concentration in European waters.[22]

We gain some measure of the new attitude in Washington by the fact that Admiral Benson soon complained to Admiral Sims in London that he was being "pushed" by Grant and the Canadians. So heavily had destroyer allocations for American home waters been cut, Benson insisted, that assignment of even five of them to Canada would "cripple our efforts abroad." Benson sought Admiralty's support in continuing to resist the Canadian request – and he got it.[23] "After consultation with Admiralty," Sims wired, "I can say unreservedly that they are in entire agreement with me in regarding as correct the [US Navy] Department's present policy and in recommending against yielding to Canadian desires."

Sims also revealed that Grant's predecessor, Admiral Browning, had himself recommended against assignment of American ships to Canadian waters on his return from Bermuda in January 1918. Part of Browning's reasoning seems rather curious: support of Canada would cause "an immediate demand for similar allocation to United States ports," which felt just as vulnerable as the foreign ports of Halifax and Sydney.[24] In this and other matters, Admiralty in London was providing the US Navy Department with fuller and more forthright information than it was passing even to the British commander-in-chief.

Had the Americans not shown Sims's signal to Admiral Grant, he would perhaps never have learned that Admiralty had decided against destroyers for the Canadian coast at least two months earlier. Grant was livid. He protested to Admiralty by telegram on 18 April by pointing out that neither he nor the Canadians had been badgering the Americans; he merely had been carrying out the Admiralty's own scheme of 3 January, which he had every reason to believe still reflected British policy. At the very least, he explained, Admiralty's bypassing of the Canadian navy undermined his own credibility. "Please," his telegram insisted, "prevent communications which might lead the United States to suppose [that] I misrepresent facts or act contrary to Admiralty wishes."[25]

The Admiralty had meanwhile made yet another major change in its assessment of Canadian requirements – again without any consultation. In January and February the Royal Navy's Air Division had considered what assistance it might give Canadians in mounting antisubmarine air patrols. Perhaps while pondering their failure to send destroyers to the western Atlantic, their lordships found that aviation would be a valuable asset. But they could spare no British resources. On 7 March 1918 they therefore cabled Ottawa a reminder that "enemy submarines may be expected to operate off the Canadian Coast in the future" and entirely surprised headquarters with the advice that the time had now come for the RCN to form its own air service.

The ambitious proposal called for development of factories to produce seaplanes and kite balloons. The latter were towed behind warships for aerial reconnaisance. Admiralty advised Ottawa to obtain special materials and labour from the United States and to get the temporary loan of American aircraft while Canadian machines were being built.[26] This unheralded new turn spun yet another web of letters, cables, and personal missions.

The Canadian navy had a new minister, C.C. Ballantyne, the Liberal businessman whom Borden had included when forming his Union government in the fall of 1917. A long-time supporter of the idea of a distinct Canadian navy, he nevertheless involved himself in the details of service affairs little more than Hazen had done. However, he did intervene as confusion and difficulties multiplied in early 1918. On learning of the proposal for aircraft, he immediately dispatched Desbarats to Washington. The deputy learned only that the us navy was itself too hard pressed by short-falls in production to offer early assistance.[27] When Admiral Grant visited Ottawa, in mid-April, he was confronted by an angry Ballantyne, who, flanked by his advisers, denounced the Admiralty's failure to provide support of any description. Grant, his ears still ringing, quickly arranged for meetings of Canadian, British, and American service representatives to see what precisely could be done about acquiring fast escorts and aircraft.[28] These were the first such joint meetings of the war.

The Allies were feeling German pressure. Already, on 11 April 1918, Field-Marshal Haig had issued his famous "Backs to the Wall" order during the Germans' second offensive on the Western Front: "Every position must be held to the last man. There must be no retirement."[29] As at Verdun, the Somme, and other great battles, casualties in March and April 1918 had been virtually equal: 331,797 Allied dead and wounded against 348,000 German. Convoy protection and anti-submarine warfare to ensure that fresh troops and supplies from North America reached the Allied armies were more important than ever.

During the initial Anglo-Canadian-American naval conference in Washington, on 20 April 1918, Captain Hose learned that the us navy was assigning two old torpedo boats and six submarine chasers for operations under his control.[30] The "subchasers" were small, 110-foot wooden craft designed for rapid wartime construction; their principle advantage lay in their ready availability in great quantity.[31] They owed their origin in large measure to an enthusiasm for yachts fostered by Assistant Secretary of the Navy Franklin Roosevelt.

Nearly three hundred of the boats had already been commissioned. Although many of them were already slated for overseas service, the us Navy Department intended that at least sixty should remain in American waters to bear the major brunt of anti-submarine escort and patrol. Over double that number were in fact ultimately employed in us waters.[32] Welcome as the sub chasers were when they arrived at Halifax in May, these little vessels were in no way the equivalent of destroyers or sloops. Still, the RCN had no choice but to employ them in long-range escort and striking force roles.

The Washington conference dealt primarily with the proposed air patrol. Hose helped draft the final conference report which established the need for four stations: small ones at Cape Race (Newfoundland) and Shelburne (Nova Scotia) and larger facilities at Halifax and Sydney. The smaller posts would operate a few kite balloons and dirigibles or perhaps even three seaplanes at Shelburne, while the larger stations were each to receive six seaplanes, four kite balloons, and three dirigibles. Quick action by all three countries – Britain, Canada, and the United States – might make it possible to commence flying operations from Sydney and Halifax by early July.

The plan called for close co-operation: Canada would develop the sites; the United States would provide the aircraft, some air crew, and training facilities; Britain would send experienced officers. Hose fervently hoped that the plan would meet its deadline: "Since the Canadian Coast Patrol contains no units or combination of vessels which are sufficiently fast or powerful in armament to operate offensively against a U-Cruiser, it will be to the Air Service that we must look for any chance of rendering such an enemy hors-de-combat."[33] Disappointment quickly set in. Seaplanes were to have formed the core of the force, but within a matter of days the United States advised that it could not dispatch them until mid-August. This proved to be the first of many delays and difficulties in all three countries which postponed the project beyond the point of utility.[34]

Hose and a group of American and British delegates to the Washington conference had meanwhile travelled to Boston to confer with the commandant of the First Naval District, Rear-Admiral Spencer S. Wood, USN, where they were joined by Admiral Kingsmill. During meetings, 22–24 April 1918, Wood offered assistance along much the same lines as the Canadians had sought a year earlier.[35] In the words of the final agreement: "The Commandant, First U.S. Naval District [will] take over Coastal Patrols, sea-patrols, protection of traffic and offensive action taken against submarines as far east as the 65th meridian (Lockeport, N.S.) including the outer part of the Bay of Fundy."[36]

The First Naval District adjusted operations of its northernmost coastal patrol to include the mouth of the Bay of Fundy and posted American lookout personnel at three Canadian lighthouses (Grand Manan, Machias Seal Island, and Gannet) on the western side of the bay.[37] The southern tip of Nova Scotia became a new American patrol section, with headquarters at Shelburne, where Canada turned over the government wharf to the US navy.[38] Because of a shortage of suitable vessels, however, operations from the Shelburne station seem not to have begun until some time after early August. A welter of problems with communications, logistics, personnel, and ships caused the delay.[39]

With such slight support, the RCN was hard-pressed to protect the resources most vital to the Allied war effort: major east coast ports and the convoys and other high-value ocean shipping that sailed from them. What, then, could be done to safeguard the large fishing fleets that operated on the rich banks from south of Yarmouth to Newfoundland's waters? Very little, it soon became clear.

As early as 1 March 1918 the Admiralty in London advised the Colonial Office of a conference that had been convened "to consider the question of Allied cooperation for the protection of fishing vessels on the Newfoundland Banks ... in view of the possibilities of hostile submarine operations off the coast of North America."[40] A British naval captain, acting on behalf of the high commissioner for Canada, had represented Canada's interests. The conference did not regard the fisheries as "liable to continual attack" but acknowledged that "the menace existed especially where the routes of steamers crossed the fishing grounds"; for this reason, "some protection, moral more than actual was advisable." The RCN was not advised in precisely these benign terms; nor was it informed that the French saw the threat as sufficiently grave to arm each of their eighty-two fishing vessels with two guns and to run them in convoy to and from the banks.[41]

In response to cables from the Colonial Office in London, Commander R.M. Stephens took up the committee's major conclusion; on 15 March 1918 he advised Admiral Kingsmill that "no protection can be afforded unless the vessels act in groups."[42] "If they fail to agree to organise in this way, the Department can then either repudiate any responsibility for them or can exercise its powers under the Defence of Canada Order to make them do so." That same day he urged the superintendent of fisheries to have his inspectors warn fishermen "that German submarine operations are anticipated on this side of the Atlantic this season"; he explained that "submarines have largely increased in size and can keep the sea for several months without returning to harbour, and that owing to the stringent countermeasures taken on the other side of the Atlantic the comparatively fair field on this side may prove attractive."[43] He proposed forming vessels into groups on the fishing grounds, with one boat acting in operational control. The superintendent directed his inspectors to "give this matter immediate attention."[44]

But organization was more easily discussed in theory than put into practice. For one thing, the concept of a "fishing fleet" reflected a higher degree of cohesion among boats than existed in fact; individual boats worked far afield according to independent schedules and season and according to the particular catch they were after. For example, Nova Scotia vessels fished not only the southern Nova Scotia coast from Brown's Bank to Banquereau Banks, and northeast to

Sable Island Bank, but also the Newfoundland Banks and the Magdalen Islands, in the Gulf of St Lawrence.

In all, the "fleet" usually consisted of 125 Canadian vessels on the Grand Banks alone, with some 80 to 100 additional boats from Newfoundland.[45] The inspector at Digby explained that "our principal vessel owners ... are of the opinion that it would be impossible to form these vessels into a fleet or group on the fishing grounds"; Pictou reported that many of the boats in his district were not easily organized and in any event "are insignificant and probably will not be subject to attack."[46] Despite this soothing advice, vessel owners preferred the constant presence of patrols.

The RCN could not oblige them. Admiralty had rejected a stop-gap proposal to recommission the old west coast depot-ships HMCS *Algerine* and *Rainbow* with reduced crews for banks patrols. In Admiralty's view, the warships would still tie up too many men and could not sustain themselves at sea for long; indeed, they carried armament too heavy for anti-submarine duties.[47] Canada had been expecting some support from the United States and France but was soon disappointed by disturbing news: the Americans intended to provide nothing to protect their own fishing fleet apart from "two gunboats of the Ice Patrol"; only one of them would be at sea at any one time, and the French patrols would be delayed at least until June for lack of armament.[48] When Admiral Grant suggested the palliative of arming Canadian fishing vessels and giving fishermen "a few days gun training at Halifax," Kingsmill could only reply that guns were simply not available.[49]

By the end of May a conference took place in Halifax between British and French representatives at which neither Canada nor Newfoundland was represented. The governor of Newfoundland did "not think this [oversight] of great importance, [for] the views of the Admiral [Grant] so far as I understand them are so much in accord with those of the Government of Newfoundland that all we should have to do is to fall in with your arrangements."[50] By 11 June Captain of Patrols Walter Hose had conferred in Halifax and Shelburne with officers of the British, French, and US navies, but little was decided except methods of communicating between ships.[51] The fact remained that patrol ships were scarce, and air patrols would often be rendered useless by fog.[52]

In the final analysis, one vessel on fish patrol was all the Canadians could manage. The situation had not improved by July, when Admiral Grant judged that the "proposed banks patrol of only one vessel on station at a time [was] too small to accomplish anything"; such vessels would be "better employed in coastal patrol and escort duties

[and] in the event of urgent need could be diverted to the Banks."[53] Walter Hose summed up the dispiriting situation in mid-September: "As matters stand at present, with the many calls that there are on the Canadian Patrol Squadron for Convoy escorts, coastal and ocean going, minesweeping and trade route patrols, that very little can be done in the matter of a constant Patrol on the Banks."[54]

In fact, shortage of ships and lack of resources and trained personnel had profoundly influenced every aspect of Canadian operations in 1918. In April there were forty-seven vessels in the east coast flotilla, including the twenty-three imperial-contract drifters and three trawlers which had arrived at Halifax the previous fall and had now been definitely allocated to the RCN.[55] This complement was less than half of the ships needed to complete the organization for the 1918 season which Hose had formulated on the basis of Admiralty's recommendations: thirty vessels at Halifax and forty-one at Sydney, for minesweeping, port defence, and convoy escort duties at each place, and another group of twenty-seven at Sydney for "striking force" duties and the St Lawrence patrol.[56]

Moreover, the ships available on the east coast in the spring of 1918 were a singularly unimpressive group. The twenty-three drifters were unsuitable for heavy-weather or long-distance operations. At least half of the larger ships, Kingsmill warned the minister, were "lame ducks." Of the nine auxiliary patrol ships, *Grilse*, *Lady Evelyn*, and *Laurentian* had never handled rough seas well, while *Canada* needed major repairs. The six "battle"-class trawlers that had been delivered the previous fall had also "not yet been proved fit for seagoing work"; this was probably a reference to machinery breakdowns that plagued these ships until the end of the war. All the remaining trawlers – seven purchased in the United States in 1917 and the three Admiralty-contract ones – were fully committed to minesweeping at Halifax.[57] In short, there were at most a half-dozen reliable ships available for extended patrols in all weathers.

Hopes for providing support to convoys and for a strengthened St Lawrence patrol therefore rested on early delivery of the remaining twenty-seven Admiralty trawlers assigned to the RCN and on the second group of six battle-class trawlers when ice cleared from the St Lawrence in May. Only seventeen trawlers actually arrived on the east coast during that month, and another ten in June. Delivery of the remainder and of the final thirteen drifters was not completed until August.[58]

None of these vessels was ready for naval duty on reaching Halifax or Sydney. Of course, any newly built ship needs a "work-up" and "shake-down" cruise before being declared operational. But these new units of Canada's naval forces needed all of that and more. The naval staffs on the east coast were not prepared for the welter of serious problems that resulted from rushed work and shortages of both materials and experienced labour in the builder's yards. Of the thirteen Admiralty trawlers that took up station at Halifax between May and July, for example, only four had boilers and engines technically certifiable as either "good" or even "fairly good." The machinery in many of the drifters appears to have been still worse. The navy had to correct defects, fit special equipment and armament, and sometimes even rebuild boilers.[59]

Despite the best efforts of patrol workshops and civilian firms in the area, naval crews all too often set sail on operations in vessels whose repairs could not be properly completed, hoping against hope that there would be no critical breakdown before additional time could be scheduled in the overcrowded yards.[60] One officer with the director of ship construction dug his way out from under an avalanche of complaints from the east coast in early August 1918 to explain the case of drifter *CD 37*. The boilers were admittedly in dreadful condition, but if the navy had refused such ships there would have been no hulls at all for the Canadian force. "In many cases the work was done by alien enemies," he claimed, "and I think that has largely contributed to the class of work which was put out."[61] He had found a scapegoat in the German émigrés who had supposedly built the ships, just as newspapers blamed the "alien spies in our midst" for the success of German submarines off the Nova Scotia coast.

Although civilian yards at Saint John and Pictou were pressed into service to augment those at Halifax and Sydney, the crush of urgent work forced postponement of even routine refits to the point where the efficiency of ships was seriously impaired.[62] The great increase in the number of ships in patrols, together with the inevitable marine accidents and unexpected major breakdowns, compounded the problems of readiness and swamped the facilities. Captain Hose reported in August, for example, that four of the older vessels at Sydney had not been drydocked for proper overhaul in thirteen months or more. Indeed, the marine slips had no available time to haul out many of the newer vessels whose hulls were becoming so badly fouled with marine growth that "the speed of many is reduced to below five knots."[63] As it turned out, major improvements to correct flaws in design could not be carried out until war's end.[64]

It was perhaps not unnatural that those responsible for building the ships tended to blame operating personnel for the defects and malfunctions. To some extent they were undoubtedly right, for the RCN desperately lacked qualified personnel in many key trades and ranks. Although too few records on manpower and training have survived to permit an authoritative account, it is none the less possible to derive the salient features of what both Kingsmill and Hose recognized as a severe manning problem.

In February 1918 some 1,518 personnel were either already serving in patrol vessels or undergoing training prior to manning new-construction ships. Included in this total were at least ninety ratings from the Royal Naval Reserve's Newfoundland division whom Admiralty had sent to man the first imperial-contract trawlers and drifters which had arrived at Halifax in the fall of 1917. Fewer than two hundred of the Canadian personnel were regular-force RCN, while the remainder had enlisted in the RNCVR. Given Kingsmill's difficulties in finding merchant seamen when expansion had begun in 1917, it is a fair assumption that a considerable proportion of these men had little or no marine experience.[65]

That, however, was only the beginning of the problem. To complete the manning of the new-construction ships due for delivery in the spring, Hose estimated he would need 734 additional personnel, for a total strength of 2,252. This figure included a 10 per cent margin of "spare" personnel who would operate the patrol workshops in Sydney and Halifax; they would also replace those who became casualties at sea or who had otherwise gone ashore on leave or for training.[66]

Kingsmill hoped that Admiralty would provide a leavening of some 345 experienced seamen. A portion would come from the Overseas Division of the RNCVR – their lordships had already agreed that some members might be returned to Canada for patrol duties – but a considerable number with special qualifications would have to be supplied from the British service. By the early summer of 1918 Admiralty appears to have dispatched no more than about two hundred men; a few dozen of them were Newfoundlanders, while the majority were Canadians from the RNCVR's Overseas Division.[67] Under the circumstances of 1918, it was nevertheless a considerable concession. In fact it admitted Admiralty's moral obligation to Canada, where some Admiralty officers had argued that the Royal Navy's own desperate manpower shortage precluded any assistance at all.[68] Still, serious shortages obliged Hose and Kingsmill to rely more heavily than they had wished on newly recruited, inexperienced men.

The extent and effect of the shortage of qualified personnel are particularly evident in the case of commanding officers for patrol vessels. Hose wanted sixty-one additional skippers, and Kingsmill asked Admiralty to supply twenty-five of them from the British service; he may have hoped to recall others from the Overseas Division of the RNCVR.[69] Once all the bartering and shuffling had ceased, Canada received thirteen skippers from overseas – four Royal Naval reservists and nine returned Canadians. Hose could just manage to cover the shortages by giving command of trawlers and drifters to nineteen officers in the more junior rank of "mate" and by assigning twelve commands to newly promoted skippers. Even the most seasoned of them had not been in the navy for more than a year.[70]

Makeshift postings to undermanned and undertrained ships were common practice. As Hose complained to headquarters: "To fill temporary vacancies of Mates in sea-going ships ... it is very frequently necessary to take a Mate out of a ship which has just come in from 16 to 20 days patrolling ... and send him to sea again at once. The officers and men of the vessels are untrained, not only in the technical knowledge required to handle the weapons ... but also in service discipline, [for they were drafted aboard ship] as hardly more than raw recruits."

So undermanned were ships and shore establishments, in fact, and so heavy was the schedule of patrols, that "it is impossible to fit in Hydrophone, Signal, Minesweeping, Depth Charges, and Gunnery Instruction, clean and refit, coal and store the ships, and also provide the work parties [to augment the understaffed base]."[71]

The stress and fatigue of life in the small, uncomfortable ships in the Canadian patrols affected efficiency, health, and morale. The caulking in the drifters and trawlers, for instance, was notoriously bad and caused intolerable living conditions below decks. The refusal of seven seamen and stokers of *TR 30* to put to sea under such conditions led to draconian measures: court martial followed by eighteen months' hard labour in Rockhead prison at Halifax. Details available about three of the sailors are revealing: none had any sea experience prior to enlisting, their service ranged from six to eighteen months, and two were still in their teens and one was just twenty.[72]

How different the fate of the Newfoundland sailors the previous February who had refused to work at the imperial rate of forty cents a day; there was no court martial, and after a brief detention they received a raise to the Canadian rate of $1.10, retroactive to their first day of arrival in Halifax.[73] The German scare that summer may well have tipped the scales against the crew of TR 30.

The effects of the heavy schedule of patrols, the mounting toll of defects, and the hectic maintenance and training activity told differently on the older merchant seamen. Thus the skipper of HMCS *Arleux* lost a tow during a tense seamanship evolution and while the accident was still under investigation collided with another patrol vessel. A merchant mariner of long experience, whose entry into the navy in 1917 had been followed by promotion, he was simply burned out at the age of fifty and was honourably discharged.[74]

The difficulties under which Canadian patrols laboured were typical of hastily organized auxiliary forces elsewhere. One affectionate memoir of the British auxiliary patrol confesses that the "trawlerman ... was a rough, tough, hardcase fellow" who did not fit the pattern that regular force officers expected.[75] Many officers, the author continues, exacerbated disciplinary problems by "foolishly attempting to use the methods on independent fishermen which had been devised only for men accustomed to the life and discipline of the Royal Navy."

American records about the US navy's submarine chasers echo much of the Canadian experience. Leaking hulls resulting from slipshod construction made life aboard most of the craft extremely unpleasant and caused one vessel nearly to founder. Poor finishing work produced an endless stream of annoying minor defects, and in one instance a life-rail gave way and caused the death of two seamen. Training of personnel was "notoriously inadequate"; vessels put to sea with officers and crew who had never before sailed out of sight of land and had never fired the gun.[76]

Yet in comparison with its British and American counterparts, the Canadian patrol operated at a special disadvantage. Practically every aspect of the auxiliary patrol was foreign to both the Canadian and Newfoundland marine community.[77] British patrols, by contrast, incorporated the peacetime fishing fleet. Their crews and shipyards were intimately familiar with the trawler and drifter classes of vessel; their minesweeping and anti-submarine tactics had grown directly out of trawler and drifter-net techniques, which were second nature to the crews. This was not the case in Canada, where fishermen put to sea in schooners whose sole machinery was perhaps a small auxiliary engine and who fished with hand-held lines from dories. The American patrol forces, for all their shortcomings, were supported by the vast resources of the regular navy.[78] Both British and American auxiliary forces operated with the knowledge that squadrons of major warships under national control could render immediate assistance. Canadians could have no such confidence in their own national waters.

While the Allies were grappling in late 1917 and early 1918 with how they might adequately but economically defend North American waters, German political and naval leaders were debating among themselves about the best means of pressing their attack. They were troubled by nagging fears that unrestricted submarine warfare – the most effective means of waging war at sea – might backfire with such damaging results on the diplomatic front as to make a satisfactory conclusion to the war still more elusive. Even as late as April 1917 Admiral von Holtzendorff still needed reminding by the state secretary of the Foreign Office that the naval war was not "an end in itself, but a means for realizing political goals."[79]

In deference to diplomatic considerations, Germany had refrained from declaring unrestricted submarine warfare in all war zones but had limited it to specific "blockade zones" (Sperrgebiete) in European waters; it had published the geographical boundaries of these zones so that neutrals would have fair warning. Working behind the scenes to achieve his ends, von Holtzendorff refined a compromise solution to the apparent political-tactical conflict in Germany's higher councils that was preventing him from deploying his ultimate weapon. Early in 1918 he began formulating the idea of a blockade-like zone off North America that he hoped would take effect by mid-May.[80]

The question was by no means trivial, for it turned on the central diplomatic issue of maritime rights. Germany, as we have seen, had steadfastly maintained that the real terrorists of the seas were not the U-boats but rather the Royal Navy. Britain, Germany claimed, was the culprit in its constant violation of neutral rights under international law by sealing off legitimate German overseas trade and suborning neutral shipping into supporting the Allied war effort. The argument had some basis in fact. In the early stages of the blockade "the British fleet was singlehandedly intercepting an average of 135 merchant ships weekly."[81] Although the United States had now entered the war, there still remained smaller neutral nations, including Norway, Denmark, and Holland, whose large shipping resources Britain was using with increasing effect in order to compensate for its own lost merchant vessels. Central to Germany's diplomacy was a clear distinction between Britain's "criminal" blockade and its own policy of blockade zones.

From a German perspective, the blockade zone offered neutrals a set of options: they could pursue non-belligerent commerce or risk their vessels on the high seas; they could face the dire consequences of attack without warning by taking direct routes across the free-fire zone or else make extensive detours; or they could make life easier for everyone concerned by simply staying completely away from all threatened waters. That was Germany's political view.

Germany's naval planners placed the emphasis rather differently. In tactical terms, they regarded the declaration of a blockade zone as primarily a means for affording safe attack conditions for the converted merchant submarines which, unlike purpose-built combat boats, could not manoeuvre rapidly on the surface or dive quickly. As a staff officer in von Holtzendorff's Operations Division explained in February 1918, u-cruisers that were forced to wage war according to prize rules – that is, to "visit and search" merchantmen – in areas already heavily controlled by Allied forces "exposed themselves to attack by submarine-traps, disguised armed merchantships."[82] This circumstance was "all the more dangerous since the poor tactical qualities of the u-cruiser make it almost defenceless against such a surprise." Ultimately, therefore, Allied strength and German weakness dictated the measure.

Von Holtzendorff had explained to the Foreign Office in mid-January that "the military necessity of splintering the enemy's defence measures" called for drawing new areas into the already declared blockade zones.[83] "The greatest prospects for success for extending the u-boat war [lay] on the east coast of the United States." Political reservations and the not yet fully developed performance capabilities of submarines, he argued, had held Germany back from this new strategy until now. His debates with a Foreign Office unconvinced of the wisdom of declaring a blockade zone off American shores would continue into late 1918. The chief of the u-Cruiser Flotilla none the less drew up ambitious proposals and plans despite his gnawing uneasiness that he would first have to attack with his converted *Deutschland*-class submarines which were really too clumsy for the job.[84] Yet there seemed little alternative to a thrust against North America. Like von Holtzendorff, the flotilla commander realized the risks in fighting against superior naval power in the waters around Britain and recognized the futility of prowling the mid-ocean, where chances of locating shipping were virtually nil.

Yet opinion within the German navy was by no means unanimous. The idea of a North American blockade zone struck Germany's most successful and famous submarine commander of the war, Kapitän-leutnant Lothar von Arnauld de la Perière, as entirely fallacious. He attacked the concept in a vigorous personal letter to a senior acquaintance in Naval Operations.[85] The u-cruiser missions in which he had participated in the Mediterranean, he argued by analogy, would have achieved far greater success without the declared block-ade zone and would have done so without antagonizing neutrals; to his mind no genuine neutrals cruised the high seas any more. His reasons were clear: an enemy forewarned by the declaration "will apply all precautionary measures – convoys, zigzag courses, escorts, boom defences – and the u-cruiser will not achieve what would otherwise be possible."

Arnauld's objections hinged on the effectiveness of the submarine's primary tactic: "The principal weapon of the u-cruiser is and remains [its] artillery, and during surface attacks the risk of bumping up against a disguised steamer that has superior fire-power cannot be avoided." In short, he urged, one should not declare a blockade zone until the area has already been "plucked clean by several cruisers, and enemy countermeasures have begun."

Passed up the line, Arnauld's letter met the ire of a bureaucracy offended by his apparent scorn of official administrative procedure. As Arnauld's exasperated acquaintance noted on the bitter staff response, "It certainly cannot harm us armchair strategists to hear the views of the frontline." No direct evidence suggests that Arnauld's letter went any further, but, as we shall see, his views were shared by Korvettenkapitän Koch, the u-Flotilla commander, who advised von Holtzendorff on North American operations.

Admiral von Holtzendorff briefed his Kaiser in the ensuing months on the importance of the North American blockade zone. By February 1918, according to the admiral's notes, the Kaiser was listening, "with great interest."[86] Von Holtzendorff reviewed with the Kaiser everything from Britain's exports to its ship construction, from Germany's tonnage war to deployment of u-cruisers; he detailed the importance of his "four economic theatres of war": the waters around Britain and the Biscay, the us east coast and the North Atlantic, the Mediterranean, and the central Atlantic, between the Azores and West Africa. The thrust of his arguments in June 1918 clarified his policy: "Disperse the enemy's defences as widely as possible and thereby weaken them."[87]

There was little doubt in Berlin and Kiel that the increased pressure of Allied countermeasures around Britain was jeopardizing Germany's prospects of victory. The chief of the u-Cruiser Flotilla addressed the proposed "blockade" of North America and enunciated the strategic view that would become doctrine: "In U-cruiser warfare it is less a matter of constantly occupying certain blockade zones than of attacking enemy trade at as many different and constantly varying points as possible, of increasing the attack zones of enemy traffic, and [thereby] forcing the enemy to decentralize his means of defence."[88]

In early March 1918, when the senior Allies had yet to decide what defence resources they would allocate to Canada, the German u-Flotilla commander was already preparing to send u-cruiser u-156 to the United States as soon as she had refitted after her Mediterranean mission.[89] The commander-in-chief of submarines was equally anxious that operations commence as soon as possible in order to "draw off to America the American escort forces active in British waters." Once cleared of American destroyers and aircraft, he believed, British waters would once again offer fresh tactical opportunities for German submarines.

Time was of the essence for the Germans. Korvettenkapitän Koch advised his admiral that the season between May and September provided the only favourable weather conditions for effective operations of the ungainly converted *Deutschland*-class u-cruisers off the North American coast. Indeed, u-151 had beat u-156 to the punch and had departed Kiel in mid-April, in order to be the first u-boat off the North American coast; in accordance with her operations orders, she had begun laying mines in Chesapeake Bay on 24 May. On 9 June Koch briefed von Holtzendorff on cruiser warfare on the North American coast and provided nautical charts of the additional areas to be mined – up to sixty miles offshore. The Americans, he anticipated, would by this time have drawn conclusions from Germany's mine warfare in British and American waters and would have taken steps to protect shipping by the introduction of protective fields, escorts, and controlled shipping lanes. u-cruiser skippers must therefore be given a free hand to undertake operations as they saw fit.

Summer fog made the Cabot Strait and Nova Scotia coast ill-suited as primary areas for u-cruiser operations unless they could be managed in passing.[90] u-151's success, his argument ran, would directly result from surprise; and surprise could be a factor only if she attacked before a blockade zone was declared. This was precisely what Arnauld had said in private. But the u-Flotilla commander went further: "In the final analysis the declaration of a blockade zone has not yet the same significance for a u-cruiser as it has for u-boat warfare. Whereas a u-boat resorts primarily to torpedo attack without prior warning and without distinguishing between [neutral and enemy] targets, a u-cruiser's primary means of attack is still artillery. This is particularly relevant to the [proposed] American blockade zone where there is possibly bound to be a series of escape clauses [in the declaration] out of consideration for Spain and other neutral states."

Here as elsewhere, German naval planners were held in check by political considerations against which they constantly strained. On 12 June 1918 the u-Flotilla commander again briefed von Holtzendorff; this time he stressed the advantages and disadvantages of declaring a blockade zone "on the North American east coast [in order to] block all accesses to the United States and Canada."[91]

Attack without warning was not only legal, he argued, it was wise. Vessels running in convoy, or armed merchantmen running alone, counted as belligerent ships and were legally subject to attack. A blockade zone was unnecessary for such targets. Neutrals caught in either situation had no escape clause to protect them. However, unarmed neutrals steaming alone – invariably showing the national flag – were a special case; for such vessels he deemed a "blockade zone essential." Otherwise the u-boat or u-cruiser was still bound by the prize rules which entailed stopping, searching, and verifying crew and manifests before destroying or capturing an offending vessel. This elaborate procedure exposed the submarine to the danger of a 'Q-ship' submarine decoy and burdened it with the responsibility of rescuing the enemy crew. At night one simply regarded all darkened ships as enemy warships and attacked accordingly.

The advantages of a blockade zone were clear. It permitted torpedo attacks against all ships in the zone and thereby protected the submarine from risk of counterattack by disguised or armed merchantmen. It permitted night torpedo attacks against all ships, even against illuminated vessels that might turn out to be neutrals. And, finally, it relieved the submarine of responsibility for the safety of the crew of sunk vessels. In short, "submarine warfare becomes considerably more effective since all vessels sighted are subject to destruction, and tricks with forged papers are excluded." However, the disadvantages of a declaration were major: "Accelerated introduction of the convoy system for all ships including neutrals, and accelerated intensification of countermeasures by naval and air forces, mines and nets." Against these, the available u-cruisers were particularly vulnerable.

The u-Flotilla commander resolved this conundrum by adopting the solution proposed by u-boat ace Arnauld de la Perière: no declaration of blockade until "about 3–4 weeks after the appearance of the first fast u-cruisers in the operations zone." By that time he would expect the Allies to have reacted with anti-submarine countermeasures and the introduction of convoys. The reference to "fast u-cruisers" reflected his hope that the first combat-designed long-range submarines would soon be available to support the converted *Deutschland*-class. He expected the new u-140 to be operating in North American waters by July. Even then, however, the blockade zone would reap full advantage only under two "absolutely necessary" conditions: there must be no exceptions and no period of grace.

On 20 June 1918 Admiral von Holtzendorff reached an apparently independent decision with far-reaching political ramifications. The long-awaited declaration of a blockade zone against North America, he wrote to the u-cruiser Flotilla and Army Headquarters, would "probably follow soon." He set forth reasons which all in his confidence shared: it had "become necessary in order to bring about as large a splintering as possible of the enemy's antisubmarine forces, and thereby relieve the pressure on our Boats in the British zone and increase their prospects of success."[92] However, he had to confess, the job required three submarines on station at a time, and he could not provide sufficient u-boats even if he weakened the Azores patrols to do so. He would none the less have to deploy all the forces he could muster.

Germany had at the time seven ocean-going u-boats of the *Deutschland*-class whose submerged displacement rated 1,857 tons; three even larger "u-ships" displaced 2,433 tons.[93] By assigning four of the u-boats and two of the u-ships to North American inshore operations – that is, over half of Germany's ocean-going submarine resources – von Holtzendorff was attempting to isolate Britain both strategically and politically from its overseas sources of support. The submarines' priorities were clear: mine the harbours, cut transatlantic cables, and attack shipping. The German navy had drawn on its intelligence sources – agents, cryptography, and captured papers – to build up a dossier on the North American coast and on Canadian and American shipping practice. On 10 June 1917, for example, u-155 (ex *U-Deutschland*) had sunk the Canada Steamships vessel *Scottish Hero* by gunfire off the Azores. She had captured not only her log but the second officer's notebook (which enabled reconstruction of the routes to Canada) and forty-five nautical charts, many of which indicated landfalls and approach points for merchant traffic.[94]

Three days after von Holtzendorff's operations memorandum, at eleven o'clock on Sunday morning, 23 June, a distressed Reichskanzler Count Georg von Hertling convened a high-level political meeting that took issue with von Holtzendorff's action. The navy, so the chancellor charged, had "presented all offices of the imperial government with a fait accompli concerning the blockade zone on the American coast."[95] Indeed, "submarines with far-reaching orders [were already] en route to America, and he found himself having to take responsibility" for a declaration in which neither he nor the Foreign Office had been invited to take part.

It was doubtless a heated session. Vice-Admiral Koch of the Admiralty Staff reviewed the reasons for the declaration and clarified the navy's position: von Holtzendorff had assumed from discussions with von Hertling that the project had been approved in principle; he had in any event by 1 March informed the Foreign Office, which had done no more than caution him against taking any prejudicial steps. Von Holtzendorff had complied. On 6 March, Koch continued, the Army General Staff (Obere Heeresleitung) had communicated to the Naval War Office its "most emphatic support" for declaring a blockade zone; by the beginning of June – in the light of u-cruiser successes off the United States – army support had been even stronger. The General Staff had urged an early declaration "in the interest of the land war" in Europe. It was therefore abundantly clear to Admiral Koch that the zone would have to "encircle the most important ports of Canadian and North American transocean shipping" and should be declared no later than 25 June. The first combat-designed u-cruiser could be in the operations zone by mid-July.

Political representatives grasped the military arguments but were shaken by their implications. In the words of State Secretary von Kühlmann, "It is always a serious matter, when political necessities must be decided under military pressure." German political strategy was once again dancing on eggs with neutral shipping. Von Kühlmann admitted that Germany "was of course at war with America" but felt constrained not to unleash submarine power in areas that could affect Germany's future economic prospects. He was particularly worried about their impact on relations with South America and Spain, whose "goodwill, with regard to the later economic war and our 'Ostpolitik', was the only salvation for the reconstruction of our foreign trade." Submarine warfare could no more guarantee success than any other instrument of politics by other means.

The shifting arguments sought a consensus, but found none. The mercurial session ended in deadlock, with the Reichskanzler setting off to brief the Kaiser at the earliest opportunity. Three days later, on 26 June 1918, von Holtzendorff himself briefed the Kaiser on key submarine matters: u-151 was returning from the North American coast after having laid mines and having operated solely according to prize rules; u-156 had departed for the United States on 18 June with orders to arrive on station in mid-July, lay mines, and "wage commerce war at first according to prize rules"; von Holtzendorff counted on being able to declare the blockade zone on 25 June and had already told his commanding officers to await the executive signal.[96]

Prospects proved even bleaker for Germany's submarine warfare in August 1918, while staff officers rehearsed the traditional litany of woe. The monthly target of 600,000 tons of shipping sunk no longer kept pace with Allied shipbuilding; Germany now required "at least 800,000 tons in order to break even."[97] This was a pipe dream. Strong

Allied countermeasures in the German blockade zone around Britain meant that over a third of all u-boats on patrol between March and July came back empty-handed.

Worse was yet to come. The German answer lay in the old refrain that von Holtzendorff had been singing since 1916 and which successive staff officers had reworked: "These enemy countermeasures must be splintered if the u-boats operating around Britain are to achieve greater individual success. u-boat warfare must therefore be carried into an area that is broad in extent, whose security of commerce the enemy values, and whose surveillance, requires powerful forces. Such an area is the North American coast. To launch the u-boat war here is our duty."

But for all this bluster and thunder, the reservations of Germany's political leadership still prevented the much desired declaration of a blockade zone which naval leaders believed they so badly needed; delayed decisions forced u-cruisers to wage commerce warfare by prize rules. For this reason, – and because of Allied success in escorting convoys – unarmed and unprotected fishing fleets became prime targets.

- 10 -
"Hun Pirate Deviltry"

The North Atlantic convoy system underwent considerable modification while the Canadian navy struggled to expand its patrols for the summer season of 1918. Yet however much changes in merchant shipping organization affected Canadian interests, the Great Powers consulted Canada little, if at all. On 20 March 1918 the British Admiralty unexpectedly gave the Canadian government a mere three weeks' notice of its intention to transfer HX convoys from Halifax to New York.[1] It had made good sense to have HX convoys originate in Halifax in 1917, when Canadian troops still constituted a substantial proportion of all reinforcements crossing the Atlantic.

However, by early 1918 nothing was so crucial to the Allied cause as the accelerated seaborne movement of American troops from North America to the Western Front. Now mobilized in the millions, they could more efficiently be embarked at American ports in fast ships whose speed would both hasten their arrival overseas and minimize the danger of submarine attack.[2] The shift to New York removed fifteen fast merchantmen from the Canadian trade that had transported high-value goods from the St Lawrence and Maritimes ports. Canada would lose this lucrative trade, thus leaving only low-profit bulk items for the Dominion's railways and ports.[3] In Admiral Grant's words, this diversion made Canadian authorities "very sore" indeed, despite the fact that Admiralty had promised them two of the "monster" transports, RMS *Olympic* and *Mauretania*, to meet Canada's immediate troop-ship needs.[4]

Coinciding as it did with word that Canada would receive no fast anti-submarine craft, news about the convoy reorganization heightened Ottawa's sense of grievance and frustration. Admiral Grant bore the brunt of Canadian criticism during his subsequent meetings with authorities in Ottawa. Yet the commander-in-chief, North America and West Indies Station, had always done his best to keep Canadians informed and was not to blame for the failure of the alliance partners to consult Canada about the defence of trade and the allocation of shipping. Indeed, he had intended to shift his flagship from Bermuda to Halifax to keep still more closely in touch; on reflection, however, he could not afford to ignore what he called the sheer "weight" of the American war effort.[5] Ultimately he had no choice but to move to Washington in March 1918 so that he could better co-ordinate the convoy system. This undoubtedly increased Canada's sense of isolation from decision-making.

All was not as black as it first appeared, for British authorities soon grew concerned about overburdening even the great port of New York. In April 1918, therefore, the British created a new series of convoys – "HC," or "Home from Canada" – that were to sail from Halifax. These consisted of "medium-speed" vessels, slower than the 13-knot "fast" ships but capable of a minimum of 11.5 knots. Admiralty thus hoped to move some 51,000 Canadian and American troops per month in the "medium-speed" ships. This would nearly double the capacity of the fast HX convoys from New York.

As the US army reluctantly conceded, large numbers of American troops might be embarked at Canadian ports; but the difficulties of moving troops over the long single-track rail link through the Maritime provinces argued for embarkation at Montreal instead of Halifax. Admiral Grant's agreement with the Americans triggered a sharp rebuke from Ottawa.[6] Since 1915, the short signal reminded him, the Canadian naval staff had opposed use of Montreal for embarking troops – and for good reason. The Canadian patrol flotilla was utterly incapable of protecting shipping on the long and vulnerable St Lawrence route.[7] On learning that American troops would make up the bulk of the Montreal embarkations, the Canadian staff withdrew its opposition; but it did so "upon the distinct understanding that Admiralty takes full and complete responsibility for the use of the St Lawrence route."[8]

The Allies quickly inaugurated the revised convoy system. The first fast convoy from New York, HX 30, sailed on 16 April. The first medium-speed convoy, HC 1, departed Halifax on 11 May. During the next five weeks medium-speed convoys transported some 56,000 troops, a figure that met Admiralty's expected monthly rate. Of these, however, 49,000 were American troops, whom US authorities still found more convenient to embark at New York and sail for convoy assembly at Halifax. There they were joined by 6,000 Canadians and 1,000 Australians. Although Admiralty had envisaged HC convoys no larger than eight or nine ships, allocation of additional medium-speed cargo ships in the St Lawrence trade actually doubled that number.[9]

Captain Walter Hose could do very little to improve anti-submarine protection for convoys until new-construction trawlers and drifters began coming down the St Lawrence when the ice cleared in late May. As it was, none of his major vessels was available for escort duty; refits, winter deployments off Saint John, and the permanent patrol off the entrance to Halifax harbour tied them down. The arrival in Halifax on 16 May of the eight patrol vessels that the US navy had promised was an especially welcome reinforcement. Unfortunately, two of them proved to be old, unseaworthy, and scarcely capable of maintaining even the inner patrol at the harbour mouth.[10]

The six submarine chasers were indispensable, however. Their good service under Canadian operational control entirely justified the view of one American officer: despite defects and the miserable conditions endured by their crew, these "excellent seaboats [were] exceptionally powerful ... vessels for their size."[11] With three 220-horse-power gasoline engines and a large fuel capacity, the boats could cruise for several days at between ten and eleven knots, with sufficient reserves of power and gasoline to accelerate when necessary to their maximum speed of approximately sixteen knots.

For this reason Hose employed them as the long-range convoy escort: he made one division of three responsible for the slow HS convoys ("Home from Sydney") and assigned the remaining division of three to the medium HC convoys. The boats remained with the convoys for up to twenty-four hours, a distance of about two hundred miles from port, before returning to their base.[12] Their greatest drawback lay in their limited fire power. Each mounted only a single six-pounder and lacked the punch that Hose so desperately wanted in the event that the u-cruisers chose to fight on the surface with their 5.9-inch guns. In other respects, however, the craft were well equipped. Their underwater arsenal included three different types of hydrophones and six heavy depth-charges. Each boat also carried long-range wireless and radio telephones for tactical communication up to a ten-mile range. The latter was a recent American innovation unknown in the Canadian fleet.

The first batches of new-construction vessels arrived in Halifax from the St Lawrence by the second week of June. This enabled Captain Hose to organize his "Forming-up Escort" properly into divisions comprising one or two trawlers and two or three drifters each. All three divisions screened the merchantmen as they began to take up their positions in the outer harbour. One division scouted a

mile ahead of the leading ships, while the other two took station on
the beams. The convoys generally left port at midday. One division
remained with the convoy for only a few hours before returning to
port for a routine lay-up, while the other two continued on until
dark. They then broke off in opposite directions – one toward Sable
Island, the other toward Shelburne – in order to conduct "Outer
Patrols" of two to three days' duration before returning to Halifax to
pick up the next convoy.[13]

   Halifax remained the assembly port for slow and medium convoys
until early July, when the navigation season opened at Montreal;
HS 47, the first convoy of the 1918 season to form up at Sydney,
departed on the ninth.[14] By that time the Sydney force had been
increased to over fifty vessels: three American submarine chasers,
nineteen Admiralty-class trawlers, twenty-two Admiralty-class drifters, three battle-class trawlers, and several New England trawlers
borrowed from Halifax for minesweeping.[15] Still, many of these vessels were not ready for operations, as they had just arrived from
the builders; five were still without guns.[16] As at Halifax, the whole
organization was in flux as Hose shuffled and reallocated his
resources to meet essential commitments.[17] The superintendent of
Halifax dockyard complained to Admiral Kingsmill that Hose's grand
design for the completed flotillas was "a very pretty one on paper"
but for the present and foreseeable future merely served to confuse
matters.[18]

   This complaint by Admiral Story signalled revival of the long-
standing controversy over who should control the Halifax flotilla after
Hose departed for his summer headquarters at Sydney in May. Captain
Hatcher had tried to settle the question in the fall of 1917; this was one
of the few instances in which he had actually exerted some influence.
The greatest threat to operational effectiveness, he had warned, was
divided authority; it exposed the command to meddling by outsiders
or infighting within the service itself. He had therefore recommended
that Hose exercise full command over the Halifax flotilla and report
directly to naval headquarters in Ottawa in both summer and winter;
but he should exercise command through a subordinate "Commander
of Patrols" at Halifax, who would be independent of the dockyard. As
for the senior officer of the dockyard, Hatcher would have restricted
his authority to small harbour craft.[19]

   In short, Hatcher had hoped that the department would give the
trusted Hose what had been denied to the offensive Coke: power to
control operations over the whole east coast. In form at least, Hatcher
succeeded. When Hose shifted his headquarters to Sydney in May
1918, Commander Percy F. Newcombe, a retired Royal Navy officer

serving in the RCN, was appointed "Senior Officer of Patrols Halifax" under Hose's command.

Newcombe was a man of indomitable spirit. Having served in waters off British Columbia in HMS *Shearwater* from 1910 to 1912, he had subsequently applied for transfer to the RCN. His recall to a war appointment with the British fleet in 1914 overtook the request. After losing a foot to an artillery shell in the Dardanelles campaign, he resubmitted his application in 1916. Kingsmill gave him command of HMCS *Niobe*, by this time the RCN's principal training depôt. In February 1918, only nine weeks before his appointment as senior officer of patrols, he entered hospital for amputation of a further section of his injured leg. Yet he took up the new job with all his usual zest – and found himself serving two masters.[20]

The forceful Admiral Story had recently replaced Captain Martin as superintendent of Halifax dockyard. Story knew his orders but was dissatisfied. It was probably he who prevailed upon Kingsmill to issue instructions that empowered Story to step in whenever Hose was absent from Halifax and assume control of the patrol vessels in any emergency – or indeed whenever Story should "consider that his interference is desirable."[21] This proviso exacerbated the problem, for the patrols were still in a chain of command entirely separate from the dockyard and were now placed under two sea commanders: Hose and Story. The fact that the order empowered Story "to interfere" underscores the ambiguity of their relationship. Looming large over both commands was yet a third: Naval Service Headquarters in Ottawa. This third dimension was crucial. Unwilling to surrender to any single commander full authority to direct east coast operations, Kingsmill personally intervened time and again.

British interception and decryption of German naval wireless transmissions had meanwhile given Operational Intelligence a clear picture of U-boat operations.[22] Early in 1918 the Admiralty in London had warned both the Canadian and American navies that German U-cruisers would almost certainly appear in the western Atlantic that spring in order to attack merchantmen assembling for convoy. Yet despite timely warnings from Operational Intelligence, the ensuing "Hun Pirate Deviltry," as the *Halifax Herald* called Germany's perfectly legitimate cruiser warfare, took North America by surprise.[23]

By the time the Germans opened their campaign in the western Atlantic in the spring of 1918, the commander-in-chief of the US Atlantic Fleet had drawn an important conclusion: "The inauguration of an intensive submarine campaign" on the North American coast "should be accepted as an admission of at least partial failure of [Germany's] submarine campaign conducted exclusively in European waters."[24] He correctly assessed "the enemy's mission [as] primarily political with the object of causing us to inaugurate such a defensive campaign as to prevent our placing our Naval Forces where they will operate to the best military advantage."

Admiral Sir Rosslyn Wemyss, Britain's first sea lord, shared the view; in fact, he recognized the westward movement as signalling complete failure of the Germans' European campaign. He had sound reasons.[25] Germany could best employ its limited number of ocean-going submarines, he argued, by concentrating on choke-points of Allied trade. As all supply routes ultimately "converged in the vicinity of England and France," it made little sense to him to disperse u-boats abroad – unless of course Allied anti-submarine measures in the European zone had already proved too dangerous to German submarine operations. Wemyss regarded the new German strategy as counsel of despair.

Canadian naval authorities could ill afford to take such a broad view. Should the u-cruisers make a concerted attack on the surface, their superior speed and formidable 15-cm (5.9-inch) guns would enable them to overwhelm the slow RCN patrol vessels; most of them mounted nothing more than a single light and short-range six-pounder or twelve-pounder gun. This meant that the army garrison based at Halifax was far more important than the army realized. Gwatkin, chief of the General Staff, continued to insist on the absolute priority of the front in Europe: men were urgently needed to replace heavy casualties in the Canadian Corps, while several thousand qualified for service were tied down in Canadian coastal forts. Home garrisons, Gwatkin was convinced, could be greatly reduced in light of the RCN's expansion and availability of support from the US navy.

But such was the lack of confidence in the fighting power of the Canadian flotilla that Admiral Story – with Admiral Grant's support – rejected both these arguments. "No naval force under the US flag is now within striking distance of [Halifax], and cannot be depended upon in case of sudden emergency." Indeed, so "very light" were the RCN vessels that in the event of a concerted attack they "would have to retire quickly behind [the heavy, long-range gunfire of the shore] batteries." The naval view prevailed. Not only was the garrison fully maintained, but the gun and searchlight crews undertook intensive training so that they could engage a surfaced or partially submerged submarine at night or in foggy weather. These were the conditions under which a u-boat was deemed most likely to attempt to enter the port.[26]

"Seiner Majestät U-Kreuzer U-151," under the command of Korvet-tenkapitän von Nostitz und Jänckendorf, departed her Baltic port of Kiel on 18 April 1918 and passed through the Kattegat and Skagerrak before rounding the Shetlands en route to the eastern US seaboard. Her ninety-four-day voyage would account for 51,929 tons sunk by torpedoes, gunnery, and scuttling charges and an additional 4,000 tons damaged by mines.[27] Though her orders encouraged her to capture valuable enemy and neutral prize vessels if the opportunity arose, her priorities for minelaying and cable-cutting forced her to forgo targets which would easily have increased her tonnage score.

The Germans had not yet learned that their lightly built and unmanoeuvrable U-cruisers were unsuited to operations against convoys. The German naval staff still regarded them as formidable vessels. In the words of their flotilla commander, they possessed "military qualities with which the old mercantile submarines cannot be compared." Buffetted by uncomfortable weather and long swells, "U-Oldenburg," as she was to have been called in her mercantile role, skirted the Great Northern Mine Barrage and edged her way across the North Atlantic.

Unfavourable weather prevented any aggressive action until early May. "Cruising in U-151 with a heavy headsea is no picnic," her first officer, Martin Niemöller, later recalled; "for the U-boat with its broad upper deck tends to drive her bows under" the oncoming waves and submerge.[28] Only by reversing engines could she regain her surface trim. Under such conditions, running submerged was more economical in a storm than running surfaced. Himself a first-class naval officer, Niemöller later received his own U-boat command and served with fellow skippers Karl Dönitz and Wilhelm Canaris in the Mediterranean. A man of intellect and religious conviction, he subsequently became a pastor in the Confessing Church and was imprisoned for his overt opposition to Hitler.

Decryption analysis at Operational Intelligence in London had provided foreknowledge of U-151's voyage.[29] Admiral William S. Sims, USN, had access to "Room 40" intelligence, though he could not reveal its source.[30] The emergency calls of U-151's victims corroborated the data the code-breakers divulged. All the evidence suggested a U-boat encroaching to within eighty miles of the Maryland coast.[31] On 16 May, US Naval Operations broadcast an alert in cipher to all bases: an enemy submarine could be encountered anywhere west of forty degrees West; ships should therefore tow paravanes against mines and show no lights except as immediately necessary to avoid collision. Most of U-151's victims were without radio and would not have received this vital information.

U-151 commenced mining operations in the entrance to Chesapeake Bay, between Cape Henry and whistle buoy 2CB, on 24 May 1918, after observing shipping and patrol patterns off Cape Henry and Cape Charles. Mines, of course, are most effective when laid in saturation – or, to use the vernacular, when they plaster coasts and estuaries. In this case, however, German long-range operations suffered a severe disadvantage. Like her sister ships, U-151 carried only fourteen mines: six in upper-deck lockers for surface operations, and eight tube-launched mines in the torpedo stowage room, for use when submerged. Although each mine carried a powerful charge of 200 pounds of TNT, there was little chance that an Allied vessel would stumble into the small area that could be sown with so few mines. And in any event, Admiralty's Operational Intelligence had already decrypted German signals warning U-151 of American barrier patrols; these stood "off Chesapeake Bay [but] apparently not beyond latitude Cape Henry." The signals recommended minelaying south of Five Fathom Bank Lightship.[32]

Avoiding heavy merchant traffic and a US cruiser engaged in gunnery practice, U-151 lay on the bottom of Chesapeake Bay in seventeen metres and awaited her chance. It came several hours later, at 9:30 p.m., when she surfaced in a calm sea and bright moonlight. Time was of the essence, and the specially designed upper-deck mine launchers and proved too slow. The crew therefore simply lined the mines along the deck and pushed them over the side at 900–1,000-metre intervals into waters 11–14 metres in depth. The U-boat's log reveals that the operation took but eight minutes at a speed of just over 18 knots. Whether this was haste or efficiency is not clear; however, the field did no damage. All of the mines were discovered either afloat or ashore between 22 June and 9 September.[33]

U-151 destroyed three sailing ships on 25 May 1918. This was the first day of her forty-eight-hour run to the Overfall lightship, where her captain intended to lay the rest of the mines.[34] The morning attack against the three-mast schooner *Hattie Dunn* (435 tons) off Winter Quarter Shoals was a swift and classic action: submerged approach to target, surface to fire warning shots, boarding and interrogation by prize crew, and eventual destruction of the vessel. The prize crew gave the schooner's skipper a receipt before setting three scuttling charges. The seven schoonermen remained prisoner aboard the submarine for eight days.

While the prize crew was still aboard *Hattie Dunn*, U-151 sighted the 1,446-ton four-mast schooner *Hauppauge* some five miles off. She was sailing in ballast from Portland, Maine, to Norfolk, Virginia. Judging by photos now in the U-boat's docket, the recently built schooner must have struck the seaman's eye as a magnificent sight as she stood under full sail in the morning light. U-151 ordered her prize crew to follow in *Hattie Dunn* and set off in pursuit. Within an hour U-151 had stopped *Hauppauge* with several shots across the bow, taken her ten-man crew prisoner, and topped up her own supplies from the schooner's stores. Shattered by scuttling charges and gunfire, the splendid ship capsized and sank.

Just then a third sailing vessel hove into view: the 325-ton three-mast schooner *Edna*, en route from Philadelphia to Cuba with 6,000 cases of oil and 4,000 cases of gasoline. She experienced submarine warfare under the same prize rules. Not only did the Germans adhere strictly to international law, but their manners were impeccable. As *Edna*'s skipper later reported: "Two German officers and four men came over the Edna's railing; they shook hands with us and greeted us just the same as they would have done men on one of their own naval vessels."[35] Scuttling charges destroyed the vessel at 4:10 p.m., and her crew of six was taken aboard the submarine. U-151 now carried twenty-three prisoners on her mission to Delaware Bay.

As the skippers of the three sailing vessels informed Kapitän von Nostitz, they had no idea that U-151 – or indeed any other German submarine – was operating on the American coast. Nor had they ever considered the possibility that U-boats would come over at all. The US navy seemed to have been keeping vital information to itself. Reassured by the apparent intelligence gap, von Nostitz felt he could still count on an element of surprise; the fact that an unidentified US naval radio station continued broadcasting its "No War Warning" signal to coastal shipping confirmed his suspicions. The schooners, of course, had sunk without a trace or a call for help. Von Nostitz therefore decided to hold his prisoners as long as possible so that they could not betray his presence. But he lashed two boats to the upper deck in order to set the crews free as soon as circumstances might permit.

The prisoners reported good treatment and reasonable amenities during their eight days aboard U-151, including an hour's exercise each day on the upper deck. The mate of *Hauppauge* found life below decks both hearty and congenial: "The food was good. In the morning we had fresh rolls and butter ... The bread was black and came in loaves about 3 feet long. We had cognac nearly all the time. They had three graphophones [record players] on board. The members of the crew were cheerful and joked with us, especially after indulging in cognac."[36] The master of *Hattie Dunn* accepted letters from the German crew to mail once he got ashore.

Toward midnight on 26 May, U-151 submerged and approached

the Overfall lightship in Delaware Bay. Navigation was easy, for the periscope picked up all the lights and beacons. Experience in Chesapeake Bay had shown that strong currents made it difficult to maintain periscope depth close inside the approaches to such deep bifurcations and frequently lifted the u-boat's bows to break surface. These were the conditions that suddenly gripped the u-boat within 600 metres of the lightship. u-151 plunged in swift eddies from 15 metres to 19 metres, then rebounded up to 10 metres and back down through periscope depth to 19 metres. The results might have been catastrophic in daylight, when observers onshore or passing ships could have readily seen and reported the submarine. Night operations were therefore imperative.

Merchant traffic passing close to the lightship dictated the pattern of mines. Just as fog began to obscure the lightship before 1 a.m. on 27 May, u-151 fixed her position for the last time and began laying the first four mines by stop-watch at intervals of 150–250 metres and in soundings of 20–22 metres. She lay on the bottom to counteract the currents while reloading and then launched the last four mines from her torpedo tubes by dead reckoning. With depth settings of 5 metres, these too were aimed at deep-draught vessels.

Heavy fog and the sirens of passing ships greeted u-151 when she surfaced, forcing her to return to the ocean bottom until she could make good her escape. Von Nostitz felt uneasy about his new weapon: "As a result of her limited manoeuvrability and submerged operating characteristics, the u-boat [was] not suitable for such operations in the close approaches to heavily frequented entrances with tidal currents."[37] She was "neither sufficiently fast nor manoeuvrable to effect an escape" when surfaced at night; nor could she cope safely with limited depths in emergencies. He required "level soundings over 20 m" so that he could dive at high speed without touching bottom and without fearing the possibility of encountering jagged, pinnacled reefs. Under peacetime conditions, underwater manoeuvres in shallow tidal waters required "the slow execution of difficult, decisive changes in depth"; if taken hastily, they risked striking bottom or breaking surface.[38]

Von Nostitz's skill in laying the mines is all the more impressive in light of his vessel's clumsiness. The unarmed 7,145-ton American steamship Herbert L. Pratt struck one of the mines on 3 June. Inbound from Mexico to Philadelphia with a full bulk cargo of crude oil, she was beached in safety before being refloated and towed to her destination. Of the seven remaining mines laid, one washed ashore and five were destroyed by us navy minesweepers. Other German minelaying cruisers followed, but their mines claimed no more than seven victims on the Atlantic coast. Significantly, however, the mere threat they imposed committed the Canadian and American naval forces to time-consuming and expensive minesweeping operations. Operational Intelligence did not obtain German data on the location of the minefields until the cessation of hostilities in November 1918.

U-151 had meanwhile executed her second mission.[39] Lying off New York on the morning of 28 May 1918, she rigged her heavy cable-cutting gear on the upper deck. This consisted of a derrick, winches, greased flexible steel wire rope, and pressure cutters capable of biting through the cable's thick protective skin and armoured strands. Shortly after 11 a.m., according to the submarine's war diary, she had cut "the southern cable of Western Union 1889." Nine hours later she cut "the southern German cable," and by 1 a.m. on the 29th she had severed "the northern German cable." These lay in depths of twenty-five fathoms.

American authorities recorded only two disrupted links: "the Central and South American Cable Company's New York–Colon" link and "the Commercial Cable Company's No. 4 Canso–New York" line. Unlike Britain, whose cable ship *Telconia* had on 5 August 1914 severed the first of five German cables that connected Germany with France, Spain, Africa, and the Americas, Germany did not have command of the sea and could not prevent the repair of U-151's labours.[40] The cable ship *Relay* had repaired the first cable by 25 June and the second by 4 July.[41]

Even "had the enemy cut all the transatlantic cables," a post-war American report concluded, "it would have been impossible for him to stop effective communication between the [US] War and Navy Departments and [US] forces in Europe."[42] This was doubtless correct. Powerful land-based transmitters, including the German-built stations at Sayville and at Tuckerton, New Jersey, which the Americans had confiscated from their German owners in 1917, could handle up to 50,000 words per day.

By 30 May 1918, U-151 lay on the steamer route from Nantucket to Fire Island and set course for the Fire Island lightship in order to establish her new patrol lines. The prevailing mists and heavy fog suggested to von Nostitz that he press north in search of fairer weather. As British decryptions of German operational signals revealed, Berlin had recommended "an attack on the shipping route off Halifax if the situation is favourable"[43] and cautioned him not to attack the Swedish vessel *Suedia*, which was en route from Buenos Aires with a minister of the German government aboard and would "put into Halifax for examination."[44] Here was a clear warning of an impending threat to Canada, but, in the event, von Nostitz's three captured merchant skippers convinced the already sea-wise commander that weather would only worsen in the higher latitudes. Thus U-151 turned southward and between 1 and 28 June she claimed twenty victims.[45] These ranged from the 124-ton Canadian schooner *Dictator* (carrying salt from Cadiz to Newfoundland) to the 5,093-ton American passenger steamer *Carolina* and the 8,173-ton British troop ship *Dwinsk*. The latter was running in ballast from Brest, France, to New York. Others were transporting petroleum products from Philadelphia to Cuba; coal and lumber from Norfolk and Jacksonville, Florida, to Rhode Island and New York; sugar from Cuba and Puerto Rico to Boston; and a variety of copra, cotton, copper, and machine parts for coastal and overseas ports as distant as Rio de Janiero.

U-151 continued to observe the prize rules meticulously. After scuttling the 1,869-ton American coastal steamer *Winneconne* and the 776-ton schooner *Isabel B. Wiley*, and torpedoing the 4,588-ton steamer *Harpathian* on 2 June, von Nostitz made provision for the safety of the crews in their lifeboats; he offered medical attention where needed, and freed his twenty-three prisoners. On 1 July he let pass a "large hospital ship fully illuminated according to [international] regulations."[46] Conscientious perhaps to a fault, he secured the safety of the crews of the Norwegian sailing vessels *Samoa* and *Kringsjaa* on 14 and 15 June by broadcasting an SOS in English with precise positions of the drifting lifeboats.[47]

His humane action brought sharp criticism at home. The flotilla commander found these signals "superfluous and pointless since the sinking had occurred only 200 miles from shore on the steamer route"; for this reason, "the crews could be regarded as rescued."[48] Admiral von Holtzendorff had been still harsher. "As understandable as such a procedure is from the human standpoint," he pointed out, "it is detrimental to the intended effect of U-boat warfare."[49] The decision was clear: "Leave rescue measures to the crews of sinking ships themselves."

U-151 had an unexpected opportunity for "pirating" war material. Certainly *U-Deutschland* had in 1916 demonstrated the effectiveness of the big submarines as freighters. Although combat equipment had reduced the capacity of the boats, they still had room to spare. On 9 June, U-151 stopped the 3,179-ton Norwegian *Vindeggan*; the Germans rigged scuttling charges aboard her and escorted her under a prize crew outside the sea lane. In a seamanship evolution comparable in complexity to the later jury-rigged fuel replenishment between the U-cruisers U-155 and U-140, von Nostitz transferred from his victim "70 tons of pure 100% electrolytic copper in bars."[50] While seaboats shuttled the cargo over to the U-boat's hold, her crew counterbalanced the increased displacement by jettisoning "water, iron ballast and trim weights" before scuttling their victim.

In von Nostitz's view the German crew had "worked superbly and fast." His flotilla commander found the evolution magnificent. Under Kophamel on an earlier mission this same u-cruiser had brought home 22 tons of copper; other boats had actually hunted for war materiel: u-156 returned with two 7.6-cm guns from the armed merchantmen she had scuttled, together with brass, zinc, and rubber from their cargo. As Admiralty's Operational Intelligence already knew from decrypted German signals, u-157 had returned with 27 tons of rubber and 5 tons of wax for war industries; u-155 had captured 45 tons of brass.[51]

Canadian newspapers were equally impressed by u-151's achievement – though for different reasons. As headlines in the *Halifax Herald* proclaimed four days after the event: "Eighty tons of copper captured by Hun Submarine."[52] The event highlighted the apparently new "Hun" policy of trying to "terrorize" both the United States and Canada.[53] For the first time since 1916, editors explained, "Germans again bring war across [the] Atlantic and with great submarines destroy ships" along the North American coast. Newspapers assumed the presence of more than one submarine. All these u-boats, they charged, had special knowledge of local waters.[54]

The stories underscored fears that German operations could have succeeded only with information from spies ashore. This was the very stuff of myth-mongering that the *Halifax Herald* exploited in its lurid attempts to whip up anti-German hysteria. Exaggerated articles contrasted with the studied sobriety of stories in the German press.[55] By this time, Allied undercover work in Germany had revealed that seven u-cruiser commanders – among them Arnauld de la Perière – were convinced of the important work that "agents in America [had accomplished] in connection with the submarine campaign" and "were expecting to be very soon ordered to proceed to waters adjacent to America."[56] Certainly, pro-German neutrals on passage through Halifax and New York had reported to German Intelligence on what they had observed, but nothing suggests that this information provided more than background colour to German plans – or the involvement of German spies.[57]

The success of the attacks on commercial shipping underscored the apparently parlous state of us naval forces.[58] Even in the early stages of the submarine's mission, American press reports had stressed the seriousness of the threat; they hinted at a possible congressional investigation of the circumstances surrounding the operations of u-151. Admiral Sims in London recoiled at the thought.

Such investigation would expose the most sensitive sources of naval intelligence by revealing that Admiralty had provided the US navy with "positive advance information" of U-151. Both he and Admiralty knew only too well that "publication of this fact would prevent similar information being obtained in future."[59]

Canadian naval authorities themselves were privy to bits of special intelligence provided by the decryption teams in London. This left little doubt that U-151 was the only submarine on the Atlantic coast at the time and that she posed no immediate threat.[60] But U-151's now widely known activity lent credence to a welter of supposed sightings; watchers claimed to have sighted everything from fully surfaced U-boats to torpedo tracks in local waters. They even panicked five merchantmen into running themselves aground while attempting to flee the "enemy" and seek safe haven in Halifax during dense fog. Naval staff subsequently detained an American troop ship in Montreal until the immediate threat had passed; and the minister for the navy appealed to the commander-in-chief, North America and West Indies Station, Admiral Grant, to provide him with destroyers. Grant expressed his amazement that uncorroborated reports had been allowed to disrupt shipping so severely.[61]

U-151 returned home to Kiel from her ninety-four-day mission on 20 July 1918. She had expended six torpedoes and 288 rounds of 15-cm shell in sinking twenty-two vessels. The mission provided the Germans with vital intelligence for U-boat warfare off North American shores: naval patrols were weak and lacked air support, ships sailed independently and without escort, and traffic both to and from the European blockade zone followed direct routes. Von Nostitz's interrogation of Allied merchant seamen suggested that things would change: shipping might well be sailed under escort and routed inshore. "Unless we declare a control zone," von Nostitz reported, "we can do nothing in future against this traffic."[62]

German Naval Staff ultimately urged declaration of the control zone against North America, only to be refused by the Kaiser himself. The measure, in the Kaiser's overriding view, had been endorsed by the German Naval War Office from a narrowly naval perspective; it had shown no concern for the political situation and was in any event premature.[63] German Admiralty released a terse press report of the submarine's success.[64]

The Americans were of course grappling with the problem of improved defences against U-cruisers. In a message to Admiral Sims, USN, Naval Operations observed that the "attacks of the U-151 [had] been directed almost entirely against unarmed ships westbound or coasting." Most seriously endangered were the "unarmed westbound ships"; these were large oceanic vessels like *Dwinsk* that the Allies could least afford to lose.[65] They crossed the Atlantic alone after having had escort cover from Britain and France only to the outer limits of "the European danger zone." Washington did not want to convoy ships further westward than absolutely necessary and did not want the Germans to force the United States to undertake any naval deployment that might mean recall of warships from overseas. However, the Americans were no less worried that "any great amount of tonnage loss off our coast would almost inevitably raise the question of continued convoys and escorts to our shores." Washington rightly felt that the problem would diminish once merchant ships were armed for self-defence.

Naval Intelligence in London detected the departure for North America of another u-cruiser, u-156, toward the end of June. Within a week, German wireless traffic revealed the departure of the purpose-built combat cruiser u-140.[66] In fact u-156, under Kapitänleutnant Richard Feldt, had departed Kiel on 16 June with specific orders to mine the approaches of New York prior to engaging in cruiser warfare in four focal areas: the Gulf of Maine and the approaches to Boston, Halifax, and Saint John.[67] She was to attempt to cut the overseas cables at Canso, Nova Scotia, and, if able to capture a prize vessel, "transform her into an auxiliary warship in support of longer operations."[68] u-140 departed on 2 July. She was commanded by Korvettenkapitän Waldemar Kophamel, who had served as first officer of *U-Deutschland* during her commercial voyage to the United States in 1916 and had also commanded u-151.

Operational Intelligence had not yet gleaned information on the precise missions and operating zones of u-140 and u-156. For this reason the u-boats' radio silence cast a pall of uncertainty over the North American inshore defences. As a precaution, Admiralty sought the advice of the commander-in-chief, North America and West Indies Station, Admiral Grant, as to what could be done in the event that submarines struck the Halifax approaches. Grant offered the now familiar scenario: despite reinforcements that might be expected from the us First Naval District, his weak forces could neither prevail against German intrusion into the port area nor provide anti-submarine escort to convoys for "any distance" to seaward.

This situation cast Admiral Grant onto a back-up plan that he had already raised with shipping authorities: redirection of any inbound shipping to alternate havens. In an emergency, therefore, ships en route to Halifax could shift to Sydney, Nova Scotia, or to New England ports, or to New York. Grant was clearly worried about the vulnerability of Halifax. It presented an unwholesome mix: regular troop-ship departures, inadequate patrols, and the expansive continental shelf, which allowed the enemy to lay mines up to 130 miles from the harbour mouth.[69]

While Grant pondered the Halifax defence problem, U-156 was approaching American waters. She would destroy twenty sailing vessels, nine steamships, and the fourteen-year-old armoured cruiser USS *San Diego*. Her propaganda effect was doubtless far greater than her tactical or strategic success. U-156 and her crew never returned from the mission. Had they done so, her log might well have provided us with colourful and detailed accounts. Its loss forces us to rely on intelligence reports, circumstantial evidence, shipping news of the day, and loss reports submitted by the merchant navies that U-156 had struck.[70]

U-156 first revealed her presence on 26 June when, ten days out of Kiel, she sank the 4,157-ton British steamship SS *Tortuguero*. On 7–8 July she destroyed two large sailing vessels some 400 miles south-east of Sable Island, Nova Scotia. There the 1,987-ton Norwegian sailing vessel *Marosa*, bearing coal from Newport News to Montevideo, experienced war according to the strict observance of the prize rules. In the words of a post-war American report: "[She] received her first warning of the presence of the submarine when a shot was fired across her bow. She hove to; the crew took to the lifeboats and rowed to the submarine where the ship's papers were examined and the officers questioned regarding the precautions taken to protect the American coast, the location of American war vessels, and the feelings of the American people in regard to war."[71]

In darkness and gathering storms the survivors set off in open boats toward Nova Scotia, sailing north-northwest against westerlies and heavy squalls. According to *Marosa*'s chief officer, the Germans "gave us no course, but told my captain to steer to westward and some one on board the submarine shouted 'Good trip and God bless you, you are 800 miles from land'." They went ashore over a week later, near midnight on 16 July, on the low, rocky Cranberry Islands, just over a mile from Cape Canso, Nova Scotia.[72] By this time the crew of the 1,729-ton Norwegian schooner *Manx King*, carrying general cargo from New York to Rio de Janeiro, had met the same fate.

These incidents fuelled the *Halifax Herald*'s anti-German hysteria. The fact that "Submarine Victims [had] Landed at Canso," the headlines for July 18 exclaimed, proved once more how close the enemy lay to Canada's defenceless shores. Editors hoped that this crisis would finally startle Nova Scotians out of their "utter unconcern" for the state of siege. Indeed, this was "the second time" since the sinking

of the Canadian sailing vessel *Dictator* on 28 June that "victims of the
Hun marine brutality have sought a haven of safety on the Nova
Scotia coast."[73] The Halifax *Morning Chronicle* reacted calmly, but the
Herald and such leading newspapers as the New York *Times* and
the Toronto *Globe* offered a ready explanation for these and other
German successes – particularly for the spectacular sinking on 1 July
1918 of the hospital ship *Llandovery Castle* off the Irish coast.[74] According to the *Herald*, it had been instigated by "Hun spies in Halifax
responsible for murder."[75]

Of course, the facts were otherwise. Although *Llandovery Castle* had
sailed from Halifax under charter from the Canadian government,
with a Canadian army medical staff, in order to evacuate overseas
casualties, her sinking was quite unrelated to German activities in
North America. Nevertheless, it seemed clear to some journalists that
"the snake is now in *our* grass."[76] The "gorilla of the sea" had now
set about his "diabolic business." Halifax's city council agreed. It
demanded the internment of all "enemy aliens" and stricter security
on the Halifax waterfront. Naval and military intelligence officers
began receiving reports of strange exchanges of light signals between
sea and shore,[77] clear evidence of "the grave peril of the 'Hun Spy'
and [the] alien enemy menace in our midst."[78] The *Halifax Herald*
soon offered $5,000 reward "for information that will lead to the
discovery of a Hun submarine base on the Nova Scotia or Bay of
Fundy shores."[79] By its own account this offer met with "universal
popular appreciation."

In the ten days that followed the sinking of her first two sailing
vessels, U-156 escaped notice while shaping course to lay mines near
the Fire Island lightship in the approaches to New York. Though USS
Harrisburg sighted her on 17 July, the Americans failed to attack; the
submarine slipped away submerged without drawing attention to her
mines. One of them claimed the 13,600-ton cruiser USS *San Diego*,
which had been based at Halifax during the winter of 1917–18 for
convoy escort duties.[80] The loss of this vessel, so "well known in
Halifax," as the *Herald* exclaimed, marked the "renewal of submarine
activity on a greater scale off the Atlantic seaboard."[81]

U-156 was brazen. During the morning of 21 July "the raider raised
a storm of excitement" on emerging from a fog bank within sight of
vacationers at Orleans on the southeastern elbow of Cape Cod,
Massachusetts; she bombarded the 435-ton tug *Perth Amboy* and her
three barges as they headed toward Vineyard Sound.[82] The *Boston
Daily Globe* published an "Extra" announcing that while "Allies have
Huns on the run" in Europe, there had been a surprising "attack by
U-boat off [the] Cape."[83] According to the war diary of the US First

Naval District: "The appearance of the raider so near the treacherous shoals and tide rips of the cape and her subsequent actions caused amazement to the thousands of eyewitnesses rather than consternation. The natives of the cape could not understand why she should waste torpedoes and shells on barges running to a coal port."[84]

The Germans' "wild shooting" at the barges and at the flying boat dispatched from the nearby US naval air station at Chatham purportedly lobbed shells among cottages ashore. Screaming headlines of the *Halifax Herald* announced this as the "first time since the beginning of the war [that] enemy shells land on American soil."[85] German newspapers took brief cognizance of the event in stories datelined New York.[86] Though the event made good copy in the Canadian and American press, it had little military significance other than to mark the path of U-156 into more northern waters. But one press report suggested otherwise: the attack had revealed as never before that the German submarine had become "the direct and most ruthless menace of the war – the sea's hidden and undiscoverable grim reaper."[87]

Although not given to apocalyptic language, Admiral Grant was alarmed. The loss of USS *San Diego* to U-156 disturbed him deeply, as did intelligence that U-140 was already approaching coastal waters.[88] No more than eighteen destroyers were available on the whole of the North American seaboard.[89] On 21 July – the same day U-156 thrilled the Cape Code cottagers – Grant summarized his precarious position for Admiralty: "Having regard to the present Military and food position in France and England, and the increasing relative importance to Germany of [her] checking the vast movement of [Allied] troops, munitions and supplies from North America, also the increased difficulties and losses to submarines operating in Home Waters [around Britain], am of the opinion [that the] present inadequate anti-submarine forces on this side can no longer be justified."

Still smarting from his embarrassment at Admiralty's sharp criticism of his earlier request for destroyers in the spring, Grant now argued that some of the new destroyers abuilding in the United States should be retained in the western Atlantic. In reopening the issue, he made it clear that he was acting with complete propriety: "I have, of course, not mentioned this [proposal] in any way to US [authorities], nor has [the] point been raised by them." He was thus all the more insulted by Admiralty's peremptory response from London: "As you are not in a position to form a true appreciation of the submarine situation generally, it is essential that you should not express any opinion to the US Authorities on the subject of retention or otherwise of US destroyers in American waters."[90]

This dashed any hope of early reinforcements. What was more, U-156's sudden appearance off Cape Cod had caught the Allied navies entirely by surprise. German signals decrypted by British intelligence had suggested that the U-boat would strike off New York and in waters to the south – a conclusion borne out by her initial attacks. Unfortunately, however, events following her unexpected appearance off Orleans did nothing to clarify the new situation. After sinking a schooner north of Cape Cod on the 22nd, she gave no hint of her presence for another ten days. In the mean time British intelligence had managed to decrypt a signal that Germany had sent her on the 22nd: if fog prevented her primary assignment in the Gulf of Maine, she was to run further south and "operate off Delaware Bay."[91] American authorities appear to have assumed that if the U-boat were indeed continuing in northern waters, she must be in the approaches to Boston. Thus on 25 July the US navy's northern hunting group – the destroyer USS *Jouett* and eighteen submarine chasers – shifted from U-156's old hunting-ground off New York and began searches based on Provincetown, Massachusetts, at the northern tip of Cape Cod.[92]

The danger to Canadian waters materialized very quickly and without warning when U-156 attacked in the Bay of Fundy instead. Her victim was the recently launched four-mast schooner *Dornfontein*. The relatively small target of 695 tons belied her significance for local industry. She had been the first vessel launched from a Saint John yard following major initiatives to rejuvenate the shipbuilding industry. She had left Saint John on 31 July with a load of lumber for Natal, South Africa, and under sailing orders issued by the naval transport officer in Saint John. In the absence of convoys and escorts, the transport officer was responsible for providing routing instructions in order to reduce the risks of enemy attack. As the war diary of the US First Naval District records, the "schooner was just getting into open sea, 25 miles off Briar Island, the westernmost point of Nova Scotia [at noon on 2 August], when the submarine rose from the water and fired two shots across the bow."[93] This and other evidence places her some seven miles south of Grand Manan Island.[94] As survivors told the Canadian press: "After taking from the ship all her valuables and foodstuffs, as well as a large quantity of gasoline, ... the Germans started a fire in her forecastle and another in her after-cabin [,] and the ship burned to the water's edge."[95] The seamen "spent five hours in the bowels of the submarine," where the Germans invited them to share a dinner of bully beef and rice. Once released, they made their way by dory to Gannet Rock, Grand Manan. One survivor described the parting scene: "When the crew of the *Dornfon-*

tein rowed away from the submarine ... the deck was swarmed with officers and men who waved their hands, calling 'Good-bye and good luck.'"[96] But for *Dornfontein*'s skipper such congeniality was hollow: the Germans "were a beastly looking set of fellows [who had] robbed us of all we had on board worth taking."[97]

The incident spawned major news stories in local newspapers such as the *Sydney Post* and the *Liverpool Advance*.[98] The Saint John *Standard* for 7 August published a human interest story based on an interview with one of the survivors, a Swede who had conversed with one of his captors aboard the submarine. The German sailor had offered a photograph of himself and a shipmate in naval uniform; the young submariner had addressed it on the back to his mother in Germany and requested the Swede to mail the photo home from Canada if he heard of the submarine being lost at sea. The *Standard* reprinted the photograph, which ultimately ended up in the hands of Naval Intelligence and never reached Germany. U-156 never reached home either.

Canadian and American naval intelligence officers sought information about the Germans' methods and equipment and interviewed the survivors of submarine attack soon after their ordeal. *Dornfontein*'s crew provided considerable detail that had to be sifted and compared with the growing corpus of data. The Germans were not above indulging in disinformation. For example, they had urged the seamen "to tell President Wilson that in six months they would have 200 submarines around this coast [,] also working around the West Coast and around Japan."[99] Some of this spurious intelligence reached the press. Significantly, the Germans never suggested that any warnings be passed to Robert Borden.

There was another aspect to "debriefing" survivors of submarine attack. Naval intelligence needed to establish just how the survivors had behaved. The master of *Dornfontein* was deemed to have failed: "[He] must have been excited, forgetting all about his instructions to destroy his papers if attacked by the enemy, until too late. After being ordered by the Commander of the Submarine to bring his papers he got frightened and complied with the request."[100]

Nor did it end there. A board of inquiry into the sinking suspended the master's certificate of competency for the duration of the war. He had allegedly "made light of his duties and responsibilities, had been guilty of neglect ... and had been gravely negligent, but not with criminal intent."[101] The decision seems draconian, one indeed easily reached from the comfort of an office ashore.

U-156 had struck at perhaps the weakest point in North American defences, the boundary between the Canadian and US sectors; it was remote from the naval bases of both countries. What was more, the Germans had delayed the raising of an alarm onshore by taking *Dornfontein*'s crew onboard. Although the lone US navy lookout at the Gannet Rock light had heard an explosion at midday on the 2nd, he could discern nothing in the fog. Not until the crew had landed on the beach at 6:40 in the morning of the 3rd could he send definite word of the sinking. Only two Allied vessels were near: the Canadian trawler HMCS *Festubert*, which happened to be in Saint John after a fisheries patrol in the Bay of Fundy, and the small American patrol vessel *Endion*.[102] USS *Jouett* and her submarine chasers immediately rushed north from Provincetown, Rhode Island, but could not reach the vicinity of the attack until the morning of the 4th.

By the time U-156 was far to the east, out in the Atlantic and working her way into the Halifax approaches. Methodically, she destroyed seven schooners – four Americans, off the southern tip of Nova Scotia on the afternoon of the 4th, and three Canadians, twenty-five miles off Shelburne and near Le Have Banks on the 4th and the morning of the 5th. Adhering to prize rules, she set their crews toward shore in dories.

If we can trust the account of a survivor of the American *Annie Perry*, the Germans were a swashbuckling lot. As reported to the *Telegraph* of Yarmouth, Nova Scotia: "The raider ransacked the Perry from stem to stern, taking all of the provisions and practically leaving no food for the crew with which to supply their dories. The sub commander also demanded the schooner's flag and papers."[103] Inclined to speak only of their work, the Germans appeared to enjoy advertising their noteworthy exploits, like the sinking of USS *San Diego*. But they were also portrayed as having been humane, providing survivors with cigarettes and brandy.[104]

Survivors landing in the port of Yarmouth, Nova Scotia, brought first news of the attacks and provided detailed stories to the town's competing newspapers, the *Herald* and the *Telegraph*. Despite the scoop, their restrained accounts made little effort to editorialize on the potentially explosive issue. Reaction was decidedly different in the provincial capital, where the *Halifax Herald* responded in its usual strident style: "Six Vessels Torpedoed by Hun Sea Wolf."[105] Its fulsome descriptions and speculations revealed the Germans' brazen panache. "After completing her devilish work for the day the submarine lay off Seal Island all night with her deck awash, and displaying a brilliant light which was distinctly seen from shore, and this morning she was still there." Newspapers would have us believe that she was communicating with her ubiquitous spies ashore. In a sensational spread on 7 August, the front page of the *Halifax Herald* listed the

"Names of 500 Austrians, Bulgarians and Germans Roaming at large in Halifax TODAY Who May Naturally Be Regarded as Spies!" How else, it asked, "did the commander of the Hun Sea Wolf get the information [about where to find victims] ... and know the psychological moment to strike his Prey?"

Some citizens in Lunenburg County became so exercised as to undertake witch-hunts of their own and watch for suspicious lights and movements during the small hours of the night. Writing to the Department of Militia and Defence in Ottawa, one hardy lady, outraged by the government's apparent inaction, spoke for her fellow-sleuths:

The men of Lunenburg are in Khaki, [away in the army, and only] the dough-heads and pro-Germans are left [here at home] ... So it is up to the women and children to be on the look out ... For Heaven's sake can nothing be done; are these devils to be allowed to carry on this work in aid of Germany and enjoy some protection and liberty as loyal British subjects? I tell you, men, if you don't take notice, we sisters, mothers, etc., who have given all will do something to those traitors, [but] in that case I suppose the 'Law' would protect the Hun and traitor, and hang its own countrymen. Send a man who is not afraid and don't herald it about as was done a few weeks ago when a detective was sent here and the traitors given every chance to keep 'Mum'.[106]

A list of denunciations followed.

The letter was not unique. In fact the colonel commanding in Halifax was so besieged by clues about the unsolvable "Lunenburg mysteries" that he himself took a very hard line: "The District Intelligence Officer is again on the warpath about this place. The Lunenburg district is a heart-break. Our small intelligence branch can do nothing to catch anyone in the act ... One thing to be done with Lunenburg is to send a really capable force of a few Secret Service Officers ... The only other possible way of doing it is to send half a company of infantry there and place the region under martial law, but I presume the politicians would not allow this."[107] Only weeks later did investigations convince him that the solution did not lie in shadow-boxing but in bridling the tongues of the gossip-mongers.[108]

Authorities onshore were unaware of the progress of U-156 around the southeastern tip of Nova Scotia toward Halifax between 3 and 5 August. None of the schooners had carried wireless, and word of their plight could not reach shore until the crews had rowed some thirty to fifty miles to nearest land. For this reason, Canadian naval intelligence was unable to sound the first warning of the attacks on the American schooners until midday on the 4th.[109] The attacks had taken place in the Gulf of Maine – the area of operations indicated in the decrypted German wireless signals – but had given no clear evidence that the U-boat was in fact headed for Halifax.

Thus USS *Jouett*'s group swept southwest of Yarmouth late on the 4th before turning back toward the coast of Maine.[110] The crew of *Nelson A.*, the first schooner sunk on Nova Scotia's Atlantic coast, did not reach land until late on the night of the 4th.[111] It was therefore not until midday on the 5th that news of this attack south of Shelburne reached the navy. By this time U-156 already lay close in to Halifax.[112] Anti-submarine patrol coverage off the coast – including the American area of responsibility, south of Lockeport, Nova Scotia – was necessarily thin. Of forty patrol craft at Halifax, one-third were not available because of breakdowns, delayed refits, and routine maintenance.[113] On 4–5 August 1918 almost all the serviceable craft were quite properly deployed in support of convoy HC-12, which departed Halifax on the afternoon of the fourth: seventeen large ships carrying 12,500 Canadian and American soldiers to the Western Front.[114]

U-156 struck the 4,867-ton Canadian tanker *Luz Blanca* in the near approaches to Halifax just before noon on 5 August 1918, only a couple of hours after having scuttled the Canadian schooners *Agnes G. Holland* and *Gladys M. Hollett* on the LeHave Bank.[115] The tanker had left Halifax in ballast for Tampico, Mexico, under charter to the Imperial Oil Co.[116] Her master had ignored instructions from naval shipping control officers to delay her departure until dusk and to proceed along evasive zigzag courses. The vessel had been free to leave nevertheless, for no specific intelligence of U-156's approach had warranted closure of the port; Halifax was included only in a broad warning zone in which submarine attacks were deemed possible.[117]

Oblivious to danger, *Luz Blanca* held a steady course through a smooth sea in clear visibility. About thirty-five miles south of the Sambro lightship, U-156 fired a torpedo into her victim's stern without warning. Here the accounts are confused: the submarine either surfaced within twenty minutes and opened fire or did not commence her gunnery assault until over two hours later.

Whatever the time-lag, *Luz Blanca* gamely took up a running gun-battle while struggling to retrace her route home under hopeless conditions. From a German perspective she had broken international law by carrying guns; moreover, her twelve-pounder gun was manned by two sailors of the Royal Naval Reserve. The submarine's gun pounded *Luz Blanca* to a burning hulk which her crew abandoned within seventeen miles of the Sambro lightship. With her wireless destroyed, she had little chance of summoning aid, but the

American steamer *F.O. Barstow* witnessed her plight and broadcast the alarm. The tanker's crew – British officers and engineers and a mixed bag of nationalities in the lower deck – had endured a blistering fusillade that killed two crew members and wounded several others. The skipper reported that all had behaved "well, except the Russians who were panick-stricken and practically useless."

Word of the attack reached Halifax dockyard at about 1345 hours, while the attack was still in progress and was retransmitted to the escort divisions returning from their overnight escort duties with troop convoy HC-12. It was also transmitted to the old American torpedo boat USS *Tingey* which had replaced the faster and more powerful HMCS *Grilse* on the harbour entrance patrol. *Grilse* had been maintained in Halifax since the earliest days of the war for just such an occasion but was now undergoing repairs at the very time she was needed.

Almost everything else that could go wrong did go wrong. The naval wireless system performed inefficiently: *Tingey*, nearest to the scene, did not receive the warning until hours later; the Canadian trawler-drifter division next handiest picked up the message promptly but failed to locate the tanker. The division commander blamed poor visibility, while Commander Newcombe in Halifax blamed poor navigation. Thus it was one of the American submarine chasers far removed from the position that first reached the tanker's hulk in the late afternoon. The Americans rescued two boatloads of survivors, but "there was neither sight nor sound of the submarine."[118]

The position of the attack lay some three hours steaming from the Halifax waterfront, and Newcombe was experiencing frustrating problems in trying to dispatch suitable vessels for a thorough anti-submarine search. Urgently needed ships were making logistic runs to distant outposts as far away as northern Newfoundland and had to be recalled by Hose in Sydney; others under repair at Dartmouth, just across Halifax harbour, could be rushed to sea, but Newcombe had no direct communication with Dartmouth and haze prevented visual signalling; he had to send messengers but had only one slow harbour craft to transport them. "It was rather like using a Cart Horse for a General's Galloper before an attack," he mused bitterly. Not until late evening, nine hours after the initial attack, could his ships begin to search the darkened scene. By this time Hose had dispatched two trawler-drifter divisions of the Sydney force to search to the northeast of Halifax.[119] By now, too, Admiral Story had pronounced the undependable torpedo boats USS *Tingey* and *DeLong* utterly useless.[120]

The front page of the *Halifax Herald* next day belted out the news in terms that would become familiar to Haligonians twenty-four years later, in 1942: "Hun sub torpedoes oil tanker off Halifax Harbour." For the Halifax reporter the incident provided a "thrilling story of the fight between the Hun sea wolf" and its desperate victim. The apparent inability of the Canadian navy to repel the threat during the subsequent days and weeks raised a crucial and not unfair question regarding national policy. In the *Herald*'s words: "What's the good of a fleet of patrols that can not catch submarines?"[121]

In fact, "catching" a lone submarine that was studiously avoiding defended shipping was – and still remains – one of the most difficult problems in maritime warfare. USS *Jouett*'s chase of 3–5 August – always a day behind U-156's actual position – demonstrated the enormous difficulty of hunting down a submarine even with the assistance of high-grade intelligence. It was precisely because of this hard-won lesson in European waters that the Allies had adopted the convoy system; for that very reason the Halifax authorities had done precisely the right thing in concentrating all available warships for the defence of the troop convoy HC-12 instead of spinning off in a "hunt-and-kill" ride toward U-156's operating area. Until the moment of the attack on *Luz Blanca*, moreover, the best intelligence had placed the submarine in the American sector.

The Canadians "in Khaki" of whom the distraught Lunenburg lady had written were meanwhile engaged in the decisive battle of 1918: the Allied offensive of 8 August at Amiens that took the Germans by complete surprise. "The enemy division in the line in front of the Canadians and the Australians were simply swept away."[122] Everywhere the Canadian Corps of three divisions in the front and one in support gained its final objective of the day. British casualties in four days of battle reached 22,000; there were 9,000 dead or wounded in the Canadian Corps. The Germans lost 75,000. The Canadians had fought with distinction: "Two VCs in two hours was a good start to the 13th Batallion's day, but other men, in other places were doing much the same without as much recognition."[123]

Back in Canada, naval authorities were assessing the *Luz Blanca* incident. The RCN's response had been anything but confident, despite the recognized difficulties in submarine detection. Newcombe had only the foggiest notion of how his vessels were deployed, and communication of his orders had been slow. The problem, he explained, lay with subordinates inexperienced in staff duties. This forced him to attend to all of his command's paper work personally, leaving little time for operational matters. Hose saw things differently.

The real problem, he advised his department, lay with Newcombe: "While zealous and energetic, [he] lacks the ability to cope with varied and numerous responsibilities." Hose recommended that Newcombe's duties be limited to ship maintenance and the manning and training depôt at Halifax.

Who, then, should be senior officer of patrols at Halifax? The choice fell on Commander John Shenton, a Royal Navy officer who had retired in Canada and who had served well on both coasts since volunteering on the outbreak of war. Thus Shenton got the job of directing all patrol operations whenever Hose was absent in Sydney. The solution bore the seeds of discontent. Shenton was not appointed subordinate to Hose but as "flag commander" to Admiral Story. Hose would now merely allocate vessels to Halifax and establish their general program, the execution of which still lay in Story's hands.[124]

The problems of command and control were not merely those of organization. Whatever the merits of Newcombe's particular complaints, the navy had far too few qualified officers, and the staffs at Halifax and Sydney were indeed overworked to the point of exhaustion. Captain Hose himself had taken ill in July, and although he recovered sufficiently by early August to "transact business at his house," he asked Kingsmill for fourteen days' leave. The arduous work of establishing the expanded patrol flotilla had worn him out: "The machinery needs a rest," he had written.[125] He immediately withdrew his request on learning of the *Luz Blanca* attack and carried on despite Kingsmill's concerns for his health.[126]

During the following weeks, when Admiral Story was feeling the strain and his chief of staff was on the verge of collapse, Kingsmill asked Admiralty for a Royal Navy captain and additional junior officers. Grant had already urged such assistance, for the Canadian dockyard had to support and co-ordinate the operations of substantial numbers of warships from three nations. By the time two British lieutenants finally arrived in October, Grant had withdrawn the request for a captain to augment the senior staff because of the lateness of the season. The overworked Canadian officers simply had to cope on their own.[127]

Senior naval officers, including both Story and Kingsmill, pressed for additional aid from the United States.[128] The minister, C.C. Ballantyne, who was then in London for the 1918 Imperial Conference, pleaded directly with Admiralty for "even one boat with longer [gun] range than the [German] submarine." This urgent request was passed to Washington, and the Americans responded. On 24 August, the old gunboat USS *Yorktown*, armed with a battery of six five-inch guns, arrived in Halifax.[129] Meanwhile, the first US navy air detachments, which had been promised in early spring, had begun to arrive in Halifax. But, as we shall see, it was early September before they could begin operational flying.

The sheer vulnerability of Halifax also persuaded the Royal Navy to provide assistance in the form of mined anti-submarine nets and personnel to train the Canadians in their use. Ironically, this was the very harbour defence that the Royal Navy had rejected years earlier. So great had been the Royal Navy's confidence in its ability to dominate the oceans that in 1904 it had abolished the army-controlled underwater defences that the opening pages of this book describe. German u-boat successes had quickly changed that attitude, and mine barriers had become one of the principal anti-submarine measures in British waters. Unfortunately, the first installations – four miles of mined nets moored thirty-six feet below the surface, on the flanks of the main shipping channel off Chebucto Head, Halifax's western headland – were not completed until three weeks before war's end.[130]

The destruction of *Luz Blanca* had an immediate impact on the trade defence system. Though still giving first priority to protection of transoceanic transport, Canadian staffs immediately tightened control over coastal traffic, most importantly by gathering ships into groups for sailing under an RCN escort. There were too few Canadian warships to allow regular, scheduled coastal convoy, but logs of auxiliary patrol vessels and trawlers leave little doubt that coastal escort of merchant shipping was a major commitment until the end of the war.[131]

u-156 virtually recast the management of transatlantic convoys as well. Within hours of the attack on *Luz Blanca*, Admiral Grant had begun diverting traffic away from Halifax. Ships outbound from ports in the St Lawrence River to join their overseas convoy in Halifax would now assemble at Sydney, at the exit of the Gulf of St Lawrence; vessels joining from American ports would gather at New York. Avoiding the Halifax approaches completely, the two sections would then rendezvous far offshore for the transatlantic voyage to Britain. This rapid reorganization was an enormously complex and exacting task. The fact that the Sydney section of convoy HC-13 sailed on 14 August – only two days later than originally scheduled – underscores the professionalism of the Canadian, British, and American control of shipping staffs.[132]

These arrangements for the HC convoys were only temporary. The rendezvous of large groups of ships far out to sea was difficult, uncertain, and dangerous; it would become more so as the autumn

fogs and storms descended on the northwest Atlantic. Drawing on
Grant's earlier advice about the advantages of the St Lawrence ports –
their distances from u-boat operating areas and excellent rail connections – Admiralty began to reroute all medium-speed ships that previously loaded at us ports. Thus Quebec became the assembly point
for HC convoys. It would be several weeks before the new plan would
take full effect. As we shall see, increased use of the St Lawrence
created serious difficulties for the RCN. But Admiralty's new convoy
orders of 8 August had none the less been timely.[133]

On that same day, decryption of German signals warned that yet
another u-cruiser would depart Germany with orders to mine the
approaches of Halifax and St John's. This was in fact the former
U-Deutschland, now known as u-155. Two days later Admiralty
became aware of another assailant: the minelayer u-117 planned to
strike off Halifax and Cape Race after initial operations in American
waters.[134] From a Canadian naval standpoint, the prospect of three
u-cruisers off Halifax meant nothing less than saturation attack.

Canadian naval authorities assumed not unnaturally that u-156
was still lurking in the Halifax approaches. In fact, she had immediately headed southwest and sunk the 3,031-ton Swedish schooner
Sydland, some 180 miles off Cape Cod, on 8 August.[135] Britain's Submarine Tracking Room attributed this attack to u-117, which was
expected to arrive at about this time. She was not far off the Allied
estimate. On 10 August, as we shall see, she ran amok among the
fishing fleet on Georges Bank, some one hundred miles from Cape
Cod, before pressing on toward the southwest. u-156, lingering in
the distant approaches off New York and Cape Cod, had meanwhile
torpedoed the 4,134-ton British steamer *Pennistone* one 11 August
and scuttled the 1,586-ton Norwegian *San Jose* on the 17th. The
British ship was a classic case of the ambushed straggler from a
convoy. The skipper of *Pennistone* spent six days aboard u-156 and
subsequently wrote a seven-page report that corroborated much that
Naval Intelligence already knew about u-cruiser submarines.[136]

The media picked up the news in stirring headlines and stories.
One account insisted that "the sub monster off Halifax [had] sunk a
big ship and murdered men."[137] Another placed the "giant u-boat
within five miles" of Halifax and announced the disturbing disinformation that "poison gas is the Hun's latest diabolical murder method
on this side of the Atlantic."[138]

More reasonable, but no less misguided, voices were raised elsewhere. The Halifax *Morning Chronicle* had bitterly denounced the
"Hun Sea Wolfs" but carried no speculation about spies ashore. In
an editorial entitled "Idle Fears," it decried the "pure sensationalism

[that had] caused a good deal of alarm in more timorous minds, and has wrought considerable mischief": "The simple truth appears to be ... that this City and Province stand less in danger of attack now than at any time since the war began. There was a period of really grave danger at the outset. German cruisers and raiders were then at large in the Atlantic. Halifax, inadequately prepared for resistance, offered a tempting mark to them. But all that has changed. The seas have been swept clean of all but underwater craft. Our forts have been adequately manned and equipped. Warships are constantly at hand."[139]

Submarines, the editors pointed out, were nothing more than an anti-shipping weapon, in no way designed for attacks against land targets. "On the whole," the editorial concluded, Nova Scotians "may sleep as peacefully and securely in their beds as if there were no such things as u-boats in existence."

Myths of secret German landings and clandestine adventures ashore prevailed – as they do to this day. When the "Hun sea wolf" attacked and sank a "large oil tanker within range of [the] guns defending New York" and the "monster sea wolf" preyed on innocent ships at close range, a fresh batch of unnerving tales appeared in the press. An unlikely story in the *Sydney Post* datelined Nantucket claimed that a "member of the pirate's crew [had] attended theatre" in New York City a couple of evenings before the *Pennistone* attack.[140] Other equally spurious accounts revealed that the German parties were scouting out Canadian defences as well. It was all grist to the mill of public opinion. Submarine activities, whether imagined or real, underscored the inability of the Canadian navy to cope with a genuine scare.

In large measure this apparent inability to deal with an inshore submarine threat was a result of the RCN's correct priority of protecting ocean shipping. Naturally, this aroused the ire of fishermen – a substantial and vocal part of the maritime community – who rightly felt that they had been abandoned. Politicians pressed the navy to alleviate the "great anxiety concerning safety of the Nova Scotia fishing vessels operating on the Banks."[141] An American union leader cabled his intentions of journeying to Nova Scotia "to organize the fishermen there for a measure of self-protection in affiliation with the Fishermen's Union of the Atlantic"; this he called "a powerful association" that had convinced Washington to introduce compensation payments for losses in war. Newspapers whipped up images of marauding Germans waylaying innocent and unarmed schooners.

Canadian naval authorities sought advice from Washington about possible American aid and wherever possible deployed a wireless-

equipped patrol to warn the fishing fleet of the "submarine menace."[142] The upshot of all this clamour was cold comfort: the Americans were helping to outfit wireless-equipped French patrol vessels
for the Banks and hoped also to commit Boston-based patrols to the
Newfoundland fishery. Strapped for resources that were already
heavily committed for convoy duty, Canadians could do little more
than reassure the fishermen that "we are doing all we can."[143]

How little this was became clear when "one of the Kaiser's Pirates"
captured a Canadian vessel and forced a Canadian warship to turn
tail.[144]

- 11 -
The Pirates'
Triumph and
Canadian Response

During the early hours of 21 August 1918 crew members of the 236-ton Canadian steam trawler *Triumph* stepped ashore from their dories in Canso, Nova Scotia, with a startling story. A prize crew from a huge German submarine had captured their vessel the previous day and had turned them loose to find their way home across sixty miles of open sea. In comments to the *Sydney Record*, the *Sydney Post*, and the *Yarmouth Telegraph*, they warned that the Germans intended to use the trawler as a raider. They were right. Indeed, according to the Berlin press, the Germans had captured nothing less than an "auxiliary cruiser."[1] The *Berliner Tageblatt* later copied a story from Geneva recounting "the wanderings of a German pirate ship in the Atlantic."[2]

Triumph had departed Portland, Maine, three days earlier to fish on the Middle Bank, some thirty miles south-southeast of Cape Canso, Nova Scotia. As the trawler lay with her side trawls down and unable to manoeuvre shortly after noon, U-156 suddenly surfaced and within two minutes had fired a shot across her bow.[3] The Canadian fishermen could do nothing but destroy their confidential books and submit. The prize crew boarded her quickly. Twenty-five minutes after the action had begun, the Germans had fitted the vessel with a wireless set and had armed her with two light guns, three or four boxes of three-pound shells, and twenty-five high explosive bombs.

Events had taken the trawlermen by complete surprise. *Triumph*'s skipper confessed to the Canadian officer who debriefed him "that nobody ever dreamed [the Germans] would do other than sink the trawler; the idea of her being captured and made use of not entering their minds as they had never heard of such a thing." He recalled little of interest except for the submarine commander's disinformation "that there were six submarines on [the] Nova Scotia Coast."

Other reports alleged that u-156 had actually "come five miles up Halifax harbour [one week earlier] and had lain for several hours in sight of the town."⁴ The supposed Halifax visit was sheer fabrication. But from a defence perspective it was technically possible; on the night of 19 August HMCS *Grilse* had tested Canadian shore defences and slipped undetected past the army forts and picket boats.⁵ By this time the *Sydney Record* had raised the question as to whether the "Cape Breton Trawler Triumph [had become a] Hun Sea Wolf."⁶

As soon as he had word of the attack on the morning of 21 August, Captain Hose ordered three auxiliary patrol ships and two trawlers to sea: *Cartier*, *Hochelaga*, and *Stadacona*, with *TR 22* and *TR 33*. All five vessels had recently completed local escort missions and were fortuitously available. The three Halifax-based American submarine chasers joined the banks patrols later that day. As soon as the Sydney forces had returned from local missions and from escorting an HC and HS convoy, they too hastened to the banks. But none of these deployments was allowed to interfere with the Canadian navy's principal tasks of shipping escort and port defence.⁷

American assistance was now substantial, if transitory. The destroyer uss *Bell*, which had escorted the New York portion of convoy HC-14 to the rendezvous off St John's, now swept over the outer banks off Nova Scotia on 21–22 August while returning to New York. uss *Jouett* and her submarine chasers began sweeping from Cape Cod to Halifax on 23 August and patrolled off Nova Scotia for the next ten days. The heavily armed gunboat uss *Yorktown*, which had arrived at Halifax on 24 August, began patrolling out to the Grand Bank of Newfoundland on the 28th. Two other American vessels – *Aztec* and *Androscoggin* – had already gone to the Newfoundland Bank. These last three ships augmented some half-dozen French motor-schooners; armed and equipped with wireless, the French ships were primarily responsible for guarding the international fishing fleets on the great banks east and southeast of St John's.⁸

Newspapers had scarcely published the disturbing news of *Triumph*'s capture when they reported assurances from Washington: "Strong forces of swift patrol boats and destroyers sped today to the North Atlantic fishing banks, where the trawler Triumph ... is reported raiding the fishing fleets. Naval officers here think recapture of her is a certainty."⁹ The us navy was clearly trying to instil confidence in the fishing community. The fishing industry had been lobbying for protection, and government food authorities had expressed concerns that further schooner losses and terror might reduce supplies of fish. Already on 17 August us Secretary of the Navy Daniels had announced increased defence measures for the fisheries. But few additional ships were actually assigned to permanent patrols on the banks. Like the Canadians, the Americans allowed no reduction of convoy escort forces.[10]

Reassuring Allied press releases were clearly intended as a psychological boost to counteract the Germans' own war of nerves against the fishermen. In the words of the US First Naval District: "Recent raids by U-boats have done little actual damage to fishing fleet taken as a whole, but much uneasiness among the men has resulted. Wives and families in some cases have induced them to remain on shore. But the American fisherman is not easily kept from the sea, and it is expected that his courage and the knowledge that the Navy is on guard will keep the fish catch up to normal."[11]

Conversations with fishermen had also convinced Hose of their determination to hang on – but for less high-minded reasons than raw courage. "It would appear," he wrote, "that there are many of them who are perfectly willing to run the risk of attack, as the business of fishing pays well; it is [only] when there is a good catch ... on board that anxiety comes."[12] Canadian schoonermen were perhaps even more practical than their Yankee brethren.

Certainly, Canadian fishermen had the government's ear throughout the crisis. From the moment of U-156's first attacks on Canadian schooners earlier in the month, the acting minister for the naval service, A.K. Maclean had pressed the east coast commands and Admiral Grant to alleviate the "great anxiety concerning safety of Nova Scotia fishing vessels."[13] Maclean was representing C.C. Ballantyne, who was then attending the Imperial Conference in London. A Liberal Unionist from Halifax whom Borden had brought into the cabinet without portfolio, Maclean had come to Halifax a few days before *Triumph*'s capture and now kept in direct touch with fishing concerns, with the dockyard, and with local MPs. Indeed, this may have been the sole reason for his trip. Although he did not interfere directly with the deployment of patrols, he did keep pressure on the navy for action and to provide information to both the industry and his colleagues.[14]

The looming presence of a senior political authority is seldom helpful to an operational headquarters – and rarely welcome. Maclean may have been an exception. His repeated emphasis on the need at least to warn fishing vessels on the banks so that their crews could make informed choices about the risk they ran may account for the care that the Canadian warships took in alerting all shipping they encountered as to the presence of U-156 and *Triumph*. It may also have been Maclean's appeals that encouraged Admiral Grant in

Washington to arrange for the French armed motor-schooners to receive the latest intelligence by wireless from Royal Navy authorities in Newfoundland and to pass warnings to Canadian and Newfoundland vessels on the Grand Bank.[15]

The patrols against U-156 and "the Pirate" *Triumph* were larger than any previous operation in Canadian waters. But the odds were very much against them. U-156's surprise appearance off Canso placed the submarine at the very centre of the vast banks that stretched southward to the Gulf of Maine, northward to the vicinity of St Pierre et Miquelon, and eastward to the Grand Banks of Newfoundland. She could strike in virtually any direction and find numerous fishing craft. And because the schooners carried no wireless, the patrols were condemned to chasing after clues that were already many hours old.

Flying her German ensign, *Triumph* went silently about her business of raiding for the next three days undisturbed. The *Halifax Herald* caught this "irony of fate": the trawler could "make a good decoy to lure former sister fishing vessels to quick destruction."[16] And so it proved. While the submarine lay hull awash nearby, the new raider sank five schooners: the American vessels *A. Piatt Andrew*, *Francis J. O'Hara Jr.*, and *Sylvania* and the Canadians *Lucille M. Schnare* and *Pasadena*; further to the north she sank the French *Notre Dame de la Garde* off Banquero Bank, seventy-five miles off Scatarie Island. The skipper of *O'Hara* described the raider's technique:

The Beam Trawler approached us under full steam. I could see that it was the Trawler *Triumph* of Halifax as we had fished alongside of him on our last trip and I knew the captain of her quite well. I did not distrust anything ... until they got within 150 yards of us when they stopped their vessel and the captain, through a megaphone ordered us to heave our vessel to. I thought the captain was joking with us ... and the first thing we knew, four shots were fired across our bow from rifles [... She] came up alongside of us and I then saw that she was manned by a German crew and had a German flag at her masthead. The captain ordered me to come aboard of his vessel with our papers ... and the Germans gave me quite a calling down for not stopping my vessel sooner, and said that if we expected him to do the right thing, we would have to do the right thing by him. He then ordered three of his men to come in the dory with me and they brought a bomb along. The bomb was a small round thing and they had it in a bag and hung it under the stern with a line ... After touching off the fuse, [they] returned to the Beam Trawler. The bomb exploded shortly after ... and the vessel went down stern first.[17]

The technique rarely varied. On one occasion, however, the French

Notre Dame de la Garde apparently saw both U-156 and *Triumph* waging war together under the British flag.[18] The Germans, as the Canadian press had correctly speculated, scuttled *Triumph* as soon as she had exhausted her coal supplies.[19]

It was now widely reported the "survivors of fishing smacks sunk by 'Triumph' [had] reach[ed] North Sydney, Gabarus, Arichat [and] Canso after hours at sea in open boats."[20] U-156 meanwhile destroyed the Canadian schooner *Uda A. Saunders*. In the fisherman's words:

The submarine came up on our bow and came right alongside, her decks awash [...] The Huns hailed us and ordered a dory alongside. I sent two men out to her in a dory and three of the raider's crew came aboard. "Don't be afraid," said the one who appeared to be in command. "We are going to sink your vessel. I will give you 10 minutes to gather up food and water enough to last you until you get ashore." One of the Boches set about storing bombs below ... [Those of us still in the schooner] had enough food and water, but the men in the dories had only their working clothes and we who were on board had only the barest necessities. The Hun commander took all my papers and the flag. We set out for the nearest shore and rowed 18 hours before landing.[21]

U-156 struck again after midnight on 25 August, about seventy miles northwest of Galantry Head on the French island of St Pierre. Sighting the 583-ton steamer *Eric* slipping without lights across a glassy sea in clear moonlight, U-156 suspected a large armed vessel and opened fire. The submarine's rapid bombardment immediately destroyed the ship's wireless and severely damaged *Eric*.[22] She proved of little value to the Germans, for she was running in ballast from St John's to Sydney under charter to the Newfoundland government. U-156 dispatched her with the usual scuttling charges and took the Canadians on board.

British communications officers reported subsequent events to Admiralty on debriefing the survivors:

On going below aboard the submarine, the wounded men from the *Eric* had their wounds dressed by a doctor, a young man about 25 years old. The crew of the *Eric* were given coffee ... and the officers were given coffee, brandy, and cigarettes. The commander of the submarine told the captain of the *Eric* that he would put him and his crew aboard the first vessel found having enough boats to accommodate them [...] About 6 a.m. the submarine ... went alongside the [Newfoundland schooner] *Willie G.* [actually Wallie G.] and the submarine commander inquired regarding the number of boats she carried. On being informed that she only carried six small dories, he [decided] that therefore he would send the *Eric*'s crew aboard the *Willie G.* and would not sink her.[23]

Later that morning of 25 August U-156 fell among a group of four fishing schooners – the Canadians *E.B. Walters, C.M. Walters,* and *Verna D. Adams* and the American *J.J. Flaherty* – which she destroyed at leisure some forty-five miles southwest of St Pierre.

It was apparently while U-156 finished this work in the early afternoon that a Canadian four-ship patrol (*Cartier, Hochelaga, Trawler 22,* and *Trawler 32*) entered the scene in line abreast at four-mile intervals. Suddenly, HMCS *Hochelaga* sighted two schooners six miles away and left the formation to head due east. Approaching to within four miles, *Hochelaga* glimpsed a submarine just as one of the schooners mysteriously "disappeared" from view. The U boat had evidently sunk the vessel and left herself open to counterattack.

The lightly armed Canadian warship faced the enemy alone. No Canadian patrol vessel had been in such a situation before, even though Admiral C.E. Kingsmill had tried to prepare them for the fray. Just two weeks earlier he had warned his small patrols about the Germans' superior fire power – "5-in or 4.1-in guns, which are usually of high velocity and long range" – and had specified the anti-submarine tactics that should be followed despite the serious risk.[24] While conceding that Canadian patrol vessels were no match for German submarines – "the surface speed of the enemy is probably twice your own" – he had directed his officers to make every effort at least to cause damage. Even if only slight, Kingsmill advised, such damage would greatly diminish the U-boat's chances of returning home through the strong British defences in the North Sea.

Hochelaga's skipper, Lieutenant Robert D. Legate, RNCVR, appears to have thought better of the idea and turned back. Perhaps he knew Captain Hose's opinion that Canadian patrols were outgunned and outmanoeuvred and "would be practically at the mercy" of the U-cruisers.[25]

Official accounts record the mitigating circumstances of his having altered course so as to rejoin his formation and warn of what he had seen. He had no means of radio communication and doubtless judged a single-handed attack against the U-cruiser sheer folly. On seeing *Hochelaga*'s course alteration and flag hoist, *Cartier* (Lieutenant McGuirk, senior officer) brought the formation around to intercept her and read her flags. Whether final consultation took place by flags or megaphones is no longer clear, but evidence at the court martial shows that when *Hochelaga* reported the "submarine bearing East," *Cartier* ordered the patrol to proceed directly toward it at full speed. *Hochelaga* held back, signalling to his senior officer in *Cartier* the greater wisdom of awaiting reinforcements. By the time the patrol reached the scene U-156 had gone.[26]

Legate had had a failure of nerve for which a man of his experience could have no excuse. Commissioned in the RNCVR in June 1915, he had seen active service since September 1914 and held sea-going commands since January 1917. A court martial held in Halifax on 5 October 1918 found that he "did not, from negligence or other default, on sight of the enemy which it was his duty to engage, use his utmost exertion to bring his ship into action."[27] The court dismissed him from the Naval Service. This was hard justice. It would have been gallant indeed had he attacked the submarine, a nobly suicidal gesture that would have lent tragic flair to Canadian naval lore.

Just before noon on 26 August, the day after the encounter with *Hochelaga* and the day of Germany's massive withdrawal along the whole Somme front, U-156 destroyed the Canadian schooner *Gloaming* in a heavy fog approximately seventy miles southwest of St Pierre. By the time the crew pulled ashore and got word to Halifax during the early morning of 28 August, U-156 was probably heading for home. She never arrived – a victim, perhaps, of an Allied mine off southern Norway while trying to break into the North Sea on 25 or 26 September.[28] During her ten days in Canadian waters she had destroyed twenty-three vessels. But only one of them – *Luz Blanca* – was a substantial steamer. Her failure was a tribute to the control of shipping organization and to the escort forces of Canada and her allies.

As we have seen, three U-cruisers – U-140, U-117, and U-155 – were following U-156: the first two close on her heels. But the concerted offensive in Canadian waters that the Allies had correctly anticipated on the basis of decrypt intelligence did not materialize. The technical shortcomings of the submarines, and the timidity of one German captain, saw to that.

Korvettenkapitän Waldemar Kophamel's U-140 departed Warnemünde for the east coast of North America on 2 July, followed nine days later by Kapitänleutnant Dröscher's U-117. U-140 had been commissioned on 28 March 1918. Displacing 1,930 tons surfaced and 2,483 submerged, U-140 was the largest "U-ship" built for combat and one of the few submarines to receive a name. She was named *Kapitänleutnant Weddigen* after the captain of U-9 which had shaken British confidence in surface fleets by sinking three Bacchanti-class cruisers in a single encounter in 1914. Kophamel had previously commanded the converted U-cruiser U-151 during her initial operations in the eastern Atlantic and had found her "an imperfect compromise."[29]

The former U-freighter's limited speed and uncertain diving performance had "precluded its utilization as a submarine in shallow waters, near the coast, and in areas even moderately patrolled." U-151's subsequent operations in North American waters bore similar results, and a report from U-152 in September 1918 would corroborate the shortcomings of the converted freighters: "The helplessness of the former mercantile submarine under present conditions [against convoys] was clearly demonstrated. Low surface and submerged speeds, bad diving characteristics in a sea, and in addition bad trim characteristics prevented [the U-cruiser] from getting close enough to the convoy and keeping contact for any length of time."[30] This was not an isolated experience. U-152's only major success was a straggler, the 5,130-ton American auxiliary cruiser *Ticonderoga* (ex-German *Kamilla Rickmers*), a slow vessel that could not keep up with her convoy.[31]

The only real hope for U-boat success lay in submarines designed for the combat role. Kophamel's new command, U-140, was just such a boat. Even so, she proved too big, clumsy, and slow for aggressive tactics of fast surface runs to locate shipping and quick dives to drive home submerged attacks; nor could she evade anti-submarine countermeasures in a way that smaller submarines had done when confronting the strengthened Allied defences in European waters. Moreover, the faulty equipment and construction that had delayed U-140's operations would continue to plague her during this, her only combat cruise.

Bearing orders to "conduct trade war near the Nantucket lightship and off New York," U-140 departed via the Kattegat and shaped course for the Shetlands; there on 11 July, poor weather conditions prevented her attacking an eight-ship convoy screened by a single Bacchanti-class cruiser. Faulty wireless prevented Kophamel from signalling the convoy's position. He continued toward US waters without radio contact. Four days later, in mid-Atlantic, three unescorted troopships – *George Washington*, *Kronprinzessin Cecilie*, and *Mauretania* – passed just beyond range. On 26 July U-140 opened her North American campaign on the high-seas route off Newport in a gun battle with the 13,967-ton British steamer *Melitia*, followed later in the day by a similar melee with the 4,147-ton *British Major*. The U-cruiser's relatively slow surface speed prevented a swift and decisive approach. Fearing that a prolonged chase would consume an excessive amount of fuel, U-140 broke off the engagement as dusk fell.

Her fortunes changed next day with a traditional attack on the unarmed 1,079-ton Portuguese three-mast barque *Porto*; she was carrying barrel staves and 600 bales of cotton to Oporto from Savannah, Georgia. The Germans took five hours to transfer stores from the sailing vessel before freeing her crew and scuttling her. Three days later, on 30 July, the boat made an unsuccessful submerged attack on the 4,947-ton American vessel *Kermanshah* some three hundred miles east of Norfolk, Virginia. Heavy swells threw the U-boat commander off his aim, while the American skipper took effective evasive action by "combing" the torpedo tracks as the lethal "fish" skimmed past his bow and stern.

The American attitude toward armed merchantmen had long since changed. Armed American as well as British freighters had become the rule. The *Kermanshah*, for example, carried a twenty-one man US naval gun's crew to man a four-inch astern and a two-pounder forward; she carried three naval wireless operators as well. Other nations were slower to follow suit. Thus, on the evening of 1 August, U-140 torpedoed the unarmed 7,029-ton Japanese steamer *Tokuyama Maru* within a day's run of Norfolk, finally sinking the crippled vessel by gun-fire next morning. Up to now Kophamel had observed "only inbound traffic," and he moved closer inshore in order "to locate the outbound important traffic," carrying vital war supplies to Europe.

Three days later, on the morning of 4 August, U-140 made an unsuccessful submerged attack against the armed 10,289-ton American tanker *O.B. Jennings* of the Standard Oil Co. about sixty miles east of Newport News, Virginia. She was inbound from Plymouth. U-140 then surfaced to open fire at an initial range of eight miles; the tanker returned fire while laying a smoke-screen and running evasive courses. The battle continued for two hours, with the submarine closing her gunnery range until shortly before noon, when she made a direct hit on the tanker's engine room and magazine and forced the crew to abandon ship. U-140 closed in to fire the coup de grâce and interrogate the survivors, who stood by in lifeboats. Over fourteen hours later, in the darkness of night, USS *Hull* rescued two boatloads of survivors and searched for more. Fearing that her prowling shape was the German submarine, survivors in a third lifeboat eluded attempts to locate them until daylight.

All survivors reached home with the exception of the tanker's second officer, who had leaped from his lifeboat to seek the relative safety of the submarine and was taken aboard as a prisoner of war. His action led some survivors in the boats to suspect him of having been a Germany spy. The myth was dispelled only after the war, when the American consul at Le Havre, France, interviewed him in January 1919 during his petition to be repatriated as a destitute American seaman. The Germans had transferred him to the prisoner-of-war camp in Karlsruhe on their return to Kiel, though not without having derived some intelligence about ship routing.

On 5 August, U-140 scuttled the 1,060-ton American sailing vessel *Stanley M. Seaman*, carrying coal from Newport News to Santo Domingo. Within sight of the Diamond Shoal lightship next day, she fired on the 3,024-ton American steamer *Merak*, bearing 5,600 tons of coal to South America. Startled by the submarine's muzzle flare flashing through the haze at a four-mile range, *Merak* turned about and ran herself aground on the shoals. U-140 approached at leisure and scuttled her once the crew had escaped. Three ships had witnessed the attack: the Diamond Shoals lightship, the British steamer *Bencleuch*, and the American *Mariner's Harbor*. The anchored lightship had attracted U-140's immediate attention by sending wireless signals of the *Merak*'s plight. U-140 sank her by gun-fire, chased and fired at *Bencleuch* without result, and never caught the third ship.

U-140 endured her first counterattack on 10 August while trying to stop the 6,062-ton Brazilian steamer *Uberaba* (ex-German *Henry Woermann*). The boat made an emergency dive to depths of seventy-five metres when the destroyer USS *Stringham*, summoned by the steamer's wireless distress calls, suddenly appeared and dropped fifteen depth charges. "Escaped undamaged," the destroyer's captain reported. In fact, however, the explosions had burst seams along the pressure hull; although not serious, the damage would ultimately persuade Kophamel to cut his mission short. Three days after the encounter with *Stringham*, U-140 engaged the USS *Pastores* in a gun duel at a range of six miles but disappeared before the American could do more than reply with five rounds of five-inch armour-piercing shell.

The first news of U-140's predations reached the Canadian public on 2 August, when the *Halifax Herald* announced the attack on *Porto* and warned that the "Hun Sea Wolf [was] still lurking in the North Atlantic waters."[32] With a random sprinkling of stories of the victims of U-156, the account gave no inkling of how many – or how few – U-boats were involved. With its usual mixture of fact and fantasy, the Halifax paper reported U-140's attack on *O.B. Jennings* "within range of guns defending New York"; it told how the "Monster Hun Sea Wolf" had supposedly destroyed the Brazilian *Uberaba*, "shelling her at 200 yards range, the ship going speedily to the bottom."[33] Such accounts heightened the impact of sensational reports of U-156 "off Halifax"; some reporters urged Britain to send its forces over to even the score against "the Kaiser's pirates."[34]

The Allies heard nothing of U-140 for a week following the attack on the USS *Pastores*. Then, on 21 August, she struck again in the distant seaward approaches of New York. Frustrated by her inability to get within torpedo range of the armed 7,523-ton British steamer *Diomed*, U-140 engaged her in a gun battle, thereby severing the vessel's steam lines and disabling her steering gear. Unable to escape or defend themselves, the merchant sailors abandoned ship. Next day U-140 launched an unsuccessful running gun battle with the 3,753-ton American cargo vessel *Pleiades*, some three hundred miles east of New York. This was the submarine's final encounter off the North American coast.

U-140 arrived in Kiel on 20 September, never to go to sea again until delivered to the Americans for experimental purposes on 23 February 1919. The destroyer USS *Dickerson* sunk her off Cape Charles, Virginia, on 22 July 1921.

Kapitänleutnant Otto Dröscher's U-117 departed Kiel on 11 July. His mission: lay mines and wage cruiser warfare off the east coast of North America – particularly off Halifax and from New York to Cape Hatteras.[35] Wherever possible, he was to bombard shipyards and docks. Dröscher stuck to his priorities – minelaying first, then cruiser warfare – so strictly that he incurred the criticism of the commander-in-chief, submarines, for failing to press home attacks on potential merchant targets until after he had accomplished his primary task.

Like the voyage of U-140, his foreshortened seventy-four-day mission was plagued with mechanical deficiencies directly attributable to poor material and workmanship in the shipyards. A faulty friction clutch frequently made him abort dives and gave rise to fears about the U-boat's ability to perform in emergencies; a malfunctioning evaporator reduced the availability of fresh water; and constantly leaking fuel tanks reduced her range and left a tell-tale oil trace visible even from the air and led to her being attacked close inshore. Dröscher had to overhaul both engines en route.

Dröscher none the less pressed on. During passage over the usual "eastern route" via the Skattegat and northward of the Shetlands, U-117 settled into battle routine in anticipation of British patrols around the Great Northern Mine Barrage. Outbound into the open Atlantic on the Great Britain–Cape Race route until 8 August, U-117 undertook unsuccessful attacks in heavy seas and swell against two lone vessels, a small cruiser, and two convoys. During one of the convoy attacks another problem came to light: a malfunctioning torpedo spun in the tube and only gradually "worked its way out." U-117 carried twenty torpedoes; five of the nine she actually fired were duds. The rest she took back home. Thanks to Canada's shipping control, she could find no major vessels in Canadian waters.

Nine fishing schooners, all American, fell victim to U-117's cruiser warfare on Georges Bank off the coast of Maine on 10 August: *Aleda May* (31 tons), *William H. Starbuck* (53 tons), *Progress* (34 tons), *Reliance* (19 tons), *Earl and Nettie* (24 tons), *Cruiser* (28 tons), *Old Time* (18 tons), *Mary E. Sennett* (27 tons), and *Katie L. Palmer* (21 tons). Dröscher interrogated some of the fishermen aboard the submarine, taking special interest in finding out the number of American soldiers then in France, the American attitude to war, and the frequency of coastal patrols.

Before scuttling the boats and releasing the crews, the Germans removed provisions and stores. In the words of the engineer of *Aleda May*, a French-Canadian named Fred Doucette: "They took onions, candles, watermelon, bananas, and meat, and cleaned out all our provisions [...] They looked like a crowd of pirates."[36] His graphic account of being raided by "pirates" was doubtless a matter of conditioned response. The engineer of u-117 provided a contrasting perspective when describing the scene some years later: "[The people in the dories] had probably assumed some imminent horrible mass murder by being rammed or mowed down with machine-gun fire. Terribly distorted were the faces that stared pleadingly toward us [...] The hostages in our submarine had at first a dreadful fear."[37]

The German account recognized the terrible irony of war, for one of the "hostages" was a German-speaking fisherman whose grandfather had emigrated to the New World. As u-117's engineer would muse in the 1930s with a "blood-and-soil" sentiment typical of the period: "Wasn't that a cruel thrust to the heart, carrying on like this against peaceful people in whose veins German blood was flowing?" The scene would repeat itself when u-117 returned home via the Newfoundland Banks.

Two days after sinking the fishing fleet on Georges Bank, u-117 torpedoed and sank the 3,875-ton Norwegian steamer *Somerstad* twenty-five miles southeast of Fire Island and some fifty miles east of New York. Inbound from Halifax, the vessel had no inkling of the imminent danger. Dröscher watched through his periscope – only 400 metres away – as the lifeboats disappeared into thick fog; he then surfaced briefly and continued submerged as dense fog continued to roll in. Several vessels hove in sight through the mists as u-117 worked her way southward to lay mines off the Barnegat on the New Jersey coast. For a while she lay on the bottom during heavy fog to avoid the risk of being rammed. Next day, in the early evening of 13 August, she torpedoed and sank the 7,127-ton American steamer *Frederick R. Kellog* thirty miles south of the Ambrose Channel lightship. Owned by the Pan-American Petroleum and Transportation Co., she was bound from Tampico, Mexico, to Boston with 7,500 barrels of crude oil. U-117's war diary records the tanker's stern sinking rapidly in thirty metres' depth, leaving one-third of the wreck above water. She was salvaged by the end of the month and saw further service. U-117 had meanwhile laid her first series of mines by the Barnegat shoals light and moved further south. She avoided all traffic until her mining operations were completed. Not until almost two months later, on 4 October 1918, did the Barnegat minefield claim her first victim: the 2,458-ton American steamer *San Saba*. By 16 October US minesweepers had destroyed all but the last mine. The 1,505-ton Cuban freighter *Chappara* struck it six days later, some ten miles from Barnegat, and sank.[38]

Early on the morning of 14 August, U-117 fired a shot that forced the crew of the 2,088-ton five-mast schooner *Dorothy B. Barrett* to abandon ship some six miles northeast of the Five Fathom Bank lightship off the Delaware River mouth. Leaving their schooner to destruction by gun-fire, the American seamen rowed their dories into shoal waters. The nearby steam trawler *Kingsfisher* took them aboard and stoutly prepared to defend herself with her three-inch gun. U-117 had now turned her attention to an unidentified tanker, when gun-fire – Dröscher first thought it was U-140 – distracted him. Dröscher turned again to silence the SOS signals of Five Fathom Bank lightship.

Just as the lightship hove into view through heavy mist, U-117 dove to avoid a distant aircraft. Lying in twenty-five metres of water, U-117 counted nine bombs in a period of fifty minutes, each one getting closer. Dröscher assumed that he could be seen from the air because of the light grey colour of his hull but feared that leaking oil and air bubbles had betrayed his position. Those aboard *Kingfisher* had watched incredulously as U-117 had pursued the tanker into shoal waters and later voiced to naval interrogators a common complaint: "If we had only had one of your fast submarine-chasing boats there[,] we would have gotten that fellow because he was in shallow water and could not turn very fast."[39] *Kingfisher* would fall victim to U-155 next month. U-117 surfaced that evening after several hours on the bottom and proceeded toward Fenwick Island Shoal lightship, south of the Delaware, to lay his second minefield.

Four hours after completion of the Fenwick minefield, at 6:30 on the morning of 15 August, U-117 had also laid her third series of mines "south of Winter Quarter lightship" and within a couple of hours had destroyed the 1,613-ton American four-mast schooner *Madrugada* by gun-fire. She bore general cargo from her home port of New York to Santos, Brazil. Not until almost six weeks later, on 29 September 1918, did the minefield claim a victim: a mine severely damaged the battleship USS *Minnesota* some twenty miles from the lightship. On 9 November the 2,873-ton naval overseas transportation vessel USS *Saetia* struck a mine ten miles south-southeast of the Fenwick shoal and sank. She had been returning from France to Philadelphia in ballast with a small contingent of army personnel. The minesweeper USS *Teal* would destroy the remaining five mines by 20 January 1919. Forced in the mean time by both unfavourable positioning and the lightship's SOS signals to forgo an attack on a steamer, U-117 eluded an aircraft and headed, submerged, for Cape Hatteras to lay her fourth and final minefield.

U-117's progress to the Wimble Shoals lightbuoy was marked by sightings of inshore coastal convoys and escorted vessels too distant for decisive attack. Scarcely had he begun to lay the Wimble minefield, however, when Dröscher observed the 6,978-ton British steamer *Mirlo* unwittingly threading her way "through the gap between the previously laid mines and the lightbuoy." Dröscher interrupted his minelaying operations in order to attack – thus winning the praise of the commander-in-chief, submarines – and torpedoed her from 400 metres. Loaded with gasoline, *Mirlo* suffered a series of fatal explosions one-half mile off the Wimble Shoal buoy. With *Mirlo* dispatched, U-117 continued to extend her line of mines toward the buoy.

The epilogue was ironic. An investigating committee rejected *Mirlo*'s assertions that she had been torpedoed and ruled instead that she had actually struck a mine.[40] This erroneous conclusion triggered the immediate minesweeping operations that cleared the field. USS *Teal* swept the nine mines clear between 18 August and 5 September 1918.

Suffering heavy oil loss from her leaking tanks, U-117 had meanwhile headed home by the shortest route: past Nova Scotia and Cape Race. Radio traffic had persuaded Dröscher that Halifax offered prime targets. But, as he wrote in his war diary, the tantalizing prospect of "heading for Halifax and waging trade war must be declined" because of shortage of fuel.

After scuttling the 2,846-ton Norwegian four-mast barque *Nordhav* off Cape Hatteras on 17 August, the submarine engaged in an unsuccessful gun battle with the Italian steamer *Ansaldo Primo* seaward of the Delaware on the 20th. Off Nova Scotia, southwest of Sable Island, she attacked the 408-ton Canadian three-mast schooner *Bianca* with gun-fire before setting scuttling charges. Had anyone stood by to watch this last vessel sink, he would have witnessed the unexpected. The load of tobacco she had been carrying from Brazil to Halifax swelled with sea water and sealed the holes in the hull. Found three days after the attack by the Boston fishing schooner *Commonwealth*, she was towed into port. The *Halifax Herald* could rejoice at this minor victory, for the "Hun Pirate Did Not Sink Bianca."[41] On 26 August, U-117 destroyed the American trawler *Rush* northeast of Sable Island, and next day she torpedoed and sank without warning the 2,555-ton Norwegian steamer *Bergsdalen*, some 110 miles southwest of Cape Race.

On 30 August 1918, U-117 sank two Canadian schooners on the Newfoundland Bank; their crew members, the German war diary records, "were without exception German-speaking German-Americans." With icebergs drifting near and the catch complete, Edward Eisenhaur's 136-ton *Elsie Porter* was returning to Le Have, Nova Scotia, when Dröscher stopped her with three rifle shots across the bow some 145 miles southeast of Cape Spear, Newfoundland.[42] Riding heavy swells under overcast skies, Dröscher allowed the schooner's crew to escape in their dories before scuttling the vessel and inviting Eisenhaur aboard the U-boat for a drink.

Three hours later, U-117 stopped Frederick Gerhardt's schooner *Potentate* and took Gerhardt, his son, and another crew member for interrogation. Dröscher's log notes nothing of this meeting, though survivors insisted that he was particularly interested in steamer routes "from Newfoundland to Canada." Gerhardt claimed to have been threatened either with pressed service as a local pilot or removal to Germany if he did not provide information. He allegedly told nothing.

Neither extreme occurred. In any event U-117 was too short of fuel to tarry. Asked why he was sinking schooners, Dröscher purportedly replied: "You are helping to feed America." Set free in their nineteen-foot flat-bottomed dory, the three men rowed the 140 miles toward shore until they met the fishing fleet three days and three nights later. Dröscher had meanwhile removed all newspapers for intelligence purposes, confiscated stores, and sunk the vessel. The summer's run of the *Halifax Herald* alone would have given him ample evidence of the psychological impact of German "frightfulness" (Schrecklichkeit) in Canadian waters. It would also have shown that their frightened potential victims were fishermen – not the high-seas shipping the U-boats wanted to find.

The St John's *Evening Telegram* did its best to turn the harrowing ordeal of *Elsie Porter*'s crew into a gentleman's adventure. Reflecting the thread of recognition among the east coast papers that the German submariners were doing their best to avoid loss of life, the *Telegram* allowed that the schoonermen had received "the very best and kindest" treatment before they were cast adrift: "Cigars, cigarettes and food in profusion were served out." Of course, *Elsie Porter*'s captain had been effectively ruined by the destruction of his ship. But the press saw it differently. He "can easily begin again. [He] is a splendid specimen of physical perfection ... He is the type of man who has built up the British Empire and made it what it is today."[43]

Because U-117 had made her fast transit of Canadian waters over a hundred miles from shore, word of her attacks did not reach authorities until twenty-four hours or more after the event. By this time there was no hope of catching her, despite patrols by Canadian, French and American vessels to distant fishing grounds.[44]

In any event, the most serious danger was of attacks by mine and torpedo against major ships off St John's. Decryptions of German wireless traffic left no doubt that this was not merely possible, but probable. Admiralty in London had no vessels to spare and appealed to Canada to provide patrols. In response the RCN deployed a force of three to five drifters and trawlers fitted with minesweeping equipment. Captain Hose also laid on a comprehensive escort program for major ships plying between Sydney and Newfoundland.[45] Meanwhile, the Admiralty had begun to reroute the valuable medium-speed ships now heading up the St Lawrence to load at Montreal. They entirely avoided the waters south of Newfoundland where U-156 and U-117 were operating and where decrypt intelligence had shown U-155 would hunt; the new route lay over the northern tip of Newfoundland via the Strait of Belle Isle.[46]

No major steamers were being sunk. But neither this fact nor efforts such as the *Evening Telegram*'s to celebrate a test of manliness did much to soften the grim reality of scores of exhausted fishermen streaming onto beaches day after day. *Triumph*'s owner had asked the government to replace his lost vessel with a navy trawler. The acting minister for the navy, A.K. Maclean, supported the idea. So too did the chairman of the Canada Food Board, who warned that the government might also have to supply additional trawlers to maintain the Atlantic fishery. Admiral Kingsmill responded by urging Deputy Minister Desbarats to press the shipyards for early completion of the second batch of twenty-four trawlers which had been ordered under Admiralty contract in July 1917. They were sorely needed, he explained, for patrol service and possibly to replace lost fishing vessels.[47]

As Kingsmill knew, Admiral Grant was doing what he could to augment the RCN flotilla by arranging for the allocation of additional drifters and trawlers from the Admiralty orders in Canadian shipyards.[48] The U-cruiser attacks had shown the vulnerability of the waters at the mouth of the Bay of Fundy and around the southern tip of Nova Scotia, and Grant also assisted the Americans in improving the virtually non-existent defences there. Having already turned over six of the Admiralty drifters to the US navy for operations in this area, in September he allocated the US navy twelve more drifters and ten of the second batch of new trawlers.[49]

The RCN's two submarines, CC-1 and CC-2, offered the only hope of engaging the German U-cruisers on anything like equal terms. In the fall of 1917, the Canadians had responded to Admiralty's request that they be made available for European waters by transferring them from Esquimalt to Halifax. But they arrived in such poor technical condition after the gruelling voyage that they had to be virtually rebuilt. In the wake of U-156's second appearance in 1918, Kingsmill immediately approved Hose's proposal that CC-2 – the only one of the two remotely ready for operations – should go to the fishing banks with a decoy schooner that would lure the enemy within torpedo range. Plans for the tactic died, however, when Canadians could not find a suitable schooner. CC-2 therefore continued with her work in the Bras d'Or Lakes, making mock attacks on CGS *Petrel* which had been outfitted as a hydrophone training vessel for operators rotated from the fleet.[50] Given the urgent need to improve anti-submarine skills, this was in fact a happy outcome especially because the Americans had long since proved the decoy trap tactic a failure: it succeeded only in alarming friendly vessels – and even drawing their fire.[51]

The armies on the Western Front in Europe were meanwhile locked in the Second Battle of Artois from 30 August to 3 September. "The crowning act was the break-through at 5 a.m. on 2 September by the 1st and 4th Canadian Divisions" with fifty-nine tanks.[52] The Germans fell back under the renewed offensive and suffered over 115,000 casualties, nearly all of them prisoners lost to the advancing armies of the British Empire. As always, the cost of Allied success – even against the weakened, retreating German forces – was heavy. From 21 August to 3 September, the British Third and Fourth armies, under which the Canadian Corps fought, lost nearly 90,000 troops killed and wounded, of which the Canadian share was some 11,000; it was in these operations that Major Georges Vanier, the future governor-general, lost his right leg.

On 2 September, the day of the Canadian Corps's break-through in northern France, the US navy's air detachment at Halifax began flying operations; the second detachment did the same at North Sydney three week later. The four HS2L flying boats at each station carried out reconnaissance and convoy escort flights of up to three hours' duration and up to sixty miles in range.

That the stations began operations so soon is a credit to their

commanding officer, Lieutenant Richard E. Byrd – later renowned
for his pioneering polar flights. Bureaucratic tangles between two
Canadian government departments – Naval Service and Public
Works – had delayed construction of the bases, and the Americans
made do with tents while carrying out a good deal of the manual
labour in preparing the sites themselves. Although several practice
bombing runs proved their bombs to be duds, at this stage of development aircraft's weapons were not crucial. (The Allies would not
develop a dependable aerial anti-submarine bomb until 1941–2).

Experience in European waters had shown that the mere presence
of escorting aircraft was affording almost perfect protection to convoys. Fearing detection and attack, u-boats submerged the moment
aircraft appeared on the horizon and were thereby prevented by
their slow underwater speed from gaining contact with the convoy.
Had the war continued into the summer of 1919, there is little doubt
that aircraft would have formed a major part of the defences in
Canadian waters. The American commitment was already large: over
five hundred officers and men served at the Halifax and North Sydney stations. The navy also experimented with kite balloons and had
begun trials towing them behind HMCS *Acadia* when the war ended.[53]

Although grateful for American assistance, Sir Robert Borden was
determined that Canada assume responsibility for its own air
defences. As he wrote Ballantyne on 31 August 1918, "At present we
are dependent upon the United States for our air protection; we
cannot very well be content with this position permanently."[54] A letter
from the Royal Air Force officer seconded to Ottawa in order to
establish the RCN's air service had roused Borden's ire.[55]

Bitterly frustrated by bureaucratic inertia both in Ottawa and in
the British services, the officer seized the panic created by the u-boat
attacks off Nova Scotia to threaten his resignation and send a final
piece of advice: barring early energetic action, the anti-submarine air
patrols should be turned over to the US navy for the duration of the
war. This did not sit well, and with Borden's prompt intervention
the wheels began to turn. An order-in-council of 5 September 1918
created the "Royal Canadian Naval Air Service"; within a few weeks
the first aircrew recruits were on their way for training in Britain and
the United States.

The immediate challenge for the RCN in September 1918 was to
defend medium-speed convoys which began sailing from Quebec at
the beginning of the month. The Admiralty's rerouting of all medium-speed convoys to the St Lawrence after the sinking of the *Luz
Blanca* had come as a complete surprise to both American and Canadian authorities. Admiral Grant had been communicating solely with

Admiralty in London on the subject, and in recommending increased use of the St Lawrence as an alternative both to Halifax and to northern US ports, Grant had emphasized that his ideas were merely proposals. For this reason, he explained, he had raised the idea neither in Washington nor in Ottawa.

But as a result of what appears to have been a genuine oversight, Admiralty assumed that the necessary consultations had taken place.[56] On reflection, Grant had no misgivings about his failure to consult the Allies about the transfer. He had thoroughly expended his patience in trying to conciliate Canadian and American authorities and to co-ordinate their diversity of service commands and shipping agencies: "I am inclined to think it as well that it was presented as a more or less accomplished fact; I do not believe, otherwise, it would ever have been assented to."[57]

Certainly Grant was aware of the Canadian staff's long-standing reluctance to dispatch fully loaded, high-value ships through the Gulf. Quebec lay some six-hundred miles from the open sea, and the enclosed waters of the Gulf favoured the submarine. The area featured many narrow choke-points, where submarines could either lay mines or lie in wait in ideal positions for picking off ships with torpedoes; as well, it provided ready access to innumerable isolated bays or broad waters where U-boats could escape counterattack. The salient facts for Grant and the Admiralty were clear: all intelligence and U-156's actual operations had indicated that the Germans were interested not in the Gulf but in the waters off Nova Scotia and south of Newfoundland. Morever, Quebec offered a great deal of flexibility for evasive routing: convoys could readily be dispatched by either the northern route or the southern, depending on the latest intelligence.[58]

Kingsmill dispatched his director of operations at Naval Service Headquarters, Commander J.P. Gibbs, RN, to Washington during the last week of August to remind Admiral Grant personally of the RCN's inability to defend the Gulf. Grant bluntly declared that "Admiralty would not hear of any alteration" and confirmed what he had already intimated by telegram: Canadian warships would have to be widely redeployed – particularly from Halifax, but also from Sydney – in order to cover the northern route into the Gulf, through the Strait of Belle Isle around the northern tip of Newfoundland, and the southern, via the Cabot Strait by passing round Newfoundland's south coast. By way of assistance, Grant could offer only fifteen Royal Navy drifters which had recently been completed at Canadian yards and confirm the offer of five of the second batch of Admiralty trawlers – whenever they became available.[59]

Firm as Admiralty had been on the transfer of the medium-speed convoys to the St Lawrence, the responsible officers were slow to provide the necessary detailed instructions about convoy HC-16. This was the first to assemble at Quebec City and was due to sail on 4 September. With only a few days to make arrangements at Quebec, the British "Port Convoy Officer" at Sydney, Rear-Admiral B.M. Chambers, RN, discovered to his horror that the Canadian staff responsible for control of shipping at Quebec amounted to a mere corporal's guard. It was a shadow of the large RCN staffs that gave him such efficient support at the Atlantic ports.

Accompanied by an intelligence officer whom he had pulled from a British cruiser at Halifax, Chambers raced up to Quebec and managed to get the convoy off on schedule. Part of the reason for his success lay in his choice of the familiar southern route through the Cabot Strait. Grant, in contrast, had preferred the northern route, through Belle Isle strait, because of its distance from the U-cruiser operating area; its use in this case would have required a great deal more staff work.[60]

There were only four vessels in the RCN flotilla with the endurance and speed to escort the HC convoys through the long Gulf passage: *Lady Evelyn*, at Sydney, and *Canada*, *Margaret*, and *Stadacona*, on harbour defence at Halifax since the destruction of *Luz Blanca*. Redeployed, they escorted HC-16 along the southern route. Beginning with convoy HC-17, which sailed from Quebec on 13 September, they escorted medium-speed convoys on the northern route at eight-day intervals until ice began to impede navigation at the end of October.[61] Meanwhile, during September, Canadians deployed a score of drifters and trawlers – all equipped with sweeps – at choke-points on both the northern and southern Gulf routes.[62]

Great as was the RCN's responsibility for the safety of the valuable medium-speed ships that sailed through the St Lawrence, the burden proved not as crushing as Kingsmill had feared. Certainly, the convoys that assembled at Quebec were as large as the ones that had sailed from Halifax – ninety-eight medium-speed ships made the St Lawrence passage in September and in October – but they carried more cargo and fewer troops: 6,017 Canadians and 12,677 Americans.[63] Although the Canadian militia promptly provided the US army with camps and embarkation facilities at Montreal when HC convoys were switched to the St Lawrence, and although the US navy had endorsed this arrangement, the US army continued to insist that it could make only limited use of the Canadian route. Grant suspected that it had its own reasons for wanting a temporary reduction in troop movements overseas.[64]

The RCN struggled during early September 1918 to meet its new commitments. The slow convoys from Sydney, for example, continued at least double the size of those in the HC series. Some 266 ships sailed in them from the beginning of September until the armistice.[65] In addition to the American submarine chasers and trawlers which had always provided long-range escorts, three slower auxiliary patrol ships, *Hochelaga*, *Cartier*, and *Acadia*, now lent their support.[66]

Canadian ports were crucial to the fully developed ocean convoy system in 1918. In September, for example, 99 ships carrying 553,211 tons of cargo cleared for overseas, as compared to 67 ships and 319,837 tons during September 1917. Nearly two-thirds of these sailings were ships from US ports that had run north to join the Sydney convoys.[67] All this activity continued in addition to the RCN's old commitments – and in the knowledge that another German U-cruiser would soon arrive.

U-155 (ex *U-Deutschland*) was the last U-boat to hunt in North American waters. She had a good record of artillery attacks against merchant vessels in European waters, a fact that had led her previous captain to endorse the U-cruiser concept of surface warfare; he did so to the neglect of the increasing emphasis on underwater combat. Korvettenkapitän Eckelmann had observed for the period September 1917 to January 1918: "The tactical attack conditions ... prove that even such clumsy and slow vessels as the former mercantile submarines, when handled correctly, are equal to their tasks both surfaced and submerged, all of which justifies the construction of even larger U-cruisers than are now in construction, since the new ones will be even more manageable than the Deutschland-cruisers."[68]

Eckelmann had argued the necessity of maintaining the U-boats' heavy 15-cm guns as well as torpedoes, so that one would always have the option of an artillery attack whenever targets were beyond torpedo firing range or too fast for a U-boat to overhaul or to gain an effective torpedo firing position. Other commanding officers had complained that U-155's lack of speed and agility had actually lost them targets. Eckelmann's successor in command of U-155 for the North American mission, Korvettenkapitän Studt, would question Eckelmann's conclusions as well. Conditions in the open Atlantic and along the North American coast offered neither the number nor the density of choke-points through which merchant traffic had to funnel. Here speed was of the essence, and U-155 was too slow.

U-155, under Studt's command, departed Kiel via the customary "eastern route" of the Skaggerak and the Shetlands on 11 August, while U-156, U-140, and U-117 were still in Canadian and American waters.[69] This was the very day on which Admiral Reinhard Scheer succeeded the aged Admiral von Holtzendorff as chief of the Admiralty Staff and assumed responsibility for submarines. Nothing indicates whether Scheer would have wished to change the u-cruisers deployments to which von Holtzendorff had in effect committed him. Studt's orders gave him the "task of waging cruiser warfare on the American coast in the area of the Nantucket lightship, and minelaying off St John's (Newfoundland) and Halifax." They also included "cable cutting northwest of Sable Island," that lonely twenty-mile-long crescent of sand situated 150 miles east-southeast of Halifax.

The orders would prove problematic. As Studt scribbled in his virtually illegible war diary: "Studying the nautical material, together with statements of the Englishman aboard the Portuguese sailing vessel Gamo [which I] sank on 31 August, lead me to believe that the harbour of St John's were I am supposed to lay mines is really St John [sic] in the Bay of Fundy."[70] The mysterious "Englishman" had advised him that the Newfoundland harbour had no major shipping. Indeed the Pilot Book also led him to conclude that St John's was an unlikely spot to lay mines: situated on an island, with a narrow entrance, shallows in the approaches, and no connections with bases.

Studt therefore concluded that the mission orders, "based on agent's information," really meant Saint John, New Brunswick, with its "connection to the Canadian Railway." Saint John had of course always figured large in Germany's pre-war strategic planning. Studt was in all things an extremely circumspect and cautious man and would take no unnecessary risks. The prospect of saving himself six hundred miles by avoiding Newfoundland altogether was appealing; in the event, once he had reached the southern tip of Nova Scotia he never really entertained the possibility of proceeding any further to Saint John.

Heavy weather while u-155 was outbound had prevented significant attacks. The scuttling in mid-Atlantic of the 315-ton Portuguese sailing vessel Gamo, en route to Lisbon from St John's with a cargo of fish, on 31 August was slight compensation for u-155's inability to effect attacks that same day on three fast vessels – among them ss France – running at high speed in an unescorted convoy. On 2 September the submarine destroyed by gun-fire the 3,560-ton Norwegian vessel Stortind, bearing railway tracks and wire from Norfolk to France.

Five days later u-155 exchanged fire with the faster 6,077-ton American steamer Frank H. Buck from an initial range of 14,000 yards. The steamer subsequently supplied graphic evidence of "a terrific explosion and black smoke" when claiming to have destroyed the submarine on her "twenty-ninth shot." u-155's log does not corroborate any damage. Almost as a consolation, u-155 scuttled that same day the 162-ton Portuguese sailing vessel *Sophia* carrying fish from St John's to Lisbon.

Pickings were random and unexpected as U-155 approached fifty degrees West: for example, her sudden and unsuccessful gunnery attack against the 4,078-ton British vessel *Monmouth*. The freighter's SOS signals confirmed information about the U-boat's position already gleaned by Operational Intelligence. As Admiral Sims wired US Naval Operations in Washington from his headquarters in London, the "submarine would be one of the two converted mercantile types which were expected to sail from Germany about the middle of August and [which] would reach the American coast about September 15" 1918.[71] The other submarine could either have been Kapitänleutnant Adolf Franz's U-152, which did not depart Kiel until 5 September, or Kapitänleutnant Arnauld de la Perière's U-139, which departed on 11 September. Both had orders to attack shipping off the North American coast; ultimately, however, both remained outside North American waters.

U-155's westward advance provided the Canadian press with evidence of further German encroachments on North America. South of Newfoundland on 12 September, U-155 torpedoed and sank the eastbound 3,245-ton Portuguese steamer *Leixoes* (ex-German *Cheruskia*). The attack without warning showed all the signs of unrestricted U-boat warfare. In the words of the Portuguese captain: "Fifteen minutes after the ship was struck the submarine appeared on the starboard beam about one-quarter mile distant. Our vessel sank in about 15 minutes and before we got alongside the submarine [...] The captain of the submarine ... spoke splendid English, very much like an American. He asked what ship it was [and] if there were any Englishmen on board ... When he ordered us to shove off he did not give us any course, neither did he give us any provisions [...] One man lost his life on the ship [...] Two other men lost their lives from exposure and cold."[72]

Five days later the *Halifax Herald* announced "Torpedoed Crew Reach Nova Scotia Port Nearly Dead" and explained that "the Portuguese steamer *Leixoes* was sent to the bottom by German submarine who with usual brutality left sailors to their fate."[73]

Whatever secrecy U-155 might have expected was lost on Friday, 13 September, some one hundred miles southeast of Sable Island, when the 4,391-ton British merchantman *Newby Hall* damaged the submarine in a running exchange of gun-fire. "It's becoming increasingly recognized," Studt complained in his log, "that U-cruisers are slow, and that a steamer can often save itself by tough resistance while running off at high speed."

Braving the submarine's high velocity and shrapnel shells, *Newby*

Hall had zigzagged at high speed and fired some fifty rounds while opening the range from 3,000 to a safe 13,000 yards. Her shots dented the submarine's armour plating and sprung rivets in the pressure-hull that led to serious leaks and temporarily made diving impossible. *Newby Hall* was equipped with wireless and raised the alarm. As her skipper reported: "Distress signals were sent out by wireless for assistance and answered immediately by United States patrol, who endeavoured to come to our assistance, but as the weather became thick and rainy we saw nothing of him. All secret books and codes were thrown overboard during the action."[74]

U-155 intercepted American war warning signals on 17 September; these indicated that an "enemy submarine was enroute to New York." Studt seems to have concluded from this that the Allies had not twigged to his Canadian mission. The contrary was in fact true. Operational Intelligence linked its decryptions with the *Newby Hall* incident and thus enabled Admiralty in London to warn naval authorities on the Canadian east coast immediately to expect minelaying off St John's (Newfoundland) and Halifax and to anticipate submarine attacks against shipping between these ports.[75]

Admiral Story at Halifax immediately deployed his most effective ships – the American submarine chasers and HMCS *Grilse*. While *Grilse* made an unusually long, three-day patrol at the harbour entrance, the American ships undertook daily patrols and hydrophone listening watches along the sea lane from Halifax to Sambro Island. All shipping sailed under escort, including air cover by the US navy flying boats.[76] Although Studt did not report observing the aircraft, he recorded the fact that "destroyers, patrol vessels" and fog had hampered his attempts at attacking merchant shipping.

Studt was in any event preoccupied with his two principal missions: minelaying and cable-cutting. On 17 September, he recorded, U-155 "laid 6 mines at one mile intervals approximately 5 miles south of Betty Island near St John." The notation is curious. U-155 went nowhere near Saint John in the Bay of Fundy and actually laid the mines off Betty Island, near Halifax.[77] By noon next day U-155 sowed her first string of four mines while running submerged "between Sambro lightship and Sambro Ledge." She lay the next two series of four mines each in lines "335 [degrees] on the intended blockade course right in front of the entrance" to the harbour. Studt's expression "in front of the entrance" should not lead us to construe that the submarine had advanced past Chebucto Head. In navigational terms the shipping route lay on a long northwest–southeast axis from Chebucto Head to the Sambro lightship. By evening U-155 lay twelve miles offshore, her work having been interrupted by the appearance of "destroyers" and numerous smaller warships, merchantmen, and sailing vessels.[78] The mines did no damage. Most broke loose from their moorings and were thus rendered "safe"; fishermen recovered several of them and received twenty-five dollar rewards from the department.

During the next two days, U-155 worked her way along the route from Halifax to the northeastern side of Sable Island in order to locate the transatlantic cable. German intelligence had rejected other alternatives: Heart's Content, Newfoundland, had little strategic value, despite being "technically the simplest to cut"; and the St Pierre cable was "too silted up after 40 years on the bottom." German intelligence regarded the cable from Halifax to Bermuda to be important as "it certainly plays a significant role in the intelligence service"; it gave secondary priority to the transatlantic cable from Halifax to Ireland.

Now working toward Sable Island, Studt sought a spot where the cable lay in a soft seabed that would not damage her experimental and apparently clumsy cutting gear.[79] Two attempts in rocky ground snapped U-155's rig; but on 19 September Studt found favourable sandy ground. His log records his "surface run on cutting course 130 [degrees] in order to begin cutting the innermost of the six northwesterly Sable Island cables in 90 meters of water." Emergency dives when exposed to "steamers, destroyers and darkened ore carriers" interrupted his work, until the tension indicator on his rig hovered in a range of "1.8–2.6 tons [and] indicated a sinewy object had been gripped and cut." Studt therefore considered it "possible that three of the cables have been sliced"; he continued to work away in the fog without any apparent further success and then headed for Nantucket.

It was in any event a hopeless task. Unknown to Studt, the Germans required fifteen cable cuttings in order to isolate Canada and Newfoundland from Britain.[80] Her cable-work completed, U-155 scuttled the American trawler *Kingfisher* on the 20th. By this time the U-boat's log records hearing public radio broadcasts about "a U-boat south of Newfoundland" and broadcasting news of troop transport departures scheduled from Halifax for 28 and 29 September. Her inability to locate major shipping gave her all the more reason to head into American waters.

U-155's American cruise seems as makeshift and haphazard as the Canadian mission had been. It leaves a record of abandoned chases and only occasional successes. She broke off running gun battles on 29 September, 2 October, and 12 October with the 2,246-ton British steamer *Reginolite*, the 9,071-ton British *Nevasa*, and the 7,409-ton

American *Amphion*, respectively. The latter battle lasted an hour, with an exchange of almost three hundred rounds. The submarine simply could not maintain speed. On 3–4 October U-155 torpedoed and sank the lone 3,838-ton Italian vessel *Alberto Treves* and scuttled the 330-ton British schooner *Industrial*, some 250 miles southeast of Nantucket Island.

On 17 October the submarine torpedoed the last ship in an unescorted convoy from New York to Marseille. This was the 6,744-ton American freighter *Lucia*. Her SOS calls were repeated by ships in convoy and answered by the USS *Fairfax*. As *Lucia*'s captain reported: "If the *Fairfax* had not arrived at the time it did [four hours after the sinking], I do not think our boats would have weathered the heavy seas, as they were all overloaded. I and my officers and crew think that great credit is due to the commanding officer and crew of the *Fairfax* in the skillful way he handled his ship in the heavy seas, and effecting the rescue of our crew without any mishaps." She was the last ship sunk by a German submarine in North American waters.

By this time submarine warfare had long since outlived its purpose. The Allies had commenced the first of four great consecutive offensives against German forces. Opening on 25 September in the Argonne, the drive pushed on into the Battle of Cambrai and St Quentin from 27 September until 10 October. The general advance pressed hard on the retreating Germans until the armistice. Even as late as 10 November, "exceptionally stubborn [German] resistance was offered near Mons [Belgium], where the German machine-gunners had orders to fight to a finish; but by dawn on the 11th the Canadian Crops had cleared the town of the enemy."[81]

Bold as the free-wheeling operations by the U-boats on the fishing banks close off Nova Scotia may have seemed in retrospective press accounts, the Germans had been running almost no risk. The little schooners were small fry that scarcely repaid the enormous effort involved in transatlantic voyages. None of the fishing vessels the Germans attacked carried radios, and news of the attacks could not reach Allied naval authorities until the boats of survivors reached shore many hours – or even days – later. Even if word of an attack had gotten out instantly, the few hours it took for the fastest warships to reach the scene of a "hit-and-run" attack allowed the U-boat ample time to escape. Experience in Europe's densely patrolled waters had shown this clearly. Although Canadian patrol vessels had had but one encounter with U-boats – and that with rather embarrassing results – their failure to locate the enemy is not surprising; much larger efforts by better-equipped American ships had also come up empty-handed.

What mattered was that over five hundred vessels had sailed for the war fronts from Canadian ports – on schedule and without loss – since u-156's first appearance off Nova Scotia in early August.[82] What was more, not one major anti-submarine vessel had to be dispatched from European waters to achieve this result. Thanks to the RCN, the Germans had succeeded in neither of their main objectives: to hamper the flow of troops and war supplies from North America and to compel the Allies to thin out their concentration of anti-submarine defences in the major theatres of war.

Far from basking in any sense of achievement in the fall of 1918, however, senior Canadian officers felt that their improvised forces was leaning over the brink of disaster. Just how deep the chasm lay is revealed in Admiral Kingsmill's comments in early September: "We have not lost any [trawlers] up to date, but at any time a submarine may sink a whole division."[83] As we shall see, the admiral and his subordinates were determined to rebuild the flotilla entirely for the 1919 season.

Undeterred by the bitter harbingers of defeat, Germany too had been pressing plans for the development of its navy. As late in the day as May 1918 high-level meetings had attempted to "clarify the question as to which types of submarine [should] be delivered in 1920."[84] Combat-proven types quite logically claimed first priority, not least because planners envisaged ordering u-boats to the maximum productive capacity the shipyards could bear. There was now no discussion about a possible end of the war – only the need for very large numbers of boats to saturate the multiplying strength of Allied anti-submarine forces. The increasing intensity of the submarine war had also spelt an end to the bold, gun-oriented tactics that had been employed in North American waters: "Strengthened [Allied] surveillance in the operations areas, increased protection of convoys, and the improved weaponry of merchant ships [now restricted] the use of a submarine's artillery, and [meant] that successes would primarily be attained with the torpedo – submerged by day, and surfaced by night." Clearly the days of the unmanoeuvrable converted mercantile boats were numbered, but the purpose-built u-cruisers, like u-140, were adequate for North American operations. Still, according to the planners, in view of Germany's "further development of the naval war, the requirement exists for a u-cruiser to reach even farther and operate in the Gulf of Mexico and off the coast of Brazil." The last vestige of the grand imperial dream of Germany's Operational Plan OP III, born of the unrealistic naval ambitions of 1898–1906, was still refusing to die.

– 12 –
Epilogue:
Mad Dreams
and Mothballs

When the Sydney flotillas began their annual migration back to Halifax for the winter in late October 1918 the total strength of the Atlantic coast patrols stood at 120 vessels: HMCS *Grilse*, HMCS *Shearwater*, the submarines *CC 1* and *CC 2*, eight auxiliary patrol ships, fifty steel trawlers, seven wooden trawlers, and fifty-one drifters. This was by no means the whole fleet. About fifty uncommissioned vessels, from motor launches to fisheries protection cruisers, were committed to domestic tasks: anti-submarine net and mine defences, convoy assembly and control of shipping, examination service, and transport of coal and stores.

By the fall of 1918 Canada's naval service had established substantial defences at both Sydney and Halifax and was escorting hundreds of valuable merchantmen through thousands of miles of the most treacherous waters in the world. This was a far cry from 1914, when the RCN had scarcely been able to maintain a presence at the entrance to Halifax harbour, its own main base.[1] Most of this expansion had occurred within eighteen months. It was achieved largely with Canadian resources and personnel at a time when these had been severely depleted by over two years' unstinting commitment to the war in Europe.

The U-cruisers had managed to sink only three large ocean-going ships in Canadian waters; they had done so under unusually favourable conditions. U-156 had caught *Luz Blanca* off Halifax because high-grade cryptographic intelligence had led the Allies not to expect an early thrust toward Nova Scotia. U-117 had the good fortune to encounter *Bergsdalen* well out to sea; the freighter was beyond the coastal focal routes where shipping was easiest to locate and outside the regularly patrolled zones. It was in just such a region that U-155 had picked off *Leixoes*. The Germans' inability to find other major vessels was the direct result of quick British, American, and Canadian action to shift assembly of HC convoys from Halifax to the St Lawrence, away from the danger area off Nova Scotia, and sail local traffic and vessels making for convoy ports in escorted groups.

Still, the events of 1918 had deeply upset senior officers of the RCN and their political masters. The appearance of the U-boats had laid bare the shortcomings of improvisation without benefit of a well-established naval organization, experienced seamen, or the most basic material resources. At the war's end, Story and Hose were still arguing over who controlled which parts of the Halifax flotilla,[2] while the department pleaded once more with Britain to provide the essential support that had been almost entirely lacking at the moment of crisis in August.[3]

Senior Canadian officers felt little sense of achievement during the late summer of 1918, only a grim foreboding about the future. Intelligence had now made it clear that the converted freighters were the principal German submarines to have crossed the Atlantic; their limited performance accounted for the scattered hit-and-run attacks. There seemed little doubt that the Germans would send over much more powerful purpose-built U-cruisers in 1919 for a determined and sustained offensive. "In the event of a U-cruiser of this type appearing off Canadian coasts," Hose warned headquarters, "there is not one vessel or any combination of vessels [in the existing flotilla] which it would be the slightest use to dispatch to the attack even if it were known exactly where to find and pick up with the U-cruiser."[4]

On 21 October 1918, the anniversary of Trafalgar, he vented his frustration by drawing up an extravagant scheme for beefing up the Canadian navy: thirty-three destroyers and four submarines were now the "minimum defence force required." In the words of the director of operations in Ottawa, the Hose plan was "quite outside the realm of practical politics."[5] He did concede, however, that Canada should construct in its own yards six large destroyers and eight submarines – provided there were "a thoroughly efficient Dockyard to keep them in repair." Kingsmill forwarded Hose's proposal to the minister with endorsement from Operations and appended a reminder: Laurier's naval program would have provided much of what was so desperately needed now.

Canada's minister for the navy had already been seeking solutions. Six weeks earlier Ballantyne had raised the question of destroyers for 1919 in a personal letter to the first sea lord, Admiral Wemyss, whom he had met during a trip to London the previous August. The visit had convinced the Canadian minister of the futility of expecting the loan of British or American destroyers. He therefore revived an old proposal: Canada should attempt to build them with help from either British or American industry. But, once again, Wemyss had to discourage the idea: assistance on the scale Canada really required, he argued, would only disrupt existing building programs.[6] For the first time, however, Admiralty did not treat the Canadian request lightly.

Admiralty's mood of optimism about the war had changed during the last months of the conflict, for the Germans had begun to reverse the downward trend of lost Allied tonnage resulting from the introduction of convoys. In June senior Allied officers had greeted the German submarine campaign against North America as an admission of German defeat in European waters, but by August and September they were beginning to recognize that the enemy had gotten second wind. Allied losses had risen from a low of seventy-eight merchant-men destroyed in June to 127 in August. This change was a result of Germany's last-ditch campaign in distant waters where defences were weak and failure of Allied anti-submarine forces in European waters to destroy more than a half-dozen u-boats per month.

This meagre toll in u-boats was not enough to counter the Germans' new submarine construction; intelligence, moreover, revealed a vastly increased German building program. So concerned was Sir Eric Geddes, first lord of the Admiralty, that he travelled to Washington in October 1918 to press the Americans to get on with their now much delayed destroyer program. It was well behind schedule; of the over 250 ships projected in 1917 they had completed only seven.[7] Among the promises offered to Geddes and his staff was an American commitment to dispatch six destroyers to Halifax early in the 1919 navigation season.[8]

Encouraging as the prospect of further support from the United States might be, Canadian officers were profoundly worried about the state of their own service. Already in September 1918 Hose had warned that the whole system of manning and training would have to be entirely revamped as soon as possible. Sparse records indicate that he had no more than "approximately two thousand" sailors – presumably ships' crews.[9] As we have seen, an unexpectedly high proportion of raw recruits were among them. Hose therefore needed a continuous flow of both new recruits and seasoned personnel to create that "considerable reserve" which experience had shown was essential for efficient operations. Moreover, he warned, no systematic training of naval forces could be achieved in the outdated and improvised facilities at Halifax; the navy needed new barracks.[10]

The inadequate and overburdened repair facilities of dockyard caused equally grave concern. As a visiting British officer reported

in October 1918, only "about 55% of the auxiliary patrols are working."[11] With a burst of zeal and energy, Hose reported, the repair
organization might just be able to refit the fleet in time for the opening
of navigation on the St Lawrence in 1919. But it would be a closely run
race.[12] As naval staff concluded, the sorry state of Halifax dockyard
formed the Achilles' heel of the whole east coast. Even if Canada's
naval service were to obtain ships significantly better than the auxiliary patrol vessels and drifters, it could not maintain them. It would
be a "waste of money doing anything to bolster up the present Yard,"
Kingsmill advised Ballantyne at the beginning of November. The
time had come to build an entirely new and expanded facility, just as
he had advised Laurier in 1909.[13]

Some British officers laid the blame for the RCN's difficulties on
poor organization and lack of resources.[14] Others blamed the Canadian bureaucracy. Two British officers who had spent considerable
time in Ottawa commented bitterly about the extent and effect of rule
by civil servants. In the words of the air force officer: "The Navy
Department have their hands quite full, know nothing about the
need of Aviation and, sometimes, one is driven to thinking, care
less; anyway the civilian element – which curiously forms the chief
element – are busy over their own little municipal affairs and are apt
to think us [military people] as somewhat of a nuisance."[15] "I am
convinced," Rear-Admiral Sir Alexander Duff observed from London, "that no sound organization of the forces in Canadian Waters
can be expected so long as the present regime at Ottawa continues."[16]

Certainly, Robert Borden was not pleased with the way the department was attending to anti-submarine defence; in the little time he
had to consider the matter during the late summer and the fall of
1918, he had collared his senior officials. Not only did he expedite
the organization of the air service personally, but he had pressed
Ballantyne to make a determined bid for destroyers for 1919. He had
also summoned Ballantyne for an earnest discussion of the "condition" of his department. Ballantyne in turn cleared the air with
Desbarats, his deputy minister.[17] Borden thought that the deputy
was one source of difficulty: "He seems to have little drive and to
be rather casual."[18] The deputy, however, placed the blame on
Kingsmill.

Captain L.G. Preston, RN, who visited Ottawa in the fall of 1918,
reported to the Admiralty that the unhappy situation was rooted in
the RCN's troubled past: "The status of the Canadian Navy is certainly
not, in the eyes of the Canadian public, the same as the status of its
Army. The naval officers employed at the Navy Department do not
appear to have any confidence in their position, and their whole

attitude shows a lack of coordination. Social and political matters
appear to present to them greater interest than the conduct of the
Department on Admiralty lines."[19] The problem could be solved, he
believed, by replacing Kingsmill with a British officer seconded from
the Royal Navy for a set term. Such an officer would therefore not
be governed by any desires for permanent employment with the
Canadian government.

There was a great deal that Preston did not understand. It was
of course true that senior British army officers with the kind of
independence he wanted for the position of director of the naval
service had done much to reform the Canadian militia; but they
had behaved outrageously in challenging civilian authority. This was
precisely the situation that had brought Laurier to enshrine the
primacy of civilian authority within the navy department. It was also
his major reason for recruiting Kingsmill, who was willing to make a
permanent commitment to Canadian service.

Laurier's arrangement had subsequently served Borden well.
When Borden's difficulties over naval policy resulted in virtual dismantling of the RCN in 1911–14, and when the circumstances of
1914–16 demanded penny-pinching policies, he had found a faithful
servant in Kingsmill. Under Desbarats's leadership, the admiral con-
scientiously held expenditures to a minimum and made no move to
embarrass the government publicly. There is ironic justice in the fact
that the very type of management that Borden had once promoted
now frustrated him in the suddenly changed conditions of 1918.

Significantly, the most senior British officer in North America, and
the one with the most experience on this continent, was much more
reluctant to condemn the Canadian department than were his colleagues and Canadian politicians. In Admiral Grant's view, much of
the confusion and ill-will in the Canadian area had been caused by
the presence of Admiral Chambers – a British officer who was not in
the Canadian chain of command.[20]

The difficulties with Chambers were, of course, symptomatic of
larger problems. Introduction of convoys in 1917 had brought Admiralty's sudden assertion of fuller and more direct control over operations in the western Atlantic and muddled lines of communication.[21]
Certainly, the commander-in-chief could be more realistic than Canadian politicians and visitors from Admiralty. Unlike them, he had
also worked closely with US navy anti-submarine forces in American
home waters, and, although he did not make the comparison, it is
clear that he believed that the American organization was as bad as
that of the RCN.

Indeed, Grant predicted that the Americans would in 1919 face

such difficulties in defending merchant shipping that they would
have to rely more on evasive routing and on the merchantman's
own defensive armament than on aggressive action by American
warships.[22] In operations, the us navy had shown "no very clearly
defined system and are subject to impulse"; American mine countermeasures were so disorganized that "a determined [German] attempt
to mine any portion of the coast would most probably meet with
considerable success." Indeed, the American "submarines available
for anti-submarine patrol are a source of danger to themselves and
an annoyance to shipping in general," while "aircraft, destroyers,
and chasers are very inexperienced and cause much trouble by their
continuous reports of attacks on and destruction of non-existent
submarines."

No one at Admiralty in 1918 was more keenly aware of the shipping
losses caused by bromidic senior officers who practised hidebound
methods, nor more impressed by the enormous difficulty in effecting
change, than was Captain Herbert Richmond. As director of training
and staff duties in London, he was still struggling to bring the archaic
Admiralty staff system into the twentieth century and had already
jeopardized his career by his frank criticism of Admiralty's failings.[23]

Not surprising, Richmond provided the most balanced assessment of the Canadians when surveying the reports about the grim
situation in Ottawa. He intuitively understood the problems as a
function of the Canadian service's troubled birth, caught as it was
between Admiralty's continued reluctance to accept the idea of
dominion navies and profound domestic political division. In
attempting to replicate itself in Canada, the Royal Navy had completely failed to understand that "it is obviously impossible to trans-
plant an ancient growth to new soil as the basis of an entirely new
organisation."[24] Canada needed, among other things, "a satisfactory
settlement of the question of where Imperial and Canadian Naval
responsibility begin and end."

Leadership was another key issue, and Richmond's perceptive
mind saw the Canadian situation much clearer than most:

It is hardly fair to expect officers untrained in Staff work and possibly ... with
a very limited experience of administrative organisation outside of ship-work
to compete with the political and other difficulties extant in Canada.

There appear to be strong party differences of opinion on the Navy question in Canada, and in consequence whole-hearted support for the Naval
Administration is not obtainable.

If this be so it would require an officer of the very greatest ability to occupy
the post of Director of the Naval Service and he would have to be supported

by a Staff of highly trained officers competent to represent their requirements unequivocally and to realise to the full what these requirements were.

At the same time the ablest Directorate and Staff will be powerless against a policy of laissez-faire or deliberate obstruction on the part of the Government.

This statement vindicated the years of Kingsmill's struggle to lead the Canadian navy with the very few experienced officers under his command. Had Richmond's thoughts been available to Canadian planners, they would have lent focus for years to come. Overtaken by events, the Canadian navy soon seemed superfluous to national security.

German Admiralty recalled all submarines on 21 October 1918, four days after U-155 had sunk the last ship to be destroyed by U-boats in North American waters; this was the very date on which Hose set out his 'Trafalgar Day' proposals for a new Canadian navy for 1919. Overshadowed by the impending armistice, of which his majesty's German submarines had gleaned only scraps of wireless information while at sea, the U-boats returned home to an uncertain future in a Germany convulsed by revolution. Indeed, it may fairly be argued that the German navy that had once emerged as an expression of empire was now "increasingly dominated by the series of military and political developments that shaped the history of Germany" itself.[25] Salient among them were Germany's impending military collapse, the democratization of the nation's political life, social conflict and internal jostling for power, and, of course, an Admirals' Rebellion that triggered the sailors' mutinies.

Admiral Scheer had abrogated unto himself the full powers of chief of the Naval War Office (Chef der Seekriegsleitung) on succeeding Admiral von Holtzendorff on 1 August 1918. He enjoyed the confidence of the officer corps and of course the loyal support of Admiral von Trotha, chief of staff of the High Seas Fleet. But both he and his officers were out of touch with tactical, social, and political realities. To be sure, he had introduced the "Scheer Programme" of building thirty-six submarines a month and had pursued a policy of submarine warfare despite President Wilson's Peace Note of 14 October which had demanded complete cessation of submarine attacks on passenger vessels in return for an armistice.

But Scheer still could not win the naval war. Nor did an armistice appeal to him and his admirals. For them it meant defeat without honour. The German navy's honour had to be saved, and the only means lay in taking his long-idle High Seas Fleet to sea against all odds. Against all wisdom, and against the desire of both the German government and the Kaiser himself, Admiral Scheer proceeded with plans for the suicidal Flottenvorstoss. This was his plan for a final, decisive battle against the British, a last-ditch heroic undertaking that reflected the primary focus of "big-ship" maritime doctrine on which the German navy had been built.

Recall of the submarines under increasing political and diplomatic pressure provided the key. Relieved of its task of supporting submarine operations, the High Seas Fleet could now regain "its operational freedom."[26] This meant freedom to attack, a role from which the fleet had shrunk since 1916. However, senior officers grossly misjudged the temper of their men. This major failure of leadership catapulted the navy into its final collapse. The sailors refused to sail; in doing so they undermined the last remnants of moral authority which the officer corps possessed. In planning to execute the Flottenvorstoss, the officers had knowingly rebelled against their government and could now no longer count on its support. Thus the German navy owed its final demise more to the paralysis of its leadership than to the strength and organization of the non-commissioned insurgents.

Assailed by its wartime enemies, and broken from within, the German Empire collapsed; the Kaiser abdicated and crossed the Dutch border, incognito, into an exile from which he would never return. In the closing days of the Imperial Navy, one German naval officer struggled through the chaos on his way from the North Sea coast to Berlin and recorded his poignant thoughts for the now almost defunct German Admiralty: "November 11 brought news of the proclamation of the Republic in Germany: confused, contradictory, impacting all the worse for this upon vacillating minds. Whether favourably or unfavourably disposed to these events, people felt one thing clearly: there is no authority up top any more, the old rights and laws are shattered."[27] And shattered they were. But even as the German fleet was dying, patriotic voices persisted in proclaiming ultimate victory and final vindication of Germany's aspirations for maritime prestige. They prophesied the day when the history of the Great War would reveal itself as "the decline and fall of British maritime tyranny," in which German u-boats would have played a major role.[28]

How different that 11 November as described in the diary of a perceptive citizen in Halifax:

Great War over. Armistice signed at 5 am Paris time ... The good news arrived at Halifax at 3.45 am.
 I awoke with faint sound of distant bells in my ear. Thought it might be

signal that [the] expected armistice had been signed, and to make sure, I was just getting out of bed when the Quinpool Road engine-house bell began to ring, and I knew it must be the good news and called out loud 'There it is!' which awoke Constance and my son. I looked out window; it was a lovely bright starlight night, with what seemed like a pinkish glow all about the horizon. Northern-lights like whiffs of smoke passing upward to about 1/3 or 1/2 way to zenith. On asking Constance the time she said it was about 4.20 am; then a steam whistle (doubtless from the Round House at Willow Park) began to blow and continued blowing for a *very* long time ... A light or two just came in on a neighbour's house. Then heard people in next house singing 'Rule Britannia,' ... Then we heard shots fired from a sporting gun nearby, followed by others at intervals; then whistles of steamers in harbour began to give long notes until these long whistlings became a bedlam of sound.[29]

The Treaty of Versailles brought Germany a reality far different from the defeat with honour that Scheer and his admirals had wished. Its peace conditions, "a more dreadful instrument for enslaving the vanquished than the world has ever seen," as former Reichskanzler von Bethmann Hollweg denounced them, harboured seeds of bitterness and shame from which another German empire would spring.[30] The treaty would trigger fresh cries in Germany for naval prestige – Seegeltung – in order to redress perceived wrongs. Indeed, the scuttling of the German fleet in Scapa Flow in 1919 provided Admiral Karl Hollweg the occasion to deliver a frothy political sermon on "the proud German oak which our old fleet represented" and which was already striking new roots in anticipating the resurrection of German naval power.

But naval prestige and naval warfare, contemporary critics like Vice-Admiral Wolfgang Wegener charged, were precisely what his country had failed to understand. Reflecting on the shortcomings of German naval thought, his rather swashbuckling, nationalistic study of 1929 charged: "Today we face the fact alone that the state in its general conduct of the war neither grasped that the whole World War was a naval war, nor that the decision lay at sea; nor did it understand what naval war meant, nor see the path on which our fleet was to be deployed. We really did not understand the sea – none of us."[31] Too rooted in Clausewitz, Germany's historically conditioned "army instincts" had blocked all naval aspirations. And naval supremacy depended on observing a radically different set of strategic principles than those applicable to a continental European army. Later German critics correctly endorsed the view.[32] Nor had German naval thinking been particularly up to date. Germany had been unprepared for even the possibility of a U-boat war; it had opened its major submarine phase in February 1915 with only twenty-one boats, only a few of which were suited to long-range operations. In the event, these innovative strategies became enmeshed in international political considerations that hampered purely military decisions.

New dreams quickly grew from the ruins. Admiral Hollweg's stirring hyperbole called on his country's youth to prepare for a rebirth of "Germanic" valour in a new destiny with sea power: "training the innate leaders (Führernaturen) and schooling those willingly led."[33] German naval literature of the inter-war years would persistently harken back to the supposedly grand old days of glory on the high seas and seek to inspire a new generation of youth with the old ideals of deep-sea chivalry.

Wresting spiritual victory from physical defeat in a retrospective of 1935, Erich Raeder, future grand admiral of the Third Reich, typified these calls. The "heroic battle" of Dogger Bank, when the British destroyed the cruiser *Blücher*, should be "for German youth, on whose achievements the destiny of the German people will one day rest, a model of genuine German military discipline, of the staunchest fulfilment of duty and valiant personal commitment, even unto self-sacrifice in the service of the Fatherland."[34]

Eberhard von Mantey, originator of the old war-plan OP III, former captain of the heavy cruiser *Freya* and the U-boat dock-ship *Vineta*, and finally a vice-admiral and naval historian, realized that new technologies and new world-wide supply routes would outdate the old concepts of naval war.[35] But he recognized that at least one central principle remained inviolable. As U-boat ace Joachim Schepke wrote in 1940, when promoting the national-socialist ideology: "A people that doesn't understand the sea will always remain a second-rate nation; the key to world power is that we Germans must go to sea on the world's oceans."[36]

Allied victory in 1918 not only put paid to one phase of German naval aspirations; it caused the rapid dismantling of Canada's naval forces. There was, it is true, an interregnum in which it appeared that the service might be established on a more solid and substantial basis. The test of war had clarified the issue of national control of armed forces over which Laurier and Borden had, for almost exclusively political reasons, fought so bitterly in 1910–14. Disillusionment at the failings of the British high command, under which the Canadian Corps fought on the Western Front, and at the Admiralty's disregard of Canadian maritime interests gradually sapped Borden's long-declared intention of re-establishing the Canadian navy in closer association with the Royal Navy.

When, at the Imperial Conference of August 1918, the Admiralty proposed more complete integration of the dominions' navies under centralized command in London, Borden joined the other premiers in rejecting the idea in favour of the existing distinctive services. He thus tacitly acknowledged the soundness of Laurier's Naval Service Act, scarcely six months before the Liberal leader died, in February 1919. Borden himself was exhausted and would retire in 1920. Although personally willing to see the fleet rebuilt in a more modern version – including fast anti-submarine vessels – of the force Laurier had proposed in 1909–10, he would not buck the deep, pervasive hostility in post-war Canada to military expenditure in general and the navy in particular.

Unlike Germany, Canada lacked the national will to develop a navy and had no myths of glory and empire with which to nourish the idea. The parliamentary debates on the Naval Service estimates of May 1919 subjected the Canadian navy's performance in the Great War to harsh scrutiny and often unjustified scorn. The object of the manipulative and sometimes parochial ploys of the British, American, and Canadian governments, the Naval Service was charged with inefficiency, blundering, unpreparedness, and financial waste.[37] Liberal opposition members from the Atlantic provinces led the attack. The Commons rang with charges of "culpable negligence" in the sinking of *Luz Blanca*, of unseaworthy vessels, and of "the officers at Halifax ... at pink teas and playing bridge whist" when the submarine attacks occurred. The navy's critics cited apparent abuses of naval discipline and the application of double standards by courts martial in their treatment of officers and men. To be sure, there were "good men in the so-called Canadian navy," as one persistent critic conceded; but they were hampered by an inflexible system in which Canadians were often subservient to the British.

Letters from constituents – some civilians, others naval officers and ratings – were read into the record of debates. They complained that "Mr. Desbarats fiddled while our fishing fleet was being sunk"; they bewailed "the enemy in our own waters, performing deeds of piracy and destruction at his own free will" while Canadian naval forces stood helplessly by. In short, asserted the Liberal member from Cape Breton North (and interim leader of the opposition), the navy minister "cannot put his finger on one single thing that his miserable navy did for the defence of the Atlantic coast that was worth tuppence ha'penny."[38] The Naval Service had been little better than a "Bum Boat Fleet." Offering an unsensational past, the navy seemed to provide no justification whatever for future development. Naval prestige was not a Canadian issue.

Naval Minister Ballantyne put up a weak defence in his often blustering and groping replies to the criticisms of his prepared speech on the new naval estimates. He offered little substantive explanation of past events, except to claim that he had "done the best [he] could with the ships the Canadian navy had."[39] He fended off charges by appealing to critics' respect for veterans who had served under trying circumstances. Ill-equipped and often ill-trained, "these men of our patrol service who have served on small trawlers and drifters in all kinds of weather, performed as good service, and deserve as much commendation for that service, as our gallant soldiers who fought in the trenches in France for all that we hold dear."[40] That was certainly true.

However, his remonstrances did not form a proud conclusion to a crucial chapter of Canada's naval history. Clinging to old myths, critics judged the value of a navy by broadsides fired and battles won. Few of Canada' achievements provided any fearsome whiff of gunpowder or the exhilaration of high-seas combat. Less important in retrospect seemed the speedy improvisation with virtually no human or material resources; less significant, the development of a significant contribution to protection of merchant shipping and coastal defence in the face of over-riding national and imperial priorities in the European theatre.

Canada's naval forces had achieved much against overwhelming odds. Despite severe shortcomings, the early years of the Naval Service laid the basis for a Canadian naval tradition in which Canadians learned the importance of the sea. Although excluded from higher councils – even within Canada – and treated by the British Admiralty with a mixture of benevolent and condescending disdain, the navy had defined and grasped its role and found an identity. But Canada's vast continental geography and limited public revenues worked against it; the political and naval predominance of Britain and the United States thwarted its aims; political squabblings at home crippled its strength. Was it any wonder, then, that the Canadian navy should become a scapegoat for a multitude of sins and be banished into the wilderness years of neglect?

The Naval Service of Canada suffered renewed setbacks in the early 1920s, by which time much of the raging passion of the years before 1914 – and the two long-time dominant players – had disappeared from politics. Politicians' profound indifference crippled the navy. Not until the late 1930s did the menace of a new war on two oceans bring a significant start in carrying out the program that senior officers had urged for twenty years. Without the dispiriting and painful struggle to keep a nucleus of the service alive during the

1920s and 1930s, the navy's achievements of the Second World War would have been far fewer and its shortcomings more marked. The commitment that sustained the service in this second "heart-breaking starvation time" was born of the frustrations of 1918, when shoe-string defences had so nearly resulted in disaster on the east coast. But the officers and men worked virtually alone in applying these lessons during the doldrum years. Unsung, and with little lore to fuel traditions, the "tin-pot navy" disappeared from the national consciousness – until war with Germany once again animated Canada's Naval Service, and the threat from another generation of "pirate" sea raiders breathed new life into old bones.

Notes

ADM   Admiralty (British)

BA-MA   Bundes-und Militärarchiv, Freiburg, iB, Federal Republic of Germany

CAR   *Canadian Annual Review*

DCER   *Documents on Canadian External Relations*

DHIST   Directorate of History, National Defence Headquarters, Ottawa

G   Old Registry files, Naval Service Headquarters

HQC   Militia and Defence Headquarters Confidential files

HQS   Militia and Defence Headquarters Secret files

MG   Manuscript Group (in NAC)

NA&WI   North America and West Indies Station

NAC   National Archives of Canada, Ottawa

NPRC   National Personnel Records Centre, Ottawa

NSC   Naval Service Headquarters Confidential files

NSHQ   Naval Service Headquarters

NSPM   Nova Scotia Provincial Museum, Halifax

NSS   Naval Service Headquarters Secret files

PABC   Provincial Archives of British Columbia, Victoria

PRO   Public Records Office, Kew, London

RG   Record Group (in NAC)

RM   Reichsmarine (Imperial German Navy, in BA-MA)

USNA   United States National Archives, Washington

USNOA   United States Navy Operational Archives, Washington, DC

PREFACE

1 George Stanley's pioneering work, *Canada's Soldiers 1604–1954: The Military History of an Unmilitary People* (1974), first formulated the concept of

Canadians as an unmilitary people. Desmond Morton (*A Military History of Canada*, 1985) correctly insists, however, that military experience is central to Canadian history.

2 Douglas, "Canadian Naval Historiography"; Sarty and Shurman, "An Historical Perspective on Canadian Naval Policy."

3 Bourne, *Britain and the Balance of Power in North America 1815–1908*, chaps. 7–8; Mackinnon, "The Imperial Fortresses in Canada."

4 Kennedy, *The Rise of the Anglo-American Antagonism 1860–1914*.

5 Messimer's popularized narrative *The Merchant U-Boat: Adventures of the 'Deutschland' 1916–1918* appeared in October 1988, after we had completed our research in Canada and abroad. It adds no new material to our perspective.

6 See, however, Sarty, "Hard Luck Flotilla," 103–25.

7 Tucker, *The Naval Service of Canada*; Schull, *The Far Distant Ships*. See, however, recent specialized studies: Boutilier, ed., *The RCN in Retrospect: 1910–1968*; Hadley, *U-Boats against Canada: German Submarines in Canadian Waters*; Milner, *North Atlantic Run: The Royal Canadian Navy and the Battle for the Convoys*; Douglas, ed., *The RCN in Transition: 1910–1985*.

8 21.7 million tons of cargo in 3,600 ships sailed in British convoys from New York and Hampton Roads.

9 Birnbaum, *Peace Moves and U-Boat Warfare*; May, *The World War and American Isolation 1914–1917*; Trask, *Captains and Cabinets: Anglo-American Naval Relations 1917–1918*; Doerries, *Washington-Berlin 1908–1917*; Herwig, *Politics of Frustration: The United States in German Naval Planning*.

10 US Navy Department, *Submarine Activities on the Atlantic Coast of the United States and Canada*; US Congress, Senate, Naval Affairs Committee, *Naval Affairs*, also known as the Sims' hearing. Messimer (*Merchant U-Boat*) focuses aspects of *U-Deutschland*.

11 For instance, Clark, *When the U-Boats Came to America*; James, *German Subs in Yankee Waters*. Even the US Naval Institute *Proceedings* succumbed to the pulp trade in 1985 by publishing W. Watts Biggers, "The Germans Are Coming!"

12 Spindler, *Der Krieg zur See*; Stegemann, *Die deutsche Marinepolitik*; Corbett and Newbolt, *Naval Operations*; Fayle, *History of the Great War: Seaborne Trade*; Hurd, *History of the Great War*. Robert M. Grant's pioneering study, *U-Boat Intelligence 1914–1918*, provides some useful but narrowly conceived coverage of North American operations, an area on which Patrick Beesly's important book (*Room 40: British Naval Intelligence 1914–1918*) sheds little light.

CHAPTER ONE

1 "Grand Torpedo Attack," Halifax *Morning Chronicle*, 7 July 1881, 1.

2 Admiralität, Berlin, to Korvettenkapitän von Wirkede, SMS *Elisabeth*, Panama, Care of German Consulate, January 1878, BA-MA: "Die Entsendung von Kriegsschiffen nach der Ost- und Westküste von Amerika," RM 1/2400, 59–83. Also "Seeminen-Uebungen 1869–1885," RM 1/2129. The initials SMS stand for "Seiner Majestät Schiff," his majesty's ship.

3 Stewart, "Sir John A. Macdonald and the Imperial Defence Commission of 1879," 123.

4 Ibid., 135; see also Stacey, *Canada and the British Army*, 187.

5 For a full account of the impact of the cruiser scares on British policy see Ranft, "Naval Defence," and Shurman, "Imperial Defence."

6 Melville, "Canada and Sea Power," 166–81; Sarty, "Silent Sentry," 48–58.

7 Admiralty to Colonial Office, 10 June 1878, file 04630, NAC, RG 9 IIA1, vol. 611.

8 Stewart, "Macdonald and the Imperial Defence Commission," 134.

9 Melville, "Canada and Sea Power," 187–8.

10 For the following see DHIST: NHS 8000 HMS Charybdis; some material was repeated in L.M., "The Young Dominion's First Warship – Charybdis," *Crowsnest* (Jan. 1955), 24–5, and "Our First Warship," *Canadian Shipping and Marine Engineering News*, March 1960, 122–3.

11 Saint John *Globe*, 26 July 1881, and Halifax *Morning Chronicle*, 2 Aug. 1881.

12 Halifax *Morning Chronicle*, 6 Sept. 1881, editorial.

13 Malcolm Colin Cameron, MP for Huron South, *Debates*, House of Commons, 27 Feb. 1882, vol. 12, 122–4.

14 Tallman, "Warships and Mackerels"; Canada, Department of Marine and Fisheries, *Special Report on the Fisheries Protection Service of Canada, During the Season of 1886* (Ottawa, 1887), iv–xix.

15 Brown, *Canada's National Policy*, 9–41, 54–90; Department of Marine and Fisheries, *Annual Reports of Fisheries Protection Service for 1886–1891*.

16 Melville, "Canada and Sea Power," chap. 8.

17 Schurman, *The Education of a Navy*; Marder, *Anatomy*, chaps. 7–8.

18 Gordon, *The Dominion Partnership*, 80–97; d'Egville, *Imperial Defence and Closer Union*, chaps. 1–3; Preston, *Canada and 'Imperial Defense,'* 96–111.

19 Charles Tupper, "Federating the Empire: A Colonial Plan," *Nineteenth Century*, 30 (Oct. 1891): 516–17; Tupper, "How to Federate the Empire: A Reply to Critics," ibid., 31 (April 1892): 528–30; Denison, *The Struggle for Imperial Unity*, 194–205; Denison, *Soldiering in Canada*.

20 H.J. Wickham, "Canada's Maritime Position and Responsibilities," 41–2; also Wickham, *Naval Defence of Canada*.

21 Wickham, "Canada's Maritime Position," 39–41.

22 *The British Empire League: Deputation to the First Lord of the Admiralty, on*

Wednesday, July 27th, 1898. In reference to Question of the Desirability of Colonial Seamen being Enrolled in the Royal Naval Reserve (London, 1898), copy in PRO, ADM 1/7573.

23 "A Colonial Naval Reserve: To Whom the Credit for the Formulation of the Scheme?" *Navy League Journal*, 3 (Nov. 1898): 169–71; Navy League in Canada (Toronto Branch) to Governor General, 14 Oct. 1889, NAC, MG 26H, reel C-4459, 187,636–8.

24 The literature on the British army, Canadian defence, and the development of the Canadian land militia is extensive. See our bibliography for selected sources: Bourne, Dennison, Gooch, Gordon, Harris, Hitsman, Mackinnon, Morton, Penlington, Preston, Stacey, and Stanley.

25 See PRO, WO 106/40/B1/5 for the army's proposals for lakes naval defence; the Leach committee's naval recommendations are summarized in Captain W.G. White, RN, "Naval Defence of the Canadian Frontier ... ," March 1899, PRO, ADM 1/7413A. Major-General E.T.H. Hutton, general officer commanding the militia, publicly commended the scheme for a lakes naval militia: Canada, Department of Militia and Defence, *Report*, year ending 31 Dec. 1898, p. 40. See also the excellent accounts in Bourne, *Britain and the Balance of Power*, 323–36, and Alvin C. Gluek, "The Invisible Revision of the Rush-Bagot Agreement," 466–84.

26 "A Colonial Naval Reserve," 169–71.

27 Committee of Imperial Defence, "Public Statement by the Chairman of the Defence Committee of the Cabinet on the 3rd December, 1896," Jan. 1905, PRO, CAB 5–1.

28 Colonial Office, Misc. No. 111, Proceedings 1897 Colonial Conference, PRO, CO 885/6, 62.

29 Gimblett, " 'Tin-Pots' or Dreadnoughts?" 45–6.

30 See, for example, Canada, House of Commons, *Debates*, 1 March 1900, 1,473; Henri Bourassa, *Grande-Bretagne et Canada: Questions actuelles* (Montreal 1902), lxxxiv–lxxxvi.

31 See papers on the Russian cruiser scare, 4 May to 8 July 1878, NAC, MG 26G, vol. 772, 219,313–8; also memorandum on the Leach Committee, ibid., vol. 773, 219,366–8.

32 "Memorandum by the Canadian Ministers concerning Defence," 11 Aug. 1902, CO Misc. 144; "Conference between the Sec of State for the Colonies and the Premiers of the Self-governing Colonies," NAC, RG 7 G 21, file 168, reel C-1366. Also the draft "Memorandum concerning Defence," London, Aug. 1902, NAC, MG 26G, reel C-1174, 219,266–8.

33 Gimblett, "Tin-Pots," chap. 3; see, especially, Préfontaine to Goudreau, 20 Dec. 1905, Laurier to Préfontaine, n.d., NAC, MG 26G, reel C-829, 104,518–21, 104,543.

34 Neatby, *Laurier*, 183–4; Gimblett, "Tin-Pots," 53–4.

35 *Morangs 1901*, 447–8.

36 Cited from *An Address Delivered by Clive Philipps-Wolley on Behalf of the Victoria-Esquimalt Branch of the Navy League ... May 14th, 1907* (Victoria, 1907), 7. See also the same comment by Macdonald's first biographer, Sir George Robert Parkin, in Parkin to Hutton, 1 May 1902, Hutton papers, NAC, reel A-480.

37 *Globe*, 25 Nov. 1902, 8.

38 *Halifax Herald*, 6 Dec. 1902, 1. For a view of a Quebec audience see Montreal *Daily Star*, 30 Oct. 1902, 5.

39 *CAR, 1903*, 267.

40 See, for example, *Montreal Gazette*, 8 Dec. 1904, 9.

41 Halifax *Morning Chronicle*, 2 Dec. 1902, 3.

42 Ibid., 28 Dec. 1904, 4.

43 Montreal *Daily Star*, 7 Dec. 1904, 4.

44 *Canadian Military Gazette*, 6 June 1905, 4–5.

45 Lyttleton to Minto, 24 Nov. 1904 (telephone); Administrator of Cda (Canada) to Lyttleton, received 2 Dec. 1904; newspaper clipping, "Ottawa 22 Dec. 1904," PRO ADM 1/7744, Grey to Seymour, 11 Feb. 1905, Grey to Lyttleton, 16 Feb. 1905, NAC, MG 271IB2, vol. 12.

46 *CAR, 1905*, 503.

47 Olivar Asselin, in *La Nationaliste*, 12 Jan. 1905, 1.

48 Great Britain, Parliament, Cd 3523, "Minutes of Proceedings of the Colonial Conference, 1907," 139–40.

49 Admiralty to C-in-C, NA&WI, 21 Feb. 1905, PRO, ADM 1/7474.

50 Spain to DM, 25 Feb. 1904, file 2914, NAC, RG 23, reel T-4020.

51 Grey to Laurier, 11 Nov. 1907, NAC, MG 11B2, vol. 2; also see Dundonald, 28 Feb. 1903, "Remarks on the Inland Waters Naval Defence of Canada," PRO, ADM 1/7576.

52 Canada, Parliament, *Royal Commission on the Civil Service*, Ottawa: King's Printer, 1909, 34.

53 Canada, Parliament, *Investigation re Department of Marine and Fisheries*, Ottawa: King's Printer, 1909, 70–3. The investigation, by Judge Walter G.P. Cassels, showed, among other things, that Spain had forged travel claims; it also suggested that he absconded with a government contractor's funds to invest in BC real estate.

54 As reported by Lord Grey to Laurier, 11 Nov. 1907; NAC, MG 27 IIB2, vol. 2.

55 Schurmann, *Corbett*, 109–10.

56 Hamilton to Willison, 16 Aug. 1908, NAC, MG 30 D 29, vol. 140.

57 Meaney, *Australian Defence*, 1.

58 Ollivier (ed.), *Colonial and Imperial Conferences*, I, 249.

59 Alan Cowpe, "The Royal Navy and the Whitehead Torpedo," in Ranft, *Technical Change*, 23–36.

60 *Spectator*, no. 3846, 15 March 1902, BA-MA: RM 3/9686.

61 Mackay, *Fisher*, 377, 444–52; Marder, *From the Dreadnought to Scapa Flow*, 1, 328–34.

62 Admiralty to Colonial Office, 20 Aug. 1908, printed in Great Britain, Parliament, "Correspondence Relating to the Naval Defence of Australia and New Zealand," Oct. 1908 (Command paper 4325).

63 Hattendorf and Hattendorf, *Bibliography*.

64 Palmer, *The Kaiser*, 69.

65 Herwig, *'Luxury' Fleet*, 40.

66 Mahan, *The Influence of Sea Power*. See Herwig, *'Luxury' Fleet*, 15–17.

67 *The Times*, 28 Oct. 1899, with the Kaiser's marginalia, BA-MA: RM 3/9686.

68 Herwig, *'Luxury' Fleet*, 38.

69 *The Times*, no. 38001, 23 April 1906, BA-MA: RM 3/9692.

70 *Spectator*, no. 4177, 18 July 1908, BA-MA: RM 3/9694.

71 Buitenhuis, *The Great War of Words*.

72 Clarke, *Voices Prophesying War*; Morris, *The Scaremongers*; Moon, "The Invasion of the United Kingdom."

73 Von Bethmann Hollweg, *Betrachtungen*, 1, 189.

74 [Hamilton], "A Navy for Canada," *Orillia Packet*, 19 Jan. 1908; see also C. Frederick Hamilton, "The Canadian Navy," *University Magazine* 8 (Oct. 1909), 375–97, and "Canadian Coast Defence," ibid., 8 (Dec. 1909), 587–602.

75 Hamilton to Willison, 31 Aug. 1907; NAC, MG D 29, vol. 18, 13,826–7.

76 Resolution of George Foster, MP for North Toronto, House of Commons, *Debates*, 29 March 1909, 3,484.

77 House of Commons, *Debates*, 29 March 1909, 3,522.

78 *Debates*, 29 March 1909, 3,489–90.

79 "Memo to Rt. Hon. Sir Wilfrid Laurier" (late 1908 or early 1909), NAC, MG 26G, vol. 772, pp 219, 359–62. For a discussion of the race see Herwig, *Luxury' Fleet*, 69–92, and Marder, *Dreadnought to Scapa Flow*, 1, 135–70. Also *CAR, 1909*, 46.

80 *CAR, 1909*, 51–5; Hamilton to Willison, 23 March 1909, NAC, MG 30D29, vol. 19, file 140.

81 Brown, *Borden*, 1, 150–5; Tucker, *Naval Service*, 1, 122–8.

82 House of Commons, *Debates*, 29 March 1909, 3,504–13.

83 Morris, *Scaremongers*, chap. 13.

84 Chancellor, "Notes ... " 20 May 1909, PRO, CO 537/571/17938.

85 See especially Robinson, minute, 4 June 1909, PRO, CO 531/571/17938; Gordon, *Dominion Partnership*, 236–7.

86 Governor General of Australia to Secretary of State for the Colonies, telegram received 4 June 1909, printed in Great Britain, Parliament, "Correspondence and Papers relating to a Conference ... on the Naval and Military Defence of the Empire, 1909," Nov. 1909 (Command paper 4948).

87 PRO, CO 532/12/16464, especially Grey to Crewe, 6 May 1909.

88 A copy of the confidential proceedings of the 1909 imperial defence conference is in NAC, MG 26G, vol. 773; see 219,706–43 and 219,761–2 on Canadian participation. Useful extracts of the proceedings have been printed in DCER, I: *1909–1918* (Ottawa, 1967), 226–45. See also Gimblett, "Tin-Pots," chap. 5.

89 Minutes, 102nd meeting of the Committee of Imperial Defence, 29 June 1909, PRO, CAB 2/27.

90 Sarty, "Trouble," 10.

91 House of Commons, *Debates*, 29 March 1909, 3,516.

92 Tucker, *Naval Service*, I, 140–1.

93 Canada, Department of the Naval Service, *Report on Naval Defence* (Ottawa, 1909).

94 For full accounts see DHIST: NHS, 26 Oct. 1961, "Brief History of HMCS Niobe," and 24 March 1961, "Brief History of HMCS Rainbow." Despite the misleading titles, these synopses are extremely detailed.

CHAPTER TWO

1 Wislicenus, *Deutschlands Seemacht sonst und jetzt*, Geleitwort.

2 For details, see Steinberg, *Yesterday's Deterrent*, and Herwig, *'Luxury' Fleet*.

3 See "Entsendung von Kriegsschiffen nach der Ost- und Westküste von Amerika," Bd. I, Feb. 1872–June 1880, BA-MA: RM 1/2398; Bd. II, July 1880–April 1888, BA-MA: RM 1/2399. "Entsendung von Kriegsschiffen ... Streitfall mit Nikaragua 26 September 1877–16 Februar 1879," BA-MA: RM 1/2890. Also "Krieg zwischen Peru, Bolivia und Chile," RM 1/2891; RM 3/11608, RM 1/2401. Also Assmann, *Die Kämpfe der kaiserlichen Marine*, and Messimer, "German Gunboats on the Yangtse."

4 For example, "Die britischen Kolonien und die deutsche Gefahr," *Berliner Tageblatt*, 10 June 1909 (from the London correspondent on 7 June 1909), BA-MA: RM 3/9694.

5 These are the so-called 'Herbstmanöver' (fall exercises) that generally took place in late summer or early fall. See BA-MA, RM 1/335–40 for the years 1882–9. Also "Herbstübungen der Manöverflotte" (1898–1912), BA-MA: RM 3/10,236–8.

6 See Weir, "Tirpitz, Technology, and Building U-Boats," 174–90.

7 "Das Angriffsmanöver auf Kiel am 11. und 12. Oktober 1903," BA-MA: RM 3/10237, p. 108.

8 "Herbstübungen der Manöverflotte," Bd. 2 (5 Sept. 1911), BA-MA: RM 3/10237.

9 This is specially true of writers of memoirs and histories in the 1930s. See, for example, Gebeschus, *Doggerbank*, 62, and von Kühlwetter, *Skagerrak*.

10 "Acta betr. Vorbereitung der Operationspläne gegen Nord-Amerika,"

BA-MA: RM 5/5960. See the pioneering study by Herwig and Trask, "Naval Operations Plans," 39–74. This article, a reworking of material in Herwig's *Politics of Frustration* (1976), continues to serve as the basis for all subsequent work on German operational plans against North America; see, for example, Lambi, *The [German] Navy*. We have re-examined all the original documents, which, however, are no longer readily accessible under the files provided by Herwig and Trask and by Lambi. We therefore indicate the new catalogue numbers used by the BA-MA.

11 Raeder, *Der Kreuzerkrieg*, I, 1–10. Also von Mantey, *Die deutschen Hilfskreuzer* (Bd. III of *Der Kreuzerkrieg*).

12 *The Influence of Seapower*, 539, cited in Raeder, *Der Kreuzerkrieg*, 3. Mahan was commenting on an assertion made by French officer Lamotte-Picquet in 1778 that "the surest means ... to conquer the English is to attack them in their commerce."

13 Raeder, *Kreuzerkrieg*, 5.

14 Weir, "Tirpitz," 178.

15 Cited in Herwig and Trask, "Naval Operations Plans," 40 and 65n2. The Kaiser's note read: "Was ich seit zehn Jahren den Ochsen von Reichsabgeordneten alle Tage gepredigt habe." Trans. M.L.H.

16 For a detailed account of legislation on the naval bills of 10 April 1898 and 14 June 1900 and the Flottennovellen of 1906, 1908, and 1912, see Militärgsschichtliches Forschungsamt, Hrsg., *Deutsche Militärgeschichte 1648–1939*, Herrsching: Manfred Pawlak, 1983, Bd. 5, Abschnitt VIII. Also Herwig, *'Luxury' Fleet*, 48.

17 Verhandlungen des Reichstags, 9. Legislaturperiode, 5. Session 1897/98, 4. Sitzung, 6. Dezember 1897, 46 A, 60 B, 60 D; Microcard edition, vol. 1, card 2. Cited also in Herwig and Trask, "Naval Operations Plans," 41. Trans. M.L.H.

18 For the provision of regular force officers to prepare copy for the press see, for example, Admiral Büchsel, Staatssekretär des Reichs-Marine-Amts, to Chef der Herbstübungsflotte, 22 Juli 1899, RM 3/10236, 19. Also "Denkschrift zum Immediatvortrag, betreffend Berichterstattung für die Presse über die Herbstmanöver," 35.

19 Marder, *Anatomy*, 55.

20 J. Meyer, "Die Propaganda des deutschen Flottenbewegung 1897–1900," Inauguraldiss., Berne 1967, 26. Cited also in Herwig and Trask, "Naval Operations Plans," 64n13. See also Paul Kennedy, "The Press, Pressure Groups and Public Opinion," in Kennedy, *The Rise of the Anglo-German Antagonism*, 87–102, and "Material für Zeitungen und Zeitschriften," 1900–14, BA-MA: RM 3/9707–9.

21 Herwig and Trask, "Naval Operations Plans," 40.

22 Scheer, *Vom Segelschiff zum U-Boot*, Vorwort.

23 R.P. Hobson, Captain, US Navy, "America Mistress of the Seas," *North*

American Review, Oct. 1902, 544–57, in "Deutschfeindliche Presseäußer-
ungen," BA-MA: RM 3/9703. See also A.G. Hales, "The Hand of the Kaiser –
Why the British sailor Is Better than the German," *Daily Express*, 9 Oct.
1901, RM 3/9703.

24 Militärgeschichtliches Forschungsamt, *Deutsche Militärgeschichte*, 6, Abschnitt VIII, 189–93.

25 "Abonnements auf Flotten-Manöverberichte," RM 3/10236, 93.

26 Draft preface to *Die Flotten-Manöver 1901*, Berlin: E.S. Mittler Verlag,
1901, BA-MA: RM 3/10236, 129.

27 Wislicenus, *Deutschlands Seemacht*.

28 B.-E., Nachrichten-Bureau, RMA, to Kapitänleutnant Brehmer, Kommandant, SM Flußkanonenboot *Tsingtau*, Tsingtau, 18 Sep. 1906, BA-MA:
RM 3/9709.

29 Boy-Ed, Nachrichten-Bureau, Reichs-Marine-Amt, to Kapitänleutnant von Rheinhaben, SMS *von der Tann*, 15 Aug. 1911, RM 3/10237,
271–2.

30 "Denkschrift: Seerüstungen der Großmächte – Stellungnahme zu dem
englischen Vorwurf, Deutschland sei der Schrittmacher im Wettrüsten
zur See gewesen," and "Denkschrift über Weiterentwicklung der Marine
nach dem Krieg," Nachlaß Vizeadmiral Hollweg (Hollweg papers), BA-MA:
RM 3/11703, 6.

31 See, for example, Paul Kennedy, "Colonies, Navies and the Balance of
Power," in *Antagonism*, 410–31.

32 Herwig, *'Luxury' Fleet*, 100.

33 Herwig and Trask, "Naval Operations Plans," 42.

34 "Themata für Winterarbeiten," in "Inspektion des Bildungswesens: Winterarbeiten der Offiziere ausschl. Akademiker 1 April 1893 – 31 Dez
1904," BA-MA: RM 27 I/9, 75–7.

35 See Lieutenant z.S.E. von Mantey, 15 June 1898, in "Acta betreffend
Vorarbeiten zu den Operationsplänen gegen Nord-Amerika Juni
1898–Juni 1911," BA-MA: RM 5/5964, 1–55.

36 Herwig and Trask observed this latter point in "Naval Operations Plans,"
68n33.

37 For example, "Besprechung der Streitkräfte der Vereinigten Staaten von
Amerika, Sommer 1906," BA-MA: RM 5/5963, 3–27. One report in this
file (p. 48) cites the case of the Pacific Fleet's USS *Marblehead*, whose crew
demonstrated in complaining of "too little vacation and poor food."

38 "Begutachtung der Winterarbeit des Leutnant von Mantey," 9 March
1898, BA-MA: RM 5/5964, 65–7. The signature and office of this handwritten manuscript are unclear.

39 "Winterarbeiten November 1895–August 1900," in "Kommando der
Marine-Station der Ostsee," BA-MA: RM 31/1853, 143.

40 Herwig and Trask, "Naval Operations Plans," 43.

41 For example, "Der Krieg," *Salzburger Chronik*, 2 May 1898, no. 98, Jg. 34.

42 "Der Krieg," *Salzburger Chronik*, 16 May 1898, no. 110, Jg. 34.

43 "Germany's Naval Programme – A Lesson for the United States," *Scientific American*, no. 13, 31 March 1900, in BA-MA: RM 3/9686.

44 "Is All Well with the Fleet? – Mr. [H.O.] Arnold-Forster's Reply," *Naval and Military Record*, no. 11, 10 Oct. 1901, BA-MA: RM 3/9687.

45 "Vorarbeiten zu den Operationsplänen gegen Nordamerika," BA-MA: RM 5/5964, 75.

46 "Vorarbeiten zu den Operationsplänen gegen Nord-Amerika," BA-MA: RM 5/5964, 100–5.

47 Herwig and Trask, "Naval Operations Plans," 45.

48 Mantey to Admiral Hollweg, 16 April 1929, in Hollweg Nachlaß, BA-MA: RM 3/11675. The eighteen-page letter harshly criticizes the German navy as inadequate and inept in preparing for war. Herwig and Trask transcribed the German in error as "planted in iron barracks" ("Kasernen" instead of "Kasten.")

49 Ruge, *In Vier Marinen*, 35. See also Theodor Plievier's novel *Des Kaisers Kulis* which created a sensation in the 1930s with its harsh criticism of conditions in the Kaiserliche Marine.

50 Kennedy, *Antagonism*, 223.

51 Tirpitz to Diederichs, 3 Dec. 1899, in "Acta betreffend Flottenerweiterungsprogramm Dezember 1899–November 1907," BA-MA: RM 5/1945.

52 "Denkschrift zum Immediatvortrag betreffend Ausarbeitungen zur Flottenvorlage über Operationen gegen England and Amerika," 20 Jan. 1900, in ibid.

53 Kptlt. von Rebeur-Paschwitz, Washington, to Staatssekretär des Reichsmarineamts, Herrn Tirpitz, Berlin, 26 Jan. 1900, "Reknogoscierung [sic] von Cape Cod und Provincetown als Stützpunkt für ein Vorgehen gegen Boston," no. 16, BA-MA: RM 5/5960, 77–83.

54 "Denkschrift zum Immediatvortrag," 26 Feb. 1900, BA-MA: RM 5/879.

55 For this and the following see documents in BA-MA: RM 5/5960, 98 ff; also Herwig and Trask, "Naval Operations Plans," 51.

56 Herwig and Trask, "Naval Operations Plans," 52.

57 Ibid., 55 and 70n63. For a critical discussion of this Stützenpunktpolitik see Hubatsch, *Die Ära Tirpitz*, 88ff.

58 Herwig, *Empire in Venezuela*, 80–109.

59 "Immediatvortrag," 14 Feb. 1903, "Stand der Operationsarbeiten der Auslands-Schiffe," BA-MA: RM 5/885, 70–4.

60 Immediatvortrag, "Krieg gegen die Vereinigten Staaten von Amerika," 21 March 1903, BA-MA: RM 5/885, 95–8.

61 Herwig and Trask, "Naval Operations Plans," 57.

62 Immediatvortrag, 4 May 1903, BA-MA: RM 5/885.

63 Immediatvortrag, 14 May 1903, BA-MA: RM 5/885.

64 Immediatvortrag, 4 April 1904, BA-MA: RM 5/886.

65 For example, "Gegenüberstellung der Seestreitkräften Deutschlands und der Vereinigten Staaten von Amerika für den Sommer 1904," BA-MA: RM 5/5961; and "Besprechung der Streitkräfte der Vereinigten Staaten von Amerika, Sommer 1906," BA-MA: RM 5/5963.

66 See the clearest copy, "O.P. III, Sommer 1906, Allgemeine Erwägungen über die Durchführung eines Seekrieges gegen die Vereinigten Staaten," in "Acta betreffend Vorbereitung der Operationspläne gegen Nordamerika," BA-MA: RM 5/5962, 7–12.

67 SMS *Panther*, 16 Sept. 1905, BA-MA: RM 5/5343, vol. 1, "U-Plätze Amerika, Okt 05–Nov. 06." Also vol. II, BA-MA: RM 5/5344, "U-Plätze Amerika, Jan 07–Juli 13."

68 Immediatvortrag, 24 March 1908, BA-MA: RM 5/893.

69 Admiral der Marine to Kommandant, SMS *Bremen*, 13 June 1907, in "England. Kolonien in Nordamerika," BA-MA: RM 5/5715.

70 "Allerhöchste Belobigung" (Allerhöchste Kabinettsordre), 15 Oct. 1907.

71 Kommandant an Chef des Admiralstabs der Marine, "Bericht über die Befestigungen in canadischen Häfen," 10 Oct. 1907, in "England. Kolonien in Nordamerika," BA-MA: RM 5/5715, 3–12.

72 Kommandant, SMS *Freya*, an Chef des Admiralstabes der Marine, 18 Feb. 1909, "Admiralstabsaufgabe über Halifax und Pensacola (Florida)," BA-MA: RM 5/5715, 14–16. Also Oberleutnant zur See von Richthofen, "Feststellung der Möglichkeit einer Passage der östlichen Einfahrt von Halifax durch kleine Kreuzer," 18 Aug. 1980 (addendum to above), BA-MA: RM 5/5715.

73 "Nine Brave Men Meet Watery Grave," *Halifax Herald*, 10 Aug. 1908, 1; also 11 Aug. 1908, 2.

74 "Men from German Warship Freya Attend Divine Service," *Halifax Herald*, 18 Aug. 1908, 5.

75 Kennedy, *Antagonism*, 262.

76 Gwatkin, Director of Operations and Staff Duties, to Chief of the General Staff, 20 March 1909; NAC, RG 24, box 2016, HQC 965, vol. 1.

77 Gwatkin to Assistant Director of Intelligence, 24 March 1909; NAC, RG 24, box 2016, HQC 965, vol. 1.

78 Ajax, *The German Pirate*.

79 District Intelligence Officer, Military District 9, Halifax, to Director of Intelligence, Ottawa, 22 March 1909; Gwatkin, for Chief of the General Staff, to General Officer Commanding, Maritime Provinces, 25 March 1909; B. General Drury, GOC, MP, to Chief of the General Staff, 29 April 1909; NAC, RG 24, box 2016, HQC, 965, vol. 1.

80 Lt. O'Hara, Corps of Guides, Quebec, to Assistant Director of Intelligence, 27 March 1909; NAC, RG 24, box 2016, HQC, 965, vol. 1.

81 Gwatkin to Captain B. White, Military Operations Branch, War Office,

London, 29 March 1909; NAC, RG 24, box 2016, HQC 965, vol. 1. The file contains notes and correspondence on the Nettlebladt case.

82 Hamilton to Willison, 9 May 1909; NAC, MG 30D29, vol. 19, file 140, 14110.

83 Gwatkin to Sir John, 29 March 1909; NAC, RG 24, box 2016, HQC 965, vol. 1.

CHAPTER THREE

1 "Rear Admiral Kingsmill Hoists His Flag on Niobe," *Halifax Herald*, 22 Oct. 1910, 1 and 2. See also advance notices in *Halifax Herald*, 21 Oct. 1910 ("The Niobe Will Arrive at ONE"), 1. for the following see also DHIST: NHS, 26 Oct. 1961, "Brief History of HMCS Niobe," and 24 March 1961, "Brief History of HMCS Rainbow." Despite the misleading titles, these synopses are extremely detailed. Also Tucker, *Naval Service*, I, 142–5.

2 *Daily Colonist*, 8 Nov. 1910.

3 *The Times*, 7 Nov. 1910.

4 Sir Graham Greene (secretary of the Admiralty), to Sir Robert Borden, 8 Aug. 1915; NAC, RG 24, vol. 4022, file NS 1062-13-14.

5 NAC, RG 24, box 5585, 1-1-20.

6 *CAR, 1909*, 88–9. On the revised Dry Dock Subsidies Act see House of Commons, *Debates*, 5 April 1910, 6279–9; 27 April 1910, 8113–5; 2 May 1910, 8687–97; 3 May 1910, 8763–70. On negotiations for the warship contracts see NAC, RG 24, vol. 5604, file NS 29-6-2 and Desbarats Papers, Folder A, DHIST.

7 Immediatvortrag, 23 October 1911, in "Die englischen Kolonialmarinen," BA-MA: RM 5/897, 228–37. A very rough draft of this Immediatvortrag is in RM 5/1160. The German consul in Montreal had been reporting the Canadian naval scene to the Reichskanzler since early 1909.

8 *CAR, 1909*, 98.

9 House of Commons, *Debates*, 3 Feb. 1910, 3012–15.

10 *Ottawa Citizen*, 9 Nov 1909; see also Mason Wade, *The French Canadians 1760–1967*, vol. 1; *1760–1911*, rev. ed. (Toronto, 1968), 565–6.

11 Lang, Kaiserlich Deutsches Konsulat, Montreal, an Reichskanzler v. Bethmann Hollweg, 27 Dezember 1909, in "Acta betreffend England. Kolonialflotten und Armeen Januar 1910–April 1919," BA-MA: RM 5/1160.

12 Lang, Kaiserlich Deutsches Konsulat, Montreal, an Reichskanzler Dr. v. Bethmann Hollweg, 7 Jan. 1910, BA-MA: RM 5/1160.

13 For this and the following see House of Commons, *Debates*, 3 Feb. 1910, 2991; 12 Jan. 1910, 1749.

14 *Debates*, 3 Feb. 1910, 2991; 19 April 1910, 7463–4.

15 P. Metternich, Kaiserlick Deutsche Botschaft, London, an Reichskanzler v. Bethmann Hollweg, 13 Jan. 1910, BA-MA: RM 5/1160.

16 Borden to McBride, 19 Nov. 1909, PABC, Add. MSS 347 (McBride Papers), vol. 1, file 1/5.

17 *Debates*, 12 Jan. 1910, 1749.

18 Willison to Borden, 22 Nov. 1909, NAC, MG 30D29, vol. 4, 2298–300; see also McBride to Borden, 8 Jan. 1910, file 1/5, PABC, Add. MSS 347, vol. 1.

19 House of Commons, *Debates*, 12 Jan. 1910, 1770–5; 3 Feb. 1910, 2955–6, 2997, 3006–10.

20 P. Metternich, Kaiserlich Deutsche Botschaft, London, to Reichskanzler, Dr. v. Bethmann Hollweg, Berlin, 5 Nov. 1910; BA-MA: RM 5/1160.

21 Roper to Kingsmill, 20 Sept. 1911; DHIST: Desbarats Papers, file B.

22 This was government's experience with the Militia Department wherein the military head was usually a British officer on loan. Desbarats to Laurier, 8 April 1910, NAC, MG 26 G, reel 1174, 219550–1; Desbarats Diary, 31 May, 1 June, 11 June 1910, NAC, MG 30E89 (G.J. Desbarats Papers), vol. 5. Thor Thorgrimsson, 22 Aug. 1966, "The Office of the Deputy Minister in the Departments Responsible for Canadian Defence," CFHQ Report No. 11, DHIST.

23 *Halifax Herald*, 31 July 1911, 1–2. Also "Preparations Have Been Fully Made at Clark's Harbor to Beach Cruiser Niobe," 2 Aug. 1911, 1–2. Subsequent issues: "Confident of Keeping Niobe Afloat" and "The Niobe to Be Towed to Halifax." For the official record see DHIST: 8000 Niobe.

24 Cited in "Preparations," *Halifax Herald*, 2 Aug. 1911, 1–2.

25 English, *The Decline of Politics*, 55–6.

26 *Debates*, 20 Nov. 1911, 63–4 (unrevised); 18 March 1912, 5463 (unrevised).

27 Marder, *Dreadnought to Scapa Flow*, I, 239–51, 272–98. See also Hough, *Former Naval Person*.

28 Churchill, *Winston S. Churchill*, II, Companion to Part 3: *1911–1914*, 1507, 1759, 1789.

29 Brown, *Borden*, I, 237–43.

30 Prime Minister to Governor General, 24 March 1913, extracts printed in DCER I, 279–81.

31 Admiralty, Oct. 1912, "The Best Method of Harbour and Coast Defence," Borden Papers, NAC, MG 26H, vol. 124, 66918.

32 Admiralty, Oct. 1912, "Supplementary Note to Memorandum on Best Method of Harbour and Coast Defence," DHIST: 81/744.

33 Admiralty, Oct. 1912, "Protection of Trade Routes in Atlantic and Pacific," Borden Papers, vol. 124, 66917; see also Churchill to Borden, 19 March 1913, and R.S. Churchill, *Churchill*, II, Companion to Part 3, 1805.

34 Immediatvortrag, 24 April 1913, BA-MA: RM 5/899.

35 Borden to Connaught, 24 March 1913; DCER, I, 280. Also Borden to Churchill, 23 March 1913, Churchill, *Churchill*, II, Companion to Part 3, 1806.

36 Borden Diary, 27 Nov. 1913, NAC, MG 26H, reel C-1864.

37 Borden Diary, 8, 15, 20 Nov. 1912.

38 *CAR, 1912*, 33–42, 44–5; "White Navy Memo" (T.W. White, June or July
    1912) NAC, MG 26H, reel C-4460, 187945–50; Sifton to White, 11 July
    1912, ibid., reel C-4348, 67191–4; Cook, *John W. Dafoe*, 58–60; Kendle,
    The Round Table Movement, 122–4.

39 Borden Diary, NAC, MG 26H, 25, 28 March, 3, 5, 6, 10, 26, 27 April, 30
    May 1913; Ross to Charles Magee, 9 April 1913, 67677; Ross, to
    Lougheed, 29 April 1913, 67678–80; Borden Papers, reel C-4349; latter
    letter printed in Borden, *Memoirs*, I, 418–9.

40 Borden to Churchill, 25 June 1913, Borden Papers, reel C-4349, 67772–5.

41 House of Commons, *Debates*, 15 March 1913, 10036–8, 10040; see also
    7 April 1913, 7238–9, and Borden's notes for his speech of 15 May:
    Memoir notes entry for 31 May 1913, 511, 514–17, 527–8, Borden Papers,
    reel C-4465.

42 Laurier to [W.S.] Fielding, 3 Feb. 1913, Laurier Papers, reel C-908,
    190437.

43 C.P. Stacey, *The Victory Campaign: The Operations in North-West Europe
    1944–1945.* (Ottawa: Queen's Printer, 1966), 94, 334, 417.

44 Lang, Kaiserlich Deutsches Konsulat für Kanada, an Reichskanzler, Dr.
    v. Bethmann Hollweg, Berlin, 22 March 1912, 5 April, 23 April, and
    22 Nov. 1912; BA-MA: RM 5/5714.

45 Loewenberg, Kaiserlich Deutsches Konsulat, an Reichskanzler, Berlin,
    9 Feb. 1912, BA-MA: RM 5/5714.

46 Immediatvortrag, 29 May 1911, BA-MA: RM 5/897. SMS *Bremen* hurriedly
    departed Montreal in late July to assist German citizens threatened by
    revolution in Haiti.

47 General Officer Commanding, MP, to Imperial German Consul, Halifax,
    15 June 1911; NAC, RG 24, box 2016, HQC 965, vol. 1.

48 Major W.A. Weeks, Corps of Guides, Charlottetown, to Assistant Director
    of Intelligence, 25 July 1911; written in response to Deputy Minister,
    Naval Service, to Deputy Minister, Militia and Defence, 18 July 1910; NAC,
    RG, box 2016, HQC 965, vol. 1.

49 "Erwiderung des Besuches der amerikanischen Schiffe (1911) in den
    Vereinigten Staaten von Amerika durch SMSS *Moltke, Stettin* und *Bremen*
    im Jahre 1912," BA-MA: RM 5/5502.

50 Bernstorff to von Bethmann Hollweg, 13 May 1912, BA-MA: RM 5/5502.

51 von Rebeur-Paschwitz to Seine Majestät den Kaiser und König, 20 June
    1912, "Militärpolitischer Bericht über den Aufenthalt Eurer Majestät
    Schiffe Moltke, Stettin und Bremen in den amerikanischen Gewässern
    vom 30. Mai bis 13. Juni," BA-MA: RM 5/5502.

52 Kommandant [Seebohm] an Seine Majestät den Kaiser, "Militärpolitischer
    Bericht über den Aufenthalt Euerer Majestät Schiff *Bremen* in Newport, R.I.
    und St. John N.B. vom 9. bis 28. Mai 1912," BA-MA: RM 5/5714. The file
    contains reports, letters, and clippings pertaining to the Saint John visit.

53 *Daily Telegraph*, 21 May 1912, in BA-MA: RM 5/5714.

54 *Standard*, 22 May 1912, BA-MA: RM 5/5714.

55 Mayor, Saint John, to Captain Seebohm, SMS Bremen, 22 May 1912, BA-MA: RM 5/5714. The honorary consul, Robert Thomson, apologized in the same vein. Seebohm replied from Newport.

56 For the following see Kommandant an Seine Majestät den Kaiser, "Militär-politischer Bericht Euerer Majestät Schiff *Viktoria Louise* über den Aufenthalt in Ponta Delgada (Azoren) von 27. August bis 8. September und in Halifax vom 17. bis 30. September 1912," Newport, RI, 9 Oct. 1912, BA-MA: RM 5/5714.

57 "The Welcome Visit ... of German Training Cruiser," *Halifax Herald*, 18 Sept. 1912, 6.

58 Boy-Ed to Staatssekretär Reichs-Marine-Amt, 8 Dec. 1912, "Canadas Beitrag für die englische Marine und die Vereinigten Staaten," BA-MA: RM 5/5714.

59 The treaty, negotiated in 1901 between the United States and Britain, and amended by the US Senate, permitted the United States to construct the canal and manage, defend, and assure the neutrality of the zone. In 1911 Britain charged that the Panama Canal Act allowed American coastal shipping toll-free use of the canal and that in passing the law the United States had contravened the previous treaty. President Taft agreed with the British view, and Congress repealed the act in 1914.

60 Lang, Kaiserlich Deutsches Konsulat, Montreal, an Reichskanzler v. Bethmann Hollweg, 9 Dec. 1912, RM 5/5714.

61 Kaiserlich Deutsches Generalkonsulat für Australia [sic], an Reichskanzler Dr. v. Bethmann Hollweg, 2 April 1913, BA-MA: RM 5/5714.

62 "Sir W. Laurier on Naval Policy – German Peril Denied," *The Times*, 30 Oct. 1913, in BA-MA: RM 3/9698. Contested was the South Bruce constituency.

63 For example, "Die kanadischen Dreadnoughts," *Deutsche Tageszeitung*, 5 June 1913, no. 278; "Die Ablehnung der kanadischen Flottenvorlage im englischen Unterhaus," *Tägliche Rundschau*, 6 June 1913, no. 259; "Churchill und die kanadischen Ueberdreadnoughts," *Neue Preußische Kreuz-Zeitung*, 25 June 1913, no. 292; "Kanadas Flotte," *Berliner Tageblatt*, 30 June 1913, no. 381; BA-MA: RM 3/9698.

64 Kommandant an Seine Majestät den Kaiser, "Militärpolitischer Bericht über den Aufenthalt EMS *Hertha* in Halifax (26. 9. bis 13.10. 1913)," 14 Oct. 1913, BA-MA: RM 5/5714.

65 Hose, "The Early Years of the Royal Canadian Navy," 19 Feb. 1960, DHIST: Hose biographical file B/3, 7–8.

66 Admiralty Fleet Orders, Oct. 1911.

67 Desbarats Diary, 2 Jan. 1912.

68 LeBlanc, "Historical Synopsis," 74; NS 18-38-2, NAC, RG 24, vol. 5592;

quote from Desbarats to minister, 12 Feb. 1913, Borden Papers, reel C-4349, 67585–90.

69 DHIST: *Niobe*, brief history, 38.

70 "Commodore Walter Hose, CBE, RCN, Director of the Naval Service of Canada," 4 *Canadian Defence Quarterly* (Oct. 1926), 8–11.

71 Hose-Kingsmill correspondence, 1909–11, quote from Hose to Kingsmill, 5 May 1910, NS 0-34178 pt. 1, NPRC.

72 Hose, "Early Years."

73 Ibid., 4–6, which quotes documents not available elsewhere; Borden to Hazen, 12 Jan. 1914; Chase-Casgraine to Pelletier, 22 Jan. 1914; Hazen to Borden, 24 Feb. 1914; Pelletier to Borden, 5 May 1914; Borden Papers, 78626, 78652, 78649–50, 78667, 786675–6, NAC, micro C-4362.

74 [?] to Kingsmill, 29 Aug. 1909, Tothill to Kingsmill, 30 Aug. 1909, NPRC, HQ 62-S.

75 Administrative friction between Militia and Marine and Fisheries is documented in HQC 365–11, NAC, RG 24, reel C-5052.

76 See NS 1014-3-1 and NS 1014-3-2, NAC, RG 24, vol. 3824; HQC 1009, pts. 1–2, PARC.

77 Sarty, "Silent Sentry," 192–3, 219–20.

78 Ibid., 220–1.

79 Admiralty, 5 May 1914, "Admiralty Comments on memorandum on 'Remarks on Naval Defence of the Atlantic Coast' ... ," NAC, Borden Papers, MG 26H, vol. 126, 68026–30.

80 Borden to Churchill, 8 June 1914, ibid., 68051.

CHAPTER FOUR

1 *Morning Chronicle*, Halifax, 8 Aug. 1914, 4. The story was only of marginal interest to Victoria's *Daily Colonist*, 7 Aug. 1914.

2 Viktor Harder, "Die ersten Vorstöße in der Nordsee," in Scheer, eds., *Die deutsche Flotte*, 13–16. Harder, a Konteradmiral twelve years later, at the time he wrote, had transited the canal between 17 and 19 August 1914.

3 Fayle, *Seaborne Trade*, I, 100–4.

4 For example, Cruisers Seen near St. Pierre," *Daily Colonist*, 3 Aug. 1914, 1.

5 von Mantey, *Die deutschen Hilfskreuzer*, 360.

6 For example, von Gottberg, *Kreuzerfahrten und U-Bootstaten*, 9.

7 Raeder, *Die Tätigkeit*, Vorwort.

8 Admiralty, *Naval Staff Monographs*, IX, 8.

9 "Notes from World War I Files re RCN Operations East Coast, 1914–18," Message, NSHQ to Captain-in Charge, Halifax, 29 July 1914, DHIST: NHS 1440–6.

10 Admiralty to Intelligence Officer, Jamaica, telegram sent 0145/5 Aug. 1914, *Naval Staff Monographs*, IX, 265.

11 Admiralty, *Naval Staff Monographs*, IX, 15, 23.

12 Ibid., 17–19, 22–3.

13 Militärgeschichtliches Forschungsamt, Hrsg. *Deutsche Militärgeschichte*, Bd. 5, Abschnitt VII, 297–303.

14 For example, *Daily Colonist*, Victoria, 6 Aug. 1914, 1.

15 Admiralty, *Naval Staff Monographs*, IX, 25.

16 Report to deputy minister, 10 Aug. 1914, NSC 1047-2-1, NAC, RG 24, vol. 3966; Ottawa to Admiralty, 10 Aug. 1918, PRO, ADM 137/37, 1036.

17 Colonial Office to governor general of Canada, 11 Aug. 1914, "European War" prints, no. 2, 75.

18 Midshipmen Malcolm Cann, RCN, John V.W. Hateway, RCN, William A. Palmer, RCN, and Arthur W. Silver, RCN. A bronze plaque at the entrance to the Coronel Memorial Library at Royal Roads Military College, Victoria, BC, commemorates their loss. It was dedicated by the lieutenant-governor of the province on 1 November 1974, the sixtieth anniversary of Coronel. An earlier commemorative plaque is in St Paul's garrison church, Esquimalt, BC.

19 Admiralty, *Naval Staff Monographs*, IX, provides the fullest account. But see also Geoffrey Bennett's masterful account *Coronel and the Falklands*.

20 Admiralty, *Naval Staff Monographs*, IX, 66–7, 69–71. Strictly speaking, his appointment was as 'rear-admiral commanding Fourth Cruiser Squadron,' the title that Cradock had retained when bringing his cruisers out in 1913. The appointment Commander-in-Chief, North America and West Indies Station, had lapsed after withdrawal of the permanent squadron from the western Atlantic in 1904–5. Phipps-Hornby sought to have the title reinstated for his appointment because it was "well known in former years, and very great weight attaches to it." See Phipps-Hornby to Admiralty, 15 Dec. 1914, PRO, ADM 137/1026.

21 "Extracts from a report to the Admiralty from the Commander-in-Chief, North America and West Indies Station," 10 June 1915, DHIST: NHS 1700–100/78.

22 Ibid.

23 Sub-committee of the inter-departmental conference, minutes, 29 July 1914, NSC 1019-1-2 pt. 1, NAC, RG 24, vol. 3852.

24 For the following, see Tucker, *Naval Service*, I, chaps. 12–13; and Sarty, "Trouble"; also "Brief History of HMCS Rainbow," NHS, 24 March 1961, DHIST.

25 *Daily Colonist*, 9 July 1914, 10.

26 For example, The German Cruiser Leipzig," *Daily Colonist*, 3 Aug. 1914, 2.

27 *Daily Colonist*, 27 Aug. 1914, 1; also 26 Aug., 1, and 29 Aug., 1.

28 Kingsmill to deputy minister, 6 Oct. 1914; Kingsmill to Story, 12 Oct. 1914 (quoted); copies in DHIST: "NHS 8000 Niobe."

29 E.g., Admiral Superintendent, Esquimalt, to NSHQ, telegram, 8 Nov. 1914, NSC 1047-7-5, NAC, RG 24, vol. 3967.

30 "Brief History of HMCS Niobe," 45–7; Department of the Naval Service, *Annual Report*, year ending 31 March 1915, 61; Tucker, *Naval Service*, 1, 242.

31 For the fullest account see "Brief History of HMCS Niobe," 50–8.

32 Admiralty, *Naval Staff Monographs*, IX, 22–3; see also the revealing discussion of Cradock's communications problems in South American waters in Bennett, *Coronel and the Falklands*, 191–3.

33 [Order-in-Council] PC 1952, 1 Aug. 1914, copy in DHIST; Department of the Naval Service, *Annual Report*, year ending 31 March 1915, 135–6.

34 [Order-in-Council] PC 2971, 28 Nov. 1914; PC 3139, 16 Dec. 1914; PC 1280, 2 June 1915, copy in DHIST.

35 Reports to deputy minister, 7 Aug. 1914, NSC, 1047-2-1, NAC, RG 24, vol. 3966; "Details Regarding Royal Canadian Navy," NS 1000-5-5, Department of the Naval Service, 16 May 1918, DHIST.

36 Governor General to HM Ambassador in Washington, 4, 5, 21, May 1915, "European War Prints," vol. III, no. 11, pp. 9, 17, 77.

37 Link, *Wilson*, 58–60.

38 Index to North America and West Indies telegrams, 17–19 Aug. 1914, PRO, ADM 137/37.

39 Hornby to Admiralty, telegram 34, 2 Oct. 1914, PRO, ADM 137/37.

40 "Historical Section Summary ... Intelligence Centre in North Atlantic," PRO, ADM 137/1026; Admiralty, to Hornby, telegrams, 1 and 2 Oct 1914; Hornby to Admiralty, telegram 34, 2 Oct. 1914, PRO, ADM 137/37; Command memo to Halifax Dockyard, 3 Dec. 1914, NSC 1023-7-3, NAC, RG 24, vol. 3857.

41 Director of intelligence division memoranda, 2 and 10 Oct. 1917, "Historical Section Summary ... Intelligence Centre in North Atlantic," PRO, ADM 137/1026.

42 Stephens to Director of the Naval Service, 10 Nov. 1914, NSC 1023-7-3, NAC, RG 24, vol. 3857; see also three telegrams between Stephens and White, 30 Sept. 1914, NS 60-W-6, NPRC.

43 Command memorandum to captain-in-charge, Halifax, 3 Dec. 1914, NSC 1023-7-3, NAC, RG 24, vol. 3857.

44 Stephens to Director of the Naval Service, 10 Nov. 1914, NSC 1023-7-3, NAC, RG 24, vol. 3857.

45 Command memorandum to captain-in-charge, Halifax, 3 Dec. 1914, NSC 1023-7-3, NAC, RG 24, vol. 3857.

46 Kingsmill, memorandum, 11 Jan. 1915, "European War Prints," vol. III, no. 9, 262–3.

47 Admiralty to Under-Secretary of State for Foreign Affairs, 5 Feb. 1915, ibid., 261–2.

48 Foreign Office to Admiralty, 18 Feb. 1914, "European War Prints," vol. III, no. 9, 263–4.

49 Notes on NS 26-2-10, NS 26-2-11, NS 26-1-12, NHS 1700–903, DHIST; deputy minister to secretary, Royal St. Lawrence Yacht Club, 31 Aug. 1914, headquarters – Story correspondence, Nov.–Dec. 1914, NS 26-2-1, NAC, RG 24, vol. 5597; Kingsmill to McBride, 3 Nov. 1914, file 804–880, PABC, GR [Government Records] 441, vol. 125.

50 Kingsmill to McBride, 3 Nov. 1914, file 804–880, PABC, GR 441, vol. 125.

51 Borden to Perley, 7 Oct. 1914; Perley to Borden, 10 Oct. 1914, cited in Tucker, *Naval Service*, I, 218–19.

52 For details on these issues see Phipps-Hornby to Admiralty, 15 Dec. 1914; Oliver, minute, 8 Jan. 1915; Admiralty to Phipps-Hornby, signal, 12 Jan. 1915; Phipps-Hornby to Admiralty, 14 June 1915, Admiralty to Phipps-Hornby, 25 July 1915, PRO, ADM 137/1026. Also Admiralty, *Naval Staff Monographs*, IX, 208.

53 Gwatkin to Rutherford, telegram, 11 Sept. 1914, HQC 95 pt. 4, NAC, RG 24, vol. 1198.

54 Phipps-Hornby to Admiralty, telegram, 15 Sept. 1914; Admiralty to Colonial Office, draft telegram, 16 Sept. 1914, PRO, ADM 137/1026.

55 Kingsmill to Phipps-Hornby, telegram, 19 Sept. 1914; Phipps-Hornby to Kingsmill, telegram, 23 Sept. 1914, NSC 1001-5-3, NAC, RG 24, vol. 6194.

56 DHIST: NHS 8000 Tuna, NS to Ballantyne, 4 Dec. 1917, NS 60-R-26. NPRC; McKee, *Yachts*, 20–3.

57 Admiralty, memorandum M-03496, 13 Nov. 1914, "European War Prints," vol. 1, no. 5, 560–1.

58 Great Britain, Admiralty, Naval Staff, *Naval Staff Monogrpahs (Historical)*, vol. IX, *Home Waters – Part II. September and October 1914* (OU 5528A) (r.p., 1924), 124–35.

59 For details see Navyard Halifax (the official message address for Halifax Navy Base) to Naval Ottawa, signal, 25 Sept. 1914, NSS 1057-1-1 pt. 1, DHIST; Department of the Naval Service, *Annual Report*, year ending 31 March 1915, 63–4; NHS notes on NS 1047-5-11, NHS 1440–11, DHIST; Phipps-Hornby to Kingsmill, 8 Jan. 1915, NS 1001–19-n4, NAC, RG 24, vol. 6197.

60 Phipps-Hornby to Kingsmill, 8 Jan. 1915, NS 1001-19-4, NAC, RG 24, vol. 6197; Kingsmill to Martin, 19 Jan. 1915, NS 1045-5-1, NAC, RG 24, vol. 3967.

61 Borden to Perley, telegram, 25 Nov. 1914, DCER, I, 59.

62 Perley to Borden, telegram, 4 Dec. 1914, DCER, I, 61.

63 See, for example, *CAR, 1914*, 497–502.

64 For an excellent summary of the Canadian economic and munitions production problem in 1914–15 see Bliss, *A Canadian Millionaire*, chap. 10.

65 Borden to Perley, telegram, 26 Nov. 1914, DCER, I, 59.
66 For details of construction see Perkins, "Canadian Vickers–Built H Class Submarines."
67 Edmonds, *A Short History*, 74–5.
68 Ellery H. Clark, "Der Erste Weltkrieg: Die Operationen zu Beginn des Krieges," von K.J. Müller übersetzt und bearbeitet, in E.B. Potter, Ch. W. Nimitz, J. Rohwer, *Seemacht*, Hrsgg. im Auftrag des Arbeitskreises für Wehrforschung von Jürgen Rohwer, Herrsching: Manfred Pawlak, 1986, 350.
69 Immediatbericht, 4 July 1916, Scheer, "Chronologische Entwicklung des U-Bootkrieges 1916," Nachlaß Konteradmiral v. Levetzow, BA-MA: N 239/15, 103.
70 "Acta betreffend Prisenordnung und Prisengericht," BA-MA: RM 3/4922, RM 3/4923.
71 For example, "U-Boote gegen Handelsschiffe," *Tägliche Rundschau*, Abend-Ausgabe, 29 Dec. 1914, Nachlaß Tirpitz (Tirpitz Papers), BA-MA: N 253/99, s. 4.
72 "British Navy and Its Work, *Daily Telegraph*, 18 May 1915, BA-MA: RM 3/9699. The British and North American press provides other examples of the war of words.
73 Nachlaß Vizeadmiral Hollweg (Hollweg Papers), BA-MA: RM 3/11679. The papers include a clipping from the *Hamburger Fremdenblatt* of 14 Nov. 1926 in which the reporter, K.E. Wiegand, describes "Mein U-Boot-Interview mit Tirpitz."
74 Bethmann Hollweg, *Betrachtungen*, II, 121.
75 "N, Seiner Exzellenz dem Herrn Staatssekretär vorzulgen, gemäß telephonischem Befehl," undated, in Tirpitz Nachlaß (Tirpitz Papers), BA-MA: N 253/99.
76 Newspaper clippings in Nachlaß Tirpitz (Tirpitz Papers), for instance, *Morning Post*, 24 Dec. 1914: "Admiral Tirpitz's Plans – Threatened Submarine Raids – Prompt American Ridicule."
77 "Denkschrift einer Weiterentwicklung der Marine nach dem Krieg," and "Erster Etat nach Friedenschluß," Nachlaß Admiral Hollweg, BA-MA: RM 3/11703, 8.

CHAPTER FIVE

1 Cited in Edmonds, *A Short History*, 145–6.
2 Jones, *The German Secret Service*, 334. See also Strother, *Fighting Germany's Spies*.
3 Buitenhuis, *The Great War of Words*, 19. See also Sanders and Taylor, *British Propaganda*.
4 For instance, *The World in a Crucible*.

5 "Acta betreffend Geheime a- und v-Angelegenheiten, Nachrichtenwesen," BA-MA: RM 5/772. These ideas were to have been presented to the Kaiser in an Immediatvortrag; no evidence suggests that this was in fact ever done.

6 "Bericht der Tätigkeit des Oberleutnants a.D. zur Helle ... als Nachrichtenoffizier für die Kaiserliche Marine," in "Acta betrefeend Europ. Krieg: Angelegenheiten s.m. Schiffe, Kreuzergeschwader an der Westküste von Amerika," BA-MA: RM 5/2229. San Francisco served as the major coaling station.

7 Korvettenkapitän Erwin Schaeffer to Staatssekretär des Reichs-Marine-Amts [v. Tirpitz], 13 Oct. 1903, "Acta betreffend Marine- und Militärattachés Feb 1903–Nov 1918," BA-MA: RM 5/287.

8 See, for example, his situation reports for 20 March 1913, 4 June 1913, and 21 Aug. through 7 Oct. 1913, in "Schriftwechsel mit dem Marine-Attaché in Washington, Juni 1913–Nov 1913," BA-MA: RM 3/2908.

9 Boy-Ed to Chef des Admiralstabs der Marine, 12 May 1915, "Schriftwechsel mit dem Marine-Attaché," BA-MA: RM 3/2912.

10 Boy-Ed to Staatssekretär des Reichsmarineamts [Tirpitz], 24 May 1914, "Die fremden Marineattachés in Washington," in "Acta betreffend dt. Marineattaché in Washington, Schriftwechsel mit RMA," BA-MA: RM 3/2910.

11 Cole, *Prince of Spies*.

12 For this and the following see the excellent account in Armstrong, "Canadian Home Defence," chap. 2, and Andrew, *Secret Service*, chap. 5. The actions of Canadian officials were more moderate and sensible than those of their British counterparts, possibly because of the Canadian's long experience with apprehended insurgency from the United States.

13 This is clear from the naval intelligence records in NAC, RG 24, vols. 3986, 4017–18.

14 Strother, *Fighting Germany's Spies*, 34.

15 Kingsmill to Chief of the Admiralty Staff, Secret Memo, 24 March 1915; DHIST: "European War, 1914," print no. 9, vol. II, item no. 625.

16 Pinkerton's to Chief Commissioner of Police, Ottawa, NAC, RG 24, vol. 3986, file NSC 1055-3-3; also Joseph Pope, Under-Secretary of State for External Affairs, to the Governor-General's Secretary, 6 March 1915; DHIST: "European War, 1914," vol. II, print no. 19, item no. 451, 475.

17 Passed by Stephens to Sherwood, Commissioner of Dominion Police, 20 March 1915; NAC, RG 24 vol. 3986, file 1055-4-1.

18 Vice-Consul C.E. Lucian Agassiz to the Admiral-in-Charge, Naval Service Headquarters, 2 June 1915; NAC, RG 24, vol. 3986, file 1055-7-3.

19 DHIST: "European War, 1914," vol. III, print no. 11, item no. 8, and enclosure 2.

20 Bennett to Governor General, 11 June 1915; DHIST: "European War, 1914," vol. III, print no. 12, item no. 289.

21 The agent, J.H. Van Koolbergen, was working with the British consul-
general and the Canadian Pacific Railway in order to stage the scenario.
See Spring Rice to Governor General, 8 Sept. 1915: DHIST: "European
War, 1914," vol. IV, print no. 15, item no. 39. Also enclosure to item 39,
H.M. Consul in San Francisco to H.M. Ambassador in Washington, 1 Sept.
1915.

22 Spring Rice, British Ambassador, Washington, to Governor-General of
Canada, cipher telegram, 17 Dec. 1914; DHIST: "European War, 1914,"
vol. II, print no. 6, item no. 1427.

23 Manfred Smuda, cited in Armin Arnold and Josef Schmidt, eds., *Reclams
Romanführer*, Stuttgart: Reclam 1978, 318.

24 Operative no. 68 to Pinkerton's, 17 March 1915; NAC, RG 24, vol. 3980,
file 1055-3-2.

25 Commissioner of Police to Cdr. Stephens, 24 April 1915; NAC, RG 24, vol.
3986, file 1055-3-2.

26 Sherwood to Under-Secretary of State for External Affairs, 2 Feb. 1915,
confidential print, "European War Prints," vol. 2, no. 8, 139; von Papen,
Memoirs, 34–5.

27 *New York American*, 25 Feb. 1915, 1–3.

28 Commander C.W. Belhairs, RN, MP, in a question to Rt Hon. Lord Robert
Cecil, Under-Secretary of State for Foreign Affairs, 31 Oct. 1916, *Parliamentary Debates*, House of Commons (United Kingdom), vol. 86, p. 1491.

29 Boy-Ed to Staatssekretär des Reichs-Marine-Amts, Berlin, 26 Feb. 1916,
in "Schriftenwechsel mit dem Marineattaché in Washington," BA-MA:
RM 3/V. 2912.

30 Boy-Ed to Chef des Admiralstabs der Marine, 12 May 1915, "Schriftwechsel mit dem Marineattaché in Washington," BA-MA: RM 3/2912.

31 Beesly, *Room 40*, 184–7.

32 See Tuchmann, *The Zimmermann Telegram*.

33 For example, "Graves Talks of U-53 Stock Deals," *New York Times*, 13 Nov.
1916, 1, 7; "Dr Graves Guarded by Grim Sentinel," *New York Times*,
14 Nov. 1916, 3; "German Newspaper Accuser of Graves," *New York
Times*, 23 Nov. 1916, 9. The Tirpitz Papers (Nachlaβ Tirpitz) contain an
American clipping on the Graves scandal, BA-MA: N 253/99.

34 See, for example, Jones, *German Secret Service*, 69–72, and Winter, *Sam
Hughes*, 120–31.

35 Captain G.H.F. Abraham, Intelligence Officer, St John's, to Governor of
Newfoundland, 31 May 1915, PRO, ADM 116/1400.

36 Colonial Office to Governor General, telegram, 9 June 1915, "European
War Prints," vol. II, no. 12, 133–4.

37 "A. Britisher," New York, to Chief Commissioner of Police, Ottawa,
undated; NAC, RG 24, vol. 4022, file NSC 1062-13-3.

38 DNS to Deputy Minister, 23 July 1915; NS 1062-13-4, NAC, RG 24, vol. 4022.

39 Commander-in-chief to Director of the Naval Service, 22 May 1916, file 1065-4-1(1), cited in Tucker, *Naval Service*, I, 247.

40 See Hough, *Former Naval Person.*

41 For the best intelligence assessment of the *Lusitania* incident see Beesly, *Room 40*, 84–122.

42 Bonar Law to Governor-General, 9 June 1915; NAC, RG 24, vol. 4022, file 1062-13-4; also DHIST: "European War, 1914," vol. III, print no. 12, item no. 261.

43 C.W. Bennett to Colonial Office, 10 June 1915; NAC, RG 24, vol. 4022, file 1062-13-4.

44 Borden to [T.W.] Crothers, 16 June 1915, NAC, MG 26H, vol. 76, 26477.

45 Ambassador Spring Rice, Washington, to Governor-General, 9 June 1915; DHIST: "European War, 1914," vol. III, print no. 12, item no. 271.

46 Navyyard to Naval Halifax (i.e. Halifax Command), 5 June 1915; "Enemy Submarine Activities," NSC 1062-13-2, NAC, RG 24, vol. 4020.

47 Consul-General, New York, to Governor-General, 11 June 1915; DHIST: "European War, 1914," vol. III, print no. 12, item no. 287.

48 Admiralty to Naval Ottawa (i.e. Naval Headquarters, Ottawa), 25 June 1915; NAC, RG 24, vol. 4022, file NS 1062-13-4.

49 Patey to Admiralty, 3 June 1915, PRO, ADM 116/1400.

50 Patey to Admiralty, no. 164 M/14, 19 July 1915; PRO, ADM 116/1400, case 20. This is the principal Admiralty file on the Canadian patrols. A convenient Canadian collection may be found in NAC, RG 25, G-1, box 1161, file 558–1915-C.

51 Patey, memorandum M/24, 4 June 1915, PRO, ADM 116/1400.

52 Patey to Connaught, 16 June 1915, copy in HQC 1686 pt. 1, NAC, RG 24, vol. 2532. Also Patey to Connaught, 17 June 1915, NAC, RG 24, vol. 4022, file NS 1062-13-4.

53 Vice-Admiral C.E. Kingsmill, DNS, to the Deputy Minister, 26 June 1915 and 30 June 1915; NAC, RG 24, vol. 4022, file NS 1062-13-4; Kingsmill to minister, 11 Aug. 1915, NS 1062-13-4, NAC, RG 24, vol. 4022; NHS notes on NS 1045-5-11, NHS 1440–11, DHIST; also NHS notes on NS 58-5-1, NHS 8000 "Premier," DHIST.

54 Stephens, "Royal Canadian Volunteer (Motor Craft Reserve)," 26 June 1915, NS 1062-13-4, NAC, RG 24, vol. 4022.

55 Patrols, Sydney, to Naval Ottawa, 2 Sept. 1915, telegram, NS 1065-2-1, NAC, RG 24, vol. 4030; J.O.B. LeBlanc, "Historical Synopsis of Organization and Development of the Royal Canadian Navy," 1937, 34, 41–4, 47–8, 52, 56, 63, 67.

56 COS (Stephens) to Kingsmill, 30 June 1915, NS 1062-13-4, NAC, RG 24, vol. 4022.

57 Desbarats Diary, NAC, MG 30E89, vol. 5.

58 Foster political diary, 3 Aug. 1915, NAC, MG 27 II D 7, vol. 4.

59 For example, NHS 8000 "Chartered Ships," NHS notes on NS 58-15-1; Desbarats Diary, 19 July 1915, NAC, MG 30E89, vol. 5.

60 McKee, *Armed Yachts*, 14–35. Also DHIST, NHS 8000 "Florence."

61 DHIST: NHS 8000, "Brief History of HMCS Grilse," 6 March 1961.

62 Kingsmill to acting minister, 10 July 1915, file NS 1062-13-4, NAC, RG 24, vol. 4022; DHIST: NHS notes on NS 58-57-2; NHS 8000 "Stadacona (ship afloat)." See also McKee, *Armed Yachts*, chap. 3.

63 Borden to George Perley [Canadian high commissioner in London], (telegram), 7 April 1915, NAC, MG 26H, reel C-4318, 39492; on Admiralty's requisitioning of Canadian merchant ships see also Robert Craig Brown, "Sir Robert Borden, the Great War and Anglo-American Relations," in John S. Moir, ed., *Character and Circumstance: Essays in Honour of Donald Grant Creighton*, Toronto: Macmillan, 1970, 215–16.

64 Smith, *Clandestine Submarines*, 102–9.

65 Cited in Patey to Admiralty, 19 July 1915, PRO, ADM 116/1400.

66 Stephens to Kingsmill, 17 June 1915, NS 1017-11-2, NAC, RG 24, vol. 3846.

67 Kingsmill to Stephens, 3 July 1915, ibid.

68 Desbarats to Borden, with enclosure, 14 June 1915; Borden to Desbarats, 15 June 1915, NAC, MG 26 H, vol. 54, 26470–4.

69 Borden to Perley, telegram, 26 May 1915, DCER I, 73; Perley, 2 July 1915 (memorandum), NAC, MG 26 H, vol. 76, 39492.

70 Kingsmill to Crowthers (Acting Minister), "The Submarine Menace and Measures to Counteract It," 10 July 1915; NAC, RG 24, vol. 4022, file NS 1062-13-4.

71 Kingsmill to Crowthers (Acting Minister), "The Submarine Menace and Measures to Counteract It," 10 July 1915; Kingsmill to commander-in-chief, 23 July 1914; NAC, RG 24, vol. 4022, file NS 1062-13-4. NHS notes from NS 1047-5-11, DHIST, NHS 1440–11; HMCS *Margaret* log, 14–17 July 1915, NAC, RG 24, vol. 7492; Stephens to Consulting Naval Engineer, 7 July 1915, enclosing "Standing Orders for St Lawrence Patrol," NS 68-53-1, NAC, RG 24, 5662; Kingsmill to Gwatkin, 28 July 1915, HQC 1686 pt. 1, NAC, RG 24, vol. 2532.

72 DHIST: 81/520/1440–6, Halifax, NS, 1905–1920, 2 September 1915, List of ships showing allocation.

73 Correspondence, July–Sept. 1915, NS 60-P-30, NPRC.

74 Smith to Kingsmill, 30 July 1915; Kingsmill to Smith, 10 Aug. 1915; Command Memorandum to Senior Naval Officer, Sydney, 17 Sept. 1915, NS 1065-2-1, NAC, RG 24, vol. 4030.

75 McLaurin to Russell, 11 Feb. 1963; DHIST: NHS 8000 *Protector*. We have edited the passage slightly.

76 See ship files DHIST: NHS 8000 series. Also Commanding Officer, HMCS *Diana*, to Captain Superintendent, Halifax, 21 Aug. 1915, NS 58-5-1, pt.

2, copy in NHS 8000 "Premier," DHIST: 81/520/1440–6, "Halifax, NS, 1905–1920," 2 Sept. 1915, List of ships showing allocation.

77 Kingsmill, "Standing Orders for St. Lawrence Patrol," June 1915 [no date given], NS 58-52-1; NAC, RG 24, vol. 5662.

78 Kingsmill to Desbarats, 26 Oct. 1915, NS 58-15-1, copy in DHIST: NHS 8000 "Sinmac"; NHS notes on NS 58-54-1, NHS 8000 "Florence"; also McKee *Armed Yachts*, 19–20; Martin to Pasco, 20 Nov. 1915, NS 58-33-5X, copy in DHIST: NHS 8000 "Sable I."

79 Kingsmill to Desbarats, 23 July 1915, NS 1062-13-4, NAC, RG 24, vol. 4022.

80 White to Borden, 14 July 1915 (telegram); Borden to White, 14 July 1915 (telegram), NAC, MG 26H, vol. 76, 39492. Borden, London, to Prime Minister's Office, Ottawa, 14 July 1915; NAC, RG 24, vol. 4022, file NS 1062-13-4. The note was received in the Intelligence Branch of the Naval Service on 23 July.

81 Stephens, COS, to DNS [Kingsmill], 5 Aug. 1915; NAC, RG 24, vol. 4022, NS 1062-13-4.

82 Troopers [War Office] to Minister Ottawa, 17 July 1915 (telegram), HQC 1686 pt. 1, NAC, RG 24, vol. 2532.

83 Patey to Admiralty, 19 July 1915, PRO, ADM 116/1400.

84 For example, Spring Rice to Intelligence Officer, St John's, 25 July 1915 (telegram), Davidson to Bonar Law, 26 July 1915, PRO, ADM 116/1400. Also situation reports, 1 and 4 Aug. 1915, NHS notes on NS 47-5-11, DHIST: NHS 1440–11; Navyard Halifax to Naval Ottawa, 2 Aug. 1915 (signal), Naval Ottawa to Navyard Halifax, 2 Aug. 1915, NS 1065-2-1, NAC, RG 24, vol. 4030; Kingsmill to Desbarats, 29 Sept. 1915, NS 1062-13-4, NAC, RG 24, vol. 4022. Kingsmill to Gwatkin, HQC 1686 pt. 1, NAC, RG 24, vol. 2532.

85 Stephens, COS, to DNS [Kingsmill], 5 Aug. 1915, NAC, RG 24, vol. 4022, NS 1062-13-4.

86 Kingsmill, "Memo for Information of Minister," 11 Aug. 1915; NAC, RG 24, vol. 4022, file 1062-13-4.

87 Kingsmill, memorandum, 10 Aug. 1915, NS 1062-13-4, NAC, RG 24, vol. 4022.

88 Historical Records Officer to Senior Canadian Naval Officer (London), "10 April 1944 HMCS Niobe 1914–1915" (copies and summaries of relevant documents in Admiralty records), NHS 1700–100/78, docket CS 43-2-1; Hazen to Borden, 9 Aug. 1915 (telegram), NAC, MG 26H, reel C-4349, 68108.

89 Graham Green to Borden, 12 Aug. 1915, NAC, MG 26H, vol. 76, 3942.

90 Borden to Hazen, telegram, 13 Aug. 1915, NS 1062-13-4, NAC, RG 24, vol. 4022; Kingsmill to Gwatkin, 13 Aug. 1915, HQC 1686 pt. 1, NAC, RG 24, vol. 2532.

91 Kingsmill to Desbarats, 28 Sept. 1915, NS 1062-13-4, NAC, RG 24, vol. 4022.

92 Desbarats to Kingsmill, 9 Oct. 1915, NS 1062-13-4, NAC, RG 24, vol. 4022. Desbarats directed Kingsmill to release all vessels under contract in order to reduce departmental expenditures.

93 Kingsmill to Desbarats, 29 Oct. 1915, NS 1062-13-4, NAC, RG 24, vol. 4022; "Chartered Ships, RCN, 1914–18," DHIST: NHS 8000 "Chartered Ships."

94 House of Commons, *Debates*, 13 March 1916, 1679.

95 A.H. Wickens to Russell, 16 Nov. 1955, DHIST: NHS 8000 "Stadacona (ship afloat)." We have corrected Wickens's idiosyncratic spelling and punctuation.

96 Edmonds, *A Short History*, 143.

97 House of Commons, *Debates*, 13 March 1916, 1686–1703.

98 Connaught to Bonar Law, 4 July 1916, with enclosures, "European War Prints," vol. VI, no. 29, 218–19, DHIST.

99 Nicholson, *Official History*, 133 5, 215.

100 Desbarats to Under Secretary of State for External Affairs, 2 March 1916, file 558–1915-C, NAC, RG 25 G-1, vol. 1161; see also Kingsmill to minister, 28 Feb. 1916, NSC 1065-4-1, NAC, RG 24, vol. 4030.

101 Desbarats to Under Secretary of State for External Affairs, 23 March 1916, file 558–1915-C, NAC, RG 24, vol 1161.

102 Oliver, minute, 4 Feb. 1916, PRO, ADM 116/1400, 139.

103 Admiralty to Colonial Office, 8 April 1916, NSC 1065-4-1, NAC, RG 24, vol. 4030.

104 Kingsmill to deputy minister, 17 April 1916, Bonar Law to Governor-General, 26 May 1915, NS 1062-12-1, NAC, RG 24, vol. 4020.

105 Maxwell, *Motor Launch Patrol*, 1–9; Smith, *Clandestine Submarines*, 117.

106 Governor General to Bonar Law, 29 Feb. 1916, "European War Prints," vol. VI, no. 26, 23A; Shea to Hazen, 9 Sept. 1916, DHIST: 81/520/1440–5 pt. 5.

107 House of Commons, *Debates*, 13 March 1916, 1678, 1680; Desbarats to Perley, 11 Feb. 1916, "European War Prints," vol. VI, no. 26, 59A.

108 *CAR, 1916*, 314–15; Historical Records Office, Senior Canadian Naval Officer (London), 1944, "The Royal Naval Canadian Volunteer Reserve: Its establishment, recruiting and some notes on its work overseas – 1916 to 1918," NHS 1700–903, DHIST (a shortened version was published under the same title in the *Royal Canadian Navy Monthly Review*, no. 26 [Feb. 1944], 26–39); House of Commons, *Debates*, 6 Aug. 1917, 4159, 4163.

CHAPTER SIX

1 See, for example, Garner, *International Law*, II, chaps. 30–7; Heinrich Pohl, Der Deutsche Unterseebootkrieg: Ein völkerrechtliches Gutachten

(unpubl. ms), Tübingen, 1923. Pohl was professor of law at the University of Tübingen.

2   "Gedanken zum U-Bootkrieg," 25 May 1915, in "U-Bootkrieg Februar 1915–Dezember 1916," BA-MA: RM 5/921.

3   Jagow to Ambassador Gerard, 22 Feb. 1915, "Auswärtiges Amt: Schrift-wechsel mit der Regierung der Vereinigten Staate von Amerika, betref-fend den Unterseebootkrieg," BA-MA: RM 8/100.

4   "Gedanken zum U-Bootkrieg," 25 May 1915.

5   For the severity of the British blockade, see Vincent, *The Politics of Hunger*.

6   See, for example, the twenty-eight notes exchanged between 4 February 1915 and 10 May 1916, in "Auswärtiges Amt: Schriftwechsel mit der Regierung der Vereinigten Staaten von Amerika, betreffend den Unter-seehandelskrieg," BA-MA: RM 8/100. Also "Notenwechsel mit Amerika, 10 Juni 1915–3 April 1917," BA-MA: RM 5/4044, and "U-Bootkrieg, Februar 1915–1916," BA-MA: RM 5/921.

7   James W. Gerard to His Excellency Mr. von Jagow, Imperial Secretary of State, Foreign Affairs, 15 May 1915, "Auswärtiges Amt: Schriftwechsel."

8   v. Tirpitz to Seine Majestät den Kaiser und König, 27 Aug. 1915, in Nachlaß Vizeadmiral Hollweg (Hollweg Papers), BA-MA: RM 3/11678. The Kaiser and the Reichskanzler had discussed, for example, *Arabic* and *Lusitania*, on 26 Aug. 1915, "U-Bootkrieg, Februar 1915–1916," BA-MA: RM 5/921.

9   Gerard to Jagow, German Foreign Office, 23 July 1915, in "Auswärtiges Amt: Schriftwechsel."

10 von Jagow, Auswärtiges Amt, to Gerard, 4 May 1916, "Auswärtiges Amt: Schriftwechsel."

11 Gerard to von Jagow, 23 July 1915, "Notenwechsel mit Amerika," BA-MA: RM 4/4044.

12 Captain Karl Boy-Ed, naval attaché, Washington, drafts for a note, 22 April 1916, "Notenwechsel mit Amerika," BA-MA: RM 5/4044. Boy-Ed spoke of the "parteiische übelwollende Neutralität gegenüber Deutsch-land" and pointed out correctly that Americans had reacted differently to the war zone declarations of Britain and Germany. The chief of the Admiralty Staff reiterated this "policy of conscious bias and conscious sup-port" of Britain – "Politik der bewußten Parteinahme und [der] bewußten Unterstützung" – on 3 April 1917, "Notenwechsel mit Amerika 10 Juni 1915–3 April 1917," BA-MA: RM 5/4044.

13 Admiral von Holtzendorff, "Über die Notwendigkeit eines baldigen Beginns des uneingeschränkten U-Boot-Krieges," Gedenkschrift des Admiralstabes, Berlin, 22 Dec. 1916, Geheimakten, "Militärische Einzel-probleme von November 1914–Oktober 1918: Blockade Englands und Friedenschluß," BA-MA: RM 3/v. 27; von Holtzendorff to Königl. General-feldmarschal, Chef des Generalstabs des Feldheeres, von Hindenburg,

22 Dec. 1916, BA-MA: RM 5/6726. Also Rössler, *Ubootbau*, 96–9; Bauer, *Reichsleitung und U-bootseinsatz*.

14 See Spindler, *Der Handelskrieg*, I, II.

15 Der Staatssekretär des Innern to Chef des Marine-Kabinetts, Herrn Kaiserlichen Admiral von Müller, 21 July 1916, "Immediatvorträge," BA-MA: RM 5/904, S. 77–82; and "Zum Immediatvortrag: Zur Randbemerkung Seiner Majestät ... über die Entstehung des Planes von Handelsschiffs-Unterseebooten," 27 July 1915, in "Europ. Krieg: Unterseeboots-Handelsschiffe," BA-MA: RM 5/2267. See also Lohmann's summary of events in König, *Die Fahrt der Deutschland*, 148–51; also König, *Fahrten der U-Deutschland*; and *Berliner Illustrierte Zeitung*, Nr. 37, XXV Jahrgang, 10 Sept. 1916, 545–7.

A number of German newspapers extolled the achievements of the Deutsche Ozean-Rhederei and *U-Deutschland* and reported essentially the same story. For an East German account see Hans-Georg Rieschke, "Handels-U-Boot 'Deutschland'," *Marine-Kalender der DDR 1981*, Berlin (Ost), 1980, 144–50. Richard Compton-Hall's well-illustrated summary (*Submarine Warfare: Monsters and Midgets*) relies on the American translation of König's first book, apparently without reference to German original sources. For notes and photographs on model-building see Karsten Eckardt, "Cargo Submarine Deutschland," 24–30. Messimer's *The Merchant U-Boat*.

16 Der Chef des Admiralstabs der Marine to Hochseekommando, Station N, 14 Aug. 1916, in "Europ. Krieg. Unterseeboots-Handelsschiffe," BA-MA: RM 5/2267.

17 The name Deutsche Ozean-Rhederei stood on the new shipping company's letterhead, copies of which may still be seen in German files; it was also on the ship's dinnerware, items of which are on display at the Maritime Museum in Bremen. Messimer refers to the firm variously as the Deutsche Ozean Reederei and German Ocean Navigation Company.

18 Staatssekretär des Innern to Chef des Marine-Kabinetts, Admiral von Müller, 21 July 1916, BA-MA: RM 5/904, S. 82.

19 For the following see Harald Fock, "Deutsche Rohstofftransport-Uboote," 46–8.

20 Because of rubber's specific gravity of 0.94, this caused no significant changes in the composition of cargo within the pressure hull itself.

21 Edwyn Gray's assertion ('*A Damned Un-English Weapon*,' 218–19) that she was sunk by British submarine G.13 does not bear scrutiny.

22 König, "Kriegs-Handelsfahrten unter See," 154–8; and Pickert, "Mit Kapitän König nach Amerika," 146–53.

23 Herzog, "Kapitän zur See Hans Rose," 387–8. A photograph in von Langsdorff's *U-Boote am Feind* shows Rose in SS uniform.

24 König, *Die Fahrt der Deutschland*, 87. See also P. König to Admiralstab der Kaiserlichen Marine, Berlin [undated Report of Proceedings], BA-MA: RM 5/2267.

25 Minutes of a meeting between Reichskanzler von Bethmann-Hollweg, Grand Admiral von Tirpitz, State Secretary of Foreign Affairs von Jagow, and Vice-Admiral Bachmann, 28 Feb. 1915, "Immediatvortrag," in "U-Bootkrieg, Februar 1915–1916": BA-MA: RM 5/921.

26 See, for example, the public summary of arguments that the *New York Times* published on 9 October 1916 (p. 3) with regard to the visit of U-53.

27 Garner, *International Law*, II, 437.

28 See, for example, "Die formelle Anerkennung der 'Deutschland' als Handelsschiff," *Berliner Tageblatt*, 17 July 1916, 2.

29 See, for example, "Die angebliche Patentklage gegen die *Deutschland*," *Berliner Tageblatt*, 14 July 1916, 2; and "Bau von Handelstauchbooten in Amerika," ibid., 17 July 1916, 2. Cf. Messimer, *The Merchant U-Boat*, 59–60.

30 See, for example, König's descriptions of events in Hans Rose, *Auftauchen!*, 55–6.

31 König, *Die Fahrt der Deutschland*, 99. See also König's more sober, but substantially similar, official report, BA-MA: RM 5/2267.

32 Von Jagow to [US Ambassador] James W. Gerard, Berlin, 8 July 1915, "Auswärtiges Amt: Schriftwechsel mit der Regierung der Vereinigten Staaten von Amerika, betreffend den Unterseehandelskrieg," BA-MA: RM 8/100.

33 Bernstorff, by cipher, to von Bethmann Hollweg, 19 July 1916, BA-MA: RM 5/2267.

34 For example, Lohmann to Toussaint, Admiralstab der Marine, 28 June 1916; Lohmann to Vanselou, Admiralstab der Marine, 8 July 1916; Lohmann to Toussaint, 7 July 1916; BA-MA: RM 5/2267.

35 "Amerikafahrt eines deutschen Handels-U-Bootes," *Berliner Tageblatt*, 1 July 1916, 1.

36 *Berliner Tageblatt*, 13 July 1916, 3.

37 Tucker, I, 235.

38 L. Persius, "Die Fahrt der 'Deutschland' und der 'Bremen' über den Ozean," *Berliner Tageblatt*, 11 July 1916, 1; and König, *Fahrten der Deutschland*, 18.

39 PRO, ADM 137/1262. This file contains the main British sources on all aspects of the cruises of *U-Deutschland* and *U-53* to the United States.

40 Commodore (Submarines), 30 June 1916, PRO, ADM 137/1262, 18.

41 Foreign Office to Sir C. Spring Rice, 1 July 1916, no. 1721, PRO, ADM 137/1262.

42 Draft of telegram to Spring Rice, suggested by Arthur Balfour, 5 July 1916, PRO, ADM 137/1262.

43 Secretary of the Admiralty to Secretary of State, Foreign Office, 18 Aug. 1916, PRO, ADM 137/1262.

44 König to Bernstorff, 20 July 1916, and Bernstorff to König, 28 July 1916, BA-MA: RM 5/2267.

45 Cited in Rose, *Auftauchen!*, 56.

46 Kaiser to Deutsche-Ozean-Rhederei, 24 Aug. 1916, BA-MA: RM 5/2267.

47 For example, "Glückliche Heimkehr der U-'Deutschland,' *Berliner Tageblatt*, 24 Aug. 1916, 1; "Vor der Einfahrt der Deutschland," and "Die Ankunft der Deutschland in Bremen," ibid., 25 Aug. 1916, 1; "Die Begrüßung der U-Deutschland in Bremen," 26 Aug. 1916, 4. Also *Berliner Illustrierte Zeitung*, 3 Sept. 1916, 526; 10 Sept. 1916, 545–6.

48 *Die Flotte*, Monatsblatt des Deutschen Flotten-Vereins, Oct. 1916, 168.

49 "Der amerikanische Botschafter Gerard über den Erfolg der Deutschland," *Berliner Tageblatt*, 25 Aug. 1916, 2.

50 Edmonds, *A Short History*, 148.

51 Ibid., 187.

52 A. Lohmann to Fregattenkapitän Toussanit, Admiralstab der Marine, 27 March 1917, BA-MA: RM 5/2267.

53 For a sampling of press speculation see the *New York Times*, 1 Oct. 1916, and 12 Oct. 1916, 2.

54 Carl W. Ackermann, "Germany's Navy Ready to Thwart Blockades," *Denver Times*, 31 Jan. 1916, BA-MA: RM 5/2861. The interview took place 31 January, with clippings forwarded to Berlin.

55 Immediatvortrag, 9 June 1916, BA-MA: RM 5/921.

56 "Sitzung in Pleß über den U-Bootkrieg," August, no. 7, BA-MA: RM 5/921.

57 This evidence of von Holtzendorff's independent action adds a new dimension to the already considerable literature on Germany's high-level meetings in late 1916 concerning unrestricted submarine warfare. Note the crucial phrase "da es sich um eine reine militärische Angelegenheit handelt, deren geplanten Durchführung den Allerhöchsten Willensaüßerungen Seiner Majestät entspricht."

58 Von Bethmann Hollweg to Hindenburg, 2 Oct. 1916, BA-MA: RM 5/921.

59 Hochseechef to Chef des Admiralstabs der Marine, 9 Sept. 1916, BA-MA: RM 5/6360. Amplified in his letter of 10 Sept. same file.

60 Von Holtzendorff to Scheer, 11 Sept. 1916, BA-MA: RM 5/6360.

61 "Allerhöchste Kabinetts-Ordre," 7 Sept. 1915, BA-MA: RM 3/2704.

62 "Telegraphische Instruktion für den Kaiserlichen Botschafter in Washington," [Count von Bernstorff], Bethmann Hollweg to Bernstorff, 25 Sept. 1916, BA-MA: RM 5/921; also Bethmann Hollweg to Hindenburg, 2 Oct. 1916, BA-MA: RM 5/921.

63 Bauer, *Als Führer der U-Boote*, 425.

64 For the following see KTB/U-53, 22 April 1916–31 May 1917, BA-MA: PG 61612; "Europ. Krieg, Kreuzerkrieg, U-53," BA-MA: RM 5/6360 (contains a wealth of correspondence and newspaper clippings); also Rose, "U-53 fährt nach Amerika," 158–85, and Rose, *Auftauchen!*

65 Garner, *International Law* 11, 430-7.

66 Cited in ibid., 431

67 Rose, "U-53 fährt nach Amerika," 162.
68 Ibid., 166.
69 "Arrival of German Submarine U-53," Commandant, Naval Station, Narragansett Bay, RI, to Navy Department (Operations), 7 Oct. 1916, USNOA,
   World War I U-Boats, microfilm by Richard von Doenhoff and Allan Rilley.
   The USN released to the press only paragraphs nos. 4 and 21 quoted
   herein. See the *New York Times*, 10 Oct. 1916, 2. The other paragraphs
   detailed technical information gathered during visits of USN officers. See
   also, "Visit of German Submarine U-53 to Newport, RI," Commander,
   Destroyer Force [Admiral Albert Gleaves, USS *Birmingham*], to Commander in Chief, Atlantic Fleet, 7 Oct. 1916, USNOA, von Doenhoff
   microfilm.
70 "Visit of German Submarine U-53 to Newport, R.I.," Commander,
   Destroyer Force, to Commander in Chief, Atlantic Fleet, 7 Oct. 1916;
   also the latter's "Supplementary Report," 9 Oct. 1916, and "Second
   Supplementary Report," 10 Oct. 1916, USNOA, von Doenhoff microfilm.
71 "Arrival of German Submarine U-53," Commandant, Naval Station,
   Narragansett Bay, RI, to Navy Department (Operations), 12 Oct. 1916,
   USNOA, von Doenhoff microfilm.
72 *New York Times*, 9 Oct. 1916, 2.
73 "Wilhelm II to Kapitänleutnant Rose, Kommandant Meines Unterseeboots
   U-53," 2 Nov. 1916, BA-MA: RM 5/6360.

CHAPTER SEVEN

 1 Spring Rice to Governor-General, 7 Oct. 1916; NAC, RG 24, vol. 4026, file
   1062-13-13, vol. 2.
 2 "Arrival of German Submarine U-53," Commandant, Naval Station, Narragansett Bay, RI, to Navy Department (Operations), 7 Oct. 1916; USNOA,
   World War I U-boats, microfilm by Richard von Doenhoff and Allan Rilley.
 3 "Europ. Krieg, Kreuzerkrieg, U-53," BA-MA: RM 5/6360.
 4 Spring Rice to Governor-General, 7 Oct. 1916; NAC, RG 24, vol. 4026, file
   1062-13-13, vol. 2.
 5 Naval to Navyard, Halifax, no. 616, 8 Oct. 1916, 06.25 hours; NAC, RG 24,
   vol. 4026, file 1062-13-13, vol. 1. Cf., for example, "Arrival of German
   Submarine U-53."
 6 P.B. German, Interdepartmental Committee, to the Military Secretary,
   Interdepartmental Committee, 8 Oct. 1916; NAC, RG 24, vol. 4026, file
   1062-13-13, vol. 1.
 7 Navyard to Naval Ottawa, no. 262, 07:20 hours, 11 Oct. 1916; NAC, RG 24,
   vol. 4026, file 1062-13-13, vol. 1.
 8 Navyard to Naval Ottawa, no. 263, 07:25 hours, 11 Oct. 1916; NAC, RG 24,
   vol. 4026, file NS 1062-13-13, vol. 1.

9   Navyard to Naval Ottawa, no. 264, 07:35 hours, 11 Oct. 1916; ibid.
10 "Zur Heimkehr von U-53," *Weser-Zeitung*, 2 Nov. 1916.
11 For example, *Salzburger Chronik*, 28 Oct. 1916, no. 247, 6.
12 Pinkerton's to Dominion Police, 8 Oct. 1916; NAC, RG 24, vol. 4026, file 1062–13–13, vol. 1.
13 Bayley to Naval Ottawa, no. 1276, 14 Oct. 1916; NAC, RG 24, vol. 4026, file 1062-13-13, vol. 1.
14 See "Visit of German Submarine U-53 to Newport, R.I.," Commandant, Naval Station, Narragansett Bay, RI, to Navy Department (Operations), 7 Oct. and 12 Oct. 1916; Commander, Destroyer Force, to Commander in Chief, Atlantic Fleet, 7 Oct. 1916; also the latter's "Supplementary Report," 9 Oct. 1916, and "Second Supplementary Report," 10 Oct. 1916. A junior officer subsequently provided a "Report of Inspection, German Naval Submarine U-53," with sketch of internal arrangement and photograph of bow: Lieutenant (jg) Marc W. Larimer, USN, to Commander Destroyer Force, Atlantic Fleet, via Commanding Officer, USS *Cumming*, 6 Nov. 1916, USNOA, von Doernoff microfilm.
15 Naval to Navyard, no. 624, 9 Oct. 1916; NAC, RG 24, vol. 4026, file 1062-13-13, vol. 1.
16 Naval to Officer-in-Charge, Cape Race [Radio], 15:00 and 15:10 hours, 8 Oct. 1916; NAC, RG 24, vol. 4026, file 1062-13-13, vol. 1.
17 Naval to Navyard no. 622, 8 Oct. 1916; ibid.
18 Gwatkin to Kingsmill, 9 Oct. 1916; NAC, RG 24, vol. 4026, file 1062-13-13, vol. 1.
19 Chief of the General Staff to General Officer Commanding, Military District No. 6, Halifax 8 Oct. 1916; NAC, RG 24, vol. 4026, file 1062-13-13, vol. 1.
20 C.E. Kingsmill, "Memo for Information of the Minister," 8 Oct. 1916; NAC, RG 24, vol. 4026, file 1062-13-13, vol. 1.
21 Patrols to Naval Ottawa, no. 775, 15 Oct. 1916; NAC, RG 24, vol. 4026.
22 Town Clerk, Pictou, to G.J. Desbarats, Deputy Minister of the Navy, 17 Oct. 1916; NAC, RG 24, vol. 4026, file 1062-13-13, vol. 1.
23 G.J. Desbarats to Town Clerk, Pictou, NS, 24 Oct. 1916; NAC, RG 24, vol. 4026.
24 Naval to Navyard, no. 632, 9 Oct. 1916; NAC, RG 24, vol. 4026, file 1062-13-13, vol. 1.
25 Commander-in-chief, North America and West Indies Station, to Naval, Ottawa, no. 244, 9 Oct. 1916; NAC, RG 24, vol. 4026, file 1062-13-13, vol. 1.
26 *Halifax Herald*, 11 Oct. 1916, 1.
27 C.E. Kingsmill to Collector of Customs, Campbelton, 12 Oct. 1916; NAC, RG 24, vol. 4026, file 1062-13-13, vol. 2.
28 "Visit of German Submarine U-53," Commander, Naval Station, Narra-

gansett Bay, RI, to Navy Department (Operations), 12 Oct. 1916; USNOA, von Doenhoff microfilm.

29 Bernstorff to Secretary of State, 8 March 1916 (note no. 8), "Auswärtiges Amt, Schriftwechsel mit der Regierung der Vereinigten Staaten von Amerika, betreffend den Unterseehandelskrieg," BA-MA: RM 8/100.

30 See, for example, *New York Times*, 9 Oct. 1916, 2.

31 War Diary, U-53; BA-MA: KTB/U-53, PG 61612.

32 For the following, see War Diary, U-53 and "Europ. Kreig, Kreuzerkrieg, U-53," BA-MA: RM 5/6360. Also, Hans Rose, *Auftauchen!* and "U-53 fährt nach Amerika." Files in PRO, ADM 137/1262 and ADM 137/4131, contain the main British sources on all aspects of the North American cruises of *U-Deutschland* and U-53. We have made judicious use of the outdated official US naval report published by the Navy Department, *German Submarine Activities*, and selected use of USN reports and eye-witness accounts in newspapers.

33 "Reporting activities of German submarine in the vicinity of Nantucket Shoals Lightvessel on October 8th, 1916," 24 Oct. 1916, District Communication Superintendent, Boston Navy Yard, to Navy Department (Operations), via Director Naval Communications; USNOA, von Doenhoff microfilm. Attached to the report are "Certified copies of all radio dispatches received, transmitted and intercepted on board Nantucket Shoals Lightvessel on October 8th, 1916."

34 As cited by Captain Boy-Ed, naval attaché, Washington, 5 Aug. 1914, in "Schriftwechsel mit dem Marine-Attaché in Washington, BA-MA: RM 3/2911.

35 "Reporting activities of German submarine in the vicinity of Nantucket Shoals Lightvessel on October 8th, 1916" [and supporting documents], District Communication Superintendent, Boston Navy Yard, to Navy Department (Operations), 24 Oct. 1916; USNOA, von Doenhoff microfilm.

36 Naval to Navyard, 8 Oct. 1916; NAC, RG 24, vol. 4026, file 1062-13-13, vol. 1. The message refers specifically to *Kansan*.

37 *New York Times*, 10 Oct. 1916, 3.

38 "Report of movements; going to assistance of crews of vessels sunk by submarine," Commanding Officer, USS *Drayton*, to Commander, Destroyer Force, Atlantic Fleet, 8 Oct. 1916; USNOA, von Doenhoff microfilm.

39 See "Statement by B.J. Shimeall, Elec. 2c (R) [radio operator aboard Nantucket Shoals lightship], to District Communication Superintendent, Boston, October 23, 1916," USNOA, von Doenhoff microfilm.

40 St John's to Naval, no. 7429, 8 Oct. 1916, gave position 41° 35′N, 69°W; Navyard to Naval, no. 7422, 8 Oct. 1916; Navyard to Naval, no. 7431, 8 Oct. 1916; NAC, RG 24, vol. 4026, file 1062-13-13, vol. 2.

41 C. Clive Bayley, British Consul-General, New York, to His Majesty's Princi-

pal Secretary, Foreign Office, London, 8 Nov. 1916, PRO, ADM 137/1262, 271. Appended to this letter (pp. 272–8) is an English translation of the Dutch captain's "Extended Marine Protest" filed under oath at the Consulate-General for the Netherlands, New York, 10 Oct. 1916. Bayley had obtained it "from certain parties" for a fee of $10.14, for which he sought reimbursement.

42 These were the USS *Aylwin, Balch, Benham, Cassin, Conyngham, Cummings, Cushing, Drayton, Ericsson, Fanning, Jarvis, McCall, McDougall, Melville, O'Brian, Palding, Porter,* and *Winslow.* The logs of these vessels (USNA, RG 24) add only minor points of detail.

43 *New York Times,* 9 Oct. 1916, 2.

44 Rose, *Auftauchen!,* 178.

45 Gerard to Jagow, 10 June 1915, "Auswärtiges Amt, Schriftenwechsel mit der Regierung der Vereinigten Staaten von Amerika, betreffend den Unterseehandelskrieg," BA-MA: RM 8/100.

46 *Halifax Herald,* 9 Oct. 1916, 1.

47 "Der U-Boot-Krieg an der kanadischen Küste," *Kölnische Zeitung,* 10 Oct. 1916.

48 *New York Times,* 10 Oct. 1916, 3.

49 Reichs-Gesetzblatt, Jahrgang 1915, Nr. 49, Para. 24. See "Acta betreffend Prisenordnung und Prisengerichtsordnung," BA-MA: RM 3/4922 and RM 3/4923. Also Allerhöchste Kabinettsordres, "Verordnung, betreffend Abänderung der Prisenordnung vom 30 September 1909 ... vom 25. Juni 1917," BA-MA: RM 3/2712.

50 Oberlandsgerichtsrat Dr. Matthiessen, "Eine Unstimmigkeit in der Prisenordnung," *Leipziger Zeitschrift für Deutsches Recht,* 1915, Nr. 22, s. 1479–82, In "Acta betreffend Prisenordnung und Prisengerichtsordnung," BA-MA: RM 3/4922.

51 U-Flotilla, 18 Oct. 1916, BA-MA: RM 5/4923, 196. Not until two months later could Admiral von Holtzendorff advise the Kaiser that the Admiralty Staff had completed the long-awaited "Guide on the Law of Trade Warfare." It was "based on the German Prize Rules, as well as on any special orders that had become necessary in the course of the war, and considered all Separate agreements with neutral states." See Immediatvortrag, 8 Dec. 1916, BA-MA: RM 5/905.

52 "Report of movements; going to assistance of crews of vessels sunk by submarine," Commanding Officer, USS *Drayton,* to Commander, Destroyer Force, Atlantic Fleet, 8 Oct. 1916; USNOA, von Doenhoff microfilm. This poorly written report might also lead the reader to construe that the megaphone message had come from U-53, but this seems unlikely.

53 The incident is recorded only in the U-boat's log, doubtless because U-53 felt itself the offended party.

54 Rose, *Auftauchen!,* 178.

55 *Telegraaf,* Amsterdam, 11 Oct. 1916, BA-MA: RM 5/6360.

56 Rose, *Auftauchen!*, 180; trans MLH.

57 Ajax, *The German Pirate*, vi. Curiously, though published in 1918, the book dealt with none of the events off the American coast.

58 BA-MA: RM 5/6360 contains clippings, press cables, and summary reports gathered by German authorities through attachés and clipping services.

59 *New York Times*, 10 Oct. 1916, 2. USS *Drayton*'s Report of Proceedings (USNOA, von Doenhoff microfilm) also documented multiple sightings.

60 For example, *New York Times*, 9 Oct. 1916, 1–3.

61 The range of debate can be ascertained in the periodicals cited for 8–12 October 1916 or in reliable summaries in the *New York Times* for the same period. See also views of Rear-Admiral Bradley A. Fiske, USN, as reported on 15 Oct. 1916 in *New York Times*, the *Sun*, and other US papers. BA-MA: RM 5/6360.

62 Harry Pratt Judson, president, University of Chicago, Professor of International Law, cited in *New York Times*, 9 Oct. 1916, 3.

63 "Aftermath of U-Boat Visit," *New York Times*, 21 Oct. 1916, BA-MA: RM 5/6360.

64 28 Oct. 1916, in "Europ. Krieg, Kreuzerkrieg, U-53," BA-MA: RM 5/6360. The version published in the *Providence Journal* was translated by the Kriegspresseamt in Berlin.

65 *Pall Mall*, 26 Oct. 1916, BA-MA: RM 5/6360.

66 For example, *Salzburger Chronik*, 12 Oct. 1916, Nr. 233, 3. Stories were datelined Montreal, 10 Oct. 1916.

67 For sample advertisements see *New York Times*, 14 Nov. 1916, 13.

68 See, for example, *New York Times*, 12 Nov. 1916, 20.

69 Foreign Office to Sir C. Spring Rice, 11 Oct. 1916, 5 p.m., no. 2766, PRO, ADM 137/1262, 297–8.

70 Spring Rice to Foreign Office, 12 Oct. 1916, 11:30 p.m., no. 3095, PRO, ADM 137/1262.

71 Foreign Office, cypher telegram to Spring Rice, 18 Oct. 1916, 8 p.m., no. 2849, PRO, ADM 137/1262, 305. Also, Foreign to Secretary of the Admiralty, 18 Oct. 1916, 304.

72 Secretary, Admiralty, to Director of Naval Services, Ottawa, 29 Jan. 1917, PRO, ADM 137/1262, 315.

73 Spring Rice to Viscount Grey of Fallodon, Foreign Office, 13 Oct. 1916, no. 812, PRO, ADM 137/1262, 365–73.

74 For example, *Berliner Tageblatt*, 10 Oct. 1916, 1. The morning and evening editions for 9–11 October are particularly detailed.

75 *Manitoba Free Press*, 9 Oct. 1916, 9.

76 *Ottawa Evening Journal*, 12 Oct. 1916, 5.

77 Under-Secretary of State for External Affairs to the Governor-General's Secretary, 31 May 1915; DHIST: "European War, 1914," vol. III, print 11, item no. 216, and enclosure.

78 Lt. Col. Ernest J. Chambers to Canadian Press Ltd., Toronto, and Western

Association Press, Winnipeg, 8 Oct. 1916; NAC, RG 24, vol. 4026, file 1062-13-13, vol. 1.

79 Chambers to Clarke, Knowles, and Livsay, Press Censors, 9 Oct. 1916; ibid.

80 Spring Rice to Administrator, 26 Oct. 1916; ibid., vol. 2; also Naval, to Navyard, 28 Oct. 1916, no. 752, 16:55 hours; G.J. Desbarats to the Under-Secretary of State for External Affairs, 30 Oct. 1916.

81 Joe E. Miller to Capt. H.H. Pegler: ibid.

82 J.D. Hazen to Admiralty, no. 799; ibid.

CHAPTER EIGHT

1 For instance, von Bethmann Hollweg, *Betrachtungen*, ii, 109.

2 Holtzendorff to Generalfeldmarschall von Hindenburg, 9 March 1917, in "U-Bootkrieg 1916–18," BA-MA: RM 5/922.

3 "Chronologische Entwicklung des U-Bootkrieges 1916," Kommando der Hochseestreitkräfte," Nachlaß Leventzow, BA-MA: N 239/15, 90–103; and "Chronologische Entwicklung ... Fortsetzung 6. Oktober 1916 bis 1. Juli 1917," Nachlaß Leventzow, BA-MA: N 239/15, 144–67.

4 For instance, Wegener, *Die Seestrategie*; Kirchhoff, *Seekriegsgeschichte*.

5 Von Bethmann Hollweg to Kaiser, 9 March 1916; BA-MA: RM 5/902.

6 Palmer, *The Kaiser*, 193–5.

7 Immediatvortrag, 9 June 1916, BA-MA: RM 5/921.

8 Von Holtzendorff, "Ein Schreiben über die Notwendigkeit eines baldigen Beginns des uneingeschränkten U-Boot-Krieges," 22 Dec. 1916; BA-MA: RM 5/6726.

9 "Sitzung zu Pleß über den U-Bootskrieg," no. 7, 31 Aug. 16, BA-MA: RM 5/921.

10 "Die Frachtraum-Verteilungsmaßnahme der englischen Regierung," von Holtzendorff an Bethmann Hollweg, Reichskanzler, 27 Aug. 1916, BA-MA: RM 8/101.

11 Bernstorff, Washington, to König, Baltimore, 28 July 1916, BA-MA: RM 5/2267. See also this file, A. Lohmann to Toussaint, 5 Sept. 1916; König to Bernstorff, 20 July 1916.

12 König (*Fahrten der U-Deutschland*, 174–6) offers scant details. Much of the voyage can be reconstructed by judicious use of a variety of newspapers against the background of official files. See, for example, the story date-lined Rotterdam in *Salzburger Volksblatt*, 7 Nov. 1916, no. 255, 2. König's undated report on the second voyage is in BA-MA: RM 5/2267. Also Messismer, *The Merchant U-Boat*, 120–36.

13 As reported in the *Providence Journal*, picked up by the Amsterdam *Handelsbladed*, and repeated in the German and Austrian press. For example, *Salzburger Volksblatt*, 14 Nov. 1916, 2.

14 See, for example, *New York Times*, 11 Nov. 1916, "Nickel from Canada on the Deutschland," and *The Times*, 13 Nov. 1916, "Canadian Nickel for Germany," in BA-MA: RM 5/2269.

15 For example, "Die Zweite Fahrt der Deutschland," *Salzburger Volksblatt*, 12 Dec. 1916, 2; *New York Times*, 1 Nov. 1916, 1, and succeeding issues throughout November.

16 *New York Times*, 3 Nov. 1916, 16; also *Army and Navy Journal*, 4 Nov. 1916. The *Daily Mirror* ("No One Allowed to Go near the U-Liner," 16 Nov. 1916) published a photograph of the 'hidden' submarine behind her barricade. BA-MA: RM 5/2268.

17 For example, Lohmann, Deutsche Ozean-Rhederei, to Admiralstab der Marine, 16 Sept. 1916; Bernstorff to Reichskanzler, 10 Nov. 1916; Reichs-Postamt to Chef des Admiralstabs der Marine, 28 Dec. 1916, BA-MA: RM 5/2267.

18 König (*Fahrten der Deutschland*, 174–6) offers little detail on this event. But see, for example, "Five Men Drown as Deutschland Crashes into Tug," *New York Times*, 18 Nov. 1916, 1; "Deutschland Held by Damage Suits," *New York Times*, 19 Nov. 1916, 2; "Deutschland May Get Away Tonight," *New York Times*, 20 Nov. 1916, 10; *Halifax Herald*, 18 Nov. 1916, 1; *Salzburger Volksblatt*, 12 Dec. 1916, 2. Also *New York Times*, 17 Nov. 1916, 1; "Submarine Deutschland Has Sailed," *Halifax Herald*, 17 Nov. 1916, 1. Cf. Messimer, *Merchant U-Boat*, 137–55.

19 "U-Boat Alarm Sent to Incoming Ships," *New York Times*, 26 Nov. 1916, 1.

20 *Halifax Herald*, 28 Nov. 1916, 1.

21 Recruiting ads: "The Royal Navy Needs Canadians," *Halifax Herald*, 7 Nov. 1916, 5; "The Royal Naval Canadian Volunteer Reserve – Overseas Division," *Halifax Herald*, 11 Nov. 1916, 14; "Admiral Jellicoe Calls for Canadians," *Halifax Herald*, 18 Nov. 1916, 9; headlines and article "5000 Canadians Will Be Recruited for Navy," *Halifax Herald*, 29 Nov. 1916, 1.

22 Admiralty to Colonial Office, 7 Nov. 1916, file M.09362/16, forwarded by Colonial Secretary (in London) to Governor-General in (Ottawa), 14 Nov. 1916, NAC, RG 25, G-1, box 1161, file 558–1915-C. "European War Prints," vol. VII, no. 33, item 294–5.

23 Borden Diary, 13 Nov. 1916, NAC, RG 24, reel C-1864.

24 Copy in NAC, RG 24, box 3831, NS 1017-10-1, vol. 1; also in DCER, I, 155–6.

25 Minute sheet 308, minuted by INS [?], 2 Jan. 1917, PRO, ADM 116/1400.

26 Admiralty to Colonial Office, 7 Jan. 1917, ibid.; copy in NS 1017-10-1, vol. 1, NAC, RG 24, box 3831.

27 Commander-in-Chief, Home Fleets, to Secretary, Admiralty, 16 Oct. 1916, PRO, ADM 137/1262, 316.

28 Secretary, Admiralty, to Director of Naval Service, Ottawa, 29 Jan. 1917, PRO, ADM 137/1262, 315.

29 Wilhelm J.R. [Kaiser Willhelm], "An Meine Marine," 1 Feb. 1917, "Allerhöchste Kabinetts-Ordres," BA-MA: RM 3/2711; also RM 5/922.

30 War Diary, U-53; BA-MA: KTB/U-53, PG 61612.

31 These were projects 46 and 47. See, for example, A. [Admiral Hebbing-haus], "Gutachtliche Äusserungen von A zu dem Projekt 47 der U.I.," in "Ubootkreuzer," BA-MA: RM 3/4914, 34–47; and B [Admiral Krafft], "Bei-trag zum Immediatvortrag, betreffend 4000t U-Kreuzer," BA-MA: RM 3/4914, 61–6.

32 Desbarats Diary, 11, 15, 16 Jan. and 14 Feb. 1917, NAC, MG 30E89, vol. 5; Director of the Naval Service, "Memorandum for the Information of the Minister," 26 Jan. 1917, NAC, MG 26H, vol. 7, 39492; Daniel G. Harris, "Canadian Warship Construction 1917–19," 149–58.

33 Marder, *Dreadnought to Scapa*, III, 324; IV, 63–5; Fayle, *Seaborne Trade*, III, 80–1, 102–3, 253. See, especially, Director of Contracts, minute, 30 Nov. 1916, PRO, ADM 116/1400.

34 Anderson, minute, 4 Feb. 1917, PRO, ADM 116/1400; Foster to Borden, telegram 21 March 1917, NS 1065-7-2, NAC, RG 24, vol. 4031; Borden to Blount, telegram, 30 March 1917, NAC, MG 26H, reel C-4314, 35454; Kings-mill to Admiralty, NS 1017-10-1, pt. 1, 22 Nov. 1917, NAC, RG 24, vol. 3831.

35 Borden to Perley, 13 and 28 Oct. 1916, DCER, I, 144–7; Governor-General to Colonial Secretary, 24 Nov. 1916, ibid., 151; Borden to Perley, 12 Nov. 1917, ibid., 184–5; W.H. Lynch to Desbarats, 11 Dec. 1917, NS 29-16-1, pt. 2, NAC, RG 24, vol. 5604; Norcross to Ballantyne, 12 Jan. 1918, NS 29-16-1, pt. 3, NAC, RG 24, vol. 5605; A.A. Wright to Desbarats, 18 Sept. 1918, NS 29-16-1, pt. 6, ibid.

36 Carson to prime minister, 8 Feb. 1917; deputy minister to Governor-General's secretary, 11 Feb. 1917; Naval to Admiralty, 13 Feb. 1917; Naval to Navyard Esquimalt, 13 Feb. 1917, NS 1065-7-2, NAC, RG 24, vol. 4031; Canada, Department of the Naval Service, *Naval Intelligence Report*, no. 11 (12 March 1917), no. 12 (19 March 1917); Historical Records Officer to Senior Canadian Naval Officer (London), 12 Jan. 1944, DHIST, NHS 1700–903; Canada, *Auditor General's Report*, year ending 31 March 1918, ZZ 246–7; NHS, "Brief History of HMCS *Rainbow*."

37 Walter Hose, "The Early Years of the Royal Canadian Navy," 19 Feb. 1960, 12, Hose Papers, file B/3, DHIST.

38 Admiralty to Commander-in-Chief, North America and West Indies Sta-tion (C-in-C, NA&WI), 13 April 1917; C-in-C, NA&WI, to NHSQ, Ottawa, 22 April 1917, NS 1001-19-4, NAC, RG 24, vol. 6197; C-in-C, NA&WI, to director of the Naval Service, 2 May 1917, NSC 1001-5-3, ibid., vol. 6194.

39 Director of the Naval Service, to C-in-C, NA&WI, 24 April and 9 May 1917; Stores, memorandum, 23 May 1917, NSC 1001-5-3, NAC, RG 24, vol. 6194.

40 Desbarats Diary, 29 May 1917, NAC, MG 30E89, vol. 5. See also Borden (in London) to prime minister's office, 24 April 1917; director of Naval

Service, memorandum, 30 May 1917, NSC 1001-5-3, NAC, RG 24, vol. 6194; c-in-c, NA&WI, general letter, 10 June 1917, PRO, ADM 137/504.

41 c-in-c, NA&WI, general letter, 29 June 1917, PRO, ADM 137/504; NHS 8000 "Premier," DHIST; McKee, *Armed Yachts*, 34; "Information Regarding Marine Defence of Defended Ports in Canada," 1 July 1917, NS 1010-11-1, NAC, RG 24, vol. 3809; HQC 1723 pts. 1–2, NAC, RG 24, vols. 2533–4; *Naval Intelligence Report*, no. 29 (16 July 1917); Stephens to Director of the Naval Service, 5 April 1917, Martin to Secretary, Department of the Naval Service, 28 July 1917, NS 1001-19-4, NAC, RG 24, vol. 6197.

42 See notes on movements, June–November 1917 from NS 1047-5-7, DHIST: NHS 8000 series by ship names. These notes are especially valuable because the original files have been destroyed.

43 Command memorandum to Commodore Patrols, 23 May 1917, Commodore Patrols to Secretary, Department of the Naval Service, 20 June 1917, NS 1065-7-3, NAC, RG 24, vol. 4023, Coke to Director of the Naval Service, 19 July 1917, NS 1065-2-1, pt. 1, NAC, RG 24, vol. 4030 (see also NS 1065-4-3).

44 Beesly, *Room 40*, 106, 110–11, 115, 120–1.

45 Kingsmill to deputy minister, 16 Jan. 1917, NS 1065-7-2, NAC, RG 24, vol. 4031.

46 Admiralty to Coke, 21 Feb. 1917, NS 1065-7-2, NAC, RG 24, vol. 4031.

47 Kingsmill to Coke, 16 April 1917, NS 1065-7-3, NAC, RG 24, vol. 4031.

48 Command memorandum to Coke, 30 april 1917, NS 1065-7-3, NAC, RG 24, vol. 4031.

49 Long to Governor-General, 22 June 1917, NS 1065-7-3, NAC, RG 24, vol. 4031.

50 Kingsmill, memorandum, 24 June 1917, NS 1065-7-3, NAC, RG 24, vol. 4031; Desbarats Diary, 27 April 1917, NAC, MG 30E89, vol. 5.

51 Kingsmill to Admiralty, 15 Aug. 1917, NS 1065-7-3, NAC, RG 24, vol. 4031.

52 Americans were as unprepared for war in the western Atlantic as in the "operational backwater" of the Caribbean. Yerxa, "The United States Navy," 182–7.

53 Fayle, *Seaborne Trade*, III, 128.

54 For this and the following, see US Congress, *Naval Investigation*, Mayo testimony, 578–7.

55 Ibid., Pratt testimony, 1230, 1329–33.

56 Dittmar and Colledge, *British Warships*, 20–1.

57 Corbett, *Naval Operations*, IV, 380.

58 Jellicoe to British naval attaché, cited in Marder, *Dreadnought to Scapa Flow*, IV, 145.

59 Cronon, *Daniels*, 132.

60 Trask, *Captains and Cabinets*, 47–9, 55; Dean C. Allard, "Anglo-American

Naval Differences During World War I," *Military Affairs*, 44 (April 1980): 75–6.

61 Admiralty, *Naval Staff History*, VIII (Home Waters, pt. VIII), 367–8; for an excellent description of factions within the department see Friedel, *Franklin D. Roosevelt*, 1, chaps. 13–19.

62 Admiralty, *Naval Staff History*, VIII, 366.

63 Browning to Admiralty, 13 April 1917, cited in *Naval Investigation*, 1333–4.

64 Berton, *Vimy*, 295.

65 Sims, *The Victory At Sea*, 1.

66 Beesly, *Room 40*, 245–6; also Sims, *Victory*, 3.

67 Morison, *Admiral Sims*.

68 Jellicoe, *The Crisis of the Naval War*, 116.

69 Sims, *Victory*, 8–9.

70 Sims to Secretary of the Navy, 14 April 1917, cited in ibid., 374–60.

71 Cronon, *Daniels*, 135.

72 Beesly, *Room 40*, 245–6. See also US Navy Department, *German Submarine Activities*, 9.

73 Sims, *Victory*, 8.

74 Cited in ibid., 9.

75 Trask, *Captains and Cabinets*, 74–7 and chap. 3; also Cronon, *Daniels*, 139, 142–5; *Naval Investigation*, Badger testimony, 1117, Pratt testimony, 1233–4.

76 *Naval Investigation*, Badger testimony, 1127; Pratt testimony, 1209–21; McKeen testimony, 1784–5.

77 Campaign Order no. 2, Submarine Force, Atlantic Fleet, USNA, RG 45, box 157, SF:1C-7; cited in Yerxa, "The United States Navy." It is not clear whether US Naval Intelligence informed the Canadians.

78 *Naval Investigation*, Badger testimony, 1144, 1162; also Maurer, "American Naval Concentration," 168–9, 172–3.

79 Ibid., 1107–9; Pratt testimony, 1235.

80 Sims to Pratt, 26 July 1917, cited in Trask, *Captains and Cabinets*, 90.

81 Notes on NSC 1065-7-4, DHIST: NHS 1550–157/1.

82 Barclay to Governor-General, 26 May 1917; Naval Ottawa, to commander-in-chief, 8 June 1917; director of Naval Service to Chief of Staff, 8 June 1917; Chief of Staff to director of the Naval Service, 8 June 1917; Naval Ottawa to British Embassy, Washington, for Stephens, 11 June 1917, NS 1065-7-3, NAC, RG 24, vol. 4031.

83 Stephens to director of the Naval Service, 15 June 1917, NS 1065-7-3, NAC, RG 24, vol. 4031. Also Stephens to Gaunt, 13 June 1917.

84 "Die allgemeine Kriegslage in ihrer jetzigen Entscheidungsphase," 30 April 1917, BA-MA: RM 5/922. For Germany's reasons for regarding it as a criminal act, see Vincent, *The Politics of Hunger*.

85 For example, "Der Staatssekretär des Innern über den U-Boot-Krieg," *Berliner Lokal-Anzeiger*, 29 April 1917, no. 216, BA-MA: RM 5/922.

86 Corbett and Newbolt, *Naval Operations*, v, 424; Great Britain, Air Ministry, Air Historical Branch, "The RAF in Maritime War," Vol. 1: "The Atlantic and Home Waters, The Prelude, April 1918 to September 1939," appendix 1.

87 Corbett and Newbolt, *Naval Operations*, v, 25–7; Fayle, *Seaborne Trade*, III, 68, 89, 92, and chap. 8.

88 Fayle, *Seaborne Trade*, III, 480.

89 Marder, *Dreadnought to Scapa Flow*, IV, 184–92.

90 See, for example, Allard, "Anglo-American Naval Differences," 78–80.

91 Marder, *Dreadnought to Scapa Flow*, IV, 269–70; Admiralty, *Atlantic Convoy System*, 153; Canada, Department of the Naval Service, *Naval Intelligence Reports*, 1917–18, includes lists of all ships that sailed in convoy from Halifax and Sydney. However, troop-ship convoys never included more than fourteen ships, and often fewer than ten.

92 Admiralty, *Atlantic Convoy System*, 126.

93 Naval Ottawa to Transports Sydney, signal 953, 3 July 1917, G. 48-48-1, NAC, RG 24, vol. 5645.

94 He had, however, been specifically enjoined to keep the commander-in-chief, North America and West Indies Station, fully informed and to follow any instructions his senior British officer might give. See Secretary of the Admiralty to Chambers, 20 July 1917 and enclosure, G. 48-48-1, NAC, RG 24, vol. 5645; see also Admiralty, *Atlantic Convoy System*, 52–3, 56, 63–5.

95 Kingsmill to deputy minister, 21 Nov. 1917, NS 1048-48-1, pt. 3, NAC, RG 24, vol. 3773; also Long to Governor General, 19 Nov. 1917, NS 1048-48-1, pt. 1, NAC, RG 24, vol. 3772.

96 Navyard Esquimalt to Naval Ottawa, personal for Kingsmill, 23 Dec. 1917; Kingsmill to minister, 18 Jan. 1918; Command memorandum, 31 Jan. 1918, HQ 60-S-3, NPRC.

97 Edmonds, *A Short History*, 252.

98 Long to Governor General, 16 Oct. 1917, G. 23-4-3 pt. 1, NAC, RG 24, reel C-5848.

99 Stephens to Kingsmill, 22 Oct. 1917, G 23-4-3 pt. 1, NAC, RG 24, reel C-5848. Also Kingsmill to minister, 25 Oct. 1917; deputy minister to under-secretary of state, External Affairs, 1 Nov. 1917, G. 23-4-3 pt. 1, NAC, RG 24, reel C-5848.

100 See, for example, W.G.D. Lund, "The Royal Canadian Navy's Quest for Autonomy in the North West Atlantic," in Boutilier, *RCN in Retrospect*, 138–57.

101 Lois Kernaghan, "Halifax Explosion," *The Canadian Encyclopedia*, 1985, II, 788.

102 Hugh MacLennan, *Barometer Rising* (Toronto: McClelland and Stewart, 1958), 187, 195. For an imaginative and authentic account of the explosion as experienced by Haligonians see 150ff.

103 Bird, *The Town That Died*, chap. 9. The initial inquiry by Mr Justice Drysdale had concluded in February 1918 that the navy had not properly regulated shipping traffic.

104 Horn, *German Naval Mutinies*, 183. Horn's study is definitive. See also his translation of *The World War I Diary of Seaman Richard Strumpf*.

105 Horn, *Naval Mutinies*, 235.

106 Scheer, 31 Dec. 1917, in "U-Bootskrieg 1916–18," BA-MA: RM 5/922.

107 Scheer, 31 Jan. 1917, BA-MA: RM 5/922.

108 Von Holtzendorff to Staatssekretär des Reichs-Marine-Amts, 9 June 1917, BA-MA: RM 5/3902.

109 For example, "Kurze Denkschrift über die militärischen Anforderungen an einen grossen U-Kreuzer als Handelszerstörer," in "Ubootskreuzer," BA-MA: RM 3/4914. See also, "UK-Verband. Kabelschneiden und Minenangelegenheiten," BA-MA: RM 5/6439.

110 Allerhöchste Kabinetts-Ordre, 22 Dec. 1917, BA-MA: RM 3/2714.

111 von Holtzendorff to von Bethmann Hollweg, 4 May 1917, BA-MA: RM 5/922.

112 *Hamlet*, III, i.

CHAPTER NINE

1 Hatcher, memorandum, 3 Oct. 1917, NS 1017-10-3; NAC, RG 24, vol. 3832.

2 Kingsmill to deputy minister, 30 Oct. 1917, NS 1017-10-3; NAC, RG 24, vol. 3832.

3 Hatcher, memorandum, 3 Oct. 1917, NS 1017-10-3, NAC, RG 24, vol. 3832.

4 Hose, 23 Sept. 1917, NS 1017-10-3; NAC, RG 24, vol. 3832.

5 Director of Naval Service to Secretary of the Admiralty, 22 Nov. 1917, NSS 1017-10-1 pt. 1; NAC, RG 24, vol. 3831; Kingsmill to deputy minister, 30 Oct. 1917, and following correspondence, NS 1017-10-3; NAC, RG 24, vol. 3832.

6 Conclusion based on extremely sparse coverage in Canadian Intelligence files of German naval operations in 1917. See, for example, NSC 1062-13-2, pt. 2; NAC, RG 24, vol. 4021.

7 Grant, *U-Boat Intelligence*, 147–8; Admiralty, Naval Staff, Intelligence Department, June 1918, "Proceedings of Enemy Submarines, Converted Mercantile Type, In the Atlantic May 1917 to April 1918 (ID 1181)," copy in file JA 2, USNA, RG 45, subject file 1911–27, box 184.

8 Rear-Admiral H.T. Mayo, USN, report on visit to England 27 Aug. to 4 Oct. 1917, printed in US Congress, Hearing, Senate 1921, *Naval Investigation*, vol. 185, pt. 2, p. 598 (Sims investigation).

9 Admiralty to Under-Secretary of State, Colonial Office, 3 Jan. 1918, NS 1017-10-1, pt. 1; NAC, RG 24, vol. 3831.

10 Admiralty memorandum M-015744, 3 Jan. 1918, NS 1017-10-1, pt. 1; NAC, RG 24, vol. 3831.

11 Browning, general letter, 1 and 30 Dec. 1917, 1 Feb. 1918, PRO, ADM 137/504; Department of the Naval Service, "Drifters Built in Canada," 3 March 1919, NS 1065-7-6, NAC, RG 24, vol. 4031.

12 Admiralty to Colonial Office, 3 Jan. 1918, NS 1017-10-1, pt. 1; NAC, RG 24, vol. 3831.

13 Hose to Secretary, Department of the Naval Service, 15 Jan. 1918, NS 1017-10-4; NAC, RG 24, vol. 3832.

14 Marder, *From the Dreadnought to Scapa Flow*, IV, 341.

15 Grant to Secretary, Department of the Naval Service, 2 March 1918, enclosing copy of his signal to Admiralty, NS 1065-7-6; NAC, RG 24, vol. 4031; Grant, general letter, 1 March 1918; PRO, ADM 137/504, ff. 316–21.

16 Minutes of 11–16 March 1918, Minute sheet no. 418; PRO, ADM 116/1400.

17 Grant, general letter, 1 April 1918; PRO, ADM 137/504, ff. 330–1.

18 Trask, *Captains and Cabinets*, 181–2.

19 "Defence against submarine attack in home waters," A Special Board to Formulate a Plan of Defense in Home Waters, to Chief of Naval Operations, 6 Feb. 1918, printed in *Naval Investigation*.

20 Grant, general letters, 1 April 1918, PRO, ADM 137/504, 331–2.

21 Grant to Naval Ottawa, signal, 18 March 1918; Grant to Naval Ottawa, signal, 3 April 1918; Naval Ottawa to Commander in Chief, Washington, 4 April 1918, NS 1065-7-6, NAC, RG 24, vol. 4031.

22 Grant, general letter, 1 April 1918, PRO, ADM 137/504, 331–2.

23 Benson to Sims, cable 4640, 01 [10?] April 1918, file KD, USNA, RG 45, subject file 1911–1927, box 221.

24 Sims to OpNav, Washington, cable 6352, 11 April 1918, file KD, USNA, RG 45, subject file 1911–1927, box 221.

25 Grant to Admiralty, telegram, 18 April 1918; PRO, ADM 116/1400, 507.

26 Admiralty to Colonial Office, letter M.02687, 7 March 1918, NSC 1017-10-7, pt. 1; NAC, RG 24, vol. 3833.

27 Desbarats Diary, 14, 18, and 19 March 1918; NAC, MG 30E89, vol. 5.

28 Grant, general letter, 3 May 1918; PRO, ADM 137/504, ff. 345–6.

29 Cited in Edmonds, *A Short History*, 306.

30 Hose to Director of Naval Service, 20 April 1918, NS 1017-10-7; NAC, RG 24, vol. 3833; Grant, general letter, 3 May 1918; PRO, ADM 137/504, f. 346.

31 Naval History Division, *Dictionary of American Naval Fighting Ships*, VI, 711–12; Friedel, *Roosevelt*, 310–11.

32 Congress, Senate, *Naval Investigation*, 1921, vol. 185, pt. 2, 1236, 1249.

33 Hose to Director of the Naval Service, 20 April 1918, NAC, RG 24, vol. 3831.

34 Hose correspondence; "Report on use of aircraft in conjunction with

Canadian patrol flotillas," Captain H.V. Haggard, RN, chief of staff, to Commander-in-Chief, NSC 1017-10-7, pt. 1; NAC, RG 24, vol. 3833 (copies of this and several other documents on the proposed Canadian air patrol are in file WA-2, USNA, RG 45, subject file 1911–1927, box 599); Grant, general letter, 3 May 1918; PRO, ADM 137/504, ff. 347–9.

35 Admiralty to Colonial Office, 3 Jan. 1918, forwarding Admiralty memorandum M-015744, 3 Jan. 1918; NAC, RG 24, box 3831, NS 1017-10-1; DHIST: NHS, 1440–11, extracts from NS 1065-7-6; NAC, RG 24, box 3833, NSC 1017-10-7, vol. 1.

36 Wood to Secretary of the Navy (Operations), 25 April 1918, enclosing "Recommendations of conference held at Boston ... ," NSC 1017-10-5, pt. 1; NAC, RG 24, vol. 3833 (copy also in file TT, USNA, RG 45, subject file 1911–1927, box 564).

37 "Machias Section," "History of the First Naval District," 25, file ZPN; USNA, RG 45, subject file 1911–1927, box 818.

38 Hose to Admiral Superintendent, Halifax, 26 June 1918; Stanwood to Commandant, First Naval District, 26 July 1918; Wood to Chief of Naval Operations, 23 Nov. 1918, file PN-1; USNA, RG 45, subject file 1911–1927, box 411.

39 District Communications Superintendent, First Naval District, to Hines, 6 July 1918; Assistant General Manager, Maritime Telephone and Telegraph, to Hines, 15 and 16 July 1918, file P-1/2; USNA, RG 38, entry 198, box 2. Also Daniels to Admiral Superintendent, Halifax, 22 May 1918; Commander-in-Chief to Naval Ottawa, signal 36, 12 July 1918; Navyard Halifax to Naval Ottawa, signal 793, 15 July 1918, NS 1065-7-6; NAC, RG 24, vol. 4031; Admiralty to Naval Ottawa, signal 672, 16 June 1918; PRO, ADM 116/1400, f. 526.

40 Secretary, Admiralty, to Under-Secretary of State, Colonial Office, NAC, RG 24, box 3832, NSC 1017-10-6. See also R.M. Stephens to Minister of the Naval Service, 13 March 1918, NAC, RG 24, box 3832, NSC 1017-10-6.

41 US CNO to US Naval Intelligence Officer, Halifax, NS, 4 April 1918, NAC, RG 24, box 3832, NSC 1017-10-6.

42 Chief of Staff to Director of the Naval Service, 15 March 1918, NAC, RG 24, box 3832, NSC 1017-10-6.

43 Chief of Staff to Superintendent of Fisheries, 15 March 1918, NAC, RG 24, box 3832, NSC 17-10-6.

44 Superintendent to Inspectors of Fisheries, Pictou and Digby, NS, 22 March 1918, NAC, RG 24, box 3832, NSC 1017-10-6.

45 Director of Naval Service to Commander-in-Chief, North America and West Indies Station (C-in-C, NA&WI) (at Washington), 29 April 1918, NAC, RG 24, box 3832, NSC 1017-10-6.

46 Inspector of Fisheries, Pictou, to Deputy Minister of the Naval Service, 30 March 1918, NAC, RG 24, box 3832, NSC 1017-10-6; and Inspector of Fisheries, Digby, to Superintendent, 15 April 1918, ibid.

47 Admiralty to Naval Ottawa, signal 140, 22 March 1918, NAC, RG 24, box 3832, NSC 1017-10-6.

48 C-in-C, NA&WI (at Washington) to Naval Ottawa, signal 21.21, 28 April 1918, NAC, RG 24, box 3832, NSC 1017-10-6; Vice-Admiral Grant, C-in-C, NA&WI, to Director of Naval Service, Ottawa, 14 May 1918, NAC, RG 24, box 3832, NSC 1017-10-6.

49 Kingsmill, to C-in-C, NA&WI, 22 May 1918, NAC, RG 24, box 3832.

50 Governor of Newfoundland to Governor General of Canada, 1 June 1918, NAC, RG 24, box 3832.

51 Captain of Patrols to the Secretary, Department of the Naval Service, 11 June 1918, NAC, RG 24, box 3832, NSC 1017-10-6.

52 Governor of Newfoundland to Governor General of Canada, 1 June 1918, NAC, RG 24, box 3832, NSC 1017-10-6.

53 Grant to Kingsmill, 3 July 1918, NAC, RG 24, box 3832, NSC 1017-10-6.

54 Captain of Patrols, Sydney, NS., to the Secretary, Department of the Naval Service, 12 Sept. 1918, NAC, RG 24, box 3832, NSC 1017-10-6.

55 "Information regarding Marine Defences of Defended Ports ... ," 1 April 1918, NS 1010-11-1; NAC, RG 24, vol. 3810.

56 Director of Naval Service to minister, 20 Feb. 1918; same to same, 21 Feb. 1918, enclosing draft of the Hose scheme; deputy minister to Under-Secretary of State for External Affairs (USSEA), 8 March 1918, enclosing "Memorandum on Organization of Atlantic Patrols [final draft of the Hose scheme]," NS 1017-10-1, pt. 1; NAC, RG 24, vol. 3831.

57 Director of Naval Service to minister (March 1918), NS 1017-10-4; NAC, RG 24, vol. 3832, "Report on condition of new TR vessels on arrival at Halifax" (July 1918), NS 29-16-1, pt. 5; NAC, RG 24, vol. 5605.

58 Hose to Secretary, Department of the Naval Service, "List of Ships and Appointments," 7 Jan. 1919, NS 29-16-1 pt. 7, copy in DHIST: NHS, 1440–11. Admiralty subsequently increased the initial allocation of trawlers from 30 to 36.

59 "Report on condition of new TR vessels on arrival at Halifax" (July 1918), NS 29-16-1, pt. 5, NAC, RG 24, vol. 5605.

60 Captain of Patrols to Secretary, Department of the Naval Service (report on condition of trawlers on arrival at Sydney), 28 June 1918, NS 29-16-1, pt. 5; NAC, RG 24, vol. 5605.

61 Skentelbery to Department of the Naval Service, 10 Aug. 1918, NS 58-12-3; NAC, RG 24, vol. 5657.

62 Canada, Auditor General, *Report* for year ending 31 March 1919, "War Appropriations Department of Naval Service," pp. ZZ 245–6, ZZ 275, ZZ 287, ZZ 289, ZZ 290–1, shows that at least fifty-eight patrol vessels were repaired or altered by civilian firms at Halifax, Sydney, Pictou, and Saint John, at a total cost of around $300,000.

63 Hose to Secretary, Department of the Naval Service, 19 Aug. 1918, NS 58-9-4; NAC, RG 24, vol. 5657.

64 Hose to Secretary, Department of the Naval Service, 13 September 1918, NS 58-9-3; NAC, RG 24, vol. 5647. Commander (G), Sydney, to Captain of Patrols, 20 Sept. 1918; Ballantyne and Welsford to Captain of Patrols, 3 Oct. 1918, NS 58-9-1; NAC, RG 24, vol. 5657.

65 Canada, Auditor General, *Report* for year ending 31 March 1919, "War Appropriations, Department of Naval Service," ZZ 284–5.

66 See table of "Manning Requirements" in "Memorandum on Organization of Atlantic Patrols," f. 87, forwarded by deputy minister, to USSEA, 8 March 1918, NS 1017-10-1, pt. 1; NAC, RG 24, vol. 3831. The accountant officer, HMCS *Niobe*, informed the chief accountant, Department of Naval Service, on 25 May 1918 (NS 58-53-30, pt. 1; NAC, RG 24, vol. 5662) that ninety Newfoundland ratings had served in the patrols since late 1917. But as the same file indicates that at least 229 Newfoundlanders ultimately served in the patrols, with very few arriving after the spring of 1918, additional Newfoundland ratings in all likelihood arrived prior to spring.

67 Admiralty to Naval Ottawa, signal, 4 July 1918, NS 1065-7-6; NAC, RG 24, vol. 4031. Also Accounting Officer, HMCS *Niobe*, to Accounting Officer HMS *Briton*, 28 Aug. 1918 (NS 58-53-30, pt. 1; NAC, RG 24, vol. 5662), lists twenty-six Newfoundlanders transferred to Canadian pay rates on 14 June 1918.

68 Minutes, 13 April–4 May 1918; PRO, ADM 116/1400, ff. 462–4.

69 Director of Naval Service to minister, 20 Feb. 1918, NS 1017-10-1, pt. 1; NAC, RG 24, vol. 3831.

70 Derived from comparison of the various listings for chief skippers, skippers and mates in Department of the Naval Service, *The Canadian Navy List*, January, April, and August 1918.

71 Hose to Secretary, Department of Naval Service, 21 Sept. 1918, NS 1065-7-12; NAC, RG 24, vol. 4032.

72 *TR 30* log, 18 July 1918; NAC, RG 24, vol. 7943; "Men of the Canadian Naval Service Tried by Court Martial," DHIST: 82/401, pt. 4.

73 Holme to Admiral Superintendent, Halifax, 13 Feb. 1918; same to same, n.d.; Admiral Superintendent, Halifax, to Secretary, Department of the Naval Service, 25 Feb. 1918; Command Memo, to Admiral Superintendent, 25 March 1918, NS 58-53-30, pt. 1; NAC, RG 24, vol. 5662.

74 File NS 47-23-A–129, NRPC.

75 Chatterton, *Auxiliary Patrol*, 48.

76 LCDR Lewis P. Clephane, USNRF, "History of the Submarine Chasers in the World War," n.d., file ZOD, USNA, RG 45, subject file 1911–1927, box 802E, 21–8.

77 For example, Director of the Naval Service to deputy minister, 30 Oct. 1917, NS 1017-10-3: NAC, RG 24, vol. 3832.

78 The engine-room personnel, for example, had "excellent training in the Navy Gas Engine School." Clephane, "History of the Submarine Chasers," file ZOD, USNA, RG 45, subject file 1911–1927, box 802E, 27.

79 Zimmermann, Auswärtiges Amt, to von Holtzendorff, 14 April 1917; and von Holtzendorff to von Bethmann Hollweg, 4 May 1917; BA-MA: RM 5/922.

80 von Holtzendorff to Auswärtiges Amt, 26 Jan. 1918, BA-MA: RM 5/3902, 144ff.

81 Vincent, *The Politics of Hunger*, 44.

82 Ops V, 2 Feb. 1918, BA-MA: RM 5/3902, 145–6 and versos.

83 von Holtzendorff to Auswärtiges Amt, 26 Jan. 1918, "U.K.-Verband," BA-MA: RM 5/3902, 144.

84 Kkpt. Koch, "Betrifft Ausdehnung des U-Kreuzerkrieges auf die Ostküste der Vereinigten Staaten," 2 Feb. 1918, BA-MA: RM 5/3902.

85 Perière to Kapitän [anon], 23 Jan. 1918, BA-MA: RM 5/3902, 149–50.

86 For example, "Zum Thronvortrag," 28 Feb. 1918, BA-MA: RM 5/907, 87–92.

87 For example, Immediatvortrag, 19 June 1918, BA-MA: RM 5/907.

88 Koch to von Holtzendorff, "Betrifft Ausdehnung des U-Kreuzerkrieges auf die Ostküste der Vereinigten Staaten," 2 Feb. 1918, BA-MA: RM 5/3902.

89 Koch to von Holtzendorff, "Vorgang: Admiralstab 2053 Op. V vom 7.11.18. Betrifft Ausdehnung des U-Kreuzerkrieges auf die Ostküste Nordamerikas," 9 March 1918, BA-MA: RM 5/3902.

90 Koch to von Holtzendorff, 9 June 1918, BA-MA: RM 5/6440.

91 Koch, Kommando des Unterseekreuzerverbandes, to von Holtzendorff, Chef des Admiralstabes der Marine, "Sperrgebiet an der nordamerikanischen Ostküste," 12 June 1918, BA-MA: RM 5/6440, 83–7.

92 von Holtzendorff to U-Kreuzer-Verband and Kommando des Heeres, 20 June 1918, BA-MA: RM 5/6440.

93 Spindler, *Der Krieg zur See*, V, 232.

94 War Diary, KTB/U-155, 23 May 1917–5 Sept. 1917; BA-MA: RM 97/1123.

95 Minutes, "Sitzung bei S.E. dem Herrn Reichskanzler am Sonntag, den 23. Juni, 11 Vm [a.m.]," 21 June 1918, BA-MA: RM 5/6440, 118–26.

96 Admiralstab Op. IV, Chef des Marinekabinetts im Gefolge Sr. Majaestät, 26 June 1918, BA-MA: RM 5/6440.

97 Kapitän z. See Horn, "Gesichtspunkte für die bisherige U-Bootskriegführung," 6 Aug. 1918, BA-MA: RM 5/6440, 180–5.

CHAPTER TEN

1 Navyard Halifax to Naval Ottawa, signal 180, NS 1048-48-1 pt. 4, NAC, RG 24, vol. 3773.

2 Admiralty, *Atlantic Convoy System*, 134.

3 Unsigned memorandum, 27 March 1918, minuted "Seen by DM and Minister," NS 1048-48-12, NAC, RG 24, vol. 3775.

4 Grant, general letter, 1 June 1918, PRO, ADM 137/504, f. 364; Naval Secretary, Interdepartmental Committee, to Military Secretary, Interdepartmental Committee, 8 April 1918, NS 1048-48-3, pt. 3, NAC, RG 24, vol. 3775.

5 Grant, general letter, 1 June 1918, PRO, ADM 137/504, 328–9.

6 Grant to Naval Ottawa, signal 0145, 27 April 1918, in Naval Secretary, Interdepartmental Committee, to Military Secretary, Interdepartmental Committee, 27 April 1918, NS 1048-48-12, NAC, RG 24, vol. 3775. Also Admiralty, *Atlantic Convoy System*, 137.

7 Naval to Britannia, signal 21.18, 27 April 1918, NS 1048-48-12, NAC, RG 24, vol. 3775.

8 Commander-in-Chief, North America and West Indies Station, to Naval Ottawa, signal 18.21, 28 April 1918, NS 1048-48-12, NAC, RG 24, vol. 3775; Ballantyne to Britannia, signal 03.05, 29 April 1918, NS 1048-48-12, NAC, RG 24, vol. 3775.

9 Admiralty, *Atlantic Convoy System*, 137, 143–4; Captain Superintendent, HMC Dockyard, Halifax, to Secretary, Department of the Naval Service, 5 Sept. 1919, enclosing "Summary of Troops Embarked in ... HC Convoys," NS 1048-48-8, pt. 2, NAC, RG 24, vol. 3775.

10 Admiral Superintendent, Halifax Dockyard, to Director of the Naval Service, 5 Aug. 1918, NS 1065-7-6, NAC, RG 24, vol. 4031. Also "*DeLong*" in US Naval Historical Division, *Dictionary*, II, 257, "*Tingey*," VII, 201; *Tingey* log, May–Nov. 1918, USNA, RG 24; no log is available for *DeLong*.

11 Lewis P. Clephane, "History of the Submarine Chasers," file ZOD, USNA RG 45, subject file 1911–1927, box 802E, 23.

12 Hose to Secretary, Department of Naval Service, 22 May 1918; Submarine Chaser Division Commander to Admiral Superintendent, Halifax Dockyard, 19 June 1918, NS 1065-7-6, NAC, RG 24, vol. 4031; logs of *SC 51* and *SC 240*, May–Nov. 1918, USNA, RG 24. The vessels were *SC 51*, *183*, *240*, *241*, *242*, and *247*.

13 Hose to Secretary, Department of the Naval Service, 12 June 1918, NS 1065-7-6, NAC, RG 24, vol. 4031.

14 Admiralty, *Atlantic Convoy System*, 137.

15 Kingsmill to Admiralty, 18 July 1918, NS 1065-7-6, NAC, RG 24, vol. 4031; NHS notes from NS 1057-4-30 and NS 1057-4-31 in DHIST: NHS 8000 "Trawlers and Drifters," pt. 2; *PV VII* log, NAC, RG 24, vol. 7761.

16 HMCS *Laurentian* log, 11 Aug. 1918, NAC, RG 24, vol. 7450.

17 HMCS *Margaret* log, July 1918, NAC, RG 24, vol. 7493; HMCS *Lady Evelyn* log, July 1918, NAC, RG 24, vol. 7444; HMCS *Stadacona* log, July 1918, NAC,

RG 24, vol. 7871; Patrols, Sydney, to Naval, Ottawa, signal 801, 5 August
1918, NS 1065-7-6, NAC, RG 24, vol. 4031.

18 Story to Kingsmill, 11 June 1918, NS 60-S-3, NPRC.

19. Hatcher [report on Atlantic patrols], 3 Oct. 1917. NS 1017-10-3, NAC, RG
24, vol. 3832.

20 NHS notes on file NS 60-N-4, in DHIST: NHS 8000 "Shearwater."

21 Confidential Naval Order No. 394, 19 June 1918, NS 1065-7-1, copy in
DHIST: NHS 1440–11. See also Naval, Ottawa, to Admiralty, signal 636,
9 March 1918, PRO, ADM 116/1400.

22 Beesly, *Room 40*, and Grant, *U-Boat Intelligence*.

23 For example, "Latest News of Hun Pirate Deviltry – More Lunenburg
Ships Destroyed," *Halifax Herald*, 27 Aug. 1918, 1.

24 C-in-C, Atlantic Fleet, to Opnav [Navy Department, Operations], "Translation of Code Despatch," 5 June 1918; USNA, RG 45, box 185, subject file
1911–27, JA-2, "Submarine Activities in Western Atlantic."

25 Wemyss's views were widely reported in the press, for example, "The
German Subs off the Atlantic Coast," *Halifax Herald*, 20 June 1918, 3.

26 Admiral Superintendent, Halifax to GOC Military District 6, 22 Feb. 1918;
NAC, RG 24, box 11,122, file 501-1-1, vol. 1; also Sarty, "Silent Sentry,"
325–35.

27 For this and the following, see the submarine's official War Diary, KTB/
U-151, BA-MA: RM 97/1114, and her operations orders, "O-Befehl für
U-151," 4 April 1918, BA-MA: RM 5/6430, 122–31. Also microfilm records
T1022, roll 30, PG 61705 in National Archives and Records Service,
Washington DC. The accounts in US Navy's Department, *German Submarine
Activities*, must be used cautiously. For contemporary intelligence assess-
ments see "Proceedings of Enemy Submarines, Converted Mercantile
Type, in the Western Atlantic, May 1917 to April 1918," Admiralty, Naval
Staff Intelligence Department, USNA RG 45, subject file 1911–1927, box
184, JA-2, ID 1181.

28 Niemöller, *Vom U-Boot zur Kanzel*, 68.

29 See "U-Boat History Sheets," PRO, ADM 137/4155.

30 Beesly, *Room 40*, 245–51.

31 US Navy, *German Submarine Activities*, (23–4), for example, mentions reports
of sightings and attacks on 19, 20, and 21 May, which U-151's war diary
does not corroborate.

32 Nauen to U-151, 14 May 1918, signal no. 166, "U-Boat History Sheets,"
PRO, ADM 137/4155.

33 US Navy, *German Submarine Activities*, 138.

34 "U.K.-Verband. Navigatorische Angaben über Hafenplätze der Vereinigten Staaten und Canada," BA-MA: RM 5/3902.

35 US Navy, *German Submarine Activities*, 27.

36 Ibid., 30.

37 War Diary, (Kriegstagebuch/u-151), 139–41.

38 War Diary, KTB/U-151, "Erfahrungen," 141.

39 For the political and tactical principles of Germany's cable warfare see "Der Kabelkrieg," BA-MA: RM 5/5962, 105–8.

40 For *Teleconia* see Beesly, *Room 40*, 2, 203.

41 US Navy, *German Submarine Activities*, 120–1.

42 Cited in ibid., 113.

43 Nauen to U-151, 6 June 1918, signal no. 193, PRO, ADM 137/4155.

44 Nauen to U-151, 15 June 1918, signal no. 198, PRO, ADM 137/4155.

45 Cf. War Diary, U-151, 113, and "Cruise of U-151," "Proceedings of Enemy Submarines, Converted Mercantile Type, in Western Atlantic," USNA, RG 45, subject file 1911–1927, box 184, JA-2, I.D. 1181, June 1918.

46 War Diary, U-151, 105.

47 War Diary, U-151, 96: "Two boats of sunken vessel 3802N 7104 W please pich up" entered in the log in English.

48 "Stellungnahme des Verbandkommandos," War Diary, U-151, 70.

49 von Holtzendorff to Scheer, Chef des Hochseestreitkräfte, Admiral Schröder, Kommandierenden Admiral des Marinekorps, 13 March 1917, BA-MA: RM 5/922.

50 War Diary, U-151, 93.

51 U-157 to Nauen, 20 March 1918, 2301 hours, PRO, ADM 137/4155, 440. I.D. 1181, "Proceedings of Enemy Submarines, Converted Mercantile Type, in the Atlantic, May 1917 to April 1918," USNA, RG 45, subject file 1911–1927, box 184, JA-2, Admiralty, Naval Staff, Intelligence Department, June 1918.

52 *Halifax Herald*, 13 June 1918. 1.

53 For example, "Hun Submarines on This Side of Atlantic Try to Terrorize U.S.," *Halifax Herald*, 4 June 1918, 1.

54 For example, "Submarine Captain ... ," *Halifax Herald*, 15 June 1918, 1. Reports erroneously identified the commander as a "Captain Neufeldt." The US Navy's report, *German Submarine Activities*, uncritically accepts similar assertions about the crew of this and other u-boats.

55 For example, *Berliner Tageblatt und Handels-Zeitung*, 6 June 1918, 1; also "Die deutschen U-Boote in amerikanischen Gewässern – Schließung der amerikanischen Häfen – Sitzung des Wilsonschen Kriegskabinetts," *Berliner Tageblatt*, 7 June 1918, 2. Beiblatt, 2; "Der transatlantische U-Kreuzer-Krieg," *Hamburger Nachrichten*, 8 June 1918, "Amerika und der u-bootkrieg," *Kreuzzeitung*, 16 June 1918.

56 Agent no. 61, to Navintel [Naval Intelligence], via Berne, Switzerland, and US State Department, 10 June 1918, "Paraphrase of Telegram," Code Room, O.N.I., 12 June 1918; USNA RG 45, subject file 1911–1927, box 185, JA-2, "Submarine Activities in Western Atlantic."

57 The "N-Stelle" intelligence office in Antwerp, for example, received regular reports from crew of Belgian and Swedish relief ships; for example, BA-MA: RM 5/2272.

58 War Diary, U-151, 89, 94–101. American wireless stations monitored by U-151 reported an escalating threat.

59 Sims to Opnav [Navy Department, Operations], 10 June 1918, USNA RG 45, subject file 1911–1927, file JA-2, "Submarine Activities in Western Atlantic," box 185.

60 For the Canadian intelligence picture in May–June 1918 see NS 1062-13-2, pt. 3, NAC, RG 24, vol. 4021; also the index of all signals to/from C-in-C, NA&WI, May–June 1918, PRO, ADM 137/478.

61 C-in-C, NA&WI, general letter, 1 Aug. 1918; PRO, ADM 137/504, ff. 399–400.

62 "Handelsverkehr und Gegenwirkung," War Diary, U-151 128. Also summarized in Arno Spindler, Der Kreig zur See, V, 251–3.

63 Memorandum, July 1918, Konteradmiral Frhr. v. Keyserlingk, Chief, Operations Group, Admiralty, Keyserlingk Papers, cited in Walter Hubatsch, Der Admiralstab, 172.

64 For example, "Neue U-Boot-Erfolge," Berliner Tageblatt und Handels-Zeitung, 24 July 1918, 1. The account gave the U-boat commander's name and listed fifteen steamers and twelve sailing vessels.

65 For the following see Opnav, Washington, to Simsadus [Admiral Sims, London], 15 June 1918, serial 7223; USNA, RG 45, Subject file 1911–1927, box 185, JA-2, "Submarine Activities in Western Atlantic."

66 Grant, U-Boat Intelligence, 152.

67 Spindler, Der Krieg zur See, V, 258–60.

68 Operations Orders, "O-Befehl für U156, BA-MA: RM 5/6431, 162–71.

69 Washington to Naval Ottawa, signal 27, 5 July 1918; NAC, RG 24, box 3773, file NS 48-48-1, vol. 3. For details of the Canadian response, told later in the account, see NAC, RG 24, box 3970, NS 1047-30-2, vol. 2; also extracts from Cdr. J. Paget Gibbs to Director of the Naval Service, 29 Aug. 1918, NAC, RG 24, vol. 4031, NS 1065-7-6.

70 See, however, Spindler, Der Krieg zur See, V; US Navy, German Submarine Activities, 50–70; KTB/U-156, "Erfahrungen," 11–14, for the period 28 Aug.–28 Oct. 1917, BA-MA: RM 97/1130.

71 US Navy German Submarine Activities, 51. The document quotes a blow-by-blow account by the vessel's skipper and chief officer. For further detailed accounts see "Captain's Statement," and "Statement of ... Chief Officer," US Naval Intelligence officer, Eastern District of Canada, Halifax, to Director of Naval Intelligence, Washington, 12 July 1918; USN Operational Archives, "U-Boat Operations in the Western Atlantic during WW I" von Doenhoff microfilm.

72 Dockyard Halifax, Nova Scotia, to Admiralty, 08:25 a.m., 17 July 1918; USN Operational Archives, von Doenhoff microfilm.

73 *Halifax Herald*, 18 July 1918, 1, 5; also "Victims of Hun Submarine Landed at Shelburne after Eight Days at Sea in Open Boat," ibid., 29 June 1918, 1, 2.

74 Ibid., 2 July 1918, 1, 3; 3 July, 1; 5 July, 1, 2, 6; 6 July, 8, 10; 8 July 6; 9 July, 1; 15 July, 6.

75 Ibid., 2 July 1918, 1; 3 July 1918, 1, 3; 5 July 1918.

76 Cf. "Idle Fears," Halifax *Morning Chronicle*, 7 Aug. 1918, 6; Colonel W.R. Lang, General Staff, 12 Dec. 1918, "Memorandum on the Reorganisation and Efficiency of the Defences of Halifax and Nova Scotia, 11 February– 11 November 1918," section XVII, NAC, RG 24, box 2323, HQS 66, vol. 10.

77 NAC, RG 24, box 2532, HQC 1686, vol. 2, 1918 correspondence; box 3970, NSC 1047-30-2, vol. 1, 1918 correspondence; box 2323, HQS 66, vol. 10, Lang, 12 Dec. 1918, memo on reorganization, section XVII.

78 *Halifax Herald*, 18 July 1918, 5.

79 Ibid., 7 Aug. 1918, 2, 3.

80 For conclusions of the US court of inquiry see US Navy, *German Submarine Activities*, 126–8.

81 *Halifax Herald*, 20 July 1918, 1.

82 US Navy, *German Submarine Activities*, 54–5.

83 *Boston Daily Globe*, Monday morning, 22 July 1918, 1. W. Watts Biggers, "The Germans Are Coming!," 39–43, provides a largely fanciful account.

84 Cited in US Navy, *German Submarine Activities*, 54–5.

85 *Halifax Herald*, 22 July 1918, 1.

86 For example, "Wieder ein U-Boot vor der amerikanischen Küste," *Berliner Tageblatt*, 25 July 1918, 2.

87 *Halifax Herald*, 25 July 1918, 1.

88 Grant to Admiralty, signal 330, 21 July 1918, PRO, ADM 137/903, 1190.

89 "Naval Craft Available," 31 July 1918, USNA, subject file 1911–1927, box 222, file KD.

90 Grant, general letter, 1 Aug. 1918, PRO, ADM 137/504, 396.

91 Nauen to U-151, 22 July (no signal number), PRO, ADM 137/4155, 432.

92 All references to the *Jouett* group are based on USS *Jouett*, log, USNA RG 24; USS *Jouett*, War Diary, USNA, RG 45; and Clephane's useful account in USNRF, "History of the Submarine Chasers in the World War," 85–93, file ZOD, USNA RG 45, subject file 1911–1927, box 802E.

93 Cited in US Navy, *German Submarine Activities*, 56.

94 Form S.A., "Particulars of Attacks on Merchant Vessels by Enemy Submarines," Dornfontein, 2 Aug. 1918; NAC, RG 24, box 4023, NSC 1062-13-10, vol. 5 (position 44° 17′N, 67° 00′W); Transports Saint John to Naval Ottawa, signal 515, 3 Aug. 1918, NAC, RG 24, box 4021, file 62-1-2, vol. 4.

95 For example, "New Brunswick Schooner Sunk by a Submarine," *Sydney Post*, 5 Aug. 1918, 1.

96 Saint John *Standard*, 7 Aug. 1918, 1.

97 "Statement of Charles Dagwell, Captain of the Schooner 'Dornfontein'," 5 Aug. 1918, US Consulate, Saint John; USN Operational Archives, "U-Boat Operations in the Western Atlantic," von Doenhoff microfilm.

98 For example, *Sydney Post*, 5 Aug. 1918, 1; *Liverpool Advance*, 7 Aug. 1918, 3.

99 "Particulars of Attacks."

100 "Ibid.

101 "Captain's Ticket Suspended," *Sydney Post*, 17 Sept. 1918, 8.

102 "Machias Section," in "History of First Naval District" file ZPN-1, USNA, RG 45, subject file 1911–1927, box 818; NHS notes on file 132-1-1, DHIST: NHS 8000 "Festubert."

103 "Statement of Charles Swain, Master of the Annie Perry," to US consul, Saint John, 17 Aug. 1918; USN Operational Archives, "U-Boat Operations," von Doenhoff microfilm. Also "The Sinking of Annie Perry," Yarmouth *Telegram*, 9 Aug. 1918, 1; "U-Boat Sinks Six Fishing Vessels," *Sydney Post*, 6 Aug. 1918, 1; "Submarine Works on Fishing Fleet," Yarmouth *Herald*, 6 Aug. 1918, 1.

104 Cited in US Navy, *German Submarine Activities*, 58.

105 *Halifax Herald*, 5 Aug. 1918, 1.

106 G. Meister to Militia Headquarters, 4 Sept. 1918, NAC, RG 24, box 2532, HQC, 1686, vol. 2.

107 Col. W.N. Land to Major F.E. Davis, Militia Headquarters, Ottawa, 11 Sept. 1918, NAC, RG 24, box 2532, HQC 1686, vol. 2.

108 Lang to Assistant Director, Military Intelligence, Ottawa, 7 Oct. 1918, NAC, RG 24, box 2532, HQC, 1686, vol. 2.

109 Navinet [Naval Intelligence Network] Halifax to Naval Ottawa, signal 40, dispatched 13.30 hours Atlantic time, 4 Aug. 1918, file 62-13-2 pt. 4, NAC, RG 24, vol. 4021.

110 "Estimate of the Submarine Situation in Western Atlantic from July 1 to and including 4 August 1918," file JA-2, USNA, RG 45, subject file 1911–1927, box 185.

111 *Yarmouth Herald*, 6 Aug. 1918, 4.

112 Naval Ottawa to Commanding Officer, HMS *Briton*, St John's dispatched 2:20 p.m., 5 Aug. 1918, file 62-13-2 pt. 4, NAC, RG 24, vol. 4021.

113 The figures are based on Hose to Secretary, Department of the Naval Service, 1 Aug. 1918, file 1065-7-6, NAC, RG 24, vol. 4031.

114 Shenton to Secretary, Department of the Naval Service, "Summary of Troops Embarked in Halifax and H.C. Convoys," 5 Sept. 1919, file 1048–48-12 pt. 2, NAC, RG 24, vol. 3775; Chambers to Commander-in-Chief, North America and West Indies, 22 Aug. 1918, PRO, ADM 137/1620, 164.

115 Form S.A., "Particulars of Attacks on Merchant Vessels by Enemy Submarines," *Gladys M. Hollett*, NSS 1062-13-10, vol. 4, NAC, RG 24, vol. 4023.

The scuttling charges only damaged *Hollett*; patrol vessels towed her into Halifax with her 2,100 barrels of herring.

116 Form S.A., "Particulars of Attacks on Merchant Vessels by Enemy Submarines," *Luz Blanca*; NAC, RG 24, box 4023, file 62-13-10, vol. 4; US Navy, *German Submarine Activities*, 58–9; Intelligence Summary, "Attack on Luz Blanca by Enemy Submarine," 7 Aug. 1918, Halifax; USN Operational Archives, von Doenhoff microfilm.

117 Dockyard Halifax to Admiralty, signal 592, 2 Aug. 1918, PRO, ADM 137/903, f. 570.

118 Newcombe to Captain of Patrols, 13 Aug. 1918, DHIST: NHS 8000 "Niobe"; *Tingey* log and *SC 240* log, 5 Aug. 1918, USNA, RG 24. The American ship was *SC 240*.

119 Newcombe to Captain of Patrols, 13 Aug. 1918, DHIST: NHS 8000 "Niobe." *CD 15* log, 5 Aug. 1918, NAC, RG 24, vol. 7157; *CD 14*, log, 5 Aug. 1918, NAC, RG 24, vol. 7155; *St. Eloi*, log, 5 Aug. 1918, NAC, RG 24, vol. 7919; Hose to Naval Ottawa, signal 801, dispatched 19:15, 5 Aug. 1918, file 1065-7-6, NAC, RG 24, vol. 4031.

120 Patrols, Sydney, to Naval Ottawa, signal 809, 6 Aug. 1918, file 1065-7-6, RG 24, vol. 4031.

121 *Halifax Herald*, 12 Aug. 1918, 2.

122 Edmonds, *A Short History*, 339–49.

123 Greenhous, "Amiens," 73–80.

124 Newcombe to Captain of Patrols, 13 Aug. 1918; Hose to Secretary, Department of the Naval Service, 14 Aug. 1918, DHIST: NHS 8000 "Niobe"; Story to Department of the Naval Service, 20 Aug. 1918, enclosing "Halifax Patrol Duties of Officers," file 1065-7-6, RG 24, vol. 4031; Shenton biographical file, DHIST.

125 Captain in charge, Sydney, to Naval Ottawa, signal, 3 Aug. 1918, NS 0–44178, pt. 1, NPRC. Hose to Kingsmill, 4 Aug. 1918.

126 Hose to Naval Ottawa, signal, 6 Aug. 1918; Kingsmill to Hose, 7 Aug. 1918, NS 0–44178, pt. 1, NPRC.

127 Grant, general letters, 1 July, 3 Sept., 1 Oct. 1918, PRO, ADM 137/504; signals, 24 Aug.–26 Sept. 1918, NS 53-6-1, pt. 2, NAC, RG 24, vol. 5651.

128 Navyard Halifax to Naval Ottawa, signal 89, 6 Aug. 1918, Haggard to C-in-C, NA&WI, 14 Aug. 1918, file 1065-7-6, NAC, RG 24, vol. 4031.

129 Admiralty to C-in-C, NA&WI, signal 348, 13 Aug. 1918, PRO, ADM 137/903, 781; *Yorktown* log, 13–24 Aug. 1918, USNA, RG 24.

130 Admiralty to Grant, telegram 367, 15 Aug. 1918, PRO, ADM 137/1619; telegrams, Navyard Halifax to Naval Ottawa, 15 Sept.–16 Oct. 1918, NS 1001-19-4, NAC, RG 24, vol. 6197. Assembly of a further sixteen miles of mined nets, some of which were intended for St John's was nearing completion at the time of the armistice.

131 In addition to the First World War logs in the 7000 series of volumes in

NAC, RG 24, see the final reports of the Canadian Control of Shipping staffs, NAC, RG 24, box 3981, file 49-2-40; Notes from file 57-4-30, DHIST: NHS 8000 "Trawlers and Drifters," vol. 2.

132 Britannia to Naval Ottawa, signal 101, 5 Aug. 1918; Naval Ottawa to Britannia, signal (no number), 6 Aug. 1918; Britannia to Naval Ottawa, signal 104, 6 Aug. 1918, same to same, signal 119, 10 Aug. 1918, file 1048-48-1, pt. 4, NAC, RG 24, vol. 3773; Navinet Halifax to Admiralty, signal 617, 6 Aug. 1918, PRO, ADM 137/903, 647; Admiralty, *Atlantic Convoy System*, 149–50.

133 Admiralty to C-in-C, NA&WI, signal 323, and to Naval Ottawa, signal 42, 8 Aug. 1918, PRO, ADM 137/903, 1212; Admiralty, *Atlantic Convoy System*, 144–5, 156.

134 Grant, *U-Boat Intelligence*, 154; Washington to Naval Ottawa, signals 101 and 104, 6 Aug. 1918; Admiralty to Naval Ottawa, signal 42, 8 Aug. 1918, NAC, RG 24, box 3773, file 48-48-1, vol. 4; US Navy, *German Submarine Activities*, 11.

135 "Interrogation of Captain A.N. Larsen," 12 Aug. 1918, USN Operational Archives, von Doenhoff microfilm; "Statement made by Captain Larson [sic] of the Swedish steamship 'Sydland'," 12 Aug. 1918, USN Operational Archives, von Doenhoff microfilm.

136 "Statement of captain of British Schooner PENISTONE [sic] bound from New York to Bordeaux," USN Operational Archives, von Doenhoff microfilm; US Navy, *German Submarine Activities*, 61–5.

137 *Halifax Herald*, 10 Aug. 1918, 1.

138 Ibid., 13 Aug. 1918. 1.

139 *Morning Chronicle*, 7 Aug. 1918, 6.

140 "Officer of U-Boat Visits New York" *Sydney Post*, 22 Aug. 1918, 6.

141 A.K. Maclean [acting minister, Marine and Fisheries], to G.J. Desbarats, 7 Aug. 1918, NAC, RG 24, box 3831, G. 1017-10-1, vol. 1; William Duff [MP], Lunenburg, NS, to A.K. Maclean, 14 Aug. 1918, Maclean to Desbarats, 22 Aug. 1918, NAC, RG 24, box 4030, NSC 1065-4-1; also ancillary signals in these files.

142 Naval Ottawa to Britannia, Washington, signal 117, 10 Aug. 1918; Washington to Naval Ottawa, signal 155, 18 Aug. 1918, signal 157, 18 Aug. 1918, signal 165, 19 Aug. 1918; NAC, RG 24, box 4030, NSC 1065-4-3.

143 For example, G.J. Desbarats, Deputy Minister of the Naval Service, to William Duff, MP, 17 Aug. 1918; Desbarats to Maclean, 21 Aug. 1918; Maclean to Desbarats, 22 Aug. 1918; Desbarats to Maclean, 23 Aug. 1918; NAC, RG 24, box 4030, NSC 1065-4-1.

144 *Halifax Herald*, 20 Aug. 1918, 1.

CHAPTER ELEVEN

1 "Ein deutscher Hilfskreuzer vor der kanadischen Küste," *Berliner Tageblatt*, 18 Aug. 1918, 2.

2 "Die Streifzüge des Hilfskreuzers 'Triumph'," ibid., 1. The quotation in the German newspaper is from *Le Matin* of Geneva.

3 "Particulars of Attacks on Merchants Vessels by Enemy Submarines," *Triumph*; NAC, RG 24, box 4023, file 62-13-2, pt. 4.

4 "U-Boat Sails up Halifax Harbor, Skipper Boasts," *Sydney Post*, 23 Aug. 1918, 1. The German boast was reported by the captain of the sunken schooner *Una P. Saunders*.

5 DHIST: NHS, 1440–6, Halifax (1905–20), vol. 1, 1–27 Aug. 1918. This early form of an opposed entry was arranged with the general officer commanding.

6 "Is Cape Breton T.R. Triumph Hun Sea Wolf?" *Sydney Record*, 22 Aug. 1918, 2; "Captured Trawler Is Now A German Raider Operating off Coast," *Sydney Post*, 22 Aug. 1918, 1, 6; "The Halifax Trawler Triumph a Raider," Yarmouth *Telegram*, 23 Aug. 1918, 2.

7 See the following logs for 20–30 August 1918: *TR 33* and *TR 30*, NAC, RG 24, vol. 7953; *Armentières*, vol. 7040; *Stadacona*, vol. 7871; *SC 240* and *SC 45*, USNA, RG 24; *Cartier*, Report of Proceedings, 24–30 Aug. 1918, DHIST: NHS 8000 "Stadacona (Ship Afloat)"; Hose to Secretary, Department of the Naval Service, 30 Aug. 1918, 1065-7-1, NAC, RG 24, vol. 4031; Patrols Halifax to Naval Ottawa, signal 342, 21 Aug. 1918, same to same, signal 351, 21 Aug. 1918, 1062-13-2, pt. 4, NAC, RG 24, vol. 4021, Patrols Sydney to Naval Ottawa, signal 16, 23 Aug. 1918, 1062-13-2, pt. 5, NAC, RG 24, vol. 4021.

8 *Yorktown* log, 24–30 Aug. 1918; *Jouett* log, 21 Aug.–3 Sept. 1918, USNA, RG 24; *Bell* War Diary 20–25 Aug. 1918, *Jouett* War Diary, 21 Aug.–3 Sept. 1918, USNA, RG 45; Britannia to Naval Ottawa, signal 179, 22 Aug. 1918, NSC 1062-13-2, pt. 5, NAC, RG 24, vol. 4021.

9 *Sydney Record*, 21 Aug. 1918, 1.

10 War Diary, [US] First Naval District, 17 Aug. 1918, file ZPN-1, USNA, RG 45, Subject file 1911–1927, box 818.

11 Ibid.

12 Hose to secretary, Department of the Naval Service, 12 Sept. 1918, NSC, 1017-10-6, NAC, RG 24, vol. 3832.

13 Maclean to Desbarats, telegram, 7 Aug. 1918, NS 1017-10-1, pt. 1, NAC, RG 24, vol. 3831; see also Naval Ottawa to Britannia, signal 117, 10 Aug. 1918, NS 1065-4-3, NAC, RG 24, vol. 4030.

14 Telegrams and correspondence, 1065-4-1, NAC, RG 24, vol. 4030.

15 Naval Ottawa to Britannia, signal 117, 10 Aug. 1918; Britannia to Naval Ottawa, signal 155, 18 Aug. 1918, NS 1065-4-3, NAC, RG 24, vol. 4040;

Duff to Maclean, telegram, 14 Aug. 1918, Maclean to Desbarats, telegram, 17 Aug. 1918, Naval Ottawa to Navyard Halifax, signal 16, 21 Aug. 1918, Maclean to Desbarats, telegram, 22 Aug. 1918, Desbarats to Maclean, signal 41, 23 Aug. 1918, NS 1065-4-1, NAC, RG 24, vol. 4030.

16 *Halifax Herald*, 22 Aug. 1918, 1.

17 "Statement of Captain Joseph P. Mesquita of the Schooner Francis J. O'Hara, regarding the loss of that vessel August 20, '18," US Naval Representative, Eastern District of Canada, Halifax, to the Director of Naval Intelligence, USN Operational Archives, RG 45, von Doenhoff microfilm; also US Navy, *German Submarine Activities*, 66–7.

18 "The French Schooner 'Notre Dame de la Garde'," O.N.D., pt. III, 20 Aug.–20 Sept. 1918, US Naval Operational Archives, von Doenhoff microfilm.

19 For example, "Has the German Raider Triumph Been Scuttled?" *Sydney Post*, 27 Aug. 1918, 3; "Has the Pirate Triumph Been Destroyed?" *Halifax Herald*, 31 Aug. 1918, 1.

20 For example, *Yarmouth Herald*, 27 Aug. 1918, 2.

21 *Gloucester Times*, 20 Aug. 1918, 1; also US Navy, *German Submarine Activities*, 67.

22 For the following, see Report of Attack on Eric, NAC, RG 24, box 4023, file 62-13-10, vol. 4; clippings from Saint John *Standard*, NAC, RG 24, box 4021, file 62-13-2, vol. 4; "Sinking of British Steamer Eric by Submarine," US Consul, St Pierre, US N Operational Archives, von Doenhoff microfilm; US Navy, *German Submarine Activities*, 68–70.

23 Uncaptioned report of British communications officer regarding SS *Eric*, 25 Aug. 1918; USN Operational Archives, RG 45, box 184, JA-2, von Doenhoff microfilm; "Sinking of British Steamer Eric" US Consul, St Pierre, 31 Aug. 1918, ibid. Also US Navy, *German Submarine Activities*, 68–9.

24 Kingsmill to Hose, 7 Aug. 1918; DHIST: "Torpedo A/S General," 81/520, 1000–973, vol. 1.

25 Hose to Secretary, Department of the Naval Service, 145 Jan. 1918, NS 1017-10-4; NAC, RG 24, vol. 3832.

26 See McKnight to Captain of Patrols, 17 Sept. 1918; DHIST: NHS 1440–6 "Halifax 1905–20." Also extracts from file 47-5-1; DHIST: NHS 8000 "Stadacona (Ship Afloat)."

27 Cited in extracts from file 47-23-L64, DHIST: NHS "Halifax 1905–20."

28 "Declaration" of three survivors of *Gloaming* before the British consul at St Pierre et Miquelon, 28 Aug. 1918, PRO, ADM 137/1618, 517; Navinet to Naval Ottawa, signal 483, 28 Aug. 1918, NS 1062-13-2, pt. 5, NAC, RG 24, vol. 4021; Grant, *U-Boat Intelligence*, 166–6.

29 "Erfahrungen, Anhang zum KTM/U151," in "Acta betreffend Technische Erfahrungen der U-Kreuzer, Mai 1918–Okt 1918," BA-MA: RM 5/2163.

30 Report of Kapitänleutnant Adolf Fritz, U-152, cited in Spindler, *Der Kreig zur See*, V, 253.

31 Ibid., 253–7. *Ticonderoga* succumbed with the loss of 213 lives after an
   exchange of eighty-three shells. See also US Navy, *German Submarine
   Activities*, 106–12.

32 *Halifax Herald*, 2 Aug. 1918, 1.

33 Ibid., 15 Aug. 1918, 1; 17 Aug. 1918, 1.

34 The expression frequently occurs; for example in the *Halifax Herald*,
   20 Aug. 1918, 1.

35 For the following see War Diary, KTB/U-117, BA-MA: RM 97/1094; Operations Orders, "O-Befehl für U117," 21 June 1918, BA-MA: RM 5/6428,
   59–67; Spindler, *Der Kreig zur See*, V, 264–5; US Navy, *German Submarine
   Activities*, 82–100.

36 Cited in US Navy *German Submarine Activities*, 83–5.

37 Beckmann, *U-Boote vor New York*, 28.

38 Cf. speculation in US Navy *German Submarine Activities*, 134.

39 Cited in ibid., 94.

40 See the erroneous judgment in ibid, 128–9.

41 *Halifax Herald*, 30 Aug. 1918, 1.

42 "Particulars of Attacks on Merchant Vessels by Enemy Submarines," *Elsie
   Porter* and *Potentate*, Form S.A. (revised June 1917); DHIST: 1650–239/
   16A. The US Navy monograph incorrectly claims *Elsie Porter's* master's
   name was W.M. Rheinhard; Reinhard was the owner.

43 St John's *Evening Telegram*, 2 Sept. 1918, 5.

44 For example, Navinet Halifax to Naval Ottawa, signal 455, 2020 hours,
   27 Aug. 1918, same to same, signal 482, 0019 hours, 28 Aug. 1918, NSS
   1062-13-2 pt. 5, NAC, RG 24, vol. 4021. Also *Stadacona* log, 26–31 Aug.
   1918, NAC, RG 24, vol. 7871.

45 Admiralty to Grant, signal 326, 9 Aug. 1918, PRO, ADM 137/903, 718; Naval
   Ottawa to Halifax, signal (no number), 11 Aug. 1918, Patrols Halifax to
   Naval Ottawa, signal 166, 12 Aug. 1918, 1065-7-6, NAC, RG 24, vol. 4031;
   DHIST: NHS notes on 1057-4-31 pt. 2 in NHS 8000 "Trawlers and Drift-
   ers," pt. 2; *Cartier*, Report of Proceedings, 25–31 Aug. 1918, and *Hochelaga*,
   Report of Proceedings, 24–30 Aug. 1918, DHIST: NHS 8000 "Stadacona
   (Ship Afloat)."

46 Admiralty to Grant, signal 401, 22 Aug. 1918, Port Convoy Officer Halifax
   to Grant, signal 711, 25 Aug. 1918, PRO, ADM 137/903, 1229, 1233.

47 Maclean to Desbarats, telegram, 22 Aug. 1918, chairman, Canada Food
   Board, to Desbarats, 3 Sept. 1918, NS 29-16-1 pt. 5, NAC, RG 24, vol.
   5605; Kingsmill to Desbarats, 6 Sept. 1918, Kingsmill to Port Arthur
   Shipbuilding Company, 11 Sept. 1918, NS 29-16-1 pt. 6, ibid.

48 DHIST: NHS notes from 1057-4-31 pt. 2, NHS 8000 "Trawlers and Drifters,"
   pt. 2; NHS notes from 29-16-1 pt. 7 in NHS 8000 "Trawlers and Drifters,"
   pt. 1; Hose to Secretary, Department of the Naval Service, "List of Ships
   and Appointments," 7 Jan. 1919, copy in DHIST: NHS 1440-11.

49 US crews took over the ships at Quebec only a few days before the armistice. Grant, general letter, 3 Sept. 1918, PRO, ADM 137/504, 110; Gibbs to Kingsmill, 29 Aug. 1918, NSC 1065-7-6, NAC, RG 24, vol. 4031.

50 Tucker, *Naval Service*, 1, 294–6; DHIST: 81/520/1440–6 "1905–20," copies of documents from NS 1047-19-4; also extracts from *Shearwater* log, Aug.–Sept. 1918.

51 Alden, "American Submarine Operations," 820–7.

52 Edmonds, *A Short History*, 356.

53 See the logs of the Halifax and North Sydney air detachments, USNA, RG 24, and also the excellent accounts in Wise, *Canadian Airmen and the First World War*, 1, 605–8, and Russell, *A History of Canadian Naval Aviation 1918–1962*, 3–7. Dave Kealy and Ted Russell have assembled a very useful digest of the relevant air service files and copies of the key documents in DHIST: NHS 1700–219.

54 Borden to Ballantyne, 31 Aug. 1918, NAC, MG 26H, reel C-4416, 136282–3.

55 Lieutenant-Colonel John T. Cull, RAF, to Kingsmill, 29 Aug. 1918, and telegrams initiated by Borden, 30 Aug. 1918, NAC, MG 26H, reel C-4416, 136276–80.

56 Grant to Admiralty, telegram 447, 9 Aug. 1918; Admiralty to Grant, telegram 350, 13 Aug. 1918; Grant to Admiralty, telegram 458, 14 Aug. 1918, PRO, ADM 137/903.

57 Grant, general letter, 3 Sept. 1918, PRO, ADM 137/504. In this instance, he was referring to the United States, but there is no doubt he felt the same way about Canada.

58 Admiralty, *Atlantic Convoy System*, III, 150, 156.

59 Gibbs to Kingsmill, 29 Aug. 1918, NS 1065-7-6, NAC, RG 24, vol. 4031. Also NHS notes on 1057-4-31, DHIST: NHS 8000 "Trawlers and Drifters," pt. 2. Only two of the trawlers actually carried out missions for the RCN prior to the armistice.

60 Chambers to Grant, 2 Sept. 1918, PRO, ADM 137/1620.

61 Naval Ottawa to Patrols Sydney, signals, 3–5 Sept. 1918; NAC, RG 24, box 4031, file 65-7-6. See also Naval Ottawa to Navyard Halifax, signal 19 Aug. 1918, and Story to Kingsmill, 20 Aug. 1918. Logs, Sept.–Oct. 1918 of *Margaret*, NAC, RG 24, vol. 7493; *Stadacona*, vol. 7871; *Lady Evelyn*, vol. 7444.

62 Hose to Secretary, Department of Naval Service, 13 Sept. 1918; Command memorandum to Hose, 17 Sept. 1918; Hose to Secretary, Department of the Naval Service, 22 Oct. 1918; Department of the Naval Service, 3 March 1919, NS 1065-7-6, NAC, RG 24, vol. 4031; NHS notes on NS 1057-4-31, DHIST: NHS 8000, "Trawlers and Drifters," pt. 2.

63 Shenton to Secretary, Department of the Naval Service, "Summary of Troops Embarked ... HC Convoys," 5 Sept. 1919, NS 1048-48-8, pt. 2, NAC, RG 24, vol. 3775.

64 Grant to Admiralty, telegram 447, 13 Aug. 1918, PRO, ADM 137/903; Naval Ottawa to Britannia, Washington, telegram 130, 13 Aug. 1918; Morres to Military Secretary, Interdepartmental Committee, 30 Aug. 1918, NS 1048-48-12, NAC, RG 24, vol. 3775; Grant, general letter, 3 Sept. 1918, PRO, ADM 137/504.

65 DHIST: Department of the Naval Service, *Naval Intelligence Reports, 1918*, 257–95.

66 DHIST: NHS notes from 1057-4-31 pt. 2, NHS 8000 "Trawlers and Drifters," pt. 2; Patrols Sydney to Naval Ottawa, signal 430, 22 Sept. 1918, 1048-48-1 pt. 4, NAC, RG 24, vol. 3773; *SC 51* log, Sept.–Oct. 1918, USNA, RG 24.

67 *Naval Intelligence Reports, 1918*, 287.

68 War Diary, KTB/U-155, Feindfahrt 6 Sept. 1917–13 Jan. 1918; BA-MA: RM 97/1124.

69 For the following, see War Diary, KTB/U-155, Feindfahrt 11 Aug.–14 Nov. 1918; BA-MA: RM 97/1125. Also Spindler, *Der Handelskrieg*, V, 257–8, and US Navy, *German Submarine Activities*, 100–6.

70 War Diary, KTB/U-155, BA-MA: RM 97/1125. Studt's handwritten copy is the only extant version. We are indebted to Dr Günther Reibhorn for his laborious deciphering of major portions of this handwritten document, much of which is too illegible to render any sense.

71 Sims to Opnav, 9 Sept. 1918, cited in US Navy, *German Submarine Activities*, 101.

72 Cited in ibid., 102.

73 *Halifax Herald*, 17 Sept. 1918, 1.

74 Cited in US Navy, *German Submarine Activities*, 102–3.

75 Navinet Halifax to Naval Ottawa, signal 732, 14 Sept. 1918, 1062-13-2 pt. 5, NAC, RG 24, vol. 4021.

76 *SC 40* and US Naval Air Station Halifax, logs, 15–23 Sept. 1918, USNA, RG 24; *Grilse* log, 16–19 Sept. 1918, NAC, RG 24, vol. 7371.

77 Wegekarte [track chart], U-155; BA-MA: RM 97/1125 K.

78 The reports of proceedings for patrol vessels (1914–18) were all "weeded," apparently in the early 1970s.

79 "U.K.-Verband, Kabelschneide- und Minenangelegenheiten, Juli 1917–August 1918," BA-MA: RM 5/6439.

80 Kennedy, "Imperial Cable Communications," 75–98. Kennedy (p. 86) lists the number of cuttings required to isolate the United Kingdom and various major colonies.

81 Edmonds, *A Short History*, 424.

82 *Naval Intelligence Reports, 1918*, 239–95.

83 Kingsmill to deputy minister, 6 Sept. 1918, NS 29-16-1 pt. 6, copy in DHIST: NHS 8000, "Trawlers and Drifters," pt. 1.

84 "Zum Thronvortrag," minutes of meeting, 14 May 1918, "Immediatvorträge," BA-MA: RM 5/907, 166–70.

CHAPTER TWELVE

1 For the uncommissioned ships see *Canadian Navy List*, Oct. 1918, 113; J.O.B. LeBlanc, "Historical Synopsis of Organization and Development of the Royal Canadian Navy," 1937, 33–73, DHIST; and "List of ships owned by, loaned to, or chartered by RCN," April 1918, Extracts from file NS 1065-1-4, DHIST.

2 Hose to Secretary, Department of the Naval Service, 21 Oct. 1918, NS 1062-13-2, pt. 6, NAC, RG 24, vol. 4021.

3 For Story's recommendations on reductions in the Halifax flotilla see Story to Kingsmill, 20 Aug. 1918, NS 1065-7-6, NAC, RG 24, vol. 4031. These seem to have been carried out; for this see Preston to Assistant Chief of the Naval Staff, 12 Oct. 1918, PRO, ADM 137/1619. See also the logs for September–October: *CD 33*, NAC, RG 24, vol. 7171; *Grilse*, vol. 7371; *SC 240*, *Yorktown*, and *Tingey*, in USNA, RG 24; NHS notes on NS 1057-4-31, DHIST: NHS 8000 "Trawlers and Drifters," pt. 2.

4 Captain of Patrols to the Secretary, Department of the Naval Service, Ottawa, 21 Oct. 1918; NAC, RG 24, vol. 4032, file 1065-7-12, vol. 1.

5 Hose to Secretary, Department of the Naval Service, 21 Oct. 1918; NAC, RG 24, vol. 4032, file 65-7-12; Kingsmill to Minister, 5 Nov. 1918, forwarding Gibb's note to the Director of the Naval Service of 28 Oct. 1918; Ballantyne to Kingsmill, 5 Nov. 1918; NAC, RG 24, vol. 4029, file 65-1-1.

6 Ballantyne to Wemyss, 11 Sept. 1918; Wemyss to Ballantyne, 28 Oct. 1918, NS 1017-10-1, pt. 1, NAC, RG 24, vol. 3831.

7 Marder, *Dreadnought to Scapa Flow*, v, 107–10; David F. Trask, *Captains and Cabinets*, chapter 8; Corbett and Newbolt, *Naval Operations* v, 428–9.

8 *Wemyss to Ballantyne, 28 Oct. 1918*, NS 1017-10-1, pt. 1, NAC, RG 24, vol. 3831.

9 Department of the Naval Service, *Annual Report for Year Ending 31 March 1919*, 13.

10 Hose to Secretary, Department of the Naval Service, 24 Sept. 1918, NS 1065-7-12, NAC, RG 24, vol. 4032.

11 Preston to Assistant Chief of the Naval Staff, 12 Oct. 1918, PRO, ADM 137/1619.

12 Hose to Secretary, Department of Naval Service, 6 Sept. 1918, NS 1065-7-13, NAC, RG 24, vol. 4032; Grant, general letter, 1 Nov. 1918, PRO, ADM 137/504. So serious were the drifters' building defects that the Canadians tried to have the Royal Navy refit them in Bermuda.

13 Kingsmill to Ballantyne, 5 Nov. 1918, endorsing Gibbs to Kingsmill, 28 Oct. 1918, NS 1065-1-1, NAC, RG 24, vol. 4029.

14 Captain L.G. Preston to Assistant Chief of the Naval Staff, 12 Oct. 1918, PRO, ADM 137/1619.

15 Lt. Col. Cull to Air Ministry, London, cited in Wise, *Canadian Airmen*, 605.

16 Duff [assistant chief of the Naval Staff, Admiralty] minute, 27 Oct. 1918, PRO, ADM 137/1619.

17 Borden Diary, 11 and 13 Sept. 1918, NAC reel C-1864; and Desbarats Diary, 16 Sept. 1918, NAC, MG 30E89, vol 5.

18 Borden Diary, 29 Aug. 1918, NAC, reel C-1864.

19 Preston to Assistant Chief of the Naval Staff, London, 12 Oct. 1918, PRO, ADM 137/1619.

20 Grant, general letter, 3 Sept. 1918, PRO, ADM 137/504.

31 Grant, general letter, 1 Oct. 1918, PRO, ADM 137/1619.

22 Grant to Admiralty, 16 Sept. 1918, ibid.

23 Hunt, *Sailor-Scholar*, chap. 3–5.

24 Richmond, minute, 22 Nov. 1918, PRO, ADM 137/1619.

25 Horn, *German Naval Mutinies*, 198.

26 KTB/Skl, "Stichworte zu stattgehabten Besprechungen des Chefs des Admiralstabes," BA-MA: PG 64726, Fasc. 4055; cited in ibid., 207.

27 Korvettenkapitän Edgar Schulze, "Bericht über den Rückmarsch der 'Abteilung Seestreitkräfte des Marinekorps' im November 1918," in "Revolution 1918," BA-MA: RM 8/1009.

28 For example, Forstmann, *U 39 auf Jagd*, 10–11.

29 Piers Diary, 11 Nov. 1918, Public Archives of Nova Scotia, MG 1, vol. 1047 (quoted with minor editing). Harry Piers was curator of the Nova Scotia Provincial Museum.

30 Von Bethmann Hollweg, *Betrachtungen*, Vorwort zum I. Teil. Germany had no alternative but to accept the treaty. See, for example, Horst Muhleisen, *Geschichte in Wissenschaft und Unterricht*, 2 (1987), 65–89, and Klaus Hildebrand, *Historische Zeitschrift*, 244 (1987), 1–28. These articles are reviewed by Dennis E. Showalter, "Military History in Germany 1986–1987: An Overview of Periodical Literature," *Military Affairs*, vol. 52, no. 3 (July 1988), 147–9.

31 Wegener, *Die Seestrategie des Weltkrieges*, 51.

32 For example, Mirow, *Der Seekrieg 1914–1918*, 155.

33 Karl Hollweg, "Der alten deutschen Flotte zum Gedächtnis," in Scheer, ed., *Die deutsche Flotte*, 169–72.

34 Erich Raeder, Preface, in Gebeschus, *Doggerbank*.

35 Von Mantey, *Die deutschen Hilfskreuzer*.

36 Joachim Schepke, *U-Bootfahrer von heute. Erzählt und gezeichnet von einem U-Boot-Kommandanten*, Berlin: In Deutschen Verlag 1940. Geleitwort.

37 House of Commons, *Debates*, 26 July 1919, 2812–52. Charges were led by William Duff (Liberal, Lunenburg), John H. Sinclair (Liberal, Antigonish and Guysborough), and Daniel D. McKenzie (Leader of the Opposition, Liberal, Cape Breton North).

38 Ibid., 26 May 1919, 2846.

39 Ibid., 2848.

40 Ibid., 2917.

Bibliography

The research for this volume derives primarily from official documents held in the archives of Canada, Federal Republic of Germany, Great Britain, and the United States. We have cited them in full in the notes. As it would unnecessarily encumber the bibliography to repeat them here, the bibliography includes a selected list of readings on which we have drawn.

Admiralty, Naval Staff, Training and Staff Duties Division. *Naval Staff Monographs (Historical). Fleet Issue.* Vol. ix, *The Atlantic Ocean 1914–1915.* London: [HMSO] Oct. 1923.
– *Naval Staff Monographs (Historical). Fleet Issue.* Vol. viii, *Home Waters – Part VIII – December 1916–April 1917.* London: [HMSO] April 1933.
Admiralty, Technical History Section. *The Atlantic Convoy System, 1917–1918.* vol. iii, pt. 14, of *The Technical History and Index.* London: Admiralty 1920.
Ajax [pseud]. *The German Pirate, His Methods and Record.* New York: George H. Doran 1918.
Alden, Carroll Storrs. "American Submarine Operations in the War." *United States Naval Institute Proceedings,* 46 (June 1920): 820–7.
Allard, Dean C. "Anglo-American Differences during World War 1." *Military Affairs* 44 (April 1980), 75–81.
Andrew, Christopher. *Secret Service: The Making of the British Intelligence Community.* London: Heinemann 1985.
Armstrong, John Griffith. "Canadian Home Defence, 1914–1917, and the Role of Major-General Willoughby Gwatkin." MA thesis, Royal Military College of Canada, 1982.
Assmann, Kurt. *Die Kämpfe der kaiserlichen Marine in den deutschen Kolonien* [Vol. i: *Tsingtau*; Vol. ii: *Deutsch-Ostafrika*]. Berlin: E.S. Mittler und Sohn 1935.
Bauer, Hermann. *Als Führer der U-Boote im Weltkrieg.* Leipzig: Koehler und Amelung 1942.

– *Reichsleitung und U-Bootseinsatz, 1914 bis 1918*. Lippoldsberg: Kloster-
   haus-Verlag 1956.
Beckmann, A. *U-Boote vor New York: Die Kriegsfahrt eines deutschen Unterseebootes
   nach Amerika*. Fifth ed. Stuttgart: Frank'sche Verlagshandlung 1931.
Beesly, Patrick. *Room 40: British Naval Intelligence 1914–1918*. Oxford:
   Oxford University Press [1982] 1984.
Bennett, Geoffrey. *Coronel and the Falklands*. London: B.T. Batsford Ltd
   1962.
Bernstorff, Johann Heinrich, Graf von. *Deutschland und Amerika: Erin-
   nungen aus dem fünfjährigen Kriege*. Berlin: Verlag von Ullstein and Co.
   1920.
– *My Three Years in America*. New York: Scribner 1920.
Berton, Pierre, *Vimy*. Toronto: McClelland and Stewart 1986.
Bethmann Hollweg, Theodore von. *Betrachtungen zum Weltkriege*. Vol. I:
   Vor dem Kriege, Berlin: Verlag von Reimar Hobbing, 1919; Vol. II:
   Während des Krieges. Berlin: Verlag von Reimar Hobbing 1922.
Biggers, W. Watts. "The Germans Are Coming!" *Proceedings*, US Naval
   Institute (June 1985): 39–43.
Bird, Michael J. *The Town That Died: The Story of the World's Greatest Man-
   Made Explosion Before Hiroshima*. London: Souvenir Press 1962.
Birnbaum, Karl. E. *Peace Moves and U-Boat Warfare: A Study of Imperial
   Germany's Policy toward the United States, April 18, 1916–January 9, 1917*
   (PHD thesis, Stockholm 1958). Hamden, Conn.: Archon Books 1970.
Bliss, Michael. *A Canadian Millionaire: The Life and Times of Sir Joseph Flavelle,
   Bart. 1858–1939*. Toronto: Macmillan 1978.
Borden, Henry, ed. *Robert Laird Borden: His Memoirs*. 2 vols. Toronto:
   Macmillan 1938.
Bourne, Kenneth. *Britain and the Balance of Power in North America
   1815–1908*. London: Longmans 1967.
Boutilier, James A., ed. *The RCN in Retrospect: 1910–1968*. Vancouver and
   London: University of British Columbia Press 1982.
Brown, Robert Craig. *Canada's National Policy 1883–1900: A Study in Cana-
   dian-American Relations*. Princeton: Princeton University Press 1964.
– *Robert Laird Borden: A Biography*. Vol. 1, *1858–1914*. Toronto: Macmillan
   1975.
Buitenhuis, Peter, *The Great War of Words: British, American and Canadian
   Propaganda, 1914–1933*. Vancouver and London: University of British
   Columbia Press 1987.
Chatterton, E. Keble. *The Auxiliary Patrol*. London: Sidgwick and Jackson
   1923.
Churchill, Randolph S. *Winston S. Churchill*. London: Heinemann 1969.
Clark, William Bell. *When the U-Boats Came to America*. Boston: Little, Brown
   1929.

Clarke, I.F. *Voices Prophesying War 1763–1884*. London: Oxford University Press 1966.

Cole, J.A. *Prince of Spies: Henri Le Caron*. London: Faber and Faber 1984.

Compton-Hall, Richard. *Submarine Warfare: Monsters and Midgets*. Poole: Blanford Press 1985.

Cook, Ramsay. *The Politics of John W. Dafoe and the Free Press*. Toronto: University of Toronto Press 1963.

Corbett, Sir Julian, and Sir Henry Newbolt. *History of the Great War: Naval Operations*. 5 vols. London: Longmans, Green 1921–9.

Cronon, E. David. *The Cabinet Diaries of Josephus Daniels 1913–1921*. Lincoln: University of Nebraska Press 1963.

Cuff, R.D., and J.L. Granatstein. *Canadian-American Relations in Wartime from the Great War to the Cold War*. Toronto: Hakkert 1975.

d'Egville, Howard. *Imperial Defense and Closer Union: A Short Record of the Life-work of the late Sir John Colomb in Connection with the Movement towards Imperial Organisation*. London: P.S. King 1913.

Denison, George T. *Soldiering in Canada: Recollections and Experiences*. Toronto: G.N. Morang 1900.

– *The Struggle for Imperial Unity: Recollections and Experiences*. London and New York: Macmillan 1909.

Dittmar, F.J., and J.J. Colledge. *British Warships 1914–1919*. London: Ian Allan 1972.

Doerries, Reinhard. *Washington–Berlin 1908–1917: die Tätigkeit des Botschafters Johann Heinrich Graf von Bernstorff vor dem Eintritt der Vereinigten Staaten von Amerika in den Ersten Weltkrieg*. Duesseldorf: Schwann 1975.

Douglas, W.A.B. "Canadian Naval Historiography." *Mariner's Mirror*, 70 (Nov. 1984): 349–62.

– ed. *The RCN in Transition: 1910–1985*. Vancouver and London: University of British Columbia Press 1988.

Eckardt, Karsten. "Cargo Submarine Deutschland." *Model Shipwright*, 63 (March 1988): 24–30.

Edmonds, James M. *A Short History of World War I*. London: Oxford University Press 1951.

English, John. *The Decline of Politics: The Conservatives and the Party System 1901–20*. Toronto: University of Toronto Press 1977.

Fayle, C. Ernest. *History of the Great War: Seaborne Trade*. 3 vols. London: John Murray 1920–4.

Fock, Harald. "Deutsche Rohstofftransport-Uboote des Ersten und Zweiten Weltkrieges," *Marineforum*, 1/2 (1982), 46–8.

Forstmann, Walter. *U 39 auf Jagd im Mittelmeer*. Foreword by Kontreadmiral Hollweg. Berlin und Wien: Ullstein 1918.

Friedel, Frank. *Franklin D. Roosevelt: The Apprenticeship*. Boston: Little, Brown 1952.

Garner, James Wilford. *International law and the World War*. Vol. II. London: Green 1920.

Gebeschus, Kurt. *Doggerbank. Kampf und Untergang des Panzerkreuzers Blücher*. Berlin: Brunnen-Verlan Willi Bischoff 1935.

Gimblett, Richard Howard. " 'Tin-Pots' or Dreadnoughts?: The Evolution of the Naval Policy of the Laurier Administration, 1896–1911." MA thesis, Trent University, 1981.

Gluek, Alvin C. "The Invisible Revision of the Rush-Bagot Agreement, 1899–1914." *Canadian Historical Reveiw*, 60 (Dec. 1979): 466–84.

Gooch, John. "Great Britain and the Defence of Canada, 1896–1914," *Journal of Imperial and Commonwealth History*, 3 (May 1975): 369–85.

Gordon, Donald C. *The Dominion Partnership in Imperial Defense 1870–1914*. Baltimore: Johns Hopkins Press 1965.

Gottberg, Otto von. *Kreuzerfahrten und U-Bootstaten*. Reihe Ullsteins Kreigsbücher. Berlin und Wien: Ullstein 1915.

Grant, Robert M. *U-Boat Intelligence 1914–1918*. London: Putnam 1969.

Gray, Edwyn. *'A Damned Un-English Weapon': The Story of Submarine Warfare 1914–1918*. London: Seeley, Service 1971.

Greenhous, Brereton. " ' ... It Was Chiefly a Canadian Battle': The Decision at Amiens, 8–11 August." *Canadian Defence Quarterly* 18, no. 2 (autumn 1988): 73–80.

Hadley, Michael L. "Inshore ASW in the Second World War: The U-Boat Experience." In *RCN in Transition: 1910–1985*, edited by W.A.B. Douglas. Vancouver: University of British Columbia Press 1988, 126–42.

– *U-Boats against Canada: German Submarines in Canadian Waters*. Montreal and Kingston: McGill-Queen's University Press 1985.

Hamilton, C. Frederick. "The Canadian Navy." *University Magazine*, 8 (Oct. 1909): 587–602.

Harris, Daniel G. "Canadian Warship Construction 1917–19: The Great Lakes and Upper St Lawrence River Areas." *Mariner's Mirror*, vol. 75, no. 2 (May 1989): 149–58.

Harris, Stephen J. *Canadian Brass: The Making of a Professional Army 1860–1939*. Toronto: University of Toronto Press 1988.

Hattendorf, John B., and Lynn C. Hattendorf. *A Bibliography of the Works of Alfred Thayer Mahan*. Newport, RI: Naval War College 1986.

Herwig, Holger H. *Germany's Vision of Empire in Venezuela*. Princeton, NJ: Princeton University Press 1986.

– *"Luxury" Fleet: The Imperial German Navy 1888–1918*. London: George Allen & Unwin 1980.

– *Politics of Frustration: The United States in German Naval Planning*. Boston and Toronto: Little, Brown 1976.

Hwerwig, Holger H. and D.F. Trask, "Naval Operations Plans between

Germany and the USA, 1898–1913: A Study of Strategic Planning in the Age of Imperialism." In *The War Plans of the Great Powers, 1880–1914*, edited by Paul M. Kennedy. London: George Allen & Unwin 1979, 39–74.

Herzog, Bodo, "Kapitän zur See Hans Rose, Ritter des Pour le Mérite, zum 100. Geburtstag." *Deutsche Soldatenjahrbuch*, 33 (1985). Deutsches Soldatenkalender, München, 1984, 387–8.

Hitsman, J. Mackay. *Safeguarding Canada 1763–1871*. Toronto: University of Toronto Press 1968.

Horn, Daniel. *The German Naval Mutinies of World War I*. New Brunswick, NJ: Rutgers University Press 1969.

– *War, Mutiny and Revolution in the German Navy: The World War I Diary of Seaman Richard Stumpf*. New Brunswick, NJ: Rutgers University Press 1967.

Hough, Richard, *Former Naval Person: Churchill and the Wars at Sea*. London: Weidenfeld and Hicolson 1985.

Hubatsch, Walther. *Der Admiralstab und die Obersten Marinebehörden in Deutschland 1848–1945*. Frankfurt am Main: Verlag für Wehrwesen Bernard & Graefe 1958.

– *Die Ära Tirpitz: Studien zur deutschen Marinepolitik 1890–1918*. Göttingen: Musterschmidt 1955.

– *Kaiserliche Marine: Aufgaben und Leistungen*. Munich: J.F. Lehmanns Verlag 1975.

Hunt, Barry D. *Sailor-Scholar: Admiral Sir Herbert Richmond 1871–1946*. Waterloo, Ont.: Wilfrid Laurier University Press 1982.

Hurd, Sir Archibald. *History of the Great War: The Merchant Navy*. 3 vols. London: Cassell 1921–9.

James, Henry J. *German Subs in Yankee Waters*. New York: Gotham House 1940.

Jellicoe, Lord. *Der U-Boot-Krieg: Englands Schwerste Stunde*. (Original: *The Submarine Peril*.) Tenth ed. Trans. Kptlt. a.D. Johannes Spieß. Berlin: Vorhut-Verlag Otto Schlegel n.d.

– *The Crisis of the Naval War*. London, New York, Toronto, and Melbourne: Cassell 1920.

Jones, John Price. *America Entangled: The Secret Plotting of German Spies in the United States and the Inside Story of the Sinking of the Lusitania*. London: Hutchinson 1917.

Jones, John Price, and Paul Merrick Hollister. *The German Secret Service in America 1914–1918*. Toronto: William Briggs 1918. [Introduction dated 1 June 1918].

Kendle, John. *The Round Table Movement and Imperial Union*. Toronto: University of Toronto Press 1975.

Kennedy, P[aul].M. "Imperial Cable Communications and Strategy, 1870–1914." In *The War Plans of the Great Powers, 1880–1914*, edited by Paul M. Kennedy. London: George Allen and Unwin 1979, 75–98.

– *The Rise of the Anglo-German Antagonism 1860–1914*. London: George Allen and Unwin 1980.

– ed. *The War Plans of the Great Powers, 1880–1914*. London: George Allen and Unwin 1979.

Kirchhoff, Hermann, Vizeadmiral. *Seekriegsgeschichte in ihren wichtigsten Abschnitten mit Berücksichtigung der Seetakitik*. Vol. VI: *Von 1910–1920*. Hannover: Hahnsche Buchhandlung 1921.

König, Paul. *Die Fahrt der Deutschland*. Berlin: Ullstein & Co. [1916] 1917. Trans. anon. *Voyage of the Deutschland*. New York: Hearst 1917.

– *Fahrten der U-Deutschland im Weltkrieg*. Berlin: Im Verlag Ullstein [1937].

– "Kriegs-Handelsfahrten unter See." In *U-Boote am Feind*, herausgg, v. Werner v. Langsdorff. Gütersloh: Verlag C. Bertelsmann 1937.

Kühlwetter, Friedrich von. *Skagerrak. Der Ruhmestag der deutschen Flotte*. Edited by H.D. Philipp. Berlin: Im Verlag Ullstein 1933.

Lake, Simon. *The Submarine in War and Peace: Its Developments and Its Possibilities*. Philadelphia and London: Lipincott 1918.

Lambi, Ivo Nikolai. *The [German] Navy and German Power Politics 1862–1914*. Boston: Allen & Unwin 1984.

Langsdorff, Werner von. *U-Boote am Feind*. Gütersloh: Verlag C. Bertelsmann 1937.

Link, Arthur S. *Wilson: The Struggle for Neutrality 1914–1915*. Princeton: Princeton University Press 1960.

Mackay, Ruddock F. *Fischer of Kilverstone*. Oxford: Oxford University Press 1973.

McKee, Fraser M. *The Armed Yachts of Canada*. Erin, Ont. Boston Mills Press 1983.

Mackinnon, C.S. "The Imperial Fortresses in Canada: Halifax and Esquimalt, 1871–1906." PHD thesis, University of Toronto, 1965.

Macpherson, Ken, and John Burgess. *The Ships of Canada's Naval Forces 1910–1981*. Don Mills, Ont.: Collins 1981.

Mahan. A.T. *The Influence of Seapower upon History 1660–1783* [1890]. Boston: Little, Brown 1932.

Mantey, Eberhard von. *Die deutschen Hilfskreuzer*, Bd. III of *Der Kreuzerkrieg in den ausländischen Gewässern*, Hrsgg, von der kriegswissenschaftlichen Abteilung der Marine, Verantwortl. Leiter Kurt Assmann Konteradmiral. Berlin: E.S. Mittler und Sohn 1937.

Marder, Arthur J. *The Anatomy of British Sea Power: A History of British Naval Policy in the Pre-Dreadnought Era. 1880–1905*. New York [1940]: Frank Cass 1964.

– *From the Dreadnought to Scapa Flow: The Royal Navy in the Fisher Era*. 5 vols. Oxford: Oxford University Press 1961–70.

May, Ernest. *The World War and American Isolation 1914–1917*. Cambridge, Mass.: Harvard University Press 1959.

Meaney, Neville, *A History of Australian Defence and Foreign Policy 1901–23*, Vol. 1,: *The Search for Security in the Pacific 1901–1914*. Sydney: Sydney University Press 1976.

Melville, Thomas Richard. "Canada and Sea Power: Canadian Naval Thought and Policy, 1860–1910." PHD thesis, Duke University, 1981.

Messimer, Dwight R. "German Gunboats on the Yangtse." *Naval History*, US Naval Institute, 1/1/1 (April 1987): 57–62.

– *The Merchant U-Boat: Adventures of the 'Deutschland' 1916–1918*. Annapolis, Md.: Naval Institute Press 1988.

Militärgeschichtliches Forschungsamt, Hrsg., *Deutsche Militärgeschichte*, 6 vols. Herrsching: Manfred Pawlak 1983.

Mirow, Jürgen. *Der Seekrieg 1914–1918 in Umrißen*. Göttingen: Musterschmidt 1976.

Moon, Howard Roy. "The Invasion of the United Kingdom: Public Controversy and Official Planning, 1888–1918." PHD thesis, University of London, 1968.

Morison, Elting E. *Admiral Sims and the Modern American Navy*. Boston: Houghton Mifflin 1942.

Morris, A.J.A. *The Scaremongers: The Advocay of War and Rearmament 1896–1914*. London: Routledge and Kegan Paul 1984.

Morton, Desmond. *A Military History of Canada*. Edmonton: Hurtig 1985.

– *Ministers and Generals: Politics and the Canadian Militia 1868–1904*. Toronto: University of Toronto Press 1970.

Neatby, Blair H. *Laurier and a Liberal Quebec: A Study in Political Management*. Toronto: University of Toronto Press 1974.

Nicholson, G.W.L. *Official History of the Canadian Army in the First World War: Canadian Expeditionary Force 1914–1919*. Ottawa: Queen's Printer 1964.

Niemöller, Martin, *Vom U-Boot zur Kanzel*. Berlin: Martin Warneck Verlag 1935.

Ollivier, Maurice, ed. *Colonial and Imperial Conferences from 1887 to 1937*. 3 vols. Ottawa: Queen's Printer 1954.

Palmer, Alan. *The Kaiser: Warlord of the Second Reich*. London: Weidenfeld and Nicolson 1978.

Papen, Franz von. *Memoirs*. Trans. by Brian Connell. London: Andre Deutsch 1952.

Parker, Gilbert. *The World in a Crucible: An Account of the Origins and Conduct of the Great War*. [New York 1915.] London: John Murray 1915.

Penlington, Norman. *Canada and Imperialism 1896–1899.* Toronto: University of Toronto Press 1965.

Perkins, J.D. "Canadian Vickers–built H Class Submarines of the Royal Navy." *Warship.* Pt. I, vol. 47, 3–9; pt. II, vol. 48 (Oct. 1988): 2–4, with drawings and photos.

Persius, L. "Die Fahrt der 'Deutschland' und der 'Bremen' über den Ozean." *Berliner Tageblatt,* 11 July 1916, 1.

Pickert, Karl, "Mit Kapitän König nach Amerika." In *U-Boote am Feind,* Hrsgg, von Werner v. Langsdorff, Gütersloh: Verlag C. Bertelsmann 1937, 146–53.

Plievier, Theodor. *Des Kaisers Kulis.* [1930.] Cologne: Kiepenheuer & Witsch 1981.

Pohl, Heinrich. "Der Deutsche Unterseebootkrieg: Ein völkerrechtliches Gutachten." MS, University of Tubingen, 1923. In M.L.H. collection.

Preston, Richard A. *Canada and 'Imperial Defense': A Study of the Origins of the British Comonwealth's Defense Organization, 1867–1919.* Durham, NC: Duke University Press 1967.

– *The Defence of the Undefended Border: Planning for War in North America 1867–1939.* Montreal and London: McGill-Queen's University Press 1977.

Raeder, Eric. *Die Tätigkeit der kleinen Kreuzer "Emden," "Königsberg," und "Karlsruhe."* Mit einem Anhang "Die Kriegsfahrt des kleinen Kreuzers 'Geier'." Bd. II of *Der Kreuzerkrieg in den ausländischen Gewässern,* [*Der Krieg zur See 1914–1918.* Hrsgg. von Eberhard von Mantey]. Berlin: E.S. Mittler und Sohn 1923.

Ranft, Brian. "The Naval Defence of British Sea-Borne Trade 1860–1905." DPHIL thesis, Oxford University, 1967.

– ed. *Technical Change and British Naval Policy 1860–1939.* London: Hodder and Stoughton 1977.

Rieschke, George, "Handels-U-Boot 'Deutschland'." *Marine Kalender der DDR 1981,* (East) Berlin (1980): 144–40.

Rose, Hans, "U-53 fährt nach Amerika." In *U-Boote am Feind.* Herausgg. von Werner von Langsdorff. Gütersloh: Verlag C. Bertelsmann 1937, 158–85.

– *Auftauchen! Kriegsfahrten von U-53.* [1931.] Third ed. Essen: Essener Verlagsanstalt 1940.

Rössler, Eberhard. *Geschichte des deutschen Ubootbaus.* Munich: J.F. Lehmanns Verlag 1975.

Ruge, Friedrich. *In Vier Marinen: Lebenserinnerungen als Beitrag zur Zeitgeschichte.* Munich: Bernard & Graefe Verlag 1979.

Russell, E.C. *A History of Canadian Naval Aviation 1918–1962.* Ottawa: Department of National Defence 1965.

Sanders, M.L., and Philip M. Taylor. *British Propaganda during the First World War, 1914–1918*. London: Macmillan 1982.

Sarty, Roger Flynn. "Hard-Luck Flotilla: The RCN's Atlantic Coast Patrol, 1914–18." In *The RCN in Transition 1910–1985*, edited by W.A.B. Douglas. Vancouver and London: University of British Columbia Press 1988, 101–25.

– "Silent Sentry: A Military and Political History of Canadian Coast Defence 1860–1945." PHD thesis, University of Toronto, 1982.

– " 'There Will Be Trouble in the North Pacific': The Defence of British Columbia in the Early Twentieth Century." *B.C. Studies*, 61 (spring 1984): 3–29.

Sarty, Roger Flynn, and Donald M. Shurman, "An Historical Perspective on Canadian Naval Policy." *Argonauta*, 4 (March 1987): 6–13.

Scheer, Reinhard, Admiral. *Die deutsche Flotte in großer Zeit*. Unter Mitwirkung deutscher Seehelden. Braunschweig and Berlin: Georg Westermann 1926.

– *Vom Segelschiff zum U-Boot*. Leipzig: Quelle und Meyer 1925.

Schurman, Donald M. *The Education of a Navy: The Development of British Naval Strategic Thought 1867–1914*. London: Cassell 1965.

– "Imperial Defence, 1868–1887: A Study in the Decisive Impulses behind the Change from 'Colonial' to 'Imperial' Defence." PHD thesis, Cambridge University, 1955.

– *Julian S. Corbett 1854–1922: Historian of British Maritime Policy from Drake to Jellicoe*. London: Royal Historical Society 1981.

Sims, William Sowden. *The Victory at Sea*. With Burton J.H. Hendrick. London: John Murray 1920.

Smith, Gaddis. *Britain's Clandestine Submarines 1914–1915*. New Haven: Yale University Press 1964.

Spindler, Arno. *Der Krieg zur See: Der Handelskrieg mit U-Booten*. Vols. 1–4, Berlin: E.S. Mittler 1932–41. Vol. 5, Berlin: E.S. Mittler 1968.

Stacey, C.P. *Canada and the British Army 1846–1871: A Study in the Practice of Responsible Government*. Rev. ed. Toronto: University of Toronto Press 1963.

Stanley, G.F.G. *Canada's Soldiers 1604–1954: The Military History of an Unmilitary People*. Toronto: Macmillan 1954.

Stegemann, Bernd. *Die deutsche Marinepolitik*. Berlin: Duncker und Humblot 1970.

Steinberg, Jonathan. *Yesterday's Deterrent: Tirpitz and the Birth of the German Battle Fleet*. London: Macdonald 1965.

Stewart, Alice R. "Sir John A. Macdonald and the Imperial Defence Commission of 1879." *Canadian Historical Review*, 35 (June 1954): 119–39.

Strother, French, *Fighting Germany's Spies*. toronto: McClelland, Goodchild and Stewart 1918. [Completed prior to Aug 1918. Also published New York: Doubleday, Page 1919.]

Tallman, Ronald Duea. "Warships and Mackerels: The North Atlantic Fisheries in Canada-American Relations, 1867–1877." PHD thesis, University of Maine, 1971.

Trask, David F. *Captains and Cabinets: Anglo-American Naval Relations 1917–1918*. Columbia, Mo.: University of Missouri Press 1972.

Tuchmann, Barbara. *The Zimmermann Telegram*. [1958] Toronto: Random House 1979.

Tucker, Gilbert Norman. *The Naval Service of Canada*. 2 vols. Ottawa: King's Printer 1952.

US Congress, Senate, Naval Affairs Committee. *Hearing before the Sub-Committee of the Committee on Naval Affairs* (short form *Naval Investigation*). 66th Cong. 2nd sess. Washington: GPO 1920.

US Naval Historical Division. *Dictionary of American Naval Fighting Ships*. Washington, DC: Department of the Navy 1976.

US Navy Department. *German Submarine Activities on the Atlantic Coast of the United States and Canada*. Washington, DC: Office of Naval Records 1920.

Vincent, C. Paul. *The Politics of Hunger: The Allied Blockade of Germany 1915–1919*. Athens, O.: Ohio University Press 1985.

Wegener, Wolfgang. *Die Seestrategie des Weltkrieges*. Berlin: E.S. Mittler 1929.

Weir, Gary E. "Tirpitz, Technology, and Building U-Boats, 1897–1916." *International History Review*, vol. 6, no. 2 (May 1984): 174–90.

Wickham, H.J. "Canada's Maritime Position and Responsibilities." *Canadian Military Institute, Selected Papers*, 6 (1894–5).

– *Naval Defence of Canada*. Toronto: Canadian Military Institute 1896.

Winter, Charles F. *The Hon. Sir Sam Hughes, Canada's War Minister 1911–1916: Recollections of Service as Military Secretary at Headquarters*. Toronto: Macmillan 1931.

Winter, J.M. *The Experience of World War I*. New York: Oxford University Press 1989.

Wise, S.F. *Canadian Airmen and the First World War: The Official HIstory of the Royal Canadian Air Force*, Vol. 1, N.p.: University of Toronto Press, in co-operation with the Department of National Defence and the Canadian Government Publishing Centre, 1980.

Wislicenus, Georg. *Deutschlands Seemacht sonst und jetzt*. Mit Bildern von Willy Stöwer. Leipzig: Fr. Wilh. Grunow [1901]. Third ed. 1909.

Yerxa, Donald A. "The United States Navy in Caribbean Waters During World War I," *Military Affairs*, 51 (Oct. 1987): 182–7.

Index

A. *Pratt Andrew*, schooner, 266

Aboukir, HMS, 117

Acadia, HMCS, 280, 283

Adams, John, 140

Admirals' Rebellion, German, 297

Admiralty, Great Britain; abolishes defensive mines, 259; allocation of ships to Canada, 208–9; and Canadian autonomy, 201; and Canadian expansion, 96, 104, 116–17, 123–4, 127–8, 129; and contracts in Canada, 208; and convoys, 200; and Dardanelles, 114; delays warning Canada, 207; discourages ship building in Canada, 100, 120–1, 129, 185, 293; and dominion navies, 296–7; erratic advice, 209; failure to advise and consult Canada, 85, 104, 112–4, 130, 178, 209–10, 215, 217, 233–4, 280; failure to support Canada, 213, 216; and fishing fleet, 217–18; full advice to USA, 215; and intelligence, 93–6, 108,

112–13; and manning, 91, 222; and patrols, 124–5, 129, 161; public confidence in, 114; and recruiting, 127, 129–30; reorganization of, 212–13; and reserve fleet, 10; and shipbuilding, 120–1, 142–3; and strategic control, 85, 116–17, 213–14; and submersible freighters, 142; and trade routes, 175, 178; and u-boat threat, 125, 129–30, 159; warns Canada, 286; *see also* Colonial Conference; Committee of Imperial Defence; Royal Canadian Navy; Royal Navy

Admiralty, German, *see* Imperial Naval Office, German agents, intelligence, 50–2, 97, 105; *see also* espionage.

Agnes B. Holland, schooner, 255

aircraft, anti-submarine, 215–17, 219, 250, 275, 279–80, 286

Alaska boundary dispute, 16

Albacore, 98

Alberto Treves, SS, 288

Aleda May, schooner, 274

Algerine, HMCS, 88, 91; and fisheries patrols, 219

Amiens, battle of, 257

Amphion, SS, 288

Androscoggin, USS, 264

Anglo-Japanese alliance of 1902, 27, 61

Annie Perry, schooner, 253

Ansaldo Primo, SS, 276

anti-submarine: air patrols for Canada, 215; aircraft 286; allied measures, 232; attacks in US waters, 175; Canadian vessels, 124–5, 128, 160, 208; escorts, 201; need for vessels in Canada, 212; and nets, 122, 159; patrols, 255; plans for air, 216–17; problems of, 257; training, 279; and US air support, 279–80

Arleux, HMCS, 187

Armada, Spanish, 23

armed merchant cruisers, 9–11, 15, 81

Armentières, HMCS, 187

armistice, 11 November 1918, 194, 297, 298–9

Arnauld de la Perière, Kapitänleutnant Lothar von, 137, 245, 285; and blockade zones, 226–7;